Unravelling the Franklin Mystery

McGill-Queen's Native and Northern Series
Bruce G. Trigger, Editor

Unravelling
the Franklin Mystery

Inuit Testimony

DAVID C. WOODMAN

McGill-Queen's University Press
Montreal & Kingston • London • Buffalo

© McGill-Queen's University Press 1991
ISBN 0-7735-0833-3

Legal deposit third quarter 1991
Bibliothèque nationale du Québec

Printed in Canada on acid-free paper

Publication of this book has been assisted by
Canada Council through its block grant
program. Funding has also been received
from Multiculturalism Canada.

Canadian Cataloguing in Publication Data

Woodman, David C. (David Charles), 1956–
Unravelling the Franklin Mystery

(McGill-Queen's native and northern series; 5)
Includes bibliographical references and index.
ISBN 0-7735-0833-3

1. Franklin, John, Sir, 1786-1847. 2. Arctic
regions – Discovery and exploration – British.
3. Inuit – Canada. 4. Great Britain –
Exploring expeditions. I. Title. II. Series.

FC3961.3.W66 1991   917.19'5041'092
C91-090224-0   G660.W66 1991

This book was typeset by
Typo Litho composition inc.
in 10/12 Palatino.

For Aglooka,

whoever he was.

Contents

Contents

Maps, Figures, and Tables

Author's Note

There are a few conventions used throughout this book with which the reader may wish to become familiar.

First and foremost is the method in which I have handled the notes. As a reader I find notes present a frustrating dilemma. Those located on the bottom of each page, while obviating the hassle of constant flipping, maddeningly disrupt the train of thought and usually aren't worth the trouble. Even worse is the tantalizing practice of including all notes in a section of their own. This is particularly galling if the author indiscriminately mixes notes which include juicy morsels of fact or opinion with ones that simply give a reference or the infuriating "ibid," for of course one must check through all the chaff in an effort not to miss any wheat.

Nevertheless, in a book which treats of highly subjective and complex material such as this, the business of notes cannot be ignored. In this book all notes are collected at the end and consist entirely of references to source material for those wishing to verify my usage or delve deeper into any aspect of the tale. The general reader who is, I presume, more interested in the content of the material than in its origin, may therefore blissfully ignore the existence of notes at all.

Next is the issue of priority. History, at least good history, can never be entirely original. Those familiar with the material will soon realize that I have drawn upon the work and ideas of all of those who have paved the way. All facts which are not readily apparent or so commonly known as to defy accreditation I have attempted to trace, usually to the original documents. However, while humbly recognizing the priority of all of the eminent scholars whose ideas have been signposts on the road, I must assume full responsibility for the conclusions reached, for the man who forms the bricks may not approve of the final building.

A thorny problem is occasionally presented by spelling. A cursory reading of the books and articles on the Franklin expedition will reveal wide differences in the spelling of various common names, place names, and native words. The native word for "white man," for example, is rendered, depending on the source, as "kobluna," "qavlunar," or other approximations to the true pronunciation. Similarly, place names are not entirely consistent – the modern "King William Island" was known as "King William's Land" long after the fact of its insularity became well known. A Glossary of common native terms and an Appendix of significant place names are included in the end matter to help the reader who is unacquainted with them. To maintain quotational accuracy, all of the original forms have been retained in material from other sources and equivalents inserted in square brackets if necessary. In the text I have somewhat arbitrarily chosen the most modern form or one which appeals most to me.

Finally, there is the related concern as to the proper name for the original inhabitants of Canada's Arctic. The French word "Esquimaux" and its English equivalent are transliterations of the Cree term "Aish-ke-um-oog," which freely translates as "raw flesh eaters." While descriptive, this is hardly polite, and I have therefore chosen the appellation which is used among the natives themselves, namely "Inuit" ("the people"). This also is found with various spellings in the sources (Innuit, etc.), often uncapitalized or incorrectly pluralized. Occasionally the whaler term "Husky" was used. Once again, quotational exactness precludes standardization and all forms will be found.

The terms "native" and "white man" are equally inexact and pejorative. Nevertheless I have used both extensively to avoid tiresome reliance on the more exact "Inuit" or "Caucasian" as other workable alternatives are rare. In neither case is their use intended to be derogatory or demeaning. As the story will amply demonstrate, the harsh dictates of the Arctic make no such petty distinctions when challenged by human beings.

Acknowledgments

In the course of the ten years it took to research this book, and the five which it took to put it in its present form, I have received generous assistance from more people than I can possibly enumerate or even remember. Many of these were nameless librarians and archivists who cheerfully helped a somewhat scruffy young man find and utilize obscure and often irreplaceable source materials. I must therefore thank those at the British Museum, Scott Polar Research Institute, and Universities of London, Toronto, British Columbia (Vancouver), and Victoria (British Columbia) for their excellent unknowing support.

Some individuals must be recognized. Mr Clive Holland of the Scott Polar Research Institute and Mr David Lewis of the British Museum, although they have undoubtedly forgotten it, were very helpful to an inquisitive "colonial."

Mrs Christine Kelly of the Royal Geographical Society has been unfailingly helpful, as was Mr Roderick Owen, himself the author of an excellent book on Franklin, who kindly invited me to lunch to discuss my ideas. Mrs Shirley of the Greenwich Maritime Museum graciously showed me through the museum's Franklin relics and allowed me to hold items of which I had only read. Dr Harold Langley, Frances Hainer, and Mr Ellis of the American Museum of Naval History (Smithsonian Institution) have been particularly helpful in meeting requests for material from the Hall Collection, within impossible deadlines.

Acknowledgments

In Canada my debt to Joan McGilvray, Philip Cercone, and Peter Blaney of McGill-Queen's University Press can only be appreciated by those unfortunates who read the manuscript in its original untutored form. Mention must also be made of Dr C.S. Houston and the two anonymous readers for the press, all of whom read the manuscript and suggested changes, deletions, and insertions while saving me from many embarrassing errors. While none of these eminent scholars totally accepted my hypothesis, their efforts nevertheless made it much more presentable. Judy Williams's exceptional editorial skill likewise vastly improved the book, not only by correcting my usage and grammar, but by pointing out where the "general" reader required overlooked background, or where more explanation was necessary to buttress a point.

My wife, Franca, who alone unswervingly believed that this book would ever see the light of day, will be able to dine out for years on my multiple obligations to her. The mapwork by my sister Deborah justifies my forbearance in not murdering her during our childhood. Finally I would like to express my thanks to my young daughters, Natalie and Laura, without whose continual distractions this book would have been completed in half the time, but with twice the heartache.

Sir John Franklin. He was not happy with this picture as he was suffering from a bad cold on the day it was taken. National Maritime Museum Greenwich. (NMM)

Lieutenant Graham Gore. Gore and party probably completed the survey of the Northwest Passage during the summer of 1847. NMM

Captain F.R.M. Crozier. After
Franklin's death, Crozier took
command and led his men
south towards the Great Fish
River. NMM

Commander James Fitzjames.
A likely candidate for
Kokleearngnun's "Aglooka."
NMM

Lieutenant H.D.T. Le Vesconte. His skeleton, recovered from Set-tu-me-nin by Hall, was identified by a gold tooth plug. NMM

Mr James Reid. Ice master of the *Erebus*, he is a possible candidate for the "Toolooah" encountered at Washington Bay. NMM

Lieutenant Hobson's men dismantling Crozier's cairn near Victory Point. National Archives of Canada (NAC) C-3468

Charles Francis Hall. During the five years that he lived with the Inuit he learned many details about the Franklin disaster. NAC C-5913

Unravelling the Franklin Mystery

Introduction

On 28 July 1845 two British exploration vessels, HMS *Erebus* and *Terror*, manned by 129 intrepid officers and seamen under the command of Sir John Franklin, were seen disappearing into the ice-pack in Davis Strait by a lonely whaling ship. They had been tasked to find the last small piece in the puzzle of the North-West Passage and travel through it to Asia. If all went well, they were expected to reappear within three years. All Europe waited anxiously.

The *Erebus* and *Terror* were never seen by white men again.

When the public eventually realized that the ill-fated expedition had run into difficulty, the outcry and effort for its rescue were unparalleled. Throughout the next decade, the largest manhunt in history was undertaken to the strident accompaniment of an unending series of headlines and editorials of argument, speculation, and, rarely, fact.

During the six-year period between 1848 and 1854, over £760,000 were expended, and in one year alone (1850) a dozen major expeditions were involved in the search. By penetrating into every likely bay and inlet (and many unlikely ones), these search expeditions succeeded in filling in the outlines of the massive and hitherto unknown Canadian Arctic Archipelago. It has been remarked with some truth that the disappearance of the Franklin expedition resulted in much more detailed and metic-

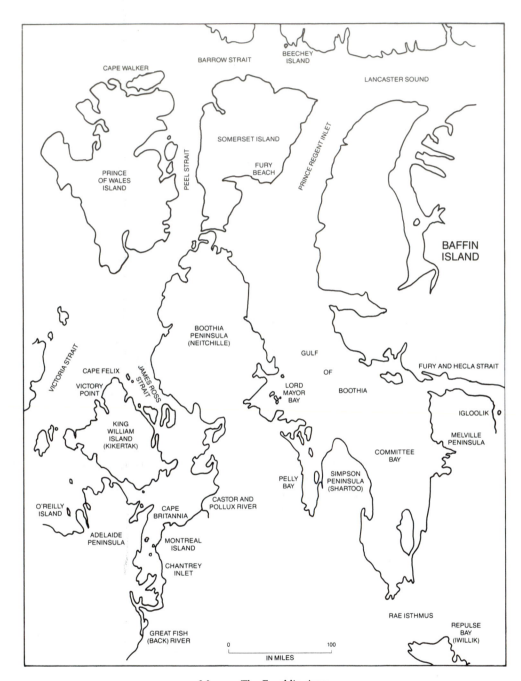

Map 1　The Franklin Area

ulous exploration than would normally have occurred if it had returned safely. However, the negative result of all of these searches was extremely disappointing to those waiting in England for news of their loved ones – or at least confirmation of their sad fate.

After nine long years, the first clues were learned by accident in 1854. Five years after this, other Europeans slowly walked along in the footsteps of the lost crews, gathered the few relics which the elements had allowed to survive, and interred the scattered bones of their comrades. Some poignant personal belongings, two brief and largely uninstructive notes, and a handful of confused and confusing native recollections were all that ever emerged. These succeeded in resolving the mystery in a very broad sense, but left much room for further interpretation. Argument as to the exact chain of events which led to the tragedy continues to this day.

Some historians contended that the ships – which have never been found by white men – sank in the deep Arctic channels, while others maintained that they had been seen riding on a large iceberg near the Newfoundland coast. Some said that Franklin and his crews had succumbed to starvation because of faulty provisioning, others concluded that they had fallen victim to murderous natives, and recently lead poisoning has been proposed as a causative factor. While most believed that none of the crew had survived the winter of 1848, some determined that a handful had eked out an existence for many years, and at least one investigator temporarily believed that survivors had been seen in the area as late as the 1860s!

The riddle of the last Franklin expedition has all of the elements required to elicit and maintain widespread interest – struggle, shipwreck, murder, massacre, cannibalism, and controversy. The story of the lost expedition has become a magnet for speculative historians, a mystery that far outstrips the contrived unfolding of fiction, and an inviting field for those who search for the elusive key, the unnoticed coincidence, or the overlooked connection which solves the problem and illuminates the truth. A quick look at the bibliography will show how fertile a field this has always proven to be. Many have combed it, some with the thoroughness of any forensic professional, many others looking hopefully for verification of far-fetched but plausible theories.

The length of time for which the Franklin mystery has maintained public interest can be attributed to the nature of the evidence as much as to the inherent human interest surrounding the tragedy. The physical evidence gathered at the scene is scanty and ambiguous. The recorded testimony of the European searchers themselves, while often useful, suffers from the fact that these men were also less than perfect in their investigative techniques and occasionally prone to make unsupported assumptions concerning what they had seen and heard.

To elicit the "true" story we must therefore weigh the untutored and often hearsay traditions of the Inuit. Some historians, believing that the remembrances of the natives are too inexact and contradictory, have ignored them. Others have built elaborate reconstructions based on them which do not accord with the "hard" evidence. Most have walked a middle path, selectively using what seemed most applicable, and attempting to minimize the assumptions which were required to make these tales fit a coherent framework.

In researching the Franklin saga, I proceeded from the assumption that all Inuit stories concerning white men should have a discoverable factual basis. Some will be found to be garbled versions of the truth, understandable misunderstandings by the Inuit, who were unfamiliar with white men and their ways, or the result of inadequacies of the interrogators, whose preconceived ideas and imperfect translations left very misleading impressions. Nevertheless, to my surprise, I managed to discover a scenario which allowed use of all of the native recollections, solved some troubling discrepancies in the physical evidence, and led to some significant new conclusions as to the fate of the beleaguered sailors.

In this, the opening address, it is perhaps appropriate to set out the main points of the case:

COMPARISON OF RECONSTRUCTIONS

Standard	Woodman
Ships direct to C. Felix.	Attempt to find shelter to east of King William Island, one ship briefly grounded.
Sir J. Franklin buried in ice.	Sir J. Franklin buried ashore near C. Felix.

Relics at Victory Pt impulsively discarded.

Abandonment to reach HBC outposts.

All die during 1848.

Ships possibly remanned.

Natives never visit Franklin's ships while manned.

One ship sinks in deep water unobserved.

Natives never see burial ashore.

Crozier dies in 1848.

Party seen by natives at Washington Bay in 1848.

Natives find relics in 1849.

Terror Bay camp established 1848.

Two boats left behind in Erebus Bay.

No records buried in vault on KWI.

Unmanned ship drifts to O'Reilly Is.

Last survivors die at Starvation Cove in 1848.

Thirty bodies found at Starvation Cove.

Adam Beck's stories of massacre disbelieved.

Peglar skeleton discovered.

Hall visits Peffer River.

Relics cached deliberately.

1848 abandonment for seasonal hunting.

Few die during 1848.

Ships definitely remanned.

Natives probably visit manned ships in 1849.

One ship sinks while natives watch.

Natives witness burial ashore.

Crozier dies in 1849.

Party seen there in 1850.

Natives find relics in 1851–2.

Terror Bay camp established 1850.

Three boats left in Erebus Bay.

Vault with records buried in Erebus Bay.

Manned ship taken to Kirkwall Is.

Last survivors leave Starvation Cove in 1851.

Fewer than ten bodies found at Starvation Cove.

Beck stories unravelled.

Armitage skeleton discovered.

Hall never sees Peffer River.

The Franklin saga is a puzzle without the prospect of complete solution. As in an involved court proceeding, the best we can hope for is to present a convincing case which, if not provable "beyond a shadow of a doubt," will be able to compete with those of other advocates. We shall re-examine evidence collected over a century ago, present new clues derived from the best new forensic technology, and review the records of the original detectives who combed the scene. Most of all, we shall cross-examine the witnesses of the events themselves, probing for inconsistencies or previously overlooked connections. Whether we can discover the "truth" about the Franklin tragedy will be up to you, the jury, to decide.

PART 1

The Evidence

Life is the art of drawing
sufficient conclusions from
insufficient evidence.
Samuel Butler

~1~

First Contact

Over one hundred years after the fact, Ohotkto told the tale of the coming of the koblunas to the land of the Netsilingmiut:[1]

One day during the summer (Sept 2, 1829) two men were fishing at "Ow-weet-tee-week" ("the place where whales abound"). This is a river to the north (Agnew River) of Neitchille, and the Inuit would often go there to fish. When the men looked out to sea they could see a large black thing, not an animal, far out to sea. It was slowly being taken to the south by the ice. They had never seen such a thing before and were much alarmed, so they returned to the place where they lived and told the others. All agreed that this must be a white-man's umiak. None of the seal-people had ever seen a kobluna, but the wife of Archnaluak, who was named Kakekagiu, had heard many stories from her sister.

This sister of Kakekagiu had been at Neyuning Eitdua (Winter Island) and Igloolik when the great eshemuta (Captain) Parree brought his two ships to the land of the Arvilingmiut (1821–3). The koblunas had spent two winters with the Arvilingmiut and had been very friendly. They had given the Inuit many fine presents of wood and iron. They were very rich in all of the things which the seal-people most lacked, and the people decided to visit the kobluna umiak when it came to rest in their country.

The Great Spirit brought the white men to a very good place, quite near Sarfak where the Tunrit ruins are. This place was later called Qavdlunarsiorfik ("the place where one meets white men"), and after the white men departed the Inuit would go there to find iron and things which the koblunas left behind.

It was near the middle of winter (8 January 1830) and the people were living quite near this place when some men went out sealing. One of these was Agliktuktoq ("he who is unclean"), and he was hunting a little to the south of the others. His dog was straining to go faster and Agliktuktoq thought that it had scented a bear so he followed as quick as he could. What the dog had smelled was not a bear but some strange men who were walking near a strange kind of house with smoke coming out of it. Greatly frightened, Agliktuktoq hurried back to the village to tell the others of the thing that he had seen.

The people gathered in the dance house to discuss the matter and the angeko (shaman) gathered his charms and his white cloak of caribou belly hide. He took a large deerskin and pegged it to the west wall of the house, had all of the lamps extinguished, then crawled behind the hide to talk to the spirits. All of the spirits said that Agliktuktoq had seen the white men, and that these were friendly and would welcome a visit from the Inuit.

The next morning everyone went to the place where the house was. Illictu and his son Toolooa (who had lost his leg to a bear) were drawn on a komotik (sledge). They found some footprints in the snow and were astonished to see their size and strange shape, and after a conference the people decided to proceed cautiously. Some said that the Great Spirit would destroy the people if they did not kill these strangers. The people hid behind some snow blocks and could see that the house was really a ship with a snow wall around it.

The hunter Niungitsoq ("the good walker") was sent alone to see what the white men would do, but when the white men started to approach him the other men, wishing to show that they were not afraid, came out from behind the snow. Two white men came forward and stopped. Then they shouted "teyma teyma" so the Inuits knew they were friends. The other white men came up and laid their weapons on the ice, and then the Inuit put down their knives and harpoons, and soon all were embracing and dancing together.

The white men took the people to their big ship and gave them each a piece of iron. Then the eshemuta asked for the hunter who had been seen the day before, and when Agliktuktoq was brought forward he took him into the big cabin and gave him an ooloo ("woman's knife"). Agliktuktoq was a great hunter and was offended by being given such a thing, but he saw a handsaw which was hanging on a nail and motioned that he would prefer that. But the eshemuta became angry and he took the ooloo back and chased Agliktuktoq out of the house emptyhanded.

John (later Sir John) Ross's published account predictably fails to mention the fact that he initially rebuffed the native "Alictu" in his quest for a handsaw. As we shall see, the sanitized accounts of affairs which were prepared for the public at home usually could not entirely be relied upon to note such little details. But the Inuit remembered.

Later relations between Ross's crew and the natives were very good. The Inuit especially liked Ross's nephew and second in command, James (later Sir James) Clark Ross. They called James "Aglooka" ("he who takes long strides"), since he always seemed to be in a hurry during his excursions from the ship.[2] Two of the hunters, Ooblooria and Pooyetta, usually went with him on his travels.

The Ross expedition had come to Prince Regent Inlet in search of a passage which would lead to the west. They hoped to be able to take their small steam-assisted vessel, the *Victory*, through such a channel and complete the North-West Passage. Unfortunately, the consistent testimony of their native guides revealed that no such outlet existed in the southern reaches of the Inlet. The natives told of a narrow passage much further north where there were strong tides (Bellot Strait), but, despite repeated attempts, James Ross could never reach it overland. It would be many years before other explorers would confirm the truth of the Inuit geographical assertions.

On one of the first of many exploratory journeys away from the ship, the Inuit guide Ooblooria took James Ross to the west across the narrow isthmus which formed the base of the Boothia Peninsula. They travelled past the large lake of Neitchille which gave the area its Inuit name and from some high ground near Padleak (Spence Bay), which James named Cape Isabella in honour of his sister, Ooblooria pointed out a "continuous open sea, or a sea free from all ice, during the summer." He told James that from the high point to the north-west no land could be seen to the westward, but that "from the south-west to the south-east, there was a tract of land connecting the ground on which we stood with Ac-cool-le and the shores of Repulse Bay."[3]

James Ross's conclusion that what he was being shown was the "great western ocean" was incorrect, for he would later travel to Kikertak ("the big island") which lay to the west. With our present knowledge we can see that Ooblooria was telling James of the ice-free channel (now Ross and Rae Straits) which separates King William Island from Boothia.

James's guide had not yet finished explaining the geographic subtleties of his land. He indicated a place far to the south-west which was called Ootgoolik. Here many Inuit lived, and the Net-silingmiut traded with these Ukjulingmiut for driftwood which accumulated on their shores. Pooyetta would later tell that Oot-goolik was many days' journey away, that there was "first an inlet to be entered [Peel Inlet], after which there were three day's journey on lakes, across some low land [King William Island]; having passed which they again arrived at salt water [Simpson Strait]; and were obliged to travel many days along the sea-coast."[4] Almost twenty years later one of Franklin's ships would be wrecked at Ootgoolik.

In the light of the later Franklin disaster the most noteworthy excursion made by James Ross occurred in May 1830. Accompanied by the mate, Abernethy, and three other men, James set out on a sledging expedition to the west. Taking two sledges, eight dogs, three weeks' provisions, and a skin boat, he hoped to be able to trace some part of the unknown coastline which still remained between Lord Mayor Bay and Point Turnagain far to the west. This latter point had been reached by Lieutenant (later Sir) John Franklin nine years before, during an expedition which had cost the lives of eleven of his twenty companions when the return across the tundra to their base had been a close-run race with starvation.

After following the now-familiar route to Cape Isabella, James Ross set out for some low land which appeared to the west. Everything was so flat and uniformly covered with snow that he had some difficulty in telling whether he was travelling over land or water, but eventually he gained the gravelly shore which he called King William's Land. On his return journey, James would wrongly conclude that King William's Land was a westward-extending peninsula connected to Boothia. The water he had traversed would be shown as "Poctes Bay" on his charts.

The small party travelled north-west along the coast until they reached Cape Felix, where the shore abruptly turned to the south-west. Ross was gratified to see no trace of land to the west, and to note that the shore trended toward Franklin's Point Turnagain. The land here was very flat, and the prospect to seaward bleak, for "the pack of ice which had, in the autumn of the last year, been pressed against that shore, consisted of the heaviest masses that I had ever seen in such a situation." Ross noted that "the lighter floes had been thrown up, on some parts of the coast, in a most extraordinary and incredible manner; turning up large quantities of the shingle before them, and, in some places, having travelled as much as half a mile beyond the limits of the highest tide mark."[5]

James Ross was thus the first white man to attain what would eventually be the most famous stretch of coastline in the entire Arctic. His "heaviest masses" and "vast extent of ocean" would be both the cause and stage of great events.

A few miles to the south, at Wall Bay, Ross stopped to consider his situation. He had left the *Victory* with twenty-one days' provision, and "considerably more than half" had been consumed in the last thirteen. The advancing summer was making for deteriorating travelling conditions and some of his men had minor injuries. Ross therefore decided to allow his men to rest here, and, accompanied by the mate Abernethy, he set off to trace the coast for a further few miles.

[We] left our station ... at eight in the evening. Being light, we now travelled quickly along the land, to the south-westward, till midnight, when, from a stranded piece of ice about forty feet high, we saw a point of land bearing south-west about fifteen miles distant, and could also trace its continuity with that in which we stood; the line forming an extensive bay, occupied by very heavy packed ice ... We now therefore unfurled our flag for the usual ceremony, and took possession of what we saw as far as the distant point, while that on which we stood was named Victory Point; being the "ne plus ultra" of our labour ... The point to the south-west was also named Cape Franklin and if that be a name which has now been conferred on more places than one, these honours, not in fact very solid when so widely shared, are beyond all thought less than the merits of that officer deserve.[6]

James Ross could never have foreseen that this lonely point would become the most famous place in the Arctic. On this sombre spring day the events which would make it so were far in the future.

On Victory Point, Ross and Abernethy hurriedly built a rock cairn six feet high and "enclosed in it a canister containing a brief account of the proceedings of the expedition since its departure from England. Such had been the custom, and to that it was our business to conform; though I must say, that we did not entertain the most remote hope that our little history would ever meet an European's eye."[7]

It would be two days short of seventeen years before another "European eye" would see the lonely cache of stones on Victory Point. That eye belonged to a boy who was nine years old when the cairn was built. It was an eye that was destined to be the first to see the last link in the North-West Passage.

At the time the interactions between the Netsilingmiut and the Rosses at Felix and Sheriff Harbours, and the short journey to the western shore of King William's Land, were not the focal point of the Rosses' expedition. In their eyes their crowning achievement was James's later journey to the location of the North Magnetic Pole, which was then located on the western Boothia shore. To those at home, the most noteworthy part of the expedition came at the end.

During the stay of the white men, the hunting had been un-usually unproductive in the vicinity of Lord Mayor Bay, and, despite their pleasure in interacting with strangers, the Inuit de-parted for better hunting grounds in 1831. The *Victory* had been shifted only four miles in 1830 (from Felix Harbour to Sheriff Harbour), and a further fourteen (to Victory, later Victoria, Har-bour) in 1831. Here it soon became obvious that she would have to be abandoned.

In August 1824, one of William Parry's ships, the *Fury*, had been wrecked on the eastern shore of Somerset Island, about two hundred miles from the place where the *Victory* was trapped. Parry had landed the *Fury*'s boats and much of her stores here at "Fury Beach" in the hope that they would prove to be of some use to a later voyager, and John Ross had supplemented his own larder there on the southbound journey. Ross now proposed that his crew drag two of their own boats to the north and leave them

in some convenient place, after which they would proceed to
Fury Beach. If Parry's boats were seaworthy the party would
attempt to reach Lancaster Sound and the annual whaling
fleet.

Some of the *Victory*'s stores were left ashore, where they would
subsequently be discovered and rejoiced over by the Inuit (who
called Victory Harbour "qilanartot" – roughly translated as "joyful
beach"). The ship itself was wrapped in chain, and Ross thought
that, in her leaky condition, she was bound to sink as soon as
the ice melted.

On 29 May 1832 John Ross and his men commenced their long
march to the north. Slowly moving their sledges and boats in
relays, they had to walk three times the straight-line distance,
but the exhausted party eventually reached Fury Beach on 1 July.
According to his crew, John was a "featherbed traveller" and
spent most of the trip perched on the provisions sledge – another
fact he neglects to mention in his published Narrative.

The men built a small shelter, which was given the imposing
name of "Somerset House." Three of the *Fury*'s boats were over-
hauled, and after a month of preparation and recuperation the
men set to sea, only to find that Lancaster Sound was choked
with ice and deserted. With no other options, they then returned
to their little thirty-one-by-sixteen-foot hut to pass their fourth
winter in the ice.

On 26 August 1833 Ross and his men were camped on the
shore of Lancaster Sound when a ship was sighted. Unfortunately, she did not see the bedraggled men and soon sailed off.
But six hours later another hove into sight and stopped to recover
her boats. She too soon set sail away, but the weary explorers
gave chase and luckily a calm descended on the fast-disappearing
ship which allowed the boats to overtake her. Having finally seen
the approaching boats, the crew of the ship launched one of their
boats to meet them.

The mate in command addressed us, by presuming that we had met
with some misfortune and lost our ship. This being answered in the
affirmative, I [John Ross] requested to know the name of his vessel,
and expressed our wish to be taken on board. I was answered that it
was "the *Isabella* of Hull, once commanded by Captain Ross;" on which
I stated that I was the identical man in question, and my people the

crew of the *Victory*. That the mate, who commanded the boat, was as much astonished at this information as he appeared to be, I do not doubt; while, with the usual blunderheadedness of men on such occasions, he assured me that I had been dead two years. I easily convinced him, however, that what ought to have been true, according to his estimate, was a somewhat premature conclusion ...[8]

Although Ross's expedition had been privately financed, the British government had been called upon, after so many years without news, to organize some effort to relieve it. The plan which was adopted called for Commander George Back, who had served on Franklin's overland expeditions, to attempt to reach the vicinity of Boothia by descending the treacherous and still unexplored "Thlew-ee-choh-degeth" or "Great Fish River." The Indians said that this would take him to the Arctic Ocean near the scene of Ross's supposed disaster. While making final preparations at Fort Reliance on Great Slave Lake, Back learned of Ross's rescue, but his orders were changed only as much as was required to make his journey one of relief rather than one of exploration.

Back and his party struggled, first, to find, then to descend, the turbulent river, and finally reached its mouth on 28 July 1834. It had taken the small party forty-two days of unremitting labour to accomplish the "violent and tortuous course of five hundred and thirty geographical miles, running through an iron-ribbed country without a single tree on the whole line of its banks, expanding into fine large lakes with clear horizons, most embarrassing to the navigator, and broken into falls, cascades, and rapids, to the number of no less than eighty three."[9]

Back encountered a large band of friendly Inuit encamped at Lake Franklin, a short distance from the river's mouth. These Utkuhikjalingmiut knew nothing of the earlier Ross expedition, but, as Ooblooria had with James Ross, they gladly told him of the surrounding geography.

Back found that the Great Fish River (now named after him) emptied into a deep inlet (Chantrey Inlet). He stopped briefly at a large island which he named Montreal, and a low sandy point of land which he called Ogle Point, both of which would figure in the later Franklin tragedy. At Ogle Point Back too was forced by lack of provisions and bad weather to consider his return. He saw two small "islands" to the north (actually the southern shore of King William Island), and named them after James Clark Ross. From what he could see, and from an imperfect understanding of what the natives had told him, Back concluded that there was probably a channel to the eastward which led to Prince Regent Inlet after all, making Boothia, in contradiction to what the Rosses had been told, into an island. This idea would die hard.

Back's return to Great Slave Lake was arduous but uneventful. He did notice that the formerly friendly natives near Lake Franklin had inexplicably become distrustful and wary, but at the time could not account for this. He later learned that some of his men, while detached from the main party, had had a fight with an Inuit party and killed three of them.[10] Back was merely puzzled when the natives "retreated with precipitation to the tents and rocks" and did not attempt to reinitiate contact. As soon as the Inuit saw that the white men would not stop, "an elderly man ran after us along the rocks ... and with loud vociferations ... bade us go away ... We perceived, infinitely to our amusement, that this was the conjuror, or wise man of the tribe ... thinking no doubt to charm us away."[11]

The old shaman's dance occurred on 31 August 1834. In 1923, eighty-nine years later, the same story was told by the grandchildren of Back's natives to Knud Rasmussen, a Danish anthropologist.

Among the Uthuhikjalingmut there is an ancient tradition that once in days gone by white men came in a boat down the Kunajik: Back River. They were the first white men that had ever been seen, friendly and good people, who bought trout for rare treasures such as knives and fish hooks. They were remarkable, smiling men, who walked about with lumps of wood in their mouths emitting smoke: they spoke in a tongue that nobody understood. Their stay at Itivnarssuk was only a brief one, then they carried their boat inland behind the rapid and rowed away down over Tahejucq: Lake Franklin. But they came back again shortly afterwards. This time they came up the river and were in a great hurry, and people were afraid of them, for it had been heard tell that one had to be cautious of white men who retraced their steps: they were dangerous and easily angered. In those times there were wise shamans among the folks, and one of the oldest spoke a magic verse that was intended to charm the white men away, far away ...[12]

This well-remembered if brief visit of Back and his men, like that of the Rosses, would have an impact on the conduct of Franklin's last expedition and on the Inuit traditions told of it.

The last white men to visit King William Island before the arrival of the doomed *Erebus* and *Terror* were sent by the Hudson's Bay Company to finally resolve whether Boothia was an island or a peninsula. The 1839 expedition of Thomas Simpson and Peter Warren Dease did not encounter any Inuit along their route, but the traces of their passage would later be confused with those of Franklin's men.

Simpson and Dease descended the Coppermine River and proceeded eastward along the unknown Arctic coast. They forced their twin boats, aptly named *Castor* and *Pollux*, through the shallow reef-filled stretches of Queen Maud Gulf, finally reaching the much-indented western shore of the Adelaide Peninsula. Although they did not know the name, they were the first white men to reach Ootgoolik.

They noted of this island-strewn area that it was "much encumbered with ice, with eleven and twelve fathoms' water; and then there appeared green sloping hills and large islands, the favourite resort of reindeer. This, after a short interval of sand, was in its turn succeeded (at Point Grant) by a large tract of shingle and limestone. It was here that the traces of Esquimaux became frequent."[13]

The terrain to the eastward became more inviting, heavily populated by game and abounding in signs of native occupation. This stretch of Arctic coastline would become, in ten years' time, the last hope for Franklin's retreating crews. The coast Simpson and Dease walked along was trending directly for Ross's Victory Point, but they were surprised to find that past Grant Point the coast turned to the eastward into a narrow strait that led them toward Back's Point Ogle. This is now called Simpson Strait.

After a brief visit to Back's camp at Montreal Island, Simpson's party crossed Chantrey Inlet to a prominent headland which they named Cape Britannia.

Just at sunrise on the 17th I climbed the bluff cape to which our course had been directed and saw the coast turn off sharply and decidedly eastward. Thence, round to the north-west, stretched a sea free from ice, and devoid of all land, except what looked like two very distant islands. On the rocky summit, about two hundred feet in height, the natives of this barren region had erected a ponderous stone slab for a landmark ...

On the beetling rock that sheltered our little camp from the sea, and forms the most commanding station on this part of the coast, we erected a conical pile of ponderous stones, fourteen feet high; which, if it be not pulled down by the natives, may defy the rage of a thousand storms. In it was placed a sealed bottle, containing an outline of our proceedings.[14]

This cairn would withstand the elements even longer than Simpson hoped. It still commanded the skyline into the 1980s, and would be one focus of the Franklin search.

The explorers persevered eastwards, each unfolding mile holding the promise of success. But the perennial problem had once again arisen – too much geography, too little summer.

It was now quite evident to us, even in our most sanguine mood, that the time was come for commencing our return to the distant Coppermine River, and that any foolhardy perseverance could only lead to the loss of the whole party ... The men were therefore directed to construct another monument in commemoration of our visit; while Mr. Dease and I walked to an eminence three miles off, to see the farther trending of the coast. Our view of the low main-shore was limited to about five miles, when it seemed to turn off more to the right. Far without lay several lofty islands; and in the northeast, more distant still, appeared some high blue land: this which we designated Cape Sir John Ross, is in all probability one of the southeastern promontories of Boothia. We could therefore hardly doubt being now arrived at that large gulph, uniformly described by the Esquimaux as containing many islands, and with numerous indentations, running down to the southward, till it approaches within forty miles of Repulse and Wager bays ... The mouth of the stream which bounded the lost career of our admirable little boats, and received their name, lies in lat. 68° 28' 23" N; long 94° 14' w.[15]

The cairn at Castor and Pollux River would also be a factor in the subsequent Franklin story.

Not content with their considerable outbound discoveries, Simpson and Dease slightly altered their homeward route. Having backtracked to Point Ogle, they branched off for further exploration, first heading down Barrow Inlet and then camping on Richardson Point, a long spit of land dividing two inlets.

From thence we crossed over on the 24th, to what had from the continent looked like islands, but which I had rightly conjectured to be part of the southern shore of Boothia. This shore we had the satisfaction of tracing, for nearly sixty miles till it turned up to the north ... only fifty seven-miles from Captain James Ross' Pillar [at Victory Point] ... The objects seen on this coast are easily enumerated. A limestone country, low and uninteresting, but abounding in reindeer, musk-cattle, and old native encampments. To seaward a good deal of ice appeared, and vast numbers of snow-geese passed high overhead in long triangular flights, bound for milder skies ... Our people erected another lofty cairn, to commemorate our discoveries; and the place was called Cape Herschel, after that distinguished astronomer.[16]

Like its counterparts at Cape Britannia and the Castor and Pollux River, this cairn at Cape Herschel would also withstand the rigours of time. The next white man to see it, nine years hence, would be in much more unfortunate circumstances.

After this short sojourn on the southern coast of "Boothia" (actually King William Island), the party recrossed the ten-mile-wide strait to Ootgoolik and noted the traces of the Inuit who lived there. Simpson thought that they must be "pretty numerous," and rightly concluded that during the summer they ventured inland to hunt caribou, while spending the winter on the coast hunting seal.

The next koblunas to visit this corner of the central Arctic would be the crews of the *Erebus* and *Terror*. They would explore the sixty-mile gap between James Ross's Victory Point and Simpson's Cape Herschel. They would eventually attempt to reach the Inuit whom Back had met at the mouth of the Great Fish River. One of their ships would be cast ashore at Ootgoolik, and some of them would meet the same natives who had seen the Rosses at Qavdlunarsiorfik. The stage was set for the single most dramatic catastrophe in the annals of Arctic exploration.

The Investigation

Dr John Rae considered the 21st of April 1854 to be an "extremely fine" day. He and his small party were passing to the south of Pelly Bay, westbound for Castor and Pollux River, in an attempt to join his earlier discoveries of 1847 to those made by Simpson and Dease in 1839. His plan was to complete the hard-fought survey of the Arctic coast of continental North America, a job which had been temporarily subordinated to the search for Franklin. Rae's purpose was strictly geographical; he thought there was "not the slightest hope of finding any traces" of Franklin's men.[1]

Rae had encountered some Inuit the day before. These natives had tried to dissuade him from proceeding west, and had pilfered some biscuit and grease. He had nevertheless bought some seal-meat from them, and on the 21st, shortly after starting on the day's march, he stopped to deposit this among the rocks. Much to Rae's annoyance, his native interpreter chose this moment to try to desert. After a "sharp race of four or five miles" the interpreter (William Ouligbuck Jr, whose native name was Mar-ko) was overtaken "crying like a baby," and eventually he was persuaded to return to camp. This delay, annoying as it must have been, allowed Rae to solve the Franklin mystery.

We had barely resumed our journey when we were met by a very intelligent Esquimaux, driving a dog sledge laden with musk ox beef.

This man at once consented to accompany us two days' journey, and in a few minutes had deposited his load on the snow, and was ready to join us ... We were now joined by another of the natives, who had been absent seal-hunting yesterday; but being anxious to see us had visited our snow house early this morning, and then followed our track. This man was very communicative, and on putting to him the usual questions as to his having seen white men before, or any ships or boats, he replied in the negative; but said that a party of kabloonans had died of starvation a long distance to the west of where we then were, and beyond a large river ...[2]

Twenty-five years later one of the native principals of this meeting, whose name Rae transcribed as Imike-pa-hu-gi-uke, was again interviewed by Charles Francis Hall; Hall, and most later writers, called him In-nook-poo-zhe-jook.

When & where was it that that [sic] you 1st saw Dr Rae?
Answers. It was when he was at Pelly Bay the last time he came into this country. *Mar-ko, Oo-ling-buk's son, was with him* ...
Ques. How many men were with Dr Rae?
Ans. Five in all – Dr Rae, Mar-ko & three white men.
Ques. Did any of the Innuits of Pelly Bay tell Dr Rae at that time when there about the white men that had died to the westward of that place?
Ans. The Pelly Bay natives didn't know anything about the white men's starving then – He In-uk (In-nook-poo-zhe-jook, I shall for brevities [sic] sake write In-k) was on his way from Neitchille to Pelly Bay when he met Dr Rae. An Innuit by the name of Ook-pik was accompanying In-k on this journey. In-k's family & Ook-pik's were with them.
Ques. Where was Dr Rae going when you met him?
Ans. Ki-ki-tuk (K.W.L.) & he In-uk went with him & party for 2 days.
Ques. Did any other Innuits go with you when you travelled 2 days with Dr Rae?
Ans. Yes & his name is See-u-ti-chu. (emphasis in original)[3]

The details of the meeting remembered by In-nook-poo-zhe-jook were in perfect accord with those of Rae.

In-k points to the land about or near where Dr Rae was on the 20th of Apr as being where he 1st saw Dr Rae ... It was where See-u-ti-chu had deposited the Musk ox meat & was on his way with dogs & sledge having on the sledge the things Dr Rae wished him to carry that he In-k came up & overtook the party. Then on In-k coming up dr [sic] Rae engaged him to go with the party for two days. Then it was that he In-k told Mar-ko about white men dying at Ki-ki-tuk K.W.L. & other places in that locality ...[4]

In-nook-poo-zhe-jook's account was remarkable in its accurate preservation of detail. He also clarified Ouligbuck's strange attempt at desertion. According to him the Pelly Bay natives had warned Mar-ko the day before that the warlike natives to the west would surely kill Rae and his companions.[5]

Both In-nook-poo-zhe-jook and See-u-ti-chu would be pivotal witnesses in the Franklin saga.

Thus did the knowledge of Franklin's fate, so long sought for, finally come to light. Six years after the *Erebus* and *Terror* had been abandoned, and three weeks after Franklin and his men had been officially pronounced dead, it was told as an offhand story by a curious Inuit who had wanted to see a white man for himself.

Rae considered this information "too vague to act upon," and, after purchasing an officer's gold cap-band, proceeded on his journey. When he returned to Pelly Bay, Rae again met In-nook-poo-zhe-jook, and he now learned more details of the dead kob-lunas. Other Inuit had relics for sale, including a silver spoon and fork embossed with an unfamiliar family crest. Rae noted that "the initials F.R.M.C. not engraved, but scratched with a sharp instrument, on the spoon, puzzled me much, as I knew not at the time, the Christian names of the officers of Sir John Franklin's Expedition; and thought that the letters above named might possibly be the initials of Captain McClure, the small c between M C being omitted."[6]

Rae did not learn for many months that the spoon which he held in his hand was marked with the initials of Francis Rawdon Moira Crozier, Captain of the *Terror*.

Had there been any doubt that the stories and relics from beyond the "great river" were from Franklin's expedition, they were soon dispelled as the Inuit brought more items to Rae's winter quarters at Repulse Bay. He acquired Franklin's Guelphic Order of Hanover and a circular plate bearing his name, silverware belonging to seven officers of the *Erebus* and five of the *Terror*, a fragment of under-vest marked "F.D.V. 6.1845" (belonging to Charles Frederick Des Voeux, Mate of the *Erebus*), parts of a gold watch which had been the property of James Reid (Ice-Master of the *Erebus*), a knife handle marked "C.H." on one side and "Hickey" on the other (Cornelius Hickey, Caulker's Mate of the *Terror*), and a certificate case on which had been scratched the letters "W M" (presumably the initials of William Mark, Able Seaman of the *Erebus*).[7]

The only papers which had survived were two pages of a devotional work entitled "The Student's Manual," and these bore no marks of ownership or any personal notes. It became obvious that the greatest source of information would be the Inuit traditions themselves. In his tent at Repulse Bay, Rae learned the details of the Franklin retreat from many different individuals. Only now did he conclude that the "great river" of which In-nook-poo-zhe-jook had spoken was actually Back's Great Fish River. His summer explorations had unknowingly taken him to within a few day's travel of the site. The stories told of the last days of the Franklin crew were heart-breaking.

In the spring, four winters past (eighteen hundred and fifty), whilst some Esquimaux families were killing seals near the northern shore of a large island, named in Arrowsmith's charts King William's Land, about forty white men were seen travelling in company southward over the ice, and dragging a boat and sledges with them. They were passing along the west shore of the above-named island. None of the party could speak the Esquimaux language so well as to be understood; but by signs the natives were led to believe that the ship or ships had been crushed by ice, and that they were then going to where they expected to find deer to shoot. From the appearance of the men – all of whom, with the exception of an officer, were hauling on the drag-ropes of the sledge, and were looking thin – they were then supposed to be getting short of provisions; and they purchased a small seal, or piece of seal, from the natives.

The officer was described as being a tall, stout, middle-aged man. When their day's journey terminated, they pitched tents to rest in.

At a later date, the same season, but previous to the disruption of the ice, the corpses of some thirty persons and some graves were discovered on the continent, and five dead bodies on an island near it, about a long day's journey to the north-west of the mouth of a large stream, which can be no other than Back's Great Fish River (named by the Esquimaux Oot-koo-hi-ca-lik), as its description, and that of the low shore in the neighbourhood of Point Ogle and Montreal Island, agree exactly with that of Sir George Back. Some of the bodies were in a tent or tents; others were under the boat, which had been turned over to form a shelter; and some lay scattered about in different directions. Of those seen on the island, it was supposed that one was that of an officer (chief), as he had a telescope strapped over his shoulders, and his double-barrelled gun lay underneath him.

From the mutilated state of many of the bodies, and the contents of the kettles, it is evident that our wretched countrymen had been driven to the last dread alternative as a means of sustaining life.

A few of the unfortunate men must have survived until the arrival of the wild fowl (say until the end of May), as shots were heard, and fish-bones and feathers of geese were noticed near the scene of the sad event.

There appears to have been an abundant store of ammunition, as the gunpowder was emptied by the natives in a heap on the ground out of the kegs or cases containing it; and a quantity of shot and ball was found below high-water mark, having probably been left on the ice close to the beach before the spring thaw commenced. There must have been a number of telescopes, guns (several of them double-barrelled), watches, compasses, &c.; all of which seem to have been broken up, as I saw pieces of these different articles with the natives, – and I purchased as many as possible ...[8]

Now that Rae had brought the elusive clue to the Franklin mystery back from the north, it was inconceivable that it would not be followed up. The British government, distracted by the Crimean War, was loath to invest any more ships and men, but the Hudson's Bay Company was asked to mount a small overland expedition to the area.

A small party, led by James Anderson and James Green Stewart, piloted their frail canoes down the turbulent Great Fish River and reached Chantrey Inlet in August 1855. They found a cairn of white men's relics and some other vestiges on Montreal Island, including two chips of wood with "Erebus" and "Mr Stanley" scratched on them, but none of the physical evidence was very illuminating. Hampered by lack of provisions and bad weather, they could not reach King William Island itself. Anderson had encountered a small group of Inuit camped near the Franklin Rapids, but owing to his lack of an interpreter could gain little from them beyond confirmation that some white men had died nearby.[9]

The stories and relics collected by Rae and Anderson convinced many in England that the complete story of the Franklin tragedy could only be learned by a search of King William Island itself. Foremost and most vocal of those demanding further effort was Franklin's widow, Jane. This indefatigable lady vowed, if the Navy should be so heartless as to abandon the quest and "unfortunately throw upon me the responsibility and the cost of sending out a vessel myself," that she would "not shrink, either from that weighty responsibility, or from the sacrifice of my entire available fortune for the purpose."[10]

The Admiralty was unmoved, and Jane, good as her word, steadfastly set about organizing a privately financed expedition. She bought and refited the yacht *Fox*, and engaged an Arctic veteran, Captain (later Admiral Sir) Leopold McClintock, to command her.

The *Fox* sailed in July 1857, stopped briefly in Greenland, and then tackled the "middle pack" of Melville Sound. Finding unexpectedly heavy ice, McClintock moored the ship to an iceberg to await a more favourable opportunity. None came. The *Fox* helplessly drifted toward the south for the entire winter and was finally released on 26 April 1858.

After a short stop in Greenland to repair his ship and refresh his crew, McClintock resumed his mission. Following in Franklin's wake, the *Fox* sailed for Cape Walker. As Franklin had done twelve years earlier, McClintock took his small ship into Peel Strait. Twenty-five miles to the south the *Fox* was frustrated by a solid barrier of ice. McClintock therefore decided to reverse course and attempt to approach King William Island by way of Prince Regent Inlet and Bellot Strait. But the western end of Bellot Strait was also impassable and the *Fox* retreated to a secure harbour at Port Kennedy. The final miles to King William Island would have to be accomplished by sledge.

In February 1859 sledging operations commenced. McClintock took one sledge and two companions (Thompson and his interpreter Petersen) along the western shore of the Boothia Peninsula. Near the Magnetic Pole they met with some Inuit who had many Franklin relics to sell. An old man named Oo-na-lee told McClintock that these had come from a place where some white people had starved to death on an island in a river which contained salmon.[11]

From these natives came information about the wrecks of one of Franklin's ships which had been "crushed by the ice out in the sea to the west of King William's Land." His informants admitted that they had not seen the white men themselves, and McClintock felt certain that Franklin's men "did not at any time land upon the Boothian shore."[12]

In April the mission commenced in earnest, although the weather was blustery and very cold with temperatures of thirty degrees below zero. McClintock and his second in command, Hobson, took ten seamen, two man-drawn sledges, and two smaller dog-drawn ones, and set off for King William Island. Near Cape Victoria they again met with Oo-na-lee and his family. McClintock now heard of a second ship which "was forced on shore by the ice, where they suppose she still remains, but is much broken. From this ship they have obtained most of their wood, &c.; and Oot-loo-lik is the name of the place where she grounded."[13] The white men concluded that "Oot-loo-lik" was some locality on the west coast of King William Island.

The natives also told that "the body of a man was found on board the ship; that he must have been a very large man, and had long teeth ... it was in the fall of the year – that is, August or September – when the ships were destroyed; that all the white men went away to the 'large river', taking a boat or boats with them, and that in the following winter their bones were found there."[14]

McClintock bought some food from the natives, and also purchased their only two dogs. He noted that Oo-na-lee "made many inquiries about the position of our ship, her size, and the number of men," and thought that "had he been able to travel so far with his wife and several young children, and without sledge or dogs, I think he certainly would have gone up to Port Kennedy; we did not give him any encouragement to do so."[15]

McClintock's two meetings with the natives were well remembered. Seven years later a native named Seepunger would tell how "a sledge with several Kob-lu-nas a few years ago came down 1st with 4 men (one an Innuit) on the ice in very cold weather & there (pointing to Cape Victoria of Rae's chart) they said many Innuits saw them. After this the same & more Koblu-nas came down with 2 sledges. They came from a ship they said that was up somewhere further north."[16]

Seepunger's wife Ki-u-tuk told "the story of her mother's father seeing white men a few years ago near Net-i-lik [Boothia] dragging a sledge." She also recalled how "the family attempted to go up to the ship but having a sick child (infant) & no dogs turned back when not far from where the ship was." The family had no dog because "the dogs (2 or 3) were sold to the white men."[17]

As with Rae's encounter with In-nook-poo-zhe-jook and See-u-ti-chu, every relevant detail preserved by McClintock was remembered by the Inuit. They knew that he had come twice, once with one sledge, once with two. They accurately preserved the details of the cold weather, the locale, and the sale of the two dogs. Since Petersen spoke their language, they assumed that he was an Inuit, and they remembered one too many white men in the first encounter, but in spite of these minor errors there is no difficulty in identifying the source of their traditions.

Having exhausted the knowledge of their informants, the white men continued south to Cape Victoria. Here the party divided, McClintock continuing south toward the Great Fish River and Montreal Island to extend Anderson's search, while Hobson took some men to explore the western shore of King William Island in search of the ship which was reported to have been cast up on the coast.

McClintock travelled down the east coast of King William Island, meeting a few Inuit near Cape Norton and Booth Point, but learned nothing new. Crossing over to Montreal Island, he found a few relics in a native cairn, but no signs of graves or other remains of a white man's camp.

Recrossing to King William Island, McClintock proceeded westward along the southern shore. He found a solitary skeleton near Gladman Point and fruitlessly dismantled Simpson's cairn at Cape Herschel in hopes of finding some record left by Franklin's retreating men. About twelve miles further on he found a cairn which had been built by Hobson. In it was a message telling of the discovery of a Franklin record at Victory Point!

This record consisted of a standard printed sheet on which James Fitzjames, Captain of the *Erebus*, had written two accounts.

The first, signed by the officers of a detached party (Gore and Des Voeux) and deposited in 1847, gave the details of the expedition's discoveries of 1845–6 and told of the departure of a small exploring party from the ships in 1847. It ended cheerfully – "All well." The more important message had been added a year later, scribbled around the margin. It told of the continued besetment of the *Erebus* and *Terror*, the death of Franklin on 11 June 1847, and the abandonment of the ships by the remaining 105 men on 22 April 1848. It was signed by Fitzjames and Crozier, and the latter had added "and start tomorrow, 26th, for Back's Fish River."

As McClintock continued north he found relics which the retreating crews had left behind. Most significant of these was a boat on a sledge which he found in Erebus Bay. It contained two skeletons. Crozier's landing-place camp at Victory Point was also easily found. At both places McClintock was shocked to note the number and variety of apparently useless things which the crew of the *Erebus* and *Terror* had brought ashore on their last march.

McClintock's return to the *Fox*, and the subsequent return to England, were relatively uneventful. The vague stories he had collected were essentially uninteresting to the British public. They added detail to Rae's account, and confirmed it, but presented little that was new. The Victory Point record and the many physical relics which had been recovered were carefully examined, but nothing more could be learned from them.

McClintock and Hobson found the record at Victory Point nine years after its deposition. Another decade would pass before the next investigator arrived on King William Island. The solitary white man who then took up the quest would pursue the truth, or at least his own vision of it, for a decade.

Charles Francis Hall was, by almost any standard, an eccentric. A burly, devout, self-educated man, he had, with varying degrees of success, been a blacksmith, engraver, printer, and publisher. His abiding passion was the Arctic, and after immersing himself in the journals of the explorers, Hall turned his not inconsiderable passion and single-minded determination to a pursuit in which he fervently believed – the rescue of Franklin survivors.

Hall read accounts of whalers who had lived comfortably with the Inuit for extended periods of time, and he reasoned that some of Franklin's men might have taken refuge among the natives as well. That any such survivors would hardly have needed twelve years to make their way to civilization did not occur to him, for he had undergone the only experience which could allow him to set aside common sense in preference to belief – a calling from God. Hall believed that he had been chosen to lead some of Franklin's men, who were still living among the Inuit, home to civilization. This belief would sustain him through privation and frustration which would have defeated a less inspired investigator.

Not surprisingly, Hall's scheme initially enlisted little support. Forced by lack of official interest to finance his one-man expedition himself, he determined to take advantage of free passage to the Arctic with the American whaling fleet. Landing on Baffin Island in 1860, Hall proposed to enlist some Inuit guides to escort him in an open boat to King William Island. Perhaps luckily for him, the natives were not over-enthusiastic, and in any case his boat had been accidentally wrecked during a storm. Hall nevertheless spent two years living with these friendly natives and he quickly became adept in their ways. While here he met the two Inuit who were to be his constant companions and friends throughout the rest of his Arctic career – Tookoolitoo and Ebierbing (also called Adlala), whom he renamed "Hannah" and "Joe."[18]

Interesting as Hall's sojourn with the Baffin Island natives had been, and necessary as indoctrination, it had been totally unproductive of any information concerning Franklin. Pausing briefly in the United States to lobby for more financial support (which he received from Henry Grinnell, a long-standing Arctic patron), Hall returned to the Arctic with his friends Tookoolitoo and Ebierbing in 1864.

This time Hall's goal was Repulse Bay, from which he hoped to be able to follow in Rae's footsteps and finally, with the aid of Inuit guides, reach King William Island. Unfortunately, owing to an error in navigation, his small entourage was mistakenly dropped by the whalers on the forbidding shore forty miles to the south of Wager Bay. Ebierbing soon found a nearby band of Inuit who welcomed the strangers, and Hall lived with these people and their chief Ouela until May 1865. From them he heard second-hand accounts of the two ships which had been lost in the ice far to the west, including one story which stated, much to his delight, that there were four men who had survived!

In July Hall moved his party to Repulse Bay, where he remained until March 1866. But he would not actually set off for King William Island for another three years. Delayed by weather, poor health, trouble in motivating the natives, and a quixotic and fruitless excursion to Melville Peninsula in search of reported white men, Hall spent four increasingly frustrating winters camped among the natives of Repulse Bay. He nevertheless spent the time profitably, questioning and cross-examining any natives he met about the lost expedition.

In March 1869 Hall finally set off on his long-awaited journey to the west. Stopping briefly in Pelly Bay, he met Seepunger and Ki-u-tuk, who told him the stories of the meetings with McClintock, heard by now familiar stories of the Franklin disaster, and obtained some relics. None of the Inuit there had ever been to King William Island, but they had friends and relations who had. Hall continued to the westward. His small party crossed the base of the Boothia Peninsula in ten days and reached Rae Strait in late April. On the eastern side of the strait Hall noticed a small group of igloos which he soon found to be littered with Franklin relics. More important, one of the inhabitants was Rae's acquaintance In-nook-poo-zhe-jook!

After meeting Rae, In-nook-poo-zhe-jook had visited King William Island in search of the white men's things, and he told Hall of finding a tent full of dead men near "Toonoonee" (Terror Bay), and of the discovery of a boat surrounded by skeletons a few miles to the east of Cape Crozier. In long interviews Hall also learned of remains which had been found unburied on a small island to the south of King William Island called "Keeuna."

While at Rae Strait Hall met two natives named Teekeeta and Ow-wer. These men had actually met with a small group of white men dragging a sledge along the shore near Washington Bay! For eight days Hall interviewed the men individually and collectively, taking copious and often verbatim notes. Here he learned that McClintock's "Ootgoolik" wreck had been found in the vicinity of O'Reilly Island and pillaged by the natives. He also learned of the initial discovery of the remains of what he presumed to have been the last survivors in a cove to the west of

Richardson Point on the northern Adelaide Peninsula. All of the tales were consistent and detailed, and much new knowledge was gained.

The season was perfect for travelling and Hall looked forward to an eventful summer of search on King William Island itself. In-nook-poo-zhe-jook readily agreed to accompany the party and act as guide. But it was not to be. Having come so far and waited so long, Hall was now shocked to hear his Inuit companions emphatically refuse to spend the summer on King William Island. They complained that the island offered poor hunting, and that the time had come to begin the homeward trip to Repulse Bay before the thaw set in. They could spare little more time for the white man's foolishness; his friends would cross over to "Kik-ertak" with him, but they would stay only one week.

Hall must have seethed in frustration. In an effort to accomplish something noteworthy he decided to make a flying visit to the nearest site where Franklin remains could be found – "Keeuna." On this small islet (now called Todd Islet) Hall found a thigh bone, which In-nook-poo-zhe-jook confirmed was part of one of the five men who had died here. Hall built a cairn over it, bitterly musing on the small return for his years of effort, and sickened to hear the natives casually remark that the bodies found here had been molested by their dogs.

In the next few days Hall crossed over to King William Island itself and visited two nearby places where the natives knew of remains. At one site the deep snow hid its secrets, but at the other his guides uncovered a complete skeleton which Hall subsequently brought back to the United States. Having accomplished all that his limited time would allow, a much-embittered Hall commenced the long trek back to Repulse Bay.

Although Hall had originally been impressed with the Inuit capacity for survival in the harshest conditions, and had been, for his time, uncharacteristically ready to adopt Inuit ways and accept their culture, he left the Arctic disillusioned with both his quest and his native hosts. Hall's great contribution to the Franklin story lies in the stories which he collected from the Inuit, some of whom had been participants in the events themselves. Although marred by his many preconceptions, assumptions, and false expectations, Hall's accounts of the detailed conversations with the natives remain the primary source of the native view of what occurred. The fact that Hall himself initially tended to believe that everything he heard could be accepted literally, and, in the end, came to the opposite conclusion that much of what he heard had been incorrect, is really irrelevant. What matters most are the words themselves.[19]

Soon after his return to the United States, Hall was inspired by another quixotic quest – the attainment of the North Pole. Now a recognized Arctic veteran, he was given command of the ship *Polaris*, and died (or was murdered) aboard her while wintering in northern Greenland. Hall therefore never organized his copious Franklin notes into a coherent "Narrative" of his experiences. It was left for an editor, J.E. Nourse, to attempt to make sense of his handwritten, jumbled, and fragmentary collection. The result would not be published until 1879.

The year before Hall's posthumous narrative was published, another expedition departed the United States. Commanded by a u.s. Army lieutenant, Frederick Schwatka, it was inspired by vague tales relayed by some whaling captains of white men still wandering the Arctic wastes. The hard-headed and practical Schwatka did not really expect to find survivors and was only mildly surprised to find that the stories had no basis in fact, but he nevertheless proceeded to take his party overland from Hudson Bay to the mouth of the Great Fish River.

Schwatka's party spent an entire summer minutely searching King William Island and Adelaide Peninsula and interviewed many of the same individuals who had told stories to Hall. The traditions which they heard generally corroborated the details given to the earlier explorers. They recovered some relics, entombed the scattered remains which they found in cairns, and left.[20]

The Schwatka expedition was the last of the nineteenth century and the last to interview actual participants in the events. In this century the matter has been taken in hand by traders, travellers, writers, and scientists. Amundsen and Larsen both took time from their pursuit of the North-West Passage to interview the natives of King William Island. Knud Rasmussen, a Danish anthropologist who studied Inuit culture in the 1920s, also spent some time with the natives of the Franklin area, hearing the old stories from the children of Hall's informants.

More recently many others have, among their other duties,

devoted time and effort to the Franklin story. Burwash, Finnie, Skinner, Gibson, Learmonth, Cooper, and Beattie, among others, have conducted informal interviews and official or unofficial searches of King William Island. All have made contributions to unravelling the mystery.

Nevertheless, little has emerged to significantly change the "standard reconstruction" of the Franklin disaster. For one hundred and forty years the account of the tragedy given to Rae by In-nook-poo-zhe-jook and See-u-ti-chu has been accepted and endorsed. As we shall see, it was a remarkably accurate recital of events. But it was not the whole story.

~3~

The Witnesses

There were no European witnesses to the final events of the Franklin disaster. Except for the few pieces of physical evidence which were laboriously gathered by later explorers, the sum total of our knowledge of what happened emerges from the folk history of the Inuit. Before placing these witnesses on the stand, therefore, we must determine how trustworthy their testimony, largely derived from their verbally conveyed traditions, will be.

One modern writer has voiced the common opinion that "the stories vary in reliability. Some of them are so plausible and fill in the gaps so perfectly that they have been deemed irrefutable truths ... Still more of the Eskimo stories have been proved to be downright lies, told mainly to please and interest the white man."[1]

Most Inuit folklore is not straightforward. The greatest volume of it consists of parables passing on the moral precepts necessary for life in the harsh Arctic environment. These often feature supernatural phenomena – giants, witches, and other such elements. For example, the native explanation for the origin of the white men amply demonstrates the Inuit capacity for original and imaginative composition. They considered all non-Inuit to be the offspring of a disobedient daughter and a dog, who had then been placed in boots and set adrift to float to their faraway lands. This tradition poses no problem to a modern historian, for few would seriously consider as fact the proposition that all non-Inuit are descended from dogs.

Other tales are more open to speculation. Vilhjalmur Stefansson had an experience which showed the nature of the legend-building process among the Inuit, and he noted a "striking example of how easy it is to be misled by native information."[2] He was told of a native hero named "Kaplavinna," a prodigious hunter of bow-head whales, who had a very large boat. As his informants were self-admittedly ignorant of the hunting of bow-head whales, and seemed unfamiliar with any type of boat except the single-person kayak, Stefansson was understandably perplexed by this tale. He "listened to these stories with great wonder and asked many questions which were readily answered, but which threw no great light on the subject."

The tale could have ended inexplicably here had not Stefansson learned that the tale of Kaplavinna had been originally told by the camp follower Natjinna. He then learned that Natjinna had first heard the tale from Natkusiak, who was one of Stefansson's own guides. Upon questioning this latter native he learned that Kaplavinna was none other than "Captain Leavitt," the skipper of the whaler *Narwal*, who had been Natkusiak's former employer. Stefansson knew Captain Leavitt personally, but had failed to make the connection with the fabled "Kaplavinna." Yet the true basis of the Inuit story, although obscured by embroidery and inexactitude, is readily apparent, and what would undoubtedly have been labelled as a fabrication or unreliable story was therefore shown to be largely truthful.[3]

Inuit stories have helped illuminate more significant mysteries than that of "Kaplavinna." While Hall was living among the Inuit of Baffin Island he interviewed a native named Koojesse, who made reference to a time "long, long ago" when "kod-lu-nas" (white men) "built a vessel on an island in the bay lower down." He also spoke of "mik-e-oo-koo-loo-oug" – small red pieces (which Hall took to be brick), as well as timber, wood chips, and other residue of the shipbuilding activity.[4] Hall realized that these stories might refer to one of Frobisher's expeditions, but felt that the "idea of a vessel having been built in those regions seemed too improbable to be entertained for a moment."[5]

Hall's companion Ebierbing remembered that, as a boy, he had seen the "oug," and that he had enjoyed making red marks on the rocks with it. He had also seen coal which had been left behind by white men. Ebierbing remembered the old people telling him that "many – a great many years ago, ships came into the Bay *Tin-nu-jok-pinq-oo-see-onq*."[6] Hall learned that the red stone had been found on two small islands, Niountelik and the nearby "Kodlunar" – "White Man's Island." Shortly after hearing these tales, Hall met two natives who actually carried some of the "oug" and verified that it was European brick.

Hall had seen brick and heard of white men's relics, but, in truth, his conclusion that these had come from Frobisher was still unproven. He continued to collect evidence. Koo-ou-le-arng informed him that the white man's coal was used by the Inuit for cooking, and when asked where it had come from replied, "Kodlunarn oomiarkchua kiete amasuadlo echar." ("A great many years ago, white men with big ship came here.")

Hall realized that the opinion that he had found Frobisher's landing place could only be confirmed by a personal visit to Niountelik. The final proof was found when he came across an excavation which proved to have been one of Frobisher's mines, although Hall noted that the Inuit, "judging only from what they saw, called it a reservoir for fresh water."[7] Hall found evidence of two mines on Kodlunar Island, as well as the foundations of a house which had been built so long ago.

On the shore of the north side of the island I found also an excavation which I called a ship's trench, for the Innuits said that was where a ship had been built by the white men. It had been dug out of stone, which was of such a nature as to yield to the persevering use of pickaxe, sledge-hammer, and the crow-bar ... A piece of iron, semi-spherical in shape, weighing twenty pounds, was discovered under the stone that had been excavated for the "ships way" and many other small pieces were also found at the head of the trench. Fragments of tile were found all over the island, and numerous other relics, indicating that civilized men had visited the place very many years ago.[8]

In every remembered detail of Frobisher's visit of three hundred years before, the Inuit were correct. Indeed, if it were not for their collective memory, the location of the Elizabethan explorer's landing place, which had, over the centuries, become a matter of dispute, might never have come to light.

Hall, with the aid of the Inuit traditions, managed to clear up another matter. Frobisher had not had amicable relations with the natives of Baffin Island. In violent clashes many of the locals had been killed, and five members of Frobisher's crew had been taken captive in retaliation. For almost three centuries the fate of these five men had been unknown to the civilized world. But the Inuit remembered.

The Inuit not only recalled the five captives, but had preserved the story of how these strangers had "wintered on shore (whether one, two, three, or more winters, could not say); that they lived among the Innuits; that they afterward built an oomien (large boat) and put a mast into her and had sails; that early in the season, before much water had appeared, they endeavoured to depart, that, in the effort, some froze their hands; but that finally they succeeded in getting into open water, and away they went, which was the last seen of them."[9]

Hall gleefully drew a parallel with the Franklin expedition: "I thought to myself, if such facts concerning an expedition which had been made nearly three hundred years ago can be preserved by the natives, and evidence of those facts obtained, what may not be gleaned of Sir John Franklin's Expedition of *only sixteen years ago?*" (emphasis in original).[10]

Amazing as it seems to people who have never cultivated the art of verbal history, the Inuit proved by this one example (among many) that their traditions were eminently trustworthy. Indeed, in a life so harsh and unchanging it would be remarkable if the natives did not seize upon any incident concerning strangers and strange occurrences as worthy of remembering and perpetuating.

As with Frobisher's "reservoirs," often a seemingly insignificant, or even bizarre, detail of a native story allows us to determine its source. In 1858 McClintock was told about a party of white men who had visited the Inuit at some time in the past. At first glance there was little to help him determine whether these were remembrances of the Franklin expedition or of some other European visitor.

Every winter [the natives] communicate with the Igloolik people. Two winters ago (1856–7) some people who lived far beyond Igloolik, in a country known as A-ka-nee, brought from there the information of white people having come in two boats, and passed a winter in snow-huts at a place called by the following names: – A-mee-lee-oke, A-wee-lik, Net-tee-lik. Our friends pointed to our whale-boat, and said the boats of the white people were like it, but larger. These whites had tents inside their snow-huts; they killed and eat [sic] reindeer and narwhal, and smoked pipes; they bought dresses from the natives; none died; in summer they all went away, taking with them two natives, a father and a son. We could not ascertain the name of the white chief, nor the interval of time since they wintered amongst the Esquimaux, as our friends could not recollect these particulars. [11]

McClintock considered that "A-ka-nee" was probably "Accoo-lee," the native name for Committee Bay in the southern reaches of Prince Regent Inlet. He also identified "A-wee-lik" with "Ay-wee-lik," which he remembered as "the name of the land about Repulse Bay." "Net-tee-lik" was readily identifiable as "Neitch-ille" or Boothia Peninsula. As John Rae had visited all of these locales during his travels, McClintock reasonably concluded that the tale probably referred to one of his visits.

The problem with this reconstruction was that when Dr Rae wintered at Repulse Bay in 1846–7 he lived in a stone house. When he again wintered there in 1853–4 he did live in snow huts, but makes no mention of having erected a tent inside them. In any case the tale cannot refer to his second visit, since Rae found no Inuit at Repulse Bay at that time and none arrived during the winter. We also know that he departed with only one native guide at that time, his interpreter William Ouligbuck Jr.

A searching look at the first winter at Repulse Bay shows how the story originated. In 1846 Rae left York Factory with ten men and two boats and arrived at Repulse Bay on the 25th of July. His men then built a one-room stone-walled hut (twenty by four-teen feet), which was grandiloquently christened "Fort Hope." This was still partially standing when visited in 1952. [12] Fort Hope was not, of course an "igloo" or snow house in the sense in which that word has entered the English language, but the Inuit used the word generically to denote any residence. [13] We could there-fore gloss over the discrepancy regarding the type of dwelling on purely linguistic grounds, but such rationalization is also sup-ported by other clues.

The seemingly irrational mention of the whites who "had tents inside their (snow) huts" is one of the most curious aspects of this particular tale. During the short intermediate season which passes for spring in the Arctic, the Inuit themselves live in hybrid structures consisting of snow-block walls and skin roof (a "kong-ma"), but such a common practice, if copied, would not have required special comment. But we find that Rae did, in fact, have a "tent" inside Fort Hope. A tarpaulin partition was apparently rigged to divide the crude stone structure into two rooms.[14] The unlikelihood of anyone bothering to erect a tent inside a perfectly sound igloo and the lack of native familiarity with subdivided dwellings conspires to expose the genesis of a seemingly un-traceable tradition.

A further detail allows us to ascribe the story to Rae's party in 1846. We know that that season he was accompanied by his interpreter, Ouligbuck, and the latter's son, William Jr (Mar-ko), and this is reflected in the Inuit statement that when the white men left they were accompanied by "two natives, a father and a son." A vague tale, told third-hand to McClintock thirteen years after the event, is shown to be true in all its particulars. More important, it is shown to contain such accurate detail as to render it identifiable beyond a shadow of a doubt.

Given that he was himself the subject of one Inuit recollection, it is interesting to learn Rae's opinion of the trustworthiness of Inuit testimony which he formed after his visits to their land.

As to the truthfulness and good memory of the Repulse Bay Eskimo, I had an excellent opportunity of testing these, because some of them, when young, had been on board Parry's ships in 1823, that is, 24 years before, and they mentioned circumstances that took place then as nearly as could be as they were told in Parry's or Captain Lyon's journal. It was the same with regard to Sir John Ross at Boothia, in 1829–32; none whom I saw, it is true, has been on board his ship the *Victory*, they, however, told me, with correctness, much that had occurred.[15]

Rasmussen, although late on the scene, was much more fluent in the native dialects than any of the earlier explorers, and was therefore a better judge of their trustworthiness. He too was very impressed by the Inuit testimony. He noted that his informants were the children of natives whose parents and grandparents had had only brief encounters with the various white explorers, and that "there has not been time to know the people they mention in the slightest; and yet so many, many years afterwards they preserve the traditions of their experiences with unembellished and sober reliability. If the particular reports of these expeditions are turned up the ancient verbal traditions will be found to be in the best agreement with the books."[16]

We have seen that the tradition concerning Agliktuktoq's encounter with the Ross expedition was preserved by the Inuit in exquisite detail, indeed in more detail than is found in John Ross's book. Rasmussen also found that the Inuit had vivid memories of the later white men who had travelled across their land, and that their traditions concerning these visits were detailed and accurate.

Of other white men who have been in their territory they remembered John Rae's visit in 1847. He was seen at the island of Qorvigjuaq (the great piss-pot) in Pelly Bay by Huluni (the wing), the father of Iggiaraarssuk's wife. The intercourse was but short; Rae was in a hurry and they could not talk with him ... Rae's next visit ... in 1854, was also remembered, and this despite the fact that on this occasion he merely passed the fjord. In exactly the same way they speak of Hall's visit in 1864, and as evidence they not only give the names of his Eskimo companions from Repulse Bay: his adoptive son Joe and the following Arviligjuarmiut: Arolaq (?), Iloratjuk (the little trout) and Niuvitsiaq (the one who is always ready to make a bargain), but the names of the men from Pelly Bay who met them are preserved, viz. Qarpik (wolverine), Talerigtoq (strong arm), and Anatlaq (vigorous evacuation).

And finally there was Schwatka's wintering on King William's Land in 1879, in connection with which they also remember the names of his companions from Chesterfield and can even indicate Pingorsaq (the ridge) on the west side of King William's Land as the place where the expedition shot most caribou.[17]

As is evident in this testimony, the recitation of names was very important to the Inuit. This is a feature which we shall use to advantage many times, and to good effect (Iggiaraarssuk's father-in-law, Huluni, met on Qorvigjuaq Island, was undoubtedly the native "A-li-ne-yuk" whom Rae encountered on Helen Island on 21 April 1847).[18]

Not only did the Inuit remember these later white explorers, they remembered Parry as well. Hall wrote that "nothing in Parry's narrative ... relating to the Eskimos of Winter Island and Igloolik but these natives [at Repulse Bay] are perfectly posted up in. Indeed, I find through my superior interpreter, Too-koo-li-too, that many deeply interesting incidents occurred at both-named places that never found their place in Parry's or Lyon's works."[19]

The events which the natives recalled of Parry's visit to Igloolik provide firm proof for their powers of observation.

This morning Erk-tu-a, the relict of E-we-rat, and old mother Ook-bar-loo, called on me [Hall]. I began my inquiries by asking Erk-tu-a to report to me all the names she could recollect of the Kob-lu-nas she saw when at Ig-loo-lik. She began and continued thus – Paree, he Esh-e-mu-ta (captain); Lyon, he Esh-e-mu-ta (captain); Par-mee, he Esh-e-mu-tar-nar (mate on Lyon's ship); Oo-liz-e (on Parry's ship); Cro-zhar [Crozier], Esh-e-mu-tar-nar (mate or some other officer not so great as a captain on Parry's ship) ... After Erk-tu-a said this much I opened Parry's work "Narrative of 2nd voyage for the discovery of a Northwest Passage," and turned to the list of officers &c, in the introduction to said work. I readily made out to whom "Par-mee" (as Erk-tu-a spoke the name) referred. Chas. Palmer was one of the lieutenants on board of Lyon's ship.[20]

Hall repeatedly asked questions about his predecessors, both out of simple interest, and as a check of native reliability.

[Hall] was much encouraged by the seeming correctness of their replies. Among these, Ar-too-a, whose age was about thirty, gave him a long account of the very serious wounds received by Ou-lig-buck, one of Dr. Rae's interpreters. Ar-too-a's story, as found in Hall's journal of the day, corresponds closely with the record given by Rae himself of the accidental wound and the healing of Ou-lig-buck ... Ar-too-a further said that he and his brothers Ou-e-la and Shu-she-ark-nook had seen Rae on each of his expeditions of 1846 and 1854, and that "although Ou-lig-buck, father and son, and most of the white men smoked, Dr. Rae never did." ... Hall was much gratified on receiving such details of incidents which occurred nearly eighteen years previous.[21]

Artooa and Shu-she-ark-nook (also spelled "Shooksheark-nook") would have been mere boys during Rae's visits, yet their recollections are accurate. Rae's Narrative reveals that Ouligbuck wounded his arm severely by falling on a dagger, and that "the whole party, with the exception of myself, were most inveterate smokers."[22] Hall, as a check on Inuit reliability, took every opportunity to compare the stories which he heard from the Inuit with the original journals of the white explorers. He found the native accuracy to be, almost without exception, uncanny.

I was present at a seal-feast at Nood-loo, where was congregated a large number of Innuits; and when through with the feast, with the aid of my "Joe" (Ebierbing), I had a talk with Ar-tung-un, in presence of all the Innuits there, for the purpose of testing the memory and accuracy of the old man. I asked him to tell me about the little dog which was on board Parry's and Lyon's ship. He said the little dog was a great favorite with everybody, and was a spotted one: one time a wolf came about the ships, and this little dog, with Parry's dog, which was a black one, ran after the wolf, when several white men hastened after the dogs to bring them back. After a while the men returned, bringing Parry's dog, but they could find nothing of the little pet dog; so all concluded that the little dog must have been killed and eaten up by the wolf. Next day some of the white men went out to see if they could find out what really had become of the little dog. When they returned they brought the head, it being all that they could find of the little dog. He could not remember the name of this dog, but on my telling him it was "Spark" he then smiled and said it sounded just like it. The old man has not only told the facts about this little dog – a terrier – as related by Lyon, whose work I have with me, but has told this much more, that the dog was spotted, and that its head was found.[23]

In assessing the Inuit testimony we cannot ignore the fact that, very rarely, the Inuit deliberately lied to the white men. Lyon considered the Inuit of Igloolik to be exceptionally truthful, noting that "when asking questions of an individual, it is but rarely that he will either advance or persist in an untruth."[24]

Complete honesty cannot be expected, however; we are, after all, dealing with human beings. The natives occasionally had personal motives to mislead explorers. One such motive was the natural desire to protect "their" relics, sources of wood, caches of meat, or other valuables. McClintock noted that, when he questioned the natives about the wreck of Franklin's ships, some of them were less than forthcoming. One old man neglected to mention that one ship had been driven ashore, presumably in an effort to protect the source of his band's wood supply.[25]

An oft-quoted case of Inuit fabrication concerned a native pilferer who was flogged by Parry at Igloolik. By the time that Hall was told of this incident the thief had become a semi-legendary hero.

Oo-oo-took, a superior an-nat-ko [shaman], was charged by Parry when at Ig-loo-lik with the crime of theft for taking a shovel, or a part of one, from alongside the ship. Parry had him taken to a place between decks [the *Fury*'s store-room passage], and his hands firmly lashed up to the mast. Then two guns were loaded and fired at him. The balls did not hit him, but one passed close to his head and lodged in the mast. The other ball went close to his loins, but did not injure him. The guns were so near his body that the powder felt hot. Parry fired one of the guns, and came very near killing himself, the ball glancing and rebounding in such a way that it passed close to his head. Another gun was about to be used in firing at Oo-oo-took, but it was found to be cracked (both barrel and stock), and, therefore, it was laid aside. Then Parry caused him to be whipped with something that was made of ropes with knots in them – cat-o'-nine-tails.

The Innuits standing around and witnessing all this wanted to help Oo-oo-took defend himself, but he said: "Let the Kob-lu-nas try to kill me; they cannot, for I am an an-nat-ko." Then Oo-oo-took's hands were untied, after which the kob-lu-nas tried to cut his head and hands off with long knives – probably swords. Every time a blow was struck, the extreme end of the knife came close to Oo-oo-took's throat; occasionally the blade came just above the crown of his head, and when the attempt was made to cut off his hands the long knife came down very near his wrists; but, after all, he was uninjured because he was a very good An-nat-ko. Some of the blows, however, did execution, cutting deep gashes in throat, head, and wrists; but each stroke, as the knife was lifted, the wounds instantly healed up, the an-nat-ko being made whole by the Good Spirit who protected him.

When Oo-oo-took was permitted to go on deck, he attempted to go ashore. He was passing out of the gangway when four men seized him; but during the struggle to free himself from further punishment, he kicked one kob-lu-na down the snow-steps, which fall nearly killed him, and the kob-lu-na suffered with a lame back for a long time. Finally, the kob-lu-na conquered him and put him down between decks, in a cold, dark place, where he kept him two days and two nights, but while so confined, one good kob-lu-na, in a very sly way, gave him something to eat; otherwise he had nothing to eat or drink.

After Oo-oo-took had been one day and one night in the dark hole, he thought he would use his power as an an-nat-ko, and destroy the vessel by splitting it through the middle from stem to stern. So he commenced calling to his aid the Good Spirit, when a great cracking noise was made, now and then, under the ship, and at the end of the two days and two nights' confinement, the kob-lu-nas, fearing from such great and terrific noises that the ship would be destroyed, let Oo-oo-took go.[26]

Needless to say, most of this was fantasy. No one tried to shoot or decapitate Oo-oo-took, and Parry's account does not mention a two-day confinement.[27] The self-promoting motive behind the shaman's account is obvious, and any fabrications and exaggerations are self-exposed by the departures from reality (such as self-healing wounds) which they embody. Yet it is difficult to see why such a harmless embroidery of what is still, in essence, a truthful tale should justify the characterization of most Inuit as liars.

The only other instance I have uncovered where the natives knowingly lied also had to do with Parry, and also had quite understandable human motives. Hall's informant Erktua was an old lady, but when she had met Parry and Lyon she had been a lively sixteen-year-old. She told Hall that both captains had been her lovers, which may or may not have been true. Other witnesses attested to the fact that Lyon, for one, left children behind him when he sailed home. What infuriated Hall was that after Erktua had seen him she started to spread the story of how she has been *his* lover as well![28] Again, it is hard to see why the sexual fantasies of an old woman should be used to invalidate Inuit testimony as a whole.

It must be admitted that at least one explorer was not entirely convinced of the Inuit propensity to truthfulness. After his disillusionment, Charles Hall often characterized his informants as "dishonest," usually in the sense that they could not forbear from pilfering some of his possessions, but occasionally in the sense of "liars." In fact, at one time or another, the suspicious and overemotional explorer felt this way about everyone! Hall was an ambitious loner, quick to take offence and with a tenacious memory for every perceived slight. He was not an easy man to love.

Hall never did or felt anything halfway. At one point he shot one of his hired whalers to death to put down what he (probably wrongly) perceived to be a mutinous threat to his life. When an autopsy of his body showed that Hall himself had acute arsenic poisoning at his death, the theory was either that the ship's doctor, a sworn enemy, had poisoned his captain, or that Hall, suspecting such a plot, had taken to treating himself and accidentally overdosed. Each of these theories has something to say about Hall's interpersonal relationships.

If his relationships with fellow white men were stormy, those with the Inuit, whose different value systems he never completely understood, were uneven. Upon meeting Ouela, Hall overflowed with his praise; months later he called him a devil and (once again) feared for his life. On hearing that Too-shoo-art-thariu had fed four Franklin survivors for a whole winter, he could not contain his admiration for the kind-heartedness of the Inuit; when he learned that the story was untrue his disdain was equally powerful.

Much of Hall's information came from In-nook-poo-zhe-jook, the same native who had met Rae, and Hall initially considered him to be "very finicky to tell the facts ... In-nook-poo-zhe-jook has a noble bearing. His whole face is an index that he has a heart kind & true. I delight in his companionship."[29] Hall, like Rae, considered In-nook-poo-zhe-jook to be "a very Intelligent Innuit – a great traveller & is a man full of the history of the latter end of Sir John Franklin's Expedition."[30]

Yet within two months Hall would write that "I believe he [In-nook-poo-zhe-jook] like the other Innuits of Nitchille will lie & *he* without any regard to consequences. He speaks truth & falsehood all intermingled so that it [is] impossible to tell which is which unless it be of matter that one questioning him knows himself the facts. And yet he is a man apparently of honest face ... It is a very great pity that the Neitchille Innuits are such consumate [sic] liars."[31]

As we shall see, In-nook-poo-zhe-jook probably never intentionally told Hall a falsehood.

In relation to the testimony dealing with the Franklin disaster, it has also been supposed that the "shame" of having "abandoned" the starving white men led the Inuit to omit or alter their testimony. This is almost certainly too simple an explanation. The natives were eminently practical people who did not have the same sensibilities as the white men when it came to death. In their harsh environment the Inuit routinely abandoned their own weak and old rather than allow them to burden the band. Infanticide, especially of baby girls, was routine and entirely comprehensible to them all. They were, therefore, not too distressed by the tragedy of Franklin's crewmen and were not averse to the expedient of disinterring and despoiling the dead Europeans for useful artifacts. Rasmussen remarked that the Inuit "did not attach great importance to the sadness of the doom of the white men: instead they emphasized the old Eskimos's [lack of] knowledge of the white men's things and sought to get what fun they could out of them."[32]

Another thing that was hard for the white men to understand was that the Inuit were not particularly concerned with the past. They found the stories of the Franklin saga interesting, but definitely not as absorbing as a caribou hunt. Two of the natives who had actually met some of Franklin's men (Teekeeta and Owwer) were interviewed briefly by Hall on his trip to King William Island. They told him what they knew, but had no interest in accompanying him to the place where the white men had died. He promised them lavish payment if they would simply remain where they were until his return, but when he arrived back at camp a week later they had gone off sealing. Only a quick decision on Hall's part to follow their tracks and cross-examine them again, during which second interview most of the valuable detail of their remembrances was obtained, allowed us to hear of this most interesting event in the retreat.

William Gibson, a later trader at the Hudson Bay Company post at Gjoa Haven, interviewed the natives of King William Island about Amundsen's sojourn there and found that their memories were impressive, but also selective.

The *Gjoa* was only a small vessel but to them she must indeed have seemed of monster proportions. Yet it is not the vessel or the ingenious equipment of the expedition which remains uppermost in their minds, but rather trifling and seemingly unimportant incidents.

The explorer's handshake – a form of greeting which was entirely new to them. The amusement derived from the reaction of various people when they were confronted for the first time in their lives with a clear reflection of their image in a large mirror, which reputedly was fastened on the back of the door leading to the ship's cabin. A naive description of the various members of the expedition, and the names by which they were known to the people. Such remembrances as these, coupled with a clear recollection of the various barter transactions in which they were intimately concerned, live to-day in the memories of the older people as they look back on the days of their youth ... Strange as it may seem, Amundsen, the man, is remembered by these simple people, not as a great explorer, but as a trader. Fourteen years ago, when I first visited Boothia Peninsula, I met an old man who looked earnestly into my eyes and assured me that he understood white men well, as he had traded with Amundsen at Gjoahavn. This experience he was ingenuously convinced would at once establish our relations on a proper footing. [33]

It is beyond doubt that the Inuit knew more about what happened in their country than many explorers were willing to grant. Unfortunately they often had difficulty in transmitting this information to the interviewers. The details which were important to the natives – the number of knives recovered, the state of the hunting at the time – were less important to the white men than the matters of number or date, things of which the Inuit had little conception. One old man confided to Rasmussen that although white men were very rich and possessed many wonderful things, they were obviously quite inferior to Inuit, and had the "strangest fancies" – just like big children. [34]

The thought processes of their informants often baffled the white men as well. Then there were the manifold complexities of the Inuit language. Many of the explorers, by omitting to mention their own difficulties with the language, give the impression in their writings of a fluency which it is unlikely that they possessed. Stefansson had a realistic idea of the difficulty of the Inuit languages and never failed to express doubt in his own abilities. [35]

It is common to hear the assertion that the Eskimo is a simple language and easy to learn, and you may meet in any town in America or Europe some person who says to you, "I had a friend who lived in Alaska (or Labrador, or Hudson's Bay) and he learned to speak Eskimo in three months." That idea of course is based on the supposition that the jargon which the white men use in dealing with the Eskimo is in reality the language of the Eskimo; but it is not, nor anything like it ... Eskimo is not only an exceedingly complicated language, but also very different from English. To put it roughly, there is no doubt that for an Englishman it would be much easier to acquire Russian, Swedish, French, and Greek than to acquire Eskimo alone. To take the only actual case the circumstances of which are fully known to me, which is of course my own, it may be said that I had a book knowledge of the Eskimo before going to the North, and I have lived for five years in houses where nothing but Eskimo was spoken. I listened to every word with all my ears, for to acquire the language has been both my chief work and my chief pastime, and yet it was only the last of the five winters that my command of the language had become such that I could follow without effort the ordinary conversations going on in the house.[36]

Stefansson was not the only one to have difficulty with Inuit dialects. In 1864, having spent four years living with the Inuit, Hall still required an interpreter for everyday conversation. Although "deeply absorbed in all that I could understand ... I must confess [it] was very little."[37]

Five years later he claimed to be able to "make myself understood by nearly every native I meet & on the other hand can to a great degree understand what they desire to communicate,"[38] yet his notes reveal that he always made use of a native interpreter and that he often misunderstood what was being said until clarified through repeated cross-questioning. In the light of Hall's published writings, Stefansson concluded that, despite his many years with the Inuit, Hall had gained only a superficial knowledge of their language.[39]

The explorers also found it hard to make allowances for the normal Inuit reticence. As we shall see, it was not uncommon for the natives to listen silently to others relate events of which they themselves had been actual participants. William Gilder, Schwatka's second in command, noted that the Inuit "seldom take the trouble to make explanations," noting that at one time Schwatka had seen a dog which he wanted, learned that its owner was named "Shiksik," and found and paid an Inuit of that name for the animal. Only later did Schwatka learn that he had paid the wrong "Shiksik." Not only had the man accepted payment for a dog which was not his own, but at the time of the original purchase "all the people looked complacently and admiringly on without a word of explanation, though they well knew the mistake."[40]

The Inuit had a perplexing, and at times infuriating, habit of answering any direct question asked, but failing to elaborate. This understandably led to the white men's resorting to "leading questions."

I questioned [Iglihsirk] to see if he knew anything about the loss of Franklin's ships. I asked him if he had ever heard that a ship had been wrecked on the east coast of Victoria Island, and what he knew about the fate of the men who had been on the ship. He said so far as he knew no ship had been wrecked *on the east coast*, but that in his father's time *two ships* had been frozen fast in the ice a *long way offshore*, beyond the east coast, and the white men on them had evidently abandoned them and all died. This was clear proof that they were familiar with Franklin's story. Had the man answered my leading question offhand, saying that one ship had been wrecked on the coast, it might have been considered one of the cases of politeness among the Eskimo, who usually answer any question in the way they think you would like to have it answered, but he had corrected me exactly in accordance with the facts already known to us, for Franklin's ships were not on the coast, but a considerable distance from it, and were abandoned before the ice broke up. (emphasis in original)[41]

The last point which must be made before we examine the stories themselves does not concern the Inuit or their capacities. It is simply that, as we know the tales, they are all as-told-to accounts, suffering or benefiting from their passage through interpreters and historians.

The competence of interpreters varied greatly. On his first expedition Rae employed William Ouligbuk (variously "Ouligback") and his son William Jr (Mar-ko). As we have seen, he employed the latter again in 1854 and considered that he was "a good interpreter but subject to fits of sulkiness, that he lied to his purpose, and that he was not too honest."[42] Before setting out on his second journey, Rae had tried to obtain the services of another interpreter, and had in fact engaged an Inuit named Munro, but Mar-ko's skill so outstripped Munro's that the latter was sent home, even though Rae considered Mar-ko "one of the greatest rascals unhung."[43]

Nevertheless, when the press in England dared to assert that Rae's information was invalidated by its passage through an unreliable interpreter, he sprang to Mar-ko's defence. He stated that his interpreter spoke English "fluently; and, perhaps, more correctly than one half of the lower classes in England or Scotland."[44] Twenty-four years later, Gilder confirmed that Ouligbuck Jr "spoke the English language like a native – that is to say, like an uneducated native," and considered that "he would prove almost invaluable as an interpreter for any expedition that expected to come much in contact with the Esquimaux, as all their dialects were understood by him."[45]

Anderson had no interpreter at all but gained his information largely through sign language. McClintock was served by Carl Petersen, who was familiar with the dialect of the Greenland natives, but was apparently unfamiliar with that of the Inuit of the central Arctic. McClintock wrote that "it was with great difficulty so much could be gleaned, the dialect being strange to Petersen, and the natives being far more inclined to ask questions than answer them."[46]

Adam Beck, another Greenland native, served John Ross as interpreter during the Franklin search and would play an important, if ambiguous, role in the Franklin saga. He was interviewed by Hall many years later and also expressed a low opinion of McClintock's interpreter Petersen. Beck, in his own broken English, stated that "Carl Petersen no speak Husky quick – not good Husky speak – small Husky speak!"[47] This opinion was endorsed by Hall, who felt that Petersen "was of little service to McClintock as an Esquimaux interpreter."[48]

Hall gathered more native testimony than any other explorer during the years which he spent with the Inuit. His faithful friends and constant companions Tookoolitoo and Ebierbing usually acted as his interpreters. Tookoolitoo and Ebierbing had spent much time among the whalers. They had visited England, and they became devoted to Hall and genuinely interested in his endeavours. As we shall repeatedly see, Hall was very prone to asking leading questions, and even more prone to jumping to conclusions based on his own preconceptions; but what he lacked in good investigative technique was somewhat compensated for in his single-minded perseverance, and his notes reveal that he often cross-examined the natives for hours, often repeating the same questions over and over again, in an effort to extract the last detail. Even Tookoolitoo became exasperated with him at times.

On asking Hannah [Tookoolitoo] to aid me in talking with old Ev-e-shuk she held a few minutes conversation with her & then I asked Hannah what the old lady had said. Hannah replied same thing that Ou-e-la had told me. But his wouldn't satisfy me so I told Hannah I wanted to know just what the old lady's story was whether the same as Ou-e-la had told or not. She replied that I had asked a thousand questions about this matter already & that she couldn't help me ask any more now. Thus it is & thus it often is that when I greatly desire to pursue my inquiries of any very important matters relative to the lost ones of Franklin's companions I have to exercise a great deal of patience & use much coaxing with my Interpreter.[49]

Despite such intermittent disagreements, Hall felt that Tookoolitoo was an excellent interpreter, "having the capacity for it far surpassing Karl [sic] Petersen," and that she would "readily accomplish the differences in language between the Innuits of Boothia and King William's Land, and that of her own people around Northumberland Inlet and Davis' Strait."[50] His journals and notebooks make clear his very real affection for her, and there can be no doubt that she faithfully reported exactly what was said. How Hall interpreted the statements is another matter.

Hall considered Tookoolitoo to be "the best interpreter of Innuit language into our vernacular that ever accompanied an Arctic expedition,"[51] but he did note that "the pronunciation of the same words by communities of Esquimaux living at considerable distance from each other and having but little intercourse, is so different that it is with difficulty they are understood one by the other." This problem is evident in his notebooks. On one occasion he noted that "at times I meet with trouble to get at precision, so difficult for my interpreter to understand the vocabulary."[52]

The widowed Ebierbing later accompanied Schwatka and Gilder to the north, and, although a less skilful interpreter than his wife had been, performed good service with them as well. Even so, Gilder noted that although "Joe" had "travelled so long with Captain Hall, and lived so many years in the United States and England," he "had but an imperfect knowledge of the English language, though he had been conversant with it almost from infancy."[53]

This is clearly a case of "people in glass houses," for both Gilder and Heinrich Klutschak, another member of Schwatka's expedition, assembled glossaries of Inuit words and commented on their language. The errors discovered therein by later experts indicate that their command of Inuit was at best marginal as well.[54]

Undoubtedly the most adept interpreter to interview the Inuit was Rasmussen. It is a pity that he was so late on the scene (1923) and that his interest in the Franklin expedition was only incidental. By the time of his arrival, two generations had passed since the Franklin disaster and many of the traditions which he was told concerning it were composite versions which had been blended and mixed during the intervening years from stories originally told to Hall and Schwatka.

It should always be borne in mind that although the pronouncements of the Inuit as recorded by these expeditions are uniformly well phrased and aptly worded, this was the work of the explorers themselves. The pidgin English and native dialect used in the original interviews was undoubtedly much less comprehensible. Adam Beck's conversation with John Ross, after years of serving as interpreter, gives a more accurate idea of the average fluency. He remarked, "Captain Phillips speak: Adam Beck lie. Sir John Ross very good man – plenty pray, plenty eat." With raw material such as this it is hardly surprising that many of the Inuit tales were garbled during transmission.

Our attempts to reconstruct the chain of events which overtook the men of Franklin's ships after April 1848 will rest largely on the testimony of the Inuit. Some writers, particularly those of the nineteenth century, have neglected such sources, emanating as they do from "balling and false savages." This is an unfair and defamatory label for people who were usually intelligent and observant witnesses. The tales which were preserved by them often contain compelling details without which a complete picture cannot be built. It is true that such tales often pose special problems and traps to puzzle the unwary analyst; they will, however, also be found to contain invaluable gems.

~4~

Omanek and Adam Beck

One of the enduring myths of the Franklin expedition is that the survivors of the *Erebus* and *Terror* may have fallen in battle with the natives. Fitzjames's short record from the cairn at Victory Point, and its cryptic comment that "the total loss by deaths in the Expedition has been to this date 9 officers and 15 men," made it apparent that something strange had occurred before the 1848 abandonment of the ships.

The high death rate, and specifically the disproportionate loss of officers, prompted Admiral (ret.) Noel Wright to publish two books in which he attempted to offer an explanation. Although not the first, Wright became the most insistent of those who sought to explain the Franklin disaster as the result of Inuit hostility. The evidence for this view came from one of the most controversial of all the Franklin witnesses – Adam Beck.

Beck's tale of a massacre emerged in 1850 when the Arctic was swarming with naval and civilian parties searching for the track of Sir John Franklin's ships. The large armada, consisting of fifteen ships under the commands of Captains Austin, Penny, De Haven, and John Ross, converged upon the Greenland coast in an attempt to pick up Franklin's trail. While near Cape York, the officers of the searching expedition were approached by Beck, a mixed-race Greenlander who had been engaged as interpreter by Captain John Ross. Beck said that he had learned these traditions from natives on the shore, and, although they were only hearsay, he was adamant that he was telling the white men exactly what had been said to him.

When [the natives] came to the ships and asked them [the people there] said they had been here four winters. Tolloit also wintered upon our land. In 1846 two ships with three masts went from our land to OMENAK; they arrived safely, but the men are dead. Two ships encompassed by the ice, otherwise they could not do. Their provisions were consumed. The men went to them; it is said they are dead. Tolloit is also dead.[1]

Beck's second story specifically mentioned a massacre.

In the winter of 1846, when snow was falling, two ships were broken up by the ice in the direction of Cape Dudley Digges, and afterwards burnt by a fierce and numerous tribe of natives. He [Beck] asserted that the ships were not whalers, and that epaulettes were worn by some of the white men; that a part of the crews were drowned; that the remainder were some time in huts or tents apart from the natives, that they had guns but no balls, were in a weak and exhausted condition, and were subsequently killed by the natives with darts and arrows.[2]

There were other variants to these tales, heard by Parker Snow of the yacht *Prince Albert*. Unfortunately, these have not been entirely preserved, but other details can be gleaned from the fragments.

In 1846 (or it might be 1847 or 1848) two English ships were lost and the crews killed. Ships were wrecked. People came on shore and were killed. Winter had set in and it was snowing. The principal [native] man's name was Mashoek. Eskimos (those who told Adam Beck) say, burnt the clothes ... Abernethy, who had been serving in the *Felix* at the time ... told Commander Inglefield that a stone cairn under which bodies had been buried had also figured in Adam Beck's tale ... This was the substance and the pith of the long and tedious statement that was elicited from him, and confirmed in appearance by many corroborating circumstances.[3]

Historians have concluded that "Mashoek" was probably the native Marshuick, whom John Ross had first encountered near

Cape York in 1818. This would indicate that Beck was not implying that Mashoek was the "principal" assailant but that he
was the "principal" informant. Apparently no attempt was made
to find or interview this man.

Beck was later presumed upon to write versions of his account
in his original language and these were preserved and forwarded
to various linguistic authorities for translation. The results were
disappointing.

The first statement, witnessed by Ross and Ommanney on 17 August
1850, was too confused to admit of a perfect translation. It enumerated
the names and abodes of Eskimos who had gone to Omenak, and contained one word which, owing to faulty spelling, could mean either
"murderers" or "many people". The translators believed that the second
meaning was correct ... then followed unintelligible words stating when
the ships set sail. The statement then said that when the ice began to
break they set sail, went to Omenak, and wintered there, for the ice
would not let them proceed. "Because there were many vessels the
Esquimaux ..." the last four words were unintelligible and to one of
them was added the syllable "gog", meaning "they say".[4]

Other copies of Beck's statements were sent to Germany and
Denmark, where they were translated by missionaries. These
men were only marginally fluent in the Greenland dialect and
their translations were inconsistent. Several passages differed so
much from one translation to another that the "intended meaning
is quite obscure, and not a few passages are so incongruous that
they seem to make no sense at all."[5]

The Europeans who heard Beck's stories at first hand tended
to feel they had been deliberately duped. Lieutenant Sherard
Osborn witnessed the original interview and expressed the common opinion concerning the "hobgoblin story" which Beck had
retold. Captain Austin also had a low opinion of Beck and considered him to be a "man in whom no faith could be placed from
his irregular conduct and, I believe, drunkenness. I think he was
about the worst description of a civilized savage I ever saw."[6]

Beck was universally ridiculed by the crews of the exploration
ships, who "reduced him to tears by telling him that he lied."
This calumny was to dog Adam Beck for the remainder of his
life and into the history books. When the fate of Franklin's un-

fortunate expedition was eventually ascertained in 1854, it was "proved" that Beck's stories had been fabrications, and his character as a liar was apparently vindicated. Yet he may have been judged too harshly.

Ten years after the Cape York fiasco, Charles Hall met Beck, and being more fluent in the Inuit language and generally more sympathetic to the natives than the British naval officers, he tried to elicit the truth of the earlier incident. He concluded that Beck had recounted "exactly what [was] told to him" and that "Commander Phillips and Carl Petersen repeatedly told Beck that he was a liar, and otherwise abused this now wreck of a man."[7]

It has generally been accepted that Beck's story had nothing to do with the Franklin expedition. The eminent Franklin scholar R.J. Cyriax concluded that Beck was a drunken coward who was trying to delay the searching squadrons on the Greenland coast in order to have an opportunity to desert before they entered the depths of the Arctic Archipelago. It is therefore a questionable tactic to begin an investigation based on Inuit testimony with such a thoroughly proven example of native fabrication from an improbable source. Yet, if what we have learned about the trustworthiness of Inuit traditions is to be believed, we should be able to sort out even Beck's improbable tales.

Some features of Beck's stories can be found in the experiences of the whalers, many of whom were wrecked in the treacherous ice of Baffin Bay. In 1830 nineteen whalers were lost here, while disaster again struck the whaling fleet in 1835. During the latter season the fleet threaded its way through the "middle ice" to the vicinity of Home Bay, only to have eleven vessels and six hundred men trapped by the ice and face the unwelcome prospect of a long and unprepared-for winter. Could Beck's disaster at "Omanek" be found here? A few miles to the south of Home Bay are two similarly shaped and identically named islets. In the local dialect they are called "Umana" which translates as "the place shaped like a heart."[8]

The first casualty of the 1835 season was the *Middleton*, which was severely nipped and abandoned by her crew before sinking. Later the *Dordon* suffered the same fate, and as she slowly filled with water the men caroused with the saved liquor until most were drunkenly sprawled on the nearby ice. Some of the *Dordon*'s sailors then lit a fire in the ship's interior to warm themselves.

This predictably got out of hand and reduced the ship to a burned-out wreck by morning. A witness described the scene the next morning as the *Dordon*'s crew came over the ice to another ship. Some of the men had "part of their hats burnt off their heads, others with trousers, boots, shoes and their very jackets burnt off" from sleeping too close to the fire. Others had "built tents on the ice to secure them from the weather, but all was of no avail, the most of them had got severely frostbitten."[9]

The wreck of the *Dordon* near an island called "Umana" may have been the source of Beck's tale. The account certainly has corroborative touches. Beck noted that the ships were "burnt by a fierce and numerous tribe," and in an alternate version he said that the "clothes" were burnt and that "part of the crews … were some time in huts or tents." We have here a concurrence with the name "Omanek" and a tale of fire, but still no tale of abandonment of an ice-fast ship or deaths due to native interaction. These elements could have been supplied by other vessels in the same fleet.

Four of the remaining ships had managed to make good an escape by November, but this still left five others to face the winter. All but one of these would eventually reach port safely, but the fate of the last ship, the *William Torr*, would be learned from the Inuit.

Nothing further was heard of the *William Torr* until 1840, when the *Norfolk* was in the Northumberland Inlet. The natives gave Captain Harrison very circumstantial details of the loss of a ship off Cape Fry in December, four years before. The story of the Eskimos was that the ship was frozen up in the land ice, and that they went out with their sledges to see her. Then a s.e. gale brought heavy drift ice down upon her and crushed in her sides; and they mentioned such details as two of the masts falling towards the land and the other to seawards. The account went on to relate that some of her crew came ashore, whilst the remainder, each with a bundle of clothes upon his back, set out to the southward over the ice, in hopes of reaching the *Jane*, which they apparently knew was iced in to the south of them. These latter, whose commander the natives declared to be a short, red-faced man (which was a good description of Captain Smith), were never heard of again. The 22 who came ashore were so badly frost-bitten that not one of them survived, though the Eskimos did the best they could for them, putting them into snow huts and feeding them on their precious seal beef.[10]

Clearly a combination of the *Dordon/William Torr* disasters could have inspired the confused Inuit stories which Beck heard. But despite the close correlation between Beck's stories and these early whaling disasters, two things argue against their being the source of the Inuit tales. Beck's statements that "the ships were not whalers" and that "the men wore epaulettes" were explicit and force us to consider that some other ship or ships may have been the true source – naval ships. There is also the problem of timing: the tales were apparently of events of the past few years, not echoes of past decades.

Only a few miles to the north of Cape York is Wolstenholme Sound, and a naval ship had indeed spent a winter there. This had occurred only the year before Beck's interview. The supply ship *North Star* had been sent to the Arctic under the command of James Saunders. She was loaded with supplies intended for Franklin's relief but failed to penetrate the heavy ice of Melville Bay and had come to winter quarters on the west coast of Greenland, anchoring near what is today called Saunders Island in Wolstenholme Sound. The *North Star* spent a relatively uneventful winter here and then left. The native name for Saunders Island was Omanek.

The *North Star* was housed over, and everything possible was done to make her warm and comfortable. Four members of the crew died but none from causes due to the climate ... they were buried on the south side of the bay ... Eskimos sometimes visited the ship, and on 28 January a native with very severely frostbitten feet was taken on board for treatment. The condition at first improved, but the patient died on 8 May. The shooting parties were able to procure only very little game – some foxes, a few wild ducks and about fifty hares. No deer were seen ... Two conspicuous beacons were erected ... and a large cairn of stones was built near the graves of the four men who had died.[11]

Here again were some elements of Beck's tale. Deaths had occurred, four white men and at least one native who had been in their care. The graves were associated with a cairn. The *North Star* was not a whaler (she was actually a converted tea clipper) and her officers did wear epaulettes. But there had been only the one ship, no interracial hostility had arisen, the men never "lived apart in tents" or apparently suffered from a lack of ammunition, and, most significantly, the ship had not been wrecked. However, the *North Star* had earlier encountered boats containing survivors of two wrecked whalers (the *Lady Jane* and *Prince of Wales*) who had been making their way south along the Greenland coast, and it was possible that some echo of these tragedies had been passed to the natives by her crew.

Was the *North Star* the source of Adam Beck's tales? Carl Petersen, who would later serve as McClintock's interpreter, questioned the Cape York natives again and learned that they had spoken to Beck but "denied having said anything about the wintering of two ships a few years previously. What they had told him, they said, was that a ship had spent the preceding winter behind Omanek (Wolstenholme) Island. She had three masts; was covered with a tent of skins (i.e. was housed in); and the captain's name was 'Sanne'. They had been on board several times and the ship had departed during the summer."[12]

This information was, of course, all true. A more cogent account of the *North Star* could hardly be asked for. Beck nevertheless persisted in his assertion that other natives had told him exactly what he had relayed. Beck was sure that the Omanek of his tale was the one with which he was most familiar – a few miles north of Cape York in Wolstenholme Sound. When the Englishmen went to the *North Star*'s wintering site and no corroborating evidence was found to support Beck's assertions, he was crestfallen, muttered that he had "lied," and wandered morosely away.

The fact that Beck did not find confirmation of the stories he had been told at Saunders Island does not disprove the traditions themselves, only that the "Omanek" of the tale was not where Beck had assumed it was. Beck apparently did not lose faith in his story, for he later swore an oath to its truthfulness in front of the magistrate at Godhavn. This worthy stated that "he had never known a native who, like Beck, had been brought up to the Christian religion, swear to the truth of a false statement."[13]

Beck believed in the story he had been told with a strange intensity. Somewhere, at "Omanek," two ships had come to grief and their crews had come ashore. A fight had occurred. "Tolloit" had died. Beck never claimed to have visited the site and quite naturally assumed that the "Omanek" referred to was Omanek Island which was only 120 miles to the north of Cape York "in the direction of Cape Dudley Digges." We have already seen one other alternative in "Umana – the heart shaped place" near Home Bay. There are others.

On the west coast of Greenland, about four hundred miles south of Cape York, lies Umanak Fjord. A small community, also called Umanak, is located here, as is a similarly named island. On the other side of the Nugssuaq Peninsula from Umanak Fjord is Disko Bay, where the *Erebus* and *Terror* transferred stores from the *Barretto Junior* before entering the ice in 1845. The association of Umanak with the *Erebus* and *Terror* is most interesting.

Franklin's ships departed from this Omanek only to be stopped by the ice near King William Island. The crews then abandoned them and lived ashore at camps near Cape Felix and in Terror Bay. Naturally their officers wore epaulettes. McClintock later heard from natives of King William Island of a burnt-through mast quite similar to that which fell from the *Dordon*. The bodies of some of the crew were associated with cairns. These were all elements of Beck's story.

Yet Beck's stories told not of ships departing from Omanek but of an arrival and subsequent massacre there. Was there another Omanek near King William Island which could tie in with Franklin's expedition?

In the 1960s the Canadian Armed Forces conducted a summer search of Taylor Island. This lies in Victoria Strait, near the drift path of the *Erebus* and *Terror*. The inspiration for this search was a native tradition that a massacre had occurred here. One of the native names for the island is "Ommanak." The expedition found no traces of Europeans on the island.[14]

Across Victoria Strait from King William Island is Victoria Island. This is the home of the the Kitlermiut Inuit. The Inuit of King William Island told Rasmussen that "in the old days a tribe was really at war with all others outside of its own hunting grounds, and many are the tales that have been handed down of strife, murder, in fact massacre. After the entry of the white man into the Hudson Bay district, perfect peace was established between the tribes in the east, but they are still at loggerheads with all tribes to the west, especially the people from Victoria Land."[15]

The natives of King William Island remembered the Kitlinermiut as "dangerous people" and "feared [them] as foot-pads who ambushed peaceful travellers,"[16] but this does not prove that they posed any threat to Franklin's men. Nevertheless, a strange tradition existed among the Kitlinermiut's descendants. Stefansson was told that some Inuit who had lived north of Minto Inlet had attacked a ship and killed some white men. According to his informant, "the white men then shot them down with guns and killed the last one." Remembering the supposed "massacre" at Taylor Island, we can only ask, like Stefansson, "What ship?"[17]

There are other candidates for Beck's Omanek as well. Rasmussen's maps in his report of the Thule Expeditions of the 1920s note many small islands of a type called "omanatluk – the heart-shaped ones," so many in fact that it seems to have been almost impossible for a European expedition to travel anywhere in the Arctic without becoming associated with one of them. One of these islands was located a few miles from John Ross's 1830s wintering place at Victory Harbour in Lord Mayor Bay. Another was in the depths of Chantrey Inlet near the mouth of the Great Fish River, and was identified by Rasmussen as King Island.[18]

So many similarly named locations, all of which were associated with white men, were bound to lead to confusion. What light can these new identifications of "Omanek" throw on Beck's tale? A line-by-line analysis of his testimony is necessary.

When I came to the ships and asked them they said they had been here four winters.

Those who believed in the Franklin origin of Beck's story pointed out that the only ships to spend a long period in the ice were the *Erebus* and *Terror*. They shrugged off the discrepancy of two years (Franklin's ships spent only two winters in the ice near King William Island before abandonment) or alternatively amended the statement by insertion of the word "ago" to translate it "had been here four winters ago" – i.e. in 1846, which was almost correct.

Others saw the "four winters" as a certain clue. Only one expedition had actually spent that long in the ice – John Ross in the *Victory*. Ross had indeed wintered four times, three times (in three different harbours) in his ship, and once at Fury Beach. But Ross's journal shows that no contact was made with the natives after the second winter, so it is hard to see how the Inuit could have known this fact.

A telling objection to Ross as the source of the tale was that he had only one ship. R.J. Cyriax thought that he could see a way around this difficulty by noting that, as well as the 150-ton *Victory*, Ross had taken the 16-ton tender *Krusenstern* to the Arctic; therefore, "Eskimos who had never seen any craft larger than their own kayaks might well have regarded him as possessing two ships."[19]

Another clue was seemingly offered by the name "Tolloit."

Tolloit also wintered upon our land.

The identity of Tolloit is uncertain. None of the officers of the *North Star* had a name which could approximate this in the manner of Saunders/Sanne. Only one European is known to have had a similar native nickname – John Ross was called "Too-loo-ah."

Those who felt that Beck was relaying a remembrance of Ross's expedition seized on this fact as proof. But there seemingly was a tradition among the Inuit of King William Island that John Ross had died with the Franklin expedition, and this considerably confuses the picture. Beck, who only served to relay the story, had no idea that "Tolloit" could refer to Ross, for his later statement that "Tolloit is also dead" would then have been patently absurd. Not only was Ross present at Cape York – he was Adam Beck's employer!

In 1846 two ships with three masts went from our land to Omenak; they arrived safely, but the men are dead. Two ships encompassed by the ice, otherwise they could not do. Their provisions were consumed. The men went to them; it is said they are dead.

Owing to the similarities between the Franklin expedition of 1845 and the Ross expedition of 1829, these ambiguous sentences can be made to fit either. In 1845 the *Erebus* and *Terror* did go to Umanak (Disko Bay) and eventually carried on to the vicinity of Taylor Island (Ommanak). They arrived safely. The men in them all eventually died, and their provisions were almost exhausted. "The men went to them" could refer to a visit to the ships by the Inuit, or, alternatively, read as "the men went from them," could be a tale of abandonment.

The *Victory* and *Krusenstern* went directly to Lord Mayor Bay (Omanaq) – not in 1846 but in 1829. They also arrived safely. The crews ran out of provisions and eventually abandoned their ship(s). The natives did not witness the abandonment and could therefore assume that the men perished (Beck only stated that "It is said they are all dead"), and that "Tolloit/Toolooah" (Ross?) was also dead.

The second story told by Beck is less amenable to explanation. It would be true of any naval expedition that "the ships were not whalers, and that epaulettes were worn by some of the white men." The statement that "part of the crews were drowned" does not fit any known expedition, although, as we shall see, a vague tradition told by a native named Kokleearngnun of a white man's ship which was overwhelmed by ice does remark that some of the men drowned. This story is usually thought to apply to either Franklin or Ross.

After the abandonment of the *Victory*, John Ross's crew spent one winter in Somerset House at Fury Beach, so it could truly be stated that they "were some time in huts or tents apart." Yet once again, apparently, there were no native witnesses to this fact. Beck's words also echo the testimony of a native woman who met Franklin's crewmen on the ice and remarked that "five of the white men put up a tent on the shore, and five remained with the boat on the ice."

The prime significance of the second tale is in the last sentence: "they had guns but no balls, were in a weak and exhausted condition, and were subsequently killed by the natives with darts and arrows." None of Ross's men were ever attacked. Were some of Franklin's?

In addition to the questionable traditions of the massacre at Taylor Island, another story of a fight was told concerning Franklin's men. According to this story, Crozier and some of his men were attacked by some Indians; Crozier was wounded, but the white men managed to drive their attackers off. Hall, to whom the story was told, came to the conclusion that "this must have occurred near the entrance of the Great Fish River." In other words the fight occurred near King Island/Omanek.

The tale of the attack on white men near the Great Fish River may have another source. It will be remembered that during Back's expedition three of his men were involved in a fight with

Inuit. Back's second in command, Dr Richard King, heard of the incident upon the expedition's return to England. King learned that the men

had fallen in during their march with a party of Esquimaux, and an affray ensued, in which three of the natives lost their lives. The men, it appeared, having surrounded a small lake to secure some wild fowl, were surprised by a party of Esquimaux, and at once retreated. The natives in following them fired a few arrows, upon which the men turned, and discharging their guns, killed three of the party, and might possibly have wounded others ... The natives, thoroughly dismayed at seeing their countrymen fall around them, fled in the greatest disorder; and the men, equally alarmed, betook themselves to flight also.[20]

According to Back's account this fight must have occurred near King Island – Omanek.

How is a garbled story constructed? The *Erebus* and *Terror* sailed to Umanak in Greenland in 1845. The *Victory* and *Krusenstern* arrived at another Omanaq in 1829. Back's men had a battle in 1834 with a small band of Inuit hunters and killed three of them near another island called "Omanaq," which is only a few miles from Montreal Island where the last Franklin relics would later be found. Many years later Hall was told that a fight occurred near there "before the white men [Franklin's crews] died," which is of course true if the story referred to Back's encounter.

All of these disparate "Omanek" tales may have been synthesized into a semi-coherent form to be subsequently told and retold. Elements of one true tale were added here, features of a similar nature there. Eventually the story was passed to the English explorers through an interpreter whose mastery of English left much to be desired. A faithful Inuit interpreter was slandered: over a century later military helicopters landed on a barren Arctic island called "Ommanak."

Even with such a seemingly unintelligible source as Adam Beck we can discern truthful roots if we look closely enough. Indeed, the problem is not that no expedition can be made to fit his tale, but that too many of them can!

We cannot know whether Beck's tales concerned the whalers at Umana/Home Bay, the *North Star* at Omanek/Saunders Island, Ross's *Victory* at Omanak/Victory Harbour, the *Erebus* and *Terror* at Ommanak/Taylor Island, George Back's encounter at Omanaq/ King Island, or some combination of these. The evidence can be interpreted in many ways and cannot convincingly stand as support for any single interpretation without further corroboration.

Here, at the start of our inquiry into the fate of Franklin's crews, we have learned some lessons which will stand us in good stead. The first is that historians have been too ready to dismiss questionable Inuit stories out of hand before investigating the clues embedded in them. The second is that those clues are often frustratingly ambiguous, but perhaps not impossibly so.

We have found an almost embarrassing number of scenarios that would fit Beck's "fabrication." At least one of these relates to the Franklin expedition, and its ramifications must be kept in mind when considering other Inuit tales. Beck's account does not allow us to definitively establish which expedition was the source, but it does cast doubt on Lieutenant Osborn's characterization of him as a "vile liar."

~5~

Poctes Bay

Adam Beck's tale of a massacre at Omanek managed to delay Austin's expedition for only one day. A few days later the little flotilla of search vessels entered Lancaster Sound and commenced their search for Franklin's trail. They were soon successful.

On the south-west shore of Devon Island a large cairn was spotted on Cape Riley. Subsequent examination of this, and of the nearby island (actually a peninsula), proved that this was where the *Erebus* and *Terror* had wintered in 1845–6. Here at Beechey Island the eager searchers found the remains of some buildings which had served as workshops and warehouses, a vast quantity of empty preserved-meat tins, a small garden, washplaces, and a shooting gallery.[1] The graves of three of Franklin's men were also discovered, although, until recently, these offered no clues as to the subsequent course of the expedition. (See appendix 4.)

No record was found which would indicate either the progress of the expedition to date or its intended course. Some searchers thought that this was a result of a hurried departure, others disagreed. Every cairn was repeatedly torn down and rebuilt and the surrounding ground excavated, but all to no avail. Several "direction posts" – boarding pikes on which had been attached boards with carved or painted pointing fingers – were found. Some searchers believed that these had originally indicated the

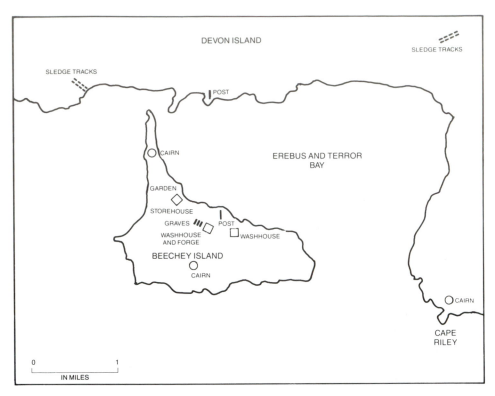

Map 2   Winter Quarters, 1845–46

place on Beechey's gravel slopes where the container with the elusive record had been deposited. Others felt they had merely indicated the location in which Franklin's ships had been anchored, remembering that Parry had set up similar posts at Igloolik to aid his crews if lost in a snowstorm.[2]

The later record recovered by McClintock on King William Island would tell of a surprisingly successful first year of effort. In 1845 the *Erebus* and *Terror* had ascended Wellington Channel to 77 degrees north and circumnavigated Cornwallis Island by means of a previously unknown channel. As this was the second prospective route offered to Franklin in his instructions, it has usually been assumed that he initially found the ice near Cape Walker, his primary objective, to have been impenetrable. Additionally, as he had to retreat somewhat to his chosen winter station at Beechey, it has also been assumed that he had probably discovered this excellent harbour before attempting Wellington Channel and kept it in mind for later use.

Except for the previously mentioned deaths of three crewmen, now known to have been by natural causes, the physical evidence at Beechey Island indicated the passage of a fairly uneventful and routine winter. The empty provision tins were initially seen to be an ominous sign, for Franklin's supplier had since come into disrepute for the quality of its product, and some observers concluded that the tinned meat provided to Franklin had here been found to be tainted. This provided a ready explanation for the disaster which all now assumed to have occurred. Debate raged over this interpretation, but recent work indicates that there is no reason to believe that any of the meat provided to the *Erebus* and *Terror* was tainted and that normal usage adequately accounts for the quantity of tins found.[3]

We now know that, after slipping from his snug winter quarters at Beechey Island, Sir John Franklin attempted to force his way to the south-west of Cape Walker, as his orders directed. If he had not discovered so in 1845, he would now learn that Cape Walker was not the western cape of Somerset Island but the eastern cape of Russell Island, and that a passage led due south between these two land masses. Passing into what Parry had initially thought was a bay, Franklin took his ships into the unknown waters of Peel Strait.

Of all of the channels which Franklin could have utilized, Peel Strait was perhaps the least favoured. Its very existence was unknown when he sailed from England in 1845. When identified as a possible route south during the subsequent search for the *Erebus* and *Terror*, the explorers were unanimous in their opinions that the lost ships could never have used it.

McClintock sledged down its eastern shore in 1849, but considered that "any attempt to force a ship down it would not only fail but lead to almost inevitable destruction in consequence of its being choked up with heavy ice."[4] In addition to this, he also thought that he could see a land barrier stretching across from Somerset to Prince of Wales Islands, confirming Parry's opinion that it was a bay. William Kennedy, specifically tasked to search the area of King William Island by Franklin's widow, also thought that he could see this non-existent land bridge. He wrote that "had the opening between Cape Walker and Cape Bunny proved a channel continuous with Victoria Strait of Rae, our proper course would have been s., on the probability of Franklin having passed through. On ascending the high land of Cape Bird, however, we observed Victoria Strait, while clear to the s., terminating distinctly, so far as we could see, in a bay, a few miles to the N. of our position ... and accordingly [we] had no alternative but to proceed westward, with a view of ascertaining whether any more promising channel existed farther w."[5]

These observations would mislead the Franklin searchers into assuming that the *Erebus* and *Terror* must be sought to the north or west of Beechey Island, and would therefore delay the discovery of their fate.

It can only be assumed that the vagaries of climate which had made 1845 such a successful year for Franklin had caused an early and tempting clearance of Peel Strait, whose promise was cruelly withdrawn by the equally early onset of winter in 1846. This, tragically, allowed the *Erebus* and *Terror* to penetrate the little-known channel, which had never before been seen free of ice, and which then closed solidly behind them for the next decade.

During the short summer of 1846 the *Erebus* and *Terror* forced their way down this hitherto unpromising strait. No signs of their passage were ever discovered, and most historians accept the idea that their voyage south was very rapid.[6] All that we know for certain is that the ships were beset on 12 September 1846 to the north-west of Cape Felix, the northernmost point of King William Island.

The standard version of the reconstructed story does not allow Franklin any divergence from a direct route between Beechey Island and the eventual position of his besetment. The thinking is that he bravely accepted the invitation of an ice-free Peel Strait and was then forced to submit to the semi-permanent and impenetrable ice-field which he found blocking his path to the west of King William Island. But surely he had other options.

As the *Erebus* and *Terror* forged their way southward, their commanders must certainly have rejoiced in their good fortune. With each passing day they approached James Ross's Victory Point, and, except for a short sixty-mile stretch between this and Simpson's Cape Herschel, the way was known from there all the way to the Pacific. Geographically they could be relatively sure that the way was clear and that the North-West Passage was theirs for the taking. But there was still one known obstacle in their way.

Franklin undoubtedly had the narratives of all of his predecessors in his library for ready reference. As he approached Cape Felix, the most relevant of these would have been James Ross's account of his exploration of northern King William Island in 1830. Here Franklin could rejoice in the "great extent of sea" which Ross had seen to the westward of Victory Point, "free from all appearance of land." It was entirely reasonable to expect that this passage would easily convey his ships to Simpson's Queen Maud Gulf and then directly to his own Cape Turnagain. Yet on the same page Ross mentioned the "heaviest masses" of ice which he had yet seen, and pack-ice which had driven ashore "as much as half a mile."[7]

As the short summer showed signs of ending, Sir John must have known that the threat from this ice was imminent. He also knew that there were no known harbours to the south-west of Cape Felix where he could hope to winter his vessels. Should he successfully navigate the unknown "gap," he would then face the narrow straits discovered by Simpson and Dease south of Victoria and Wollaston Land. These offered no protection for large unwieldy ships until the discovery of Cambridge Bay by Collinson in 1852. If the *Erebus* and *Terror* defeated the "heavy masses" of ice in Victoria Strait, they would presumably be standing themselves into peril by searching for a perhaps non-existent shelter.

The explorers could feel pleased with the progress of the expedition in the first two years. They had unlocked the secrets of both Wellington Channel and Peel "Sound." They could be relatively confident of the successful outcome of a further season, a season which would probably result in the long-awaited conquest of the North-West Passage. Surely it was now time to find a winter haven from which they could safely emerge in 1848 to complete the quest.

A quick look at James Ross's maps (as drawn by Arrowsmith), would have shown that there was a safe refuge only a few miles to the east of Cape Felix. This was "Poctes Bay." In fact, Ross had mentioned finding two natural harbours in the area, one of which was an "excellent harbour, could such a harbour ever be of any use: and its entrance, which is two miles wide, is divided in the middle by an islet that would effectually cover it from the invasion of heavy ice."[8]

It may have been that Franklin could have made use of such a harbour.

Ross's guide Ooblooria had told him that this narrow strip of water was a "continuous open sea, or a sea free of all ice during the summer,"[9] and modern evidence indicates that the one-year ice which forms here is among the first to break up and the last to reappear.[10]

Even more enticing was the possibility that "Poctes Bay" was in fact an open channel which eventually connected to Simpson Strait. James Ross had obtained only imperfect and questionable views of its southern shore during his return trip, and Franklin's charts probably showed the southern reaches of the bay as a dotted line, indicating that an opening might be found there.[11]

In John Ross's Narrative, buried in the Appendix, he even mentioned the possibility that King William's Land might be an island![12] If this were found to be so, not only would an ice-free channel to the east bypass the hazards of Victoria Strait, but the question of the peninsularity of Boothia, which had confounded both Back and Simpson, would be resolved.

We now know that "Poctes Bay" is in fact the northern entrance of James Ross Strait, and that Ooblooria was more accurate than James Ross in his geography. This is the preferred route through the "southern" North-West Passage (the only one passable by small wooden ships), and was later used successfully by Amundsen, Larsen, and others. It has often been remarked that James Ross's error in thinking that this waterway was closed to the south indirectly led to the Franklin tragedy by forcing Franklin to choose the unforgiving ice-pack to the west. Few have considered that, with the threat of a fast-approaching winter, even a misnamed "bay" would have been welcome to Franklin. Did he attempt to use it?

Although the general opinion when Franklin sailed was that King William's Land was a westward-extending peninsula of Boothia (itself thought to be an island, separated from the continent by Simpson Strait), there was no proof that this was so. To fail to clarify such a confused situation, when the time and resources were so conveniently at hand, would have been unthinkable to Franklin. As a prudent commander he must have realized that an escape route might eventually be of use, and if the supposed isthmus between Boothia and King William's Land was non-existent, as indeed it is, the resulting passage would lead to Simpson Strait, which almost everyone believed led both westward toward success, and eastward – toward home.

Sir John Barrow published a book in 1846 which clearly indicated the state of the geographical knowledge available to Franklin when he left England. Barrow also believed that there was a channel leading around King William Island to the east which opened "into the lower part of Prince Regent Inlet: should this be so, it will form the continuation of [James Ross] strait, through which not only a single ship and boats, but whole fleets, may pass."[13]

Barrow was such a devout believer in the idea that "Poctes Bay" was in fact a strait that he refused to accept the contrary views of his contemporaries. He endeavoured to "correct the erroneous impressions which the Report of a Select Committee of the House of Commons is calculated to convey," a report which he considered to be "founded on the most absurd nonsense." In opposition to this report he assured his readers that a passage did exist between Prince Regent Inlet and the western sea, probably including Ross Strait, and that any assertion to the contrary "has since been proved to be wholly incorrect."[14]

Franklin must have been aware of the importance of determining the true nature of this tiny unexplored corner. But if he took his ships into the northern reaches of "Poctes Bay" he would almost unavoidably have found himself in difficulties, for the treacherous shoals would soon have confounded his deeply laden and rather clumsy ships. They would quickly have found themselves enmeshed in what has traditionally been one of the most unforgiving parts of the Arctic.

Ten miles to the east of Cape Felix lies the first obstacle to confront any vessel entering Ross Strait – the Clarence Islands. Interestingly, there is an Inuit tradition of a white man's cairn on one of them.[15] Neither James Ross nor any other nineteenth-century explorer ever crossed over to these almost invisible islands. Could this cairn be a relic of Franklin's men?

The Clarence Islands are only the first of the difficulties of Ross Strait. Three modern expeditions all bore witness to the next hazard – the Matty Island shoals. In 1941, the RCMP vessel *St Roch* successfully navigated the North-West Passage from west to east, her route taking her through these waters. Here Captain Larsen, in his own words, "nearly lost the ship, as the waters were full of shoals."[16]

Thirty-six years later, Willy de Roos took his small yacht *Williwaw* through Ross Strait and noted the same reef "lying along the northern coast of Matty Island ... Before long the depth is down to three fathoms."[17] Three fathoms equals eighteen feet. When the *Erebus* and *Terror* left Greenland they drew seventeen.

Larsen in the *St Roch* and de Roos in *Williwaw* managed to avoid the hazards of the Matty Island reef partly because they had the previous experience of Roald Amundsen to guide them. In 1903, during his famous transit, Amundsen's little vessel, the *Gjoa*, encountered difficulties in the same area. Having previously touched bottom in the shallows of Ross Strait, the *Gjoa* found herself inextricably enmeshed in shoal water.

Shortly after [hitting bottom], we struck again, got off, and grounded again, this time for good ... The bank we had grounded on was a large submerged reef, branching out in all directions. It extended towards the west [sic] towards Boothia, as far as I could see. The land right to leeward was probably Matty Island ...

With a few tons of ballast the *Gjoa* had a draft of six feet. Loaded as she was, she drew 10 feet 2 inches ... We were compelled to lighten the vessel as much as possible. First of all we threw over 25 of our heaviest cases. They contained dog's pemmican, and weighed nearly 4 hundredweight each. Then we threw out all the other cases of deck-cargo on one side, to get the vessel to heel over as much as possible ... We were near a little island to the north of Matty Island.[18]

The weather deteriorated and the next day the stranded *Gjoa* was pounded by a heavy sea in a full gale. The crew attempted to kedge off with a bower anchor, and later set the sails to assist in powering the vessel forward over the shallow bar. Amundsen had to decide whether to abandon his suffering ship before she foundered. He gave the order to clear away the boats and load them with provisions, rifles, and ammunition, until "Lund, who stood nearest, asked whether we might not make a last attempt by casting the remainder of the deck-cargo overboard ... We set to in pairs, and cases of 4 cwt were flung over the rail like trusses of hay."[19]

Although it is not expressly stated, this second section of "deck-cargo" was presumably more of the dog pemmican, as the cases were identical in weight. The lightened ship forced her way over the reef and her false keel was dislodged. Amundsen "expected every moment to see her planks scattered on the sea," but the valiant *Gjoa* managed to continue her momentous journey without further damage.

Was there another victim, an earlier victim, of these deceptive waters?

One of the most unlikely of the Inuit tales was told to Major L.T. Burwash in 1929. Burwash was told by the Netsilingmiut that they "had for many years been aware of the fact that the wreck of a large vessel lay submerged off the northeastern extremity of Matty Island."[20] Since it was such a late-sprouting and unsupported story it has usually been dismissed out of hand by the reviewers. However, it is so simply and straightforwardly told, and has such telling internal consistency, that it is hard to discount entirely.

Two natives named Enukshakak and Nowya, whom Burwash described as of "apparently more than sixty years of age," gave further details.

When they were both young men, possibly twenty years of age, they were hunting on the ice in the area immediately northeast of Matty Island. When crossing a low flat island they came across a cache of wooden cases, carefully piled near the center of the island, and about three hundred feet from the water. As described by them this cache covered an area twenty feet long and five feet broad and was taller than they were (more than five feet). The cache consisted of wooden cases which contained materials unknown to them, all of which were enclosed in tin canisters, some of which were painted red ...

They said that on the outside of the pile of the boxes the wood appeared old but the parts sheltered from the weather were still quite new. All of the boxes were opened by the natives and the wooden cases divided for the manufacture of arrows. Enukshakak's share was eleven cases, Nowya's nine and their friend two, making twenty two cases in all. After the wood had been divided they opened the tin containers but found them to contain materials of which they had no knowledge. In a number they found a white powder which they called "white man's snow" ... since learning more about the white man's supplies they have come to the conclusion that some of the cases contained flour, some ship's biscuits, and some preserved meats, probably pemmican.

They also secured at this time a number of planks which they described as being approximately ten inches wide and three inches thick and more than fifteen feet long. These they found washed up on the shore of the island upon which they had found the cache and on the shore of a larger island nearby. Before the time of the finding of the cache on the island the natives had frequently found wood (which from their description consisted of barrel staves) and thin iron (apparently barrel hoops) at various points along the coastlines in this area.

The wreck itself, which had long been known to the natives, lay beneath the water about three quarters of a mile off the coast of the island upon which the cache was found ...

[Enukshakak and Nowya] gave it as their opinion that the boxes had been put on the island by white men who had come on the ship which lay on the reef offshore ...[21]

Burwash was very impressed by the tale – a rare eyewitness account – and Enukshakak and Nowya offered to take him to the site of their cache. His informants reported that "a few years ago when they had last visited the island only the marks of rusty tins were to be seen," but when Burwash visited the scene in April 1929, he found "a low flat terrain still covered with snow" and was therefore unable to verify the story.

Burwash concluded that the wreck must be that of either the *Erebus* or the *Terror*. This idea presented problems. Since one ship was known to have been destroyed in Victoria Strait, Burwash surmised that the other had either drifted or been taken through Simpson Strait and north to Matty Island – practically circumnavigating King William Island! Predictably, this idea was generally felt to be extremely improbable, and in the absence of any corroboration it was quietly dropped.

The close agreement between the "wreck" of the *Gjoa* and the tale told by the two natives has led most commentators to the opinion that the tale, if not entirely spurious, is a late echo of Amundsen's ordeal. However, it must be noted that the details of the stories do not entirely mesh.

The locale is hardly as significant as it would at first appear. We have seen that the system of shoals and reefs near Matty Island hold a menace for any vessels attempting the passage. Also the current which flows through Ross Strait is southerly, so Matty Island would be a likely place for debris to accumulate if drifting from the north (the drift would work against Burwash's supposed circumnavigation).

The packing cases seem conclusive at first – Amundsen ditched twenty-five and the natives found twenty-two – but it must be remembered that the crew of the *Gjoa* subsequently jettisoned the other half of their deck-cargo as well. In any event, cases which were hastily tossed overboard could hardly be expected to neatly arrange and stack themselves three hundred feet from the water. Also, the contents of the cargo – dog pemmican – would probably not have been carefully canned, and could not possibly be confused with flour or ship's biscuit. We also recall that the tins found were "painted red," which, coincidentally, was the colour of those supplied to Franklin.

There is also a problem with timing. If Enukshakak and Nowya were really sixty years of age in 1929 (and Burwash, having spent much of his life among the Inuit, should be a trustworthy judge), then they were in their twenties long before the *Gjoa* came to the north.

Finally there is the question of wreckage. When the natives mention debris from a wreck which "lay beneath the water," and tell of fifteen-foot-long planks and barrels that were washed ashore, we remember that the *Gjoa* suffered only minor damage, jettisoned no barrels, and continued on her voyage.

The *Gjoa* was not wrecked at Matty Island, but we also know that the *Erebus* and *Terror* were intact in 1848, at which time they were trapped in Victoria Strait. How can we explain the native "wreck"?

If either the *Erebus* or the *Terror* grounded on one of the shoals while searching for Poctes Bay in 1846, we could expect that an effort would be made to lighten her. Presumably some of her stores would be offloaded onto a nearby beach by making use of the ship's boats. The largest of these would have been one of the four thirty-foot whaleboats with which each vessel was supplied. These were larger than a typical Inuit "umiak," the largest type of boat in their experience.

Although the explorer's ships were larger still, the natives are known to have called these "umiaks" as well. The native use of the same word for "large boat" and "ship" could be a key to the solution to the question. It is conceivable that a whaleboat could have been nipped while transferring stores between a grounded ship and the nearest island. In the shallow water around Matty Island, only a boat of this size would be likely to lie "beneath the water" without showing any superstructure and yet remain within sight of the surface.

The loss of a boat would also explain why the carefully arranged cache of crates was abandoned when the mother ship was finally freed. Presumably the drifting ice prevented the surviving boats from returning for it.

This hypothetical chain of events would explain the native tale of a "wreck" without invoking the *Gjoa* or forcing the *Erebus* or *Terror* to drift miraculously around King William Island. The evidence for such a theory is admittedly circumstantial and ambiguous, but it would explain an otherwise inexplicable Inuit remembrance.

The most common objection to Enukshakak and Nowya's tale seems to be that it is too recent and that no other mention exists of a wreck which Burwash stated to have been "long known to the natives." There seems to be no independent corroboration. Or is there?

The east coast of King William Island was away from the focus of European attention, and the only explorer to pass this way before Burwash was McClintock. McClintock barely mentions his trip past Matty Island, but what he does say is interesting. In May of 1859 he crossed over to the south-west point of Matty Island, where he found "a deserted village of nearly twenty snow huts, besides several others, within a few miles on either side of it; in all of them I found shavings or chips of different kinds of wood from the lost expedition."[22]

McClintock had earlier learned of a small islet near the southeast tip of Matty Island called "Owut-ta" where the natives traditionally congregated, and he next went in search of it. He did not find the islet, but on another nearby he again found some deserted igloos. He regretted the absence of these Inuit, for "from the quantity of wood chips about the huts, they probably had visited the stranded ship alluded to by the last Esquimaux we had met."[23]

He was impressed by the amount of wood shavings which he found, and rightly so, for they were evidence of a larger amount of wood than he had noted in the possession of any other Inuit. Few natives were rich enough in this precious commodity to be able to afford the abandonment of any of it, even "shavings." McClintock evidently thought that the wood was the remains of one of Franklin's ships. But we can now ask whether this amount of wood, associated with a small offshore islet near Matty Island, could have come from another wreck, one which lay much nearer, or from Burwash's cases and barrel staves.

It was near here that the natives offered McClintock "a heavy sledge made of two short stout pieces of curved wood" which he thought that "no mere boat could have furnished them with." On the map of King William Island which Burwash included with his report he indicated that he had also found "relics" on a small islet to the south of Matty Island. In the latter case no reference to the nature of these relics is made.

Part of the reason that Burwash's tale of a wreck near Matty Island met such stiff resistance is undoubtedly his interpretation of the facts which were conveyed to him. His theory that the wreck must be of either the *Erebus* or the *Terror* was bound to be questioned. As we shall see, the eventual fate of both of the ships was thought to be known. That a ship which was known to have been abandoned in Victoria Strait could drift completely around King William Island against contrary currents was far-fetched, and so Burwash was forced to the conclusion that some remnant of the crews had brought the ship hither. This was altogether too much to accept on the basis of one unsubstantiated and questionable Inuit account.

Yet the "wreck" at Matty Island may have occurred much earlier in the story. The detour of the *Erebus* and *Terror* into "Poctes Bay" in search of a winter haven seems reasonable, and the end result of such a detour – the grounding of at least one of Franklin's unwieldy ships – almost inevitable. The loss of a boat which had been used to lighten the grounded ship is admittedly conjectural, but it would explain the Inuit story of a "wreck" which was completely submerged in the shallow water, and would also take care of the discrepancy between "neatly stacked boxes" of flour and Amundsen's cases of "dog pemmican" which were tossed overboard in the height of a storm.

Franklin may have attempted to make use of James Ross's "excellent harbour" in the lee of the Tennant Islands. If so, the evidence can be read to indicate that he was unsuccessful in this, and that he was then forced to try to penetrate the "heaviest masses" of ice in Victoria Strait which Ross had warned him about. This would mean that the eventual tragedy was caused, not by a grievous error of judgment on Franklin's part as has usually been concluded, but by the inescapable dictates of geography.

~6~

A Season of Search

We will probably never know whether the *Erebus* and *Terror* originally attempted to force a passage southwards in Ross Strait or whether the "wreck" at Matty Island is no more than a confused echo of Amundsen's *Gjoa*. As with much of the story of the Franklin expedition, we can make Inuit testimony fit several scenarios.

Fitzjames does tell us in his 1847 and 1848 Victory Point record that "HM Ships *Erebus* and *Terror* wintered in the Ice in Lat. 70°5 N Long 98°23 W ... having been beset since 12th Sept. 1846," and that "Sir John Franklin died on the 11th June 1847," but his short note gives no information as to what else happened during this pivotal period.

The *Erebus* and *Terror* were now in a precarious position. Having failed in an attempt to bring his ships to a secure winter harbour (if any attempt had been made), Franklin would now have to experience the strain of a winter in the exposed pack-ice. The *Terror* had suffered through a similar situation in 1836–7 (as had Lieutenant Gore), and only barely managed to survive. Of the discomforts, trials, and frustrations of the winter of 1846–7 we have no record.

Despite the hazardous position of his ships (or perhaps because of it), we know that during the following spring of 1847 Franklin sent Gore, Des Voeux, and six seamen on an exploratory journey. This was in direct accord with his orders, which noted that "the ascertaining [of] the true geographical position of the different points of land near which you may pass so far as can be effected without detention of the ships in their progress westward … must prove valuable and interesting to the science of our country."[1]

In light of this directive, it is only natural that Sir John would in turn remark that he would "of course dispatch parties in boats and by land to examine into and to find out passages in places where it may be difficult and only productive of delay in taking the ships."[2] Hall was certain that Franklin did not waste his time while his ships were locked in the ice.

To my mind, it appears reasonable that Sir John Franklin's expedition was not idle after getting beset as it did … as the spring of 1847 opened, it is altogether likely that exploring parties were started off, one at least down the west coast of King William's Land, to connect the discoveries of Sir John Ross' expedition with those of Dease and Simpson, while another, quite likely, proceeded down the east coast to connect discoveries that had been made by the same expeditions. Of course King William's Land was found to be an island, and the whole coast of the mainland (Boothia) from Cape Porter to Castor and Pollux River, was most undoubtedly explored …[3]

The first of Hall's suspected expeditions – that to trace the west coast of King William Island – we know to have been undertaken by Gore and Des Voeux. We do not know if they completed the survey of the North-West Passage, although it is generally assumed that they would persevere as far as Simpson's cairn at Cape Herschel. The records at Victory Point and Back (now Gore) Point are the only certain proof of their effort. The other exploration – that of the eastern coast – appears at first glance to be less urgent, and most authorities doubt whether it actually took place.

Yet we cannot lose sight of the situation which Franklin faced that winter. He was in the classic position of a man at the crossroads: to the south Cape Felix was a sharp arrow dividing two channels, either of which might yield success. It is possible that the reefs at Matty Island had already thwarted his first attempt to explore the eastern passage; however, he would still have no proof as to what lay in the bottom of "Poctes Bay."

Temporarily secure in the pack, Franklin knew what perils the capricious ice could summon and he therefore had a more than passing need to discover the true nature of that small geographical area where the expeditions of Ross, Simpson, and Back had come so close to touching. Here might lie his salvation.

It must be admitted that excellent reasons for an eastern expedition do not constitute proof that one was actually undertaken. Only the faintest clues in support of this idea exist. An old cairn, not of Inuit design, was found by Learmonth and Sturrock near the end of Peel Inlet. This deep inlet on the east coast was one of the main Inuit routes toward their hunting grounds to the south, yet if this cairn actually was built by white men they were almost certainly crewmen of the *Erebus* and *Terror*, for James Ross did not venture so far south and McClintock passed by the inlet without entering it.[4]

One positive relic of white men was found on the east coast of King William Island a few miles to the south of Peel Inlet. In-nook-poo-zhe-jook told Hall that an Inuit hunter had found a "knife (a butcher knife) of same kind as others that had been found of those who died on & about that Island, under some stones. On asking In-uk to point out the place where this knife was found he pointed to Livingston Point s. side of Latrobe Bay."[5]

As McClintock was the only white man to have passed this point, Hall further interrogated In-nook-poo-zhe-jook as to this find. When asked if the knife could have been deposited by McClintock, In-nook-poo-zhe-jook said no, but added that McClintock had placed a revolver under a stone in another place "far off from there." In this he was perfectly correct. In March 1859 McClintock built a cache on Boothia in which he hid some blubber, articles for barter, and two revolvers. Although his cache had been buried under four feet of snow, it was almost immediately discovered by the Inuit, and the revolvers had been taken.[6]

The name of the original thief was not recorded, but so detailed was the Inuit knowledge of white men's relics that In-nook-poo-zhe-jook could tell Hall, ten years after the event, that one of the revolvers had recently come into the possession of Koong-on-e-lik, a native of Pelly Bay.[7]

In light of this further proof of the native knowledge about the white men's relics, we can safely conclude that In-nook-poo-zhe-jook was probably correct in asserting that McClintock had not left a knife on the eastern shore of King William Island. This does not, of course, prove that Franklin's men themselves placed it there – it was more likely hidden by a native than from one. Nevertheless Seepunger told Hall that Franklin's men tried to go down the west coast of King William Island, but that "some turned back & doubled Cape Felix & went down on the E. side." In-nook-poo-zhe-jook similarly told him that "the Innuits had seen enough to satisfy them that some of those white men went one way, others in another direction & so on. They do not think they all kept together."[8]

An old cairn and a knife are indeed scant proof of an eastern exploring party from the *Erebus* and *Terror*. Hall, being subject to ready acceptance of any Inuit testimony as support for his own preconceptions, may not be the best witness on this particular question. But he was not the only proponent of the "eastern search" idea, and the other was the most respected interviewer of all.

Knud Rasmussen apparently had enough information from the Inuit to lead him to the same conclusion. Rasmussen never published this conclusion himself; we learn of it through an old Arctic hand, Andy Bahr, who knew the Danish explorer in his later travels.

Rasmussen, after years of study and delving into the history of the Huskies [Inuit] had arrived at the one way to make a successful hunt for [Franklin] records ... You see how all the parties concentrated on the west. Look, they even went down as far as the mainland of Canada. But every one of them was on the wrong trail according to Rasmussen, and I believe he had the right dope ... Now it strikes me that Knud Rasmussen's theory is sound; that instead of the entire party striking out along the west coast for aid, the main body ... headed down the east side of the island. Natives had always camped there on their hunting trips ... Nobody could get information from the Huskies as completely as Rasmussen, and I have told you his deduction after years of study of the question.[9]

We will never know what formed the basis for Rasmussen's theory that some of Franklin's men had traversed the east coast of King William Island. But if such a journey took place, it is not surprising that only faint echoes of it remain. On the western shore, 105 men traversed ninety miles of coastline. Their camp-sites and skeletons clearly marked their retreat and this area was then repeatedly and meticulously combed for clues. But a small surveying party similar to Gore's group of "2 officers and 6 men" would hardly be productive of a long trail of artifacts along the eastern shore. Since later searchers have entirely ignored this locale in favour of the more historically rewarding and important west coast, it could be expected that little would remain to mark such an effort.

If an eastern expedition is problematical, we still have ample evidence that, Gore's excursion aside, Franklin's men were not entirely confined to their ships during the summer of 1847. When the *Erebus* and *Terror* were beset, the nearest land lay to the south at Cape Felix, the northernmost point of King William Island. Here they established a camp.

The camp ... had apparently been occupied for some time by a party consisting of about twelve officers and men. Three small tents were used; they were lying flat when found by Lieutenant Hobson, and beneath them lay bearskin and blankets. Boarding pikes had apparently served as tent poles. Three fireplaces were near the tents.

Under one tent, which was smaller than the others, and had presumably been occupied by officers, lay the remains of an ensign, a parcel which contained some packets of needles (perhaps intended as presents for Eskimos), some shot, fragments of clothing, etc. Other relics found by Lieutenant Hobson at the camp included matches; scraps of wood partially burnt; ptarmigan feathers, broken pipes; some tobacco; a copper cooking-stove apparently made on board; pieces of broken china; a badge from a marine's shako; old clothing, two pike heads etc. No article was marked with a name or initials.[10]

Schwatka and Gilder revisited this camp in 1879. Schwatka noted "many red cans marked 'Goldner's Patent', and cups, with a large proportion of broken porter bottles and crockery,"[11] while Gilder remarked on "a torn down cairn, and a quantity of canvas and coarse red woolen stuff, pieces of blue cloth, broken bottles ... a piece of an ornamental tea cup, and cans of preserved potatoes."[12] The presence of crockery, tinned potatoes, and wine bottles led Klutschak to remark wryly that Franklin's men had lived better at their camp than Schwatka's party did.

This was not an entirely frivolous observation. A party large enough to require three tents and settled enough to afford the luxury of china teacups and "a large proportion" of wine bottles was not simply passing through. Even though every group proceeding south from the vessels would undoubtedly utilize such a convenient site for their first night's rest, and each would, like careless campers, contribute to the accumulated debris, there can be little doubt that at some time a party paused here. They were in no extremity, for they left tins of food behind. What where they doing?

Schwatka proposed that the camp was occupied during the summer of 1847 by a construction party which had been sent ashore to build cairns. He based this idea on the fact that near Cape Felix he had found a very large cairn, seven feet high and three feet in diameter at the base, which he concluded must have been used as an important marker of some sort. He concluded that "it must have been visible from the ships with a good marine glass, it was probably a monument erected to establish and measure the rate of drift."[13]

This explanation does not ring true. Franklin must have had a very good marine telescope indeed for a seven-foot marker built of stone to be visible from a distance of fifteen miles. In addition, the *Erebus* and *Terror* are known to have drifted only nineteen miles between September 1846 and April 1848, and that was probably not a uniform drift but the result of the erratic movements of the ice-field during the "breakup" of 1847. It seems more likely that the cairn served as a landmark for those making their way from the ships to the low shore.

This was not the only cairn to be found near Cape Felix by Schwatka. Gilder noted that his commander discovered another about three miles south of Cape Felix, that it, like its predecessor, had been torn down, but that "in the first course of stones, covered and protected by those thrown from the top, he found a piece of paper with a carefully drawn hand upon it, the index finger pointing at the time in a southerly direction." Gilder further noted that "the bottom part of the paper, on which rested the stone which held it in place, had completely rotted off, so if there had ever been any writing on it that too had disappeared."[14]

Hobson had found a similar cairn twenty years earlier. He discovered a "very large cairn" a short distance to the westward of Cape Felix, the top of which had fallen down. It still contained a piece of then-blank paper which had been carefully folded up, and among the tumbled stones two broken bottles were found which he thought might once have contained records.[15]

During the twenty-year interval between Hobson's and Schwatka's visits, the cairns had been visited by the Inuit. The Pelly Bay native Seepunger told Hall in 1866 that he and his uncle had visited northern King William Island and pointed out his route on a chart. They had gone "direct from the upper part of Pelly Bay overland to Spence Bay, and thence across the ice to Ki-ki-tung, passing the south point of Matty Island, and thence northwest."[16] Seepunger had not gone to King William Island in search of white men's relics but "for sealing," yet soon after reaching shore he had found a cairn.

See-pung-er, three years before, had visited King William's Land. He told Hall that he had seen, near Shar-too ... a very high and singular E-nook-shoo-yer (monument), built by kob-lu-nas, of stones, and having at its top a piece of wood something like a hand pointing in a certain direction. He had also seen a monument about the height of a tall man, at another point somewhere between Port Parry and Cape Sabine. When asked whether he had thrown this pile down, he answered, "Only enough of it to find something within." And when further closely questioned, he said that what he found was the small tin-cup which he had just given to Too-koo-li-too; that a tight top had fitted it; and that it was thickly and tightly wrapped up and tied, and had been found full of just such looking stuff as the paper on which Hall had been writing; but, he added, "this stuff was good for nothing to Innuits, and so was given to the children, or thrown away. He said further that he and his uncle had spent one night near this monument, wrapping themselves up in blankets taken from a pile of white men's clothing found there, and that a kob-lu-na's skeleton lay by the pile.[17]

Seepunger's account of his finds is in perfect agreement with the discoveries of McClintock and Schwatka. The pile of white men's clothing which he found was the same one discovered by Hobson at Victory Point a few years before. The presence of a skeleton near this pile surprised Hall; Schwatka would find it only eleven years later. In-nook-poo-zhe-jook later confirmed the site by pointing to Victory Point on a chart as "where See-pung-er & his uncle found the In-nook-shook (monument) that had been erected by white men & that about this they found many things that belonged to Kob-lu-nas."[18]

When Hall showed Seepunger a copy of Fitzjames's record, Seepunger remarked that the paper he had found was similar to it – with both printed and written words. This too may have been found at Victory Point; McClintock left a copy of Fitzjames's original record behind, but as Schwatka's party found this still tightly wrapped and tied with a ribbon it is possible that Seepunger found a similar form in one of the other cairns near Cape Felix.[19]

That more than one record had been left near Cape Felix is almost certain. Schwatka's paper with the pointing hand and Hobson's bleached sheet had probably each originally contained reports from Franklin's men. The pointing wooden hand on Seepunger's Enook-shoo-yer was also intended to direct searchers to something significant nearby. What was being indicated?

The camp at Cape Felix was manned during the summer of 1847. It was quite large, and was occupied for considerable periods of time. Presumably it was a suitable place to take the scientific observations, and served as an advance post for the exploring parties which Franklin sent out to chart the surrounding territory. It might also have served a more sombre purpose.

In 1949, Inspector H. Larsen noted "two small islets" about a mile north of Cape Felix. These are presumably low-lying reefs, as they are shown on most charts as "existence doubtful," yet Larsen noted with interest that a native tradition "believed that Sir John Franklin's grave might be on one of these islets."[20] He repeatedly tried to follow up this story, but was defeated by fog and bad weather which prevented him from approaching the site. No other explorers are known to have attempted to search these islets.

There are few other places which would so admirably serve as the burial place of Sir John. A thriving camp had been established nearby, and the "islets" would have been the nearest land to the ships at the time of Franklin's death. Yet few modern writers have ever given any credence to the tradition.

The search for Franklin's grave has been the "holy grail" of every investigator from McClintock to the present day. None have had success. The predominant opinion seems to be that it

is almost inconceivable that Franklin's men would not have conveyed his body ashore for burial, but that if they did so they
picked such an out-of-the-way spot, or they marked it so poorly,
that no later searcher has managed to uncover it.

Is there any evidence that the men of the *Erebus* and *Terror*
buried their comrades ashore at Cape Felix? Seepunger told Hall
that "another Eskimo before him had found a tin case with papers
in it" at Cape Felix and that this native had also found "the dead
bodies of three white men there."[21] It was not until recently that
physical evidence was found to support this claim.

At Cape Felix Larsen found the remains of a human skull embedded in
moss between some rocks on a ridge about a half mile from the sea.
These remains were examined at Ottawa and found to be parts of the
skull of a single individual, slightly built, of white race, and aged about
twenty five years. He was undoubtedly one of the officers or men of
the *Erebus* and *Terror* ... Larsen's discovery is of great interest, for none
of the previous searchers has found the bones of members of the Franklin expedition anywhere on King William Island to the north of Crozier's
cairn. For this reason it has hitherto been generally believed that Franklin
himself and the officers and men, who presumably died on board the
ships ... were buried at sea.

This discovery shows however, and Larsen believes, that some may
have been buried on land although, as he states, the finding of bones
or graves would be only accidental, for the terrain is difficult to examine
and any crosses or memorials would long ago have been removed by
the Eskimos.[22]

We remember the Enookshooyers – one with a wooden pointing finger, another with one drawn on paper. We also recall the
relics discovered at the camp at Cape Felix – the remains of an
ensign, a packet of sewing needles, and pikestaffs with their
heads missing. Could the monuments have been designed to
direct searchers to a gravesite? Was the ensign ever draped over
a coffin? Were the pikestaffs utilized to make a stretcher and the
needles used to sew up a shroud?

Some of the men who died while the *Erebus* and *Terror* were
beset were undoubtedly brought ashore and buried at the closest
point of land – Cape Felix. Was Franklin's body similarly treated?
If so, the grave has probably been pillaged and his bones scat-

tered. Only if a future search for Larsen's "islets" is successful can we hold out much hope that Franklin's grave will be found.

Thanks to Fitzjames's additions to his Victory Point record, we know of the main events in the history of the *Erebus* and *Terror* between the besetment in 1846 and the abandonment in 1848 – Gore's journey and Franklin's death. But even these simple facts have offered fertile ground for speculation, and on closer examination Fitzjames's account is itself full of mysteries.

Handwriting analysis shows that Commander Fitzjames wrote both accounts on the position sheet – that of the 1847 expedition and the amendment from the following year. The initial message was simple: "– of May 1847, Party consisting of 2 officers and 6 men left the ships on Monday the 24th of May 1847." Gore and Des Voeux then signed their names to the prepared sheet. The identity of the six seamen is not known. Similarly, the number of "form letters" Fitzjames made up for Gore's use is unknown; two have been found, but others were presumably destroyed by the Inuit. But careful study of the forms which were recovered shows some interesting features.

Slight differences in the colour and texture of the ink which Fitzjames used allowed Cyriax to note that "the day of the month was [originally] omitted from the head of both records, doubtless because he [Fitzjames] did not know at the time of writing on which days Lieutenant Gore would deposit them," but that in 1848 Fitzjames reopened the Victory Point tin and completed the date "by inserting the '28' in front of 'May'. As the tins were sealed with solder before the party left the ships [in 1847], it was evidently intended that the date should not be inserted."[23]

The assumption that the 28th was the day of deposition of the Victory Point record may not be correct. The two memoranda were hurriedly written, possibly on the morning of the party's planned departure, the 24th of May. As Gore and Des Voeux signed their own names but Fitzjames wrote the words denoting their ranks, we can see that the number of men involved and their leaders had already been chosen, as was the planned day of departure. But if Gore's party left the *Erebus* on the 24th, why did he take four days to travel the forty miles to Victory Point? It is probable that he spent the first night at the Cape Felix campsite, but this would still leave three days to accomplish the relatively short fifteen-mile journey to reach Ross's cairn. Almost exactly seventeen years before Gore's trip, in May 1830, James Ross had walked from his camp near Cape Felix to Victory Point in only four hours.

Another fact which argues against the idea that the 28th was the day of deposition is the realization that Gore deposited other records during his exploratory trip in 1847. Since we know that Gore was already dead when Fitzjames filled in the "28" (he is referred to as "the late" in the 1848 addition), Gore would have to have remembered the date of each record drop and passed these dates on to Fitzjames. A year later Fitzjames would then have to have remembered such an insignificant detail and decided to enter it on the Victory Point record. As each of Gore's records was deposited at a different time, this would require a considerable effort of memory on Fitzjames's part.

What Fitzjames is more likely to have remembered is that the party which had planned to depart on the 24th had actually been delayed to the 28th.

After filling in the "28" at the top of Gore's record, Fitzjames wrote the addition around the margin which would tell of the abandonment of the ships. Here he again mentioned the deposition of Gore's document: "this paper was found by Lt. Irving under the cairn supposed to have been built by Sir James Ross 4 miles to the northward in 1831 – where it had been deposited by the late Commander Gore in May June 1847."

Here, by originally writing "May" and then making a correction to "June," Fitzjames shows that the deposition could not have occurred on the 28th of the former month. Unless this is another error, it would imply that Gore could not have left the ships much before the last days of May. Indeed, the correction seems to indicate that Fitzjames had originally forgotten that the party had been delayed. Gore's record had been soldered into its cylinder before he left the ship and no amendments had been foreseen. Evidently it had not been considered necessary to break them open and correct the "left the ships on Monday 24th May" when the departure was delayed for a few days. Adverse weather could have caused such a delay, but there is a better conjecture.

It is the universal custom on vessels of the Royal Navy that all written correspondence, regardless of the originator, is signed by the Commanding Officer. It is therefore likely that Fitzjames would have shown these records to Franklin for his signature and approval. Sir John is known to have signed a similar form which had been tossed overboard on 30 June 1845 (and which was later recovered on the coast of Greenland), and presumably he would normally have signed these documents as well. But he did not.

Sir John Richardson stated that "Franklin had signed his own name but had not written the word 'Sir' immediately preceding his name."[24] Closer examination shows that the good doctor was mistaken, for Franklin's signature is not in his usual handwriting in either of the King William Island records, both of which are in Fitzjames's style.

When he wrote the narrative, Fitzjames had also crossed over the rank "Commander" in the official signature block. Since this was his own rank, his doing so could be taken to indicate that he did not intend to sign the documents himself, but was preparing them for Franklin. This would be consistent with normal practice. Yet the signature block remained blank on both copies. Why didn't Franklin sign?

Franklin died on 11 June 1847, and it therefore seems reasonable to conclude that he may have been incapacitated on 24 May when the records were prepared. Some writers have assumed a much more sudden collapse on his part, pointing out that Fitzjames wrote "All Well" on the 24th, but this I believe to be a much too literal reading. "All Well" referred to the general state of the expedition rather than the health or otherwise of any individual. Even if Franklin had been seriously ill in May it would hardly have been seemly for Fitzjames to include this in a general note.

Franklin's accident, whatever its nature, may have occurred on the 24th itself. Perhaps the occurrence delayed the departure of Gore's party for a few days. Yet it is tolerably certain that Gore's party did eventually depart on their search before Franklin's death, regardless of his state of health. The general opinion seems to be that Gore reached Simpson's cairn at Cape Herschel and thus confirmed that the *Erebus* and *Terror* were at the gates of a true North-West Passage. The question then arises – did he return with this information before Franklin died?

One of the enduring traditions of the Franklin expedition is that Gore confirmed the existence of the last link in the fabled passage in time to whisper the news of this final triumph in the ear of his dying Commander. However touchingly dramatic such a scenario may seem, there is, once again, only circumstantial evidence to support it.

We do not know how efficiently Gore and his party marched. If we assume that the two records which he deposited at Victory Point and Gore Point were one day's march apart, we are faced with the disturbing fact that these points are separated by only about six miles. But this is as the crow flies, and a glance at a chart will show that to reach the second point Gore and his party presumably had to complete the circuit around the deep indentation of Collinson Inlet – about twenty miles over the ground.

If Gore did manage a twenty-mile daily pace he would have reached Victory Point on the second day after leaving the ships. At this rate he would have required twelve days to reach Cape Herschel from the besieged vessels and then return. Even if the party did not depart until the 28th of May, this would allow them to regain the ships on the 9th of June – two days before Franklin's death.

Set against this purely speculative reasoning is the curious fact that, in the 1848 additions to Gore's document, Fitzjames refers to "the late *Commander* Gore." When Gore departed England he was first lieutenant of the *Erebus* and, although he had been promoted to Commander, in absentia, on 9 November 1846, he was still signing himself "Lieutenant" as late as May 1847. Between the time that he sailed and the first of March 1854 (when the crews of the *Erebus* and *Terror* were officially proclaimed to have died), Gore would actually be promoted again – to Captain.[25] Yet this was the perogative of the Admiralty; only for the most meritorious service could a "field-promotion" be given.

The fact that Commander Fitzjames signed himself "Captain" in the record amendments misled some writers into believing that Crozier had promoted both senior officers of the *Erebus* upon assuming command. But Captain is both the rank above Commander and the legal title of any man in command of a vessel (in this case the *Erebus*), regardless of his naval rank. Many Lieutenants were "Captains" of their own ships. Both Commander Fitzjames and Lieutenant Gore held rank appropriate for their positions after Franklin's death.

Keeping in mind that in the 1840s there were many senior officers in the Royal Navy on peacetime "half pay" with little chance of promotion, it is very unlikely that either Crozier or Fitzjames would have felt himself in a position to promote Gore to Commander. This leaves only the supposition that Franklin must have survived long enough to welcome "Lieutenant" Gore back from his momentous discovery, and bestowed greater rank on him for his efforts.

In truth, except for the fact that it occurred, we know nothing concrete about Gore's exploration. We are unsure as to when it departed, when it arrived back, or how far it managed to travel. The fact that neither Gore nor Des Voeux was living the next year might lead one to theorize that this party met with some accident and failed to return to the ships, but the reference to "Commander" Gore tends to nullify this. I think, however, that some slight misfortune did overtake Gore's party.

If one draws a straight line from Victory Point to Simpson Strait, one finds that it crosses the Graham Gore Peninsula, which separates Erebus Bay from Terror Bay. A short cut across the base of this peninsula saves anyone travelling this coast from the arduous forty-mile journey which would be necessary if the coast was followed. The Inuit and later explorers usually made use of this detour. Schwatka utilized this route twice during his search, and remarked that after the cheerless ice-strewn coasts of Erebus Bay the chain of lakes across the base of the peninsula had "soft mossy banks" which "were often perfect beds of gay and brilliant flowers."[26] As we shall see, there is evidence to suggest that Crozier's men also may have utilized this path after abandoning the ships. This would suggest that Gore had discovered its existence in 1847.

Only one lone skeleton was found to the west of this short cut. Schwatka found a single grave near Cape Crozier at the far western extreme of the peninsula.[27] While this has always been assumed to have been one of the 1848 marchers, it may have been that of one of Gore's original party of 1847 – perhaps poor Des Voeux – as this was the only party that would have been unaware of the short cut.

Except for the brief mention of Gore's excursion and Franklin's death, nothing is said in the Victory Point record about the events of the fateful first year spent in the ice. The relics found at Cape Felix are tantalizing but inconclusive. The Inuit were still unaware of the presence of the *Erebus* and *Terror* in their territory, and they have no tales of this time. We have seen that even the written words of one of the principals in the drama are not unambiguous, and that much detective work is needed in an attempt to gain a more complete view of what *could* have happened. Nevertheless, in 1847 Fitzjames could still write that all was "well." It would be the last year that that would be true.

~7~

Crozier's Choice

Whether or not Lieutenant Gore returned to the ships in time to tell Franklin of the successful accomplishment of the North-West Passage, like so many other questions, must remain unanswered. It is certain that he (or some of his party) did safely return from their summer excursion, for otherwise Crozier would not have known that Gore's record had been left in Ross's cairn.

The next winter, that of 1847–8, was the critical point of the expedition. We have no record of it beyond Fitzjames's later addition to the Victory Point record, which noted the sombre fact that as of April 1848 "the total loss by deaths in the Expedition has been to this date 9 officers and 15 men." Had rescue come at this time, the expedition would still have had the dubious honour of possessing the highest death rate in the history of British Arctic exploration.

This extremely high mortality has remained a mystery. Wright, noting the disproportionate number of officers, concluded that an officer-rich exploring party had been ambushed by the Inuit.[1] Others, with a more generous outlook, felt that the officers had possibly over-exerted themselves in an effort to care for their men, perhaps by exposing themselves to the elements while hunting.[2] Without further information such speculations remain largely idle.

Fitzjames's Victory Point record indicates that by April 1848 the *Erebus* and *Terror* had drifted from Cape Felix to a position

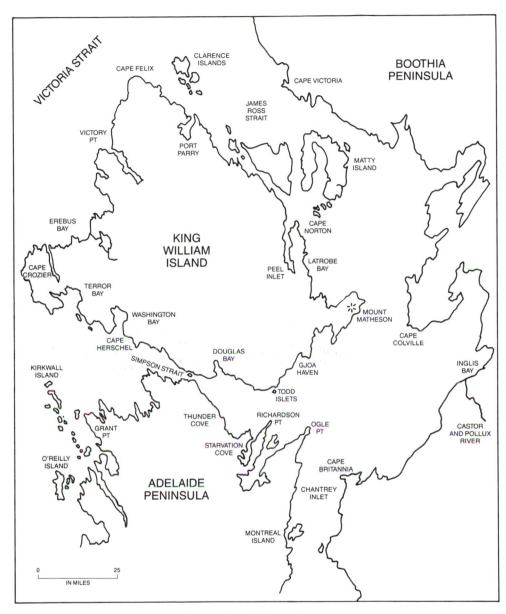

Map 3   King William Island

well out in the ice-stream of Victoria Strait. Breakup and possible release could not be expected until late July, and, failing that, the men would be unable to survive another winter.

The ships had been provisioned with food for 137 men for three years (1092 days), but as only 129 men actually entered the ice, and only 105 of these were still alive in April, it is probable that shortage of food was not yet a pressing problem. It was felt that the food loaded in Greenland was probably sufficient to sustain Franklin's men until May 1849 "without serious inconvenience," and this would of course have been augmented by hunting, as Franklin had intended and as the evidence at Beechey Island indicated.[3] The Inuit would tell that when one of the ships was later found there were still full tins of food aboard.

Although the men of the *Erebus* and *Terror* were not starving in April 1848, there was obviously something wrong. In spite of recent work by Dr Owen Beattie which indicates that lead poisoning may have been a contributing factor (see appendix 4), there is little doubt that the primary problem facing Crozier was an outbreak of scurvy, caused by a lack of vitamin c, among his men.

In 1845 the causes and treatment for scurvy were still in doubt. Bad food, poor ventilation, lack of exercise, and improper personal hygiene were all still considered to play a part. Almost every Arctic expedition had experienced the disease to some extent, however, and it was generally held that fresh food was an effective treatment.

Crozier now considered the strategy successfully employed by John Ross and his crew from the *Victory* sixteen years before – the abandonment of the ships in an attempt to reach help. The spring abandonment was obviously not a hastily made decision. Although there is no certain evidence, prudence and precedent would strongly indicate that advance parties established caches of supplies ashore for the later use of the main body. Some of the recovered relics – specially made cooking stoves, homemade socks, and improvised sunglasses made from wire mesh or coloured glass – also show that the men had had time to prepare for their march. The boats and sledges found by McClintock and Schwatka had been extensively modified in an effort to reduce their weight, and, although there is no evidence to prove that these were brought ashore at this time, the general consensus of opinion favours that view.

There also exists an uncertain but interesting snippet of documentary evidence. Some personal papers written by Petty Officer Harry Peglar of the *Terror* were recovered by McClintock from a skeleton found near Gladman Point. These consisted mainly of lower-deck doggerel and some incomplete and incomprehensible fragments. One section of the sheets is, however, of particular interest, for the following words can be made out

We will have his new boots in middel watch has we have got some very hard ground to heave [illegible] shall want some grog to wet houer issel. All my art Tom for I to do think [illegible] time [illegible] I clozes [illegible] should lay [illegible] and [illegible] the 21st night a gread[4]

Although it would be improper to make too much out of such an incomplete chain of words, one could easily read: "We shall have his new boots in middle watch [i.e.: midnight to 4 am] as we have got some very hard ground to heave [we] shall want some grog to wet [our whistles]. All my [heart] Tom for I to[o] do think [it is] time [to go]. I [close and] should lay [= go] [aft? up?] and [?] The 21st night [agreed]."

This connection of an impending journey over "hard ground" with the "21st night" is very suggestive, since we know that the *Erebus* and *Terror* were abandoned on 22 April. This was a Saturday, and, more important, in 1848 it was the day before Easter. Noting this fact, some have considered that the ships were abandoned at short notice, probably in a "convulsion caused by the devastations of a pressure ridge."[5] Yet the sheer volume and variety of the equipment which Crozier's men carried ashore seem to betoken an orderly abandonment.

The fact that Crozier and his men left their ships so early in the year has caused considerable debate. Most contemporaries felt that it would have been preferable to wait until July or August in order to make use of the boats in the open water then usually found near the shore. A.H. Markham expressed the general view.

The necessity for abandoning the ships so early in the season seems somewhat unaccountable; it may have been due to the fact that they were running short of provisions on board, or, which is quite possible, to their anxiety to make an early start. It is estimated that they were not able to carry away with them on their sledges provisions for more than about forty days, so that even had they succeeded in reaching the continent of America, they would have been without food for a considerable time ... It would therefore, it seems, have been better for them to have deferred the abandonment of their ships till the month of May, when they would have had warmer weather for travelling.[6]

In light of these opinions, still found among modern commentators, Crozier's fatal attempt to march his large contingent south appears to be the desperate gamble of a stupid man. Yet Crozier was an Arctic veteran, and both he and Fitzjames appear from their correspondence to have been intelligent and competent leaders.

And yet the one inescapable fact of the Franklin disaster is that Crozier and Fitzjames took their men ashore at the end of April 1848. Why?

There are few things as inconstant as Arctic weather patterns, and therefore it is impossible to assert with confidence what conditions were like in 1848. The Inuit told Hall that "the two winters the two ships were at Neitch-ille were very cold ... there was no summer between the two winters," a fact which Rae, who was travelling only a hundred and fifty miles to the east, confirmed in his journal.[7] Nevertheless, it is generally agreed that the best travelling conditions in the Arctic are found during the very short intermediate seasons (hardly deserving of the names "spring" or "autumn"), for the Arctic "summer" – June through September – is not particularly hospitable. Schwatka's party spent the summer of 1879 on King William Island and often bewailed the vast expanses of watery mud, and the lack of cushioning snow over the boot-shredding gravel beaches. They noted that travel became particularly difficult after the level band of shore ice melted. Like most later explorers they travelled at night to avoid the harsh glare of the sun, which caused both snow-blindness and sunburn, and to escape the hordes of mosquitoes which swarmed from the marshes.[8]

On the other hand, April, after the winter storms and darkness have passed, is usually a good time for sledge travel. In 1859 McClintock left the *Fox* on 2 April and returned on 19 June. He experienced bad weather throughout, but seems to have been most inconvenienced by May gales, which he found "unseasonal," and the onset of warm weather in June.[9]

David Irwin, who walked alone across the Canadian Arctic in the 1930s, also found April weather agreeable. Despite being delayed for three days on the Adelaide Peninsula by a blizzard, Irwin took only fifteen days to travel from Queen Maud Gulf to Matty Island, and crossed King William Island in five. [10]

Yet even with ideal travelling conditions the problems facing Crozier and his men were daunting. Some idea of the enormity of the task before them can be gained by tabulating the results obtained by other parties which had left their ships to explore the Arctic by sledge. [11]

Table 1
Land Excursions in the Arctic

Expedition	No. of men	Provisions for	Average miles per day	Distance (stat. miles)
Parry (June 1820)	13	21 days	12	120
Lyon (1822)	8	21 days	16	180
Lyon (June 1823)	3	31 days	8.5	130
Parry (June 1828)	28	71 days	12.5	569
Ross (May 1830)	5	21 days	14	400
Ross (abandonment)	18	42 days	10	300*
Crozier (1848)	105	?	?	650

* Ross's march from Victoria Harbour to Fury Beach only; direct distance of 180 miles, 300 covered by Ross.

Even more significant is the fact that Franklin's men had apparently obtained decidedly mixed results during previous sledging attempts at Beechey Island. Two of the sledges used at that time were left behind and later found to be "very crude structures, one of which had been used for transporting stones." Osborn thought that the deep grooves cut into the permafrost there showed "how little Franklin's people were impressed with the importance of rendering their travelling equipment light and portable, both as a means of exploration whilst their ships were imprisoned, and to enable them to escape if their ships were destroyed." He noted that the greatest distance that any of the sledge crews had travelled in 1845–6 was twenty miles. [12]

Could Crozier and Fitzjames really have though that their men could reach Great Slave Lake?

If the reason for abandonment was to reach help, then Crozier was almost certainly headed in the wrong direction. At the same time that Crozier was taking his men south, James Clark Ross was bringing the *Enterprise* and *Investigator* into Prince Regent Inlet with a search and relief party.

While formulating relief plans after Franklin's disappearance, the Admiralty canvassed the resident experts on their opinion as to what Franklin was likely to do if beset. James Clark Ross was sure that if he was compelled to abandon the *Erebus* and *Terror*, Franklin would try to reach Baffin Bay, the Mackenzie River, or the Coppermine, "whichever was the nearest," and that his "intimate knowledge of the impossibility of ascending the Great Fish River, or, of procuring food for his large party when crossing the Barren Grounds, would prevent his going there."[13]

Sir George Back, who better than anyone knew the difficulties of the river which would later bear his name, was equally emphatic. He wholly rejected "all and every idea of any attempts on the part of Sir John Franklin to send boats or detachments over the ice to any point of the mainland eastward of the Mackenzie River, because I can say from experience that no toilworn and exhausted party could have the least chance of existence by going there."[14]

When the fate of Crozier's men became known, many "experts," with the advantage of hindsight, found it hard to understand his reasoning. John Rae, himself the foremost proponent of living off the land, was sure that Franklin's men could have survived if only they had marched north.

What struck me at the time, as it does still, was the great mistake made by Franklin's party in attempting to save themselves by retreating to the Hudson's Bay Company territories. We should have thought that the fearful sufferings undergone by Franklin and his companions, Richardson and Back, on a former short journey through those barren grounds, would have deterred inexperienced men from attempting such a thing, when the well known route to Fury Beach – certainly much more accessible than any of the Hudson's Bay Company's settlements, and by which the Rosses escaped in 1832 + 33 – was open to them. The distance from their ships to Fury Beach was very little greater than that from where Ross' vessel was abandoned to the same place, and Franklin and his officers must have known that an immense stock of provisions still remained at the place where the *Fury* was wrecked, and where, even so late as 1859, an immense stock … remained.[15]

But Rae's assertion that an "immense stock" remained at Fury Beach was not altogether true. The *Fury* had had a complement of seventy-five officers and men and only a portion – probably less than half – of her stores remained when she was wrecked. Some of these were taken aboard by the *Hecla*, and the remainder, possibly a year's supply, had been left on the beach. This had subsequently been utilized by Ross and the *Victory*'s crew, both on their southbound journey, when they had taken "a sufficiency of stores and provisions to complete our outfit for two years and ten months," and again upon their retreat from their imprisoned vessel.[16]

So efficiently had Ross raided this bounty of Fury Beach that he wondered what they would subsist on if forced to return. The last of the preserved meat had been eaten.[17] When the crew of the *Victory* finally departed Fury Beach they made an inventory of what had been left behind, noting that "30 casks of flour, each weighing 504 lbs, and 12 casks of 336 lbs; 11 casks of sugar, each weighing 372 lbs; a few kegs of lime juice, and a large quantity of parsnips, carrots, soups etc" remained, "but not a single canister of meat" was left behind.[18]

Although substantial, even that amount of food would have been ineffective in restoring the health of 105 scurvy-ridden men. In the fifteen years between Ross's departure from Fury Beach and Crozier's abandonment of the *Erebus* and *Terror*, this cache had probably been undisturbed. Even so, the officers of Franklin's ships could not have known that, and they would have been indiscreet in assuming it, for "it was rumoured before Franklin sailed, and he is said to have believed, that the stores had been removed by the crews of some whaling ships. There was also possibility of the depot having been plundered by Eskimos."[19]

That these rumours were unfounded, or at least exaggerated, is proven by the fact that in later years the depot was found to be intact. In 1849 a party dispatched by James Ross from Port Leopold found Somerset House intact and confirmed that the *Fury*'s provisions were still there.[20] When Lieutenant Bellot visited the site in 1851–2 he doubted that the stores could have been of much use to Franklin's men, for he found that "the provisions found here consist solely of vegetables" and considered the biscuit to be "too damaged to be fit for use." He specifically remarked on the lack of any meat.[21]

Nevertheless Sir Albert H. Markham, who visited Fury Beach in 1873, thought that the stores would have been perfectly adequate to sustain Crozier's party through one winter. Markham agreed with Rae that had Crozier brought his crews to Prince Regent Inlet in 1848 they would have been rescued by James Ross's party the next year.[22]

The depot at Fury Beach was well known to Crozier, who as midshipman in the *Hecla* had been present at its deposition, and was also familiar to Thomas Blanky, Ice Master of the *Terror*, who had lived through one winter there while serving with Ross. Why didn't Crozier use it?

Faced with the impossibility of reaching help to the south, and the fact that he did not attempt to utilize Fury Beach to the north, we return again to the problem of why Crozier decided to "start on tomorrow to Back's Fish River." P.F. Cooper felt that Crozier had no choice but to attempt to reach the nearest source of fresh meat in an attempt to revive his crews.[23]

Franklin's old comrade Richardson also thought that this was the most reasonable alternative facing the survivors of the *Erebus* and *Terror*. He felt that "the object in going so early in the spring to Back's River, was to kill a sufficiency of fish, birds and deer, to enable the party to pursue the voyage to the Coppermine and Mackenzie River, in their boats, during the summer."[24]

Gibson felt that Crozier had taken the only course open to him.

The southerly route he doubtless believed to abound in game, especially the desirable caribou, and there was the chance of receiving some assistance from the different groups of natives as he fell in with them. What he needed most urgently was fresh game of any kind in order to stem the rising tide of scurvy. Every other consideration had to be subordinated to this pressing necessity otherwise the disease was immitigable and imminent disaster a certainty. This is most likely the factor which influenced him in attempting a retreat up the Great Fish River in preference to the northeastward.

Crozier was correct in assuming that game was plentiful to the southward; that is during the late spring and summer months. At the height of the summer season the marshes and tundra a short distance inland on the continent are alive with wild life. Swans circle over the larger lakes on the look-out for nesting and feeding places. Every pond is occupied by the predominant eider duck. Brant and Canada grey geese, as well as a variety of other water fowl, are to be seen on the swampy flats. Groups of caribou, browsing on the summer herbage, dot the plains. In the lagoons, in the creek mouths, in the lakes, a fine variety of Arctic salmon and trout are universally common.[25]

That Crozier intended to descend on a small ill-equipped Hudson's Bay Company outpost with his famished party after a two-month ascent of one of the most treacherous rivers in the Canadian Arctic is almost beyond belief. That he attempted to lead his men to the mouth of that river in order to replenish his larder seems much more reasonable. The libraries of the *Erebus* and *Terror* would have supported such a decision. Throughout his travels, George Back had noted herds of "two or three hundred deer (caribou), and apart from them herds of musk oxen" and later "hundreds of geese," and again "the deer, which were plentiful as usual."[26]

On his arrival at the mouth of the Great Fish River, Back had found a substantial, and apparently thriving, band of Inuit. He did not determine their exact number but considered "about sixty or seventy would probably be near the truth."[27] Surely if seventy Inuit could support themselves on the resources of the country one hundred well-armed Englishmen could do the same.

If further proof of the area's fecundity had been required, Crozier could have found it in Simpson's Narrative. Simpson noted many signs of native hunting on Adelaide Peninsula, where he "judged these people to be pretty numerous ... and that each family, or little band, has its inland beat, to which they resort in summer to hunt reindeer."[28]

Later explorers confirmed that Crozier's idea had been sound. McClintock noted that while further north his party had managed to shoot only one bear and a few birds, but that as he approached the Great Fish River traces of caribou became more common. He managed to kill one out of a herd of eight "reindeer" that he saw near Montreal Island and noted that here there was "more vegetation than upon King William Island, or any other Arctic land I have yet seen."[29]

Twenty years later, Schwatka and his party lived almost entirely on the game which they could procure. He remarked of the great herds of caribou, which he encountered during their yearly migration across Simpson Strait, that "the 'tuktoo' were so thick that one was not compelled to hunt them. Securing a favorable place to lay [sic] in wait, in course of a short time, they would soon hunt the hunters ... Returning inland we passed some five hundred reindeer grazing on the low hills, and I encountered, for the first time in my life, the singular phenomenon of game being so thick that it was almost impossible to hunt them."[30]

Unfortunately, to reach the fertile hunting grounds, Crozier's men would have to first traverse the barren west coast of King William Island, far from the caribou migration path. Here the Inuit rarely ventured, and then only after seals. The British sailors did not possess the skills to hunt these. McClintock offers graphic testimony to the conditions faced by Crozier's men.

The coast we marched along was extremely low – a mere series of ridges of limestone shingle, almost destitute of fossils. The only tracks of animals seen were those of a bear and a few foxes – the only living creatures a few willow grouse. Traces even of the wandering Esquimaux became much less frequent after leaving Cape Herschel. Here were found only a few circles of stones, the sites of tenting-places, but so moss-grown as to be of great age. The prospect to seaward was not less forbidding – a rugged surface of crushed-up pack, including much heavy ice. In these shallow ice-covered seas, seals are but seldom found: and it is highly probable that all animal life in them is as scarce as upon the land.[31]

Having travelled the coast during the same season as the men from the *Erebus* and *Terror*, McClintock could easily picture his friends' plight.

Nothing can exceed the gloom and desolation of the western coast of King William Island: Hobson and myself had some considerable experience of it; his sojourn there exceeded a month; its climate seems different from that of the eastern coast; it is more exposed to northwest winds, and the air was almost constantly loaded with chilling fogs ... [It] is for the most part extremely barren, and its surface dotted over with innumerable ponds and lakes. It is not by any means the "land abounding with reindeer and musk oxen" which we expected to find: the natives told us there were none of the latter and very few of the former upon it.[32]

Schwatka and Gilder, both ex-soldiers, were skilful hunters, and their Inuit guide Toolooah was almost phenomenally so, accounting for "a score of 232 reindeer ... besides a number of seal, musk-ox and polar bear" during a sojourn of ten months. The Americans managed to provision themselves adequately even on the west coast by hunting wildfowl and seals, and although they once ran out of meat while searching the desolate shores of Erebus Bay in July, Toolooah managed to kill three caribou the same day.[33]

On the south coast the prospects for game improved. At Terror Bay the game was "very plentiful," while in early September Schwatka noted that "a thousand deer passed within that many yards" and on the following days "the number was no less."[34]

It has often been remarked that if Crozier had only dispersed his men into small hunting groups they might have had a chance at survival. Yet it is improper to extrapolate this conclusion from the hunting success of small exploring parties such as Schwatka's. The food requirements of Crozier's 105 men would have been of a completely different order of magnitude. As we shall see, there is evidence that Crozier's men did reach the fertile hunting grounds of southern King William Island in July, and that they hunted and fished there. Unfortunately they were either too numerous, too late in the season, or too awkward as hunters to bring Crozier's plan to a successful conclusion. Had they met some of the natives and enlisted their support while the caribou were plentiful, the outcome of the expedition would have been quite different. Perhaps.

Victory Point

On 25 April 1848, Crozier's surviving men, having abandoned the *Erebus* and *Terror*, reached the bleak western coast of King William Island. Astronomical observations indicated that they were at the place which James Ross had dubbed "Victory Point" eighteen years before. Even though they had landed in a shallow bay quite different from Ross's description, a fruitless search was made for his cairn. Someone remembered that Lieutenant Gore had left a note the previous year on a small point two miles to the north (Ross's actual point),[1] and Lieutenant Irving volunteered to fetch it.

In his dark and cold tent, Commander Fitzjames opened the previously soldered tin and added some supplementary information in the margins.

[25th April 1]848 HM Ships Terror and Erebus were deserted on the 22nd April 5 leagues NNW of this [hav]ing been beset since 12th Sept. 1846. The Officers & Crews consisting of 105 souls under the command [of Cap]tain F.R.M. Crozier landed here – in Lat. 69° 37' 42" Long. 98° 41' [This] paper was found by Lt. Irving under the cairn supposed to have been built by Sir James Ross in 1831 – where it had been deposited (4 miles to the northward) – by the late Commander Gore in May June 1847. Sir James Ross' pillar has not however been found and the paper has been transferred to this position which is that in which Sir J Ross pillar was erected – Sir John Franklin died on the 11th June 1847 and

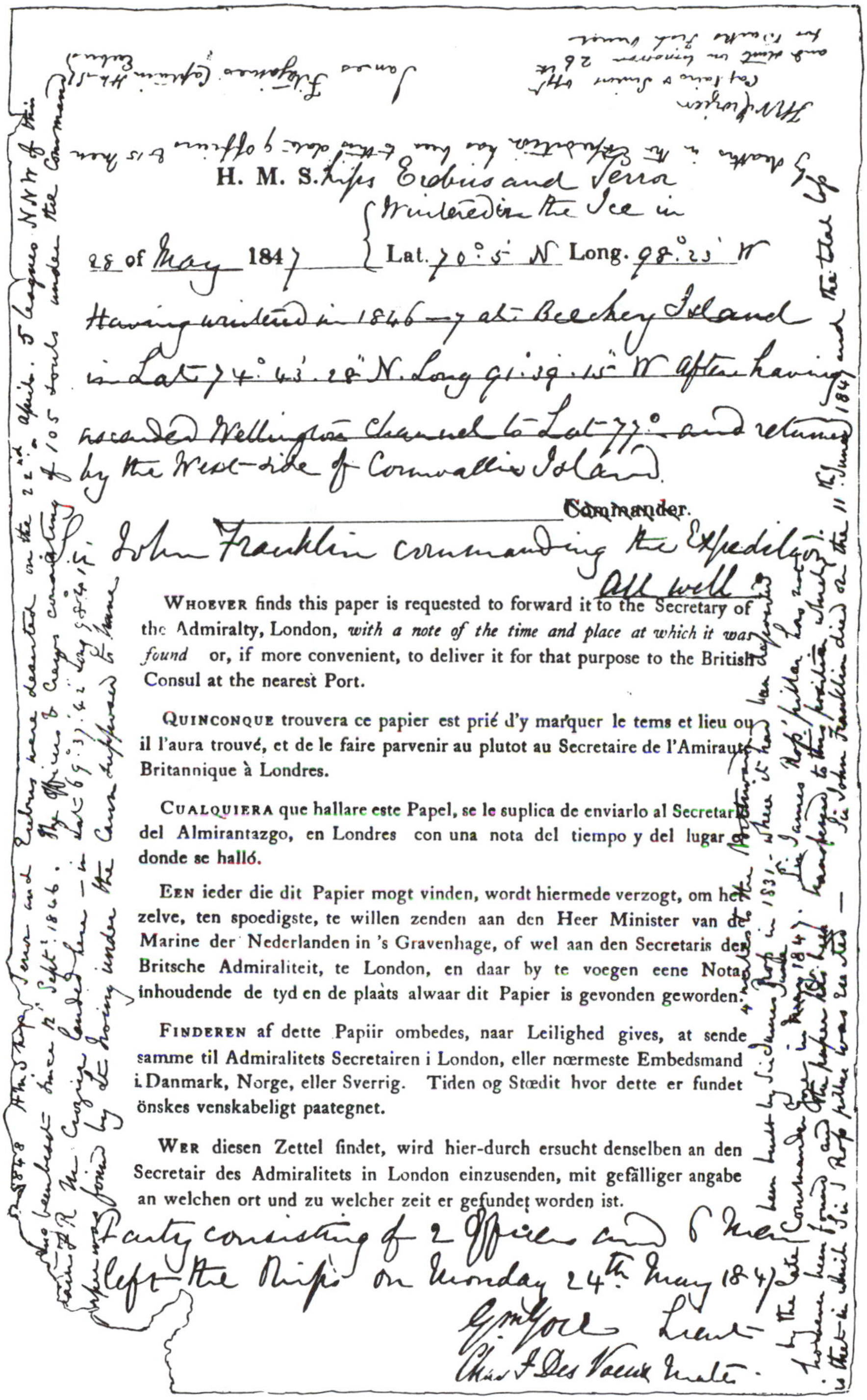

H. M. S. Ships *Erebus and Terror*
{ Wintered in the Ice in

28 of May 1847 { Lat. 70° 5′ N Long. 98° 23′ W

Having wintered in 1846—7 at Beechey Island
in Lat 74° 43′ 28″ N. Long 91 39 15″ W after having
ascended Wellington Channel to Lat 77° and returned
by the West side of Cornwallis Island

_____ Commander.
Sir John Franklin commanding the Expedition
All well

WHOEVER finds this paper is requested to forward it to the Secretary of
the Admiralty, London, *with a note of the time and place at which it was
found* or, if more convenient, to deliver it for that purpose to the British
Consul at the nearest Port.

QUINCONQUE trouvera ce papier est prié d'y marquer le tems et lieu ou
il l'aura trouvé, et de le faire parvenir au plutot au Secretaire de l'Amirauté
Britannique à Londres.

CUALQUIERA que hallare este Papel, se le suplica de enviarlo al Secretario
del Almirantazgo, en Londres con una nota del tiempo y del lugar en
donde se halló.

EEN ieder die dit Papier mogt vinden, wordt hiermede verzogt, om het
zelve, ten spoedigste, te willen zenden aan den Heer Minister van de
Marine der Nederlanden in 's Gravenhage, of wel aan den Secretaris der
Britsche Admiraliteit, te London, en daar by te voegen eene Nota
inhoudende de tyd en de plaats alwaar dit Papier is gevonden geworden.

FINDEREN af dette Papiir ombedes, naar Leilighed gives, at sende
samme til Admiralitets Secretairen i London, eller nærmeste Embedsmand
i Danmark, Norge, eller Sverrig. Tiden og Stædit hvor dette er fundet
önskes venskabeligt paategnet.

WER diesen Zettel findet, wird hier-durch ersucht denselben an den
Secretair des Admiralitets in London einzusenden, mit gefälliger angabe
an welchen ort und zu welcher zeit er gefundet worden ist.

Party consisting of 2 Officers and 6 Men
left the Ships on Monday 24th May 1847

Gm Gore Lieut
Chas F Des Voeux Mate.

Figure 1 The Victory Point Record. This is the only written record recovered from
the Franklin expedition. Fitzjames originally erred by writing that the ships had
"wintered in 1846–7 at Beechey Island"; it should have read "1845–6." He apparently
did not notice this error when he added the marginal information in 1848, which
tells of the besetment of the ships to the north of King William Island "since 12th
Sept 1846." (National Maritime Museum)

the total loss by deaths in the Expedition has been to this date 9 officers & 15 men.

A curious fact is that the *Terror* was mentioned first, making it the senior ship. This was in direct contradiction to Article 21 of Franklin's orders, which, upon his death, directed that the next in line, in this case Crozier, "take the command of the *Erebus* placing the officer of the expedition who may next be then in seniority to him in command of the *Terror*." Apparently neither Crozier nor Fitzjames could see much point in switching ships.

Fitzjames signed himself "Captain HMS Erebus" and then passed the form to Crozier, who appended his signature "Captain & Senior Offr" and added an important postcript: "and start on tomorrow, 26th, for Backs Fish River."

It is perhaps significant that it was only on a last-minute impulse that Crozier made mention of his present intentions. Evidently Fitzjames had been going to ignore the matter completely.

The cylinder containing this record had not been soldered up again; I [McClintock] suppose they had not the means of doing so ... Brief as these records are, we must needs be contented with them; they are perfect models of official brevity. No log-book could be more provokingly laconic. Yet that ANY RECORD AT ALL should be deposited after the abandonment of the ships, does not seem to have been intended; and we should feel the more thankful to Captains Crozier and Fitzjames, to whom we are indebted for the invaluable supplement; and our gratitude ought to be all the greater when we remember that the ink had to be thawed, and that writing in a tent during an April day in the Arctic regions is by no means an easy task. (emphasis in original)[2]

Fitzjames's short account is indeed tantalizing, and has been the object of intense scrutiny. The first to question it was McClintock. He knew that 134 men had left England on the *Erebus* and *Terror* and therefore queried the casualty figures (105 + 24 = 129). He later learned that five "invalids" had been sent home from Greenland.

Nevertheless, Fitzjames had made errors in his account. The cairn from which Irving had fetched Gore's record was not four miles to the northward but a mere two and a half, although the weary Irving undoubtedly felt as if he had walked eight. It has been repeatedly pointed out that Fitzjames failed to correct the initial error which he had made when filling out the form for Gore's trip the year before. He had then written that the *Erebus* and *Terror* had "wintered in 1846–7" at Beechey rather than 1845–6. He was also in error when he wrote that Sir James Ross had built his cairn in 1831 – it had actually been built in 1830. Fitzjames was obviously unaware of the enduring importance of his short record – or of the scholarly effort which it would inspire.

The exact nature of the disaster which befell these retreating crewmen after they left Victory Point is still a matter of debate. As we have seen, the discovery of so many empty preserved-meat tins at Beechey Island initially led to the supposition that this staple of their diet had been contaminated and that consequently starvation had overtaken them. Yet evidence shows that they did not lack food in early 1848, and full tins of meat were found along their retreat and in the wrecks of the ships. The natives also invariably stated that the men did not die from starvation but because they were "sick."

Similarly, there can be little doubt as to the illness which afflicted many of the men. Graphic native descriptions of the state of the corpses, with hard blackened mouths and gums, give unmistakable evidence that vitamin c deficiency – scurvy – was rampant among them. Yet this may not be the complete answer. The evidence from other Arctic expeditions shows that "Arctic sickness" was not simply the product of a lack of a single vitamin.

Arctic scurvy was probably a group of diseases, perhaps caused not only by deficiency of ascorbic acid [vitamin c] but also other essential factors such as niacin, riboflavin, or thiamine ... Psychiatric and psychological disorders loom large in Arctic expeditions. The colloquial terms "bush fever", "cabin fever", and others, are illustrations. Isolation, sensory deprivation, and continuous environmental stress, can lead to hallucinations, withdrawal, and a syndrome like schizophrenia. Among other disorders that are likely to occur in extreme cold are infectious diseases such as dysentery, a variety of dermatoses, and food poisoning such as tularaemia from undercooked wild game that acts as the vector.[3]

As we have seen, the recent work of Dr Owen Beattie and his associates considers that lead poisoning might have been another possible contributing cause. While noting that "bone tissue changes attributable to scurvy" were universally found in the remains from King William Island, Beattie concluded that "the problems of lead intoxication, compounded by the severe effects of scurvy, could have formed a lethal combination" which contributed to the castastrophe.[4] Lead poisoning would undoubtedly have complicated any efforts to abandon the ships, for some of its effects include anorexia, weakness, fatigue, stupor, paranoia, and anemia. (See appendix 4.)

Some conception of the health of Crozier's crewmen, or at least the opinion of his own doctors as to that state of health, may be afforded by one of the relics recovered from Victory Point. Here Hobson found a small medicine chest which had been left behind. It contained twenty-three bottles, most of them still full and unopened, bandages, and other necessities for minor medical problems.

Extensive analysis of the medicines found here indicates that the doctors of the *Erebus* and *Terror* had armed themselves solely with preventatives and cures for such common complaints as cough, gout and gouty disorders, rheumatism, snow-blindness, and diarrhoea. Nothing more can be confidently concluded from such an assortment of medicines then that they had been thorough in their preparations for the journey.[5]

The Fitzjames record and the medicine chest were only two of the interesting things found at Victory Point. McClintock described the other relics.

A great quantity and variety of things lay strewed about the cairn, such as even in their three days' march from the ships the retreating crews found it impossible to carry further. Amongst these were four heavy sets of boat's cooking stoves, pickaxes, shovels, iron hoops, old canvas, a large single block, about four feet of a copper lightning conductor, long pieces of hollow brass curtain rods, a small case of selected medicines containing about twenty-four phials, the contents in a wonderful state of preservation; a deep [i.e.: dip] circle by Robinson, with two needles, bar magnets, and light horizontal needle all complete – the whole weighing only nine pounds; and even a small sextant engraved with the name of "Frederick Hornby" lying beside the cairn without its case ...

The clothing left by the retreating crews ... formed a huge heap four feet high; every article was searched, but the pockets were empty, and not one of all these articles were marked, – indeed sailor's warm clothing seldom is. Two canteens, the property of marines, were found, one marked "88 Co. Wm. Hedges", and the other "89 Co. Wm. Hether". A small panniken made out of a two-pound preserved-meat tin had scratched on it "W. Mark".[6]

McClintock endorsed Hobson's conclusion that the profusion of articles found at Victory Point had been carelessly abandoned and that Crozier's men, now aware that they were retreating for their lives, had abandoned everything which was considered superfluous. This assessment of the evidence has never been seriously questioned, although some commentators have found it curious that the men would laboriously traverse broken ice for three days before disposing of such "junk." An alternative reading of the evidence was proposed in 1956 by G.F. Lamb.

Some writers have supposed that the crews set out on their long march to the mainland with a mass of unnecessary gear, and then, by the time they reached the coast of King William's Land, found it necessary to discard a great many inessentials. It is more reasonable to presuppose that neither Crozier nor his fellow officers were fools, and that there was never any intention of taking this mass of material on a long march. It is likely that one or both of the ships was so endangered by the ice that it was decided to remove all kinds of portable goods to a depot on the nearest part of the coast, which was at Point Victory.[7]

It does seem strange that, with the possible exception of the cooking stoves, none of the relics found here seem to have been particularly weighty. A four-foot length of lightning conductor and hollow brass curtain rods are of questionable utility, but stoves, extra clothing, a medicine case, and navigational equipment such as the "small" sextant and dip circle (which weighed only nine pounds) might have been of future use.

The medicine chest itself may offer another clue that the men intended to return, for Cyriax noted that it "contained poisons that would have been extremely dangerous to Eskimos or other unskilled persons" and that "any medical officer with a sense of responsibility would have emptied all the drugs onto the ground."[8] Unwilling to embrace the notion of a planned retreat, Cyriax could only conclude that the Franklin doctors must have felt that the Inuit did not inhabit or regularly visit the north-west coast of King William Island, – a fact which was later proven to be true, but which would have been an unwarranted assumption in 1848. Such a rationale is not as inherently logical as a belief that the medicines were being preserved for later use.

If the still-fresh men of Crozier's party felt burdened by the "impedimenta" found only fifteen miles from their ships, one should perhaps find a steady trail of abandoned articles along their route further south. But this is not so. Cairns and graves mark some of their nightly camping places, but, with the exceptions of the sledge-borne boats in Erebus Bay and, presumably, the encampment even further south at Terror Bay (seen only by the Inuit), no similar accumulation of material was found.

If one concludes that the men intended to return to the ships a different light is thrown on these articles. There is no reason for carrying heavy cooking stoves to shore if one is simply re-treating, but if a return is expected then this is the type of article which it would be prudent to leave "en cache." An outfit of navigational instruments would also be useful. Likewise there is little reason to pile discarded clothing neatly unless one foresees a later use for it.

If these articles were not hastily abandoned but carefully deposited there should be some trace of evidence that efforts were made to protect them from the elements. McClintock laconically mentioned that he found "old canvas" at the site and also noted "part of a canvas tent."[9] Twenty years later, a few yards from the pile of now-rotted clothes, Schwatka found cordage and concluded that "a tent had evidently been erected near this pile of waste material, its bottom being cushioned with blankets."[10]

In 1930 Burwash visited the site and found traces of the encampment here. He confirmed McClintock's observations, finding "what had evidently been stone caches and possibly walls of a rectangular tent" and "the remains of a linen tent" nearby.[11]

It is probable that canvas covers were initially erected over the detritus left on the beach, but this does not necessarily imply that Crozier intended to utilize the site himself. John Ross had abandoned the Victory, and McClure the Investigator, with no thought of return; yet both had established caches of useful items in the hope that some later explorers might find them. That a tent was left behind at Victory Point is perhaps more significant

116

– a standing tent could be expected to survive for a few weeks until Crozier's return, but would be torn to ribbons by the first winter gale.

The greatest objection to the idea that a cache was made at Victory Point is the lack of any food here. As the Inuit reported finding full tins on the wreck of one of Franklin's ships, it would seemingly have been more sensible to transport these to the shore in case the vessels were damaged during the summer or drifted away. The lack of food requires piling assumption on assumption – that some of Crozier's men had actually recovered it when returning to the ships. Is there any evidence of a return?

The return to the ships of at least part of the crew during the summer of 1848 has been widely proposed and cautiously accepted by some historians. The first to consider the question was McClintock. While examining the boat and sledge in Erebus Bay, he was "astonished to find that the sledge was directed to the N.E., exactly for the next point of land for which we ourselves were travelling"; "a little reflection led me to satisfy to my own mind at least, that the boat was returning to the ships."[12]

Hall endorsed McClintock's opinion that the *Erebus* and *Terror* had been remanned after the abandonment of 1848, but as his belief was based on Inuit testimony it was less readily accepted. These native traditions will be dealt with shortly.

The first physical evidence supporting such an idea was discovered by the Schwatka expedition at Crozier's landing place at Victory Point. While Schwatka and Gilder, misled by a garbled story, examined Collinson Inlet, they sent Klutschak and Melms to examine McClintock's cairn. The latter two men easily found Crozier's encampment, but the most surprising discovery was that of a grave.

The grave was identified as that of an officer, since "in the grave was found the object-glass of a marine telescope, and a few officer's gilt-buttons stamped with an anchor and surrounded by a crown. Under the head was a colored silk handkerchief, still in a fair state of preservation."[13] On the edge of the grave a medal was found which had been a "Second Mathematical Prize, Royal Naval College." The significance was in the recipient, for it had been "Awarded to John Irving, Midsummer 1830."

The presence of this medal does not actually prove that the grave was Irving's. The medal was not found in the grave itself but "upon one of the stones at the foot of the grave," and it was "thickly covered with grime, and was so much the color of the clay stone on which it rested as to nearly escape detection." [14] Nevertheless, it had rested in its present position long enough to leave a mark on the underlying rock, [15] and most commentators have accepted the unanimous opinion of the finders that it had originally come from the grave. It was probably Irving's skeleton, beside a "pile of clothes," that Seepunger and his uncle had seen. [16]

Irving had been described by Crozier as "a diligent hard-working fellow." [17] He entered the Service at the age of thirteen and was noted for his academic skill, but by 1834 he considered that, his "prospects in the Navy having become so bad that I can hardly do worse than remain in it," he should leave and join his father as a settler in the new colony of New South Wales. The life on a sheep farm was apparently not satisfying, for in 1842 he re-enrolled and managed to secure a berth aboard Franklin's ships through the influence of Sir George Clerk, a friend of his father (probably supported by an endorsement from his old shipmate Graham Gore). [18] When the ships stopped at Stromness on the outward passage, it had been particularly remarked that "Lieutenant Irving was very conspicuous among the officers ... by his greater appearance of manly strength and calm decision – one apparently well fitted for the hardships foreseen but not dreaded." [19]

By a happy coincidence, Irving was the only living officer, besides themselves, who was mentioned by name in Fitzjames and Crozier's record. He had been sent to fetch Gore's account from the northern cairn. And yet here was his grave! It seems inconceivable that Irving would have been dispatched to retrieve the record in Gore's cairn if he had been seriously ill. It is also of note that he apparently played a role in Fitzjames's composition of the amended version of this record which was found in the cairn at Victory Point.

The second entry contains four emendations. Two of these were evidently, and the other two presumably, made by Fitzjames. He wrote the figure "5", in the phrase "5 leagues NNW of this", over another figure, which appears to be a "3". When stating the month in which Gore had deposited the record in 1847, Fitzjames first wrote "May" but deleted May and replaced it by June. He inserted the phrase "4 miles to the Northward" into the text by means of a caret. Lastly where he referred to the cairn from which Irving had just taken the record, deposited there by Gore in 1847, he evidently intended to say that Irving had found the record "in" the cairn, and he put down "in" but then he wrote "under" over "in", and the way in which the words are spaced shows that he made this alteration at once. It thus seems possible that ... Fitzjames read out aloud what he was writing down, and that the last two emendations mentioned above were suggested by Irving himself.[20]

Of course, Irving may have died of an accident between the time he returned to camp and the departure of Crozier's party, but the easiest and most likely way to interpret the evidence is to assume that Irving was, at a later date, a member of a return detachment. Schwatka himself was sure of this interpretation. He noted that the body was encased in "many pieces of coarsely stitched canvas, showing that this had been used as a receptacle for the body when interred. From this fact I inferred that the body had never been buried from the ships, where sufficient work ... could have been procured to construct a coffin; but that Lieut. Irving belonged to a party that had returned to the ships, after it had become evident that all could not escape."[21]

The existence of the "Irving" grave at Victory Point demonstrates that the "retreat" of the crews of the *Erebus* and *Terror* did not follow the simple script set out for it. The natives indicated that Franklin's men did not march as a single party, and some of them may have returned to the ships. If the last event did take place, then there is reason to suppose that some of these men may have survived 1848 and been involved in further adventures. One thing is clear. What happened to Crozier's men cannot be resolved by reference to Fitzjames's record or the scattered and uninformative physical relics alone. After Victory Point we are forced, for better or worse, to consider the testimony of those who were eyewitnesses of the events which overtook the beleaguered men – the Inuit.

PART 2

The Testimony

When you have eliminated the
impossible, whatever remains, however
improbable, must be the truth.
Sir Arthur Conan Doyle
(Sherlock Holmes)

~9~

Incident at Teekeenu

Whether bound for the Great Fish River to hunt or to find a route to civilization, when the retreating crews left Victory Point they disappeared into the mists. They left a few carefully tended graves between Cape Jane Franklin and Cape Crozier, but of course we cannot be sure whether these men died while proceeding southward. Up to the latter point the evidence seems consistent that they followed their original intention and marched as a large disciplined body, burying their weaker comrades as they fell.

Those historians who discount the utility of native testimony and rely wholly on the single record left by Fitzjames assert that the men followed the scenario set out in that record until they eventually succumbed to their weakness before reaching the Great Fish River. Such a script ignores the presence of "Irving's" grave at Victory Point as well as some other physical evidence which cannot easily be fitted into the standard reconstruction. The Inuit testimony undercuts such a scenario even more.

Most of the commentators on the Franklin expedition have realized that *something* unplanned happened during the march southwards. Few have agreed what it was. We have seen that Rasmussen, according to Irwin, believed that "the main body, including the leader, crossed ... and headed down the east side of the island."[1] Burwash thought that "half or more of the party were sent back to the ships, while the others, probably the more exhausted, either moved ahead slowly or remained in camp."[2]

The Inuit themselves confirmed that the white men did not long march as a single large group. Hall was told that "there were a good many men together starving some started off from the main body of starving ones & never came back again. Every once in awhile a part of the great many would go away & not return again."[3]

In an effort to unravel the situation, we must sort carefully through the physical evidence and testimony looking for connecting threads. The physical evidence itself will sometimes be found to have been misrepresented or misreported, and "tradition" has occasionally replaced the critical assessment of possibilities.

The Fitzjames record tells us what the retreating sailors *intended* to do. Their scattered remains give us an indication of what *some of them* actually did. There is also the testimony of the men and women who actually saw them do it.

Of all of the verbal Inuit traditions, the tale of the meeting with survivors on the march is the only one which has been universally accepted among historians. This tale is the pivot on which all reconstructions must turn. It was undoubtedly a much-told and popular story among the Inuit, and was the source from which many later hearsay versions were distilled.

The story was originally told to Hall during May 1869 by two eyewitnesses – Teekeeta and Ow-wer. He asked them to repeat their tale many times and the different versions of the meeting with the white men at "Teekeenu" were remarkably, if not absolutely, consistent. Many versions of the tale exist. The longest and most detailed account was recorded on 18 May 1869, and the following is a literal transcription, complete with spelling errors, naming inconsistencies, and occasional insertions, of Hall's original field notes of that day.

Tuk-ke-ta and Ow-wer now tell that they with Too-shoo-art-thar-u [sic] and Mong-er, the latter now at Neitchille, were on the west shore of Kikituk (K.W.L.) with their families sealing, & this a long time ago. They were getting ready to move – the time in the morning & the sun high – when Tuk-ke-ta saw something in the distance on the smooth ice that looked white & thought it was a bear. The company had got all ready to start travelling on the land. Soon as Tuk-ke-ta saw this something white, he told his companions of it, when all waited, hoping it was a bear. As they watched, the white object grew larger, for it was coming down towards them. They saw the white thing moving along in the direction of the coast, turning in a kind of circling way just as the little bay turned. At length they began to see many black objects moving along with what they had first espied as white in the distance. The object that they 1st had seen as white proved to be a sail raised on the boat & as this got nearer saw this sail shake in the wind. On seeing what they did, the object grew plainer and they thought of white men and began to be afraid.

As the company of men (strangers) & what they were drawing got quite near, 2 men came on ahead of all & were walking on the ice & were getting near where the Innuits were standing looking out, which was on the land, the 2 men (Koblunas) came walking up to where they were. Too-shoo-art-thar-u and Ow-wer started to meet them, walking there on the ice. When they came to a crack in the ice, they stopped for the two white men to come up. Then the 2 white men came close to Ow-wer and Too-shoo-art-thar-u. One had a gun which he carried in his arms. The crack in the ice separated the meeting natives. The man that carried the gun stopped behind – a little back, while the other man came as close up to Ow-wer & Too-shoo-art-thar-u as the crack in the ice would allow him. The man that came up to the crack had nothing in his hands or on his shoulder. As he stopped, he cried out "C'hi-mo". The first man that came up then spoke to the man a little behind, when he laid the gun down and came up at once along side the 1st man.

The 1st man then showed that he had an oo-loo when he stooped down beside the ice crack which divided the white men from the Innuits & began cutting the ice with a peculiar kind of circling motion with the oo-loo (Civilization mincing-knife or Innuit women's knife). This peculiar motion now showed by Ow-wer with his oo-loo on the snow floor of the igloo. At the same time, or rather right after this man had made these "chippings" or "scratchings" (as you call it) on the ice, he put his hand up to his mouth and lowered it all the way down his neck and breast, as if to say he wanted to get something to eat. Then the two white men moved along the one side, till they found a place where they could pass over to the 2 Innuits – Ow-wer & Too-shoo-art-thar-u. On the 2 Kabloonas (white men) getting to them, the 1st man, who was Aglooka, spoke to them, saying, "Man-nik-too-me", at the same time stroking 1st one & then the other down the breast, and also shook hands with each, repeating "Man-nik-too-me" several times. The other man with Aglooka did all the same in stroking the breast, shaking hands & speaking "Man-ik-too-me".

After this salutation Aglooka tried to speak with them, but of all he then said, they could only make out one word I-wil-ik. Here some 15-20 minutes have been spent in Ow-wer's describing in pantomimic way just how Aglooka appeared and repeating his words.[4]

This initial description of the meeting between Ow-wer and Too-shoo-art-thariu and the two advancing white men could hardly be bettered. A few things should be noted. The Inuit are unaware of the white men's presence in their country and are initially afraid of contact with them. They therefore send their two most intrepid hunters to a safe location (across a crack in the ice) to meet the two white men, who advance to meet them. One of these is obviously an officer; he orders the second man, who initially covers him with a firearm, to lay down his gun and join him by the ice. This unnamed officer is henceforth called "Aglooka" by the Inuit.

Aglooka pointed with his hand to the southward & eastward & at the same time repeating the word I-wil-ik. The Innuits could not understand whether he wanted them to show him the way there or that he was going there. He then made a motion to the northward & spoke the word oo-me-en, making them to understand there were 2 ships in that direction; which had, as they supposed, been crushed in the ice. As Aglooka pointed to the N., drawing his hand & arm from that direction he slowly moved his body in a falling direction and all at once dropped his head side ways into his hand, at the same time making a kind of combination of whirring, buzzing & wind blowing noise. This the pantomimic representation of ships being crushed in the ice. While Aglooka was talking and making motions, the other men Innuits came to where they were.

After this first interview the two men went ashore with the Innuits. While Aglooka was trying to talk with the Innuits (Ow-wer & Too-shoo-art-thar-u), the party with the boat and one other sledge passed by going a little lower down to a point or cape of the little bay where they then were. On getting ashore Aglooka wanted everything – every pack opened & opened them himself, the dogs' saddle bag packs, the women's packs and the men's packs, for everything was ready for making a journey across the land. Aglooka wanted meat & for this he wanted every pack opened. The Innuits were all willing he should do as he did.

After each man Innuit had given him some seal meat, it was all put on a (one) dog's back & then by the request of Aglooka all 4 Innuit men with the dog laden with meat went down with Aglooka and the man with him to where the men and the boat where, the men erecting a tent. As they approached the tent, one man came out to meet them. Aglooka spoke to the men when he and the Innuits were near the tent. The men along side the tent and the men alongside of the boat stood in line holding up their arms and open hands above their heads, showing they had nothing (that is no weapons) about them.[5]

In another version, Ow-wer noted that "trouble thought to be among the men; but not so. They were putting up the tent and stopped, staring at the Innuits. When [Aglooka] spoke to them then, they at once resumed their work."[6] The Inuit, unfamiliar with naval discipline, probably considered the "harsh" tone of Aglooka's orders to his men to indicate "trouble," but later learned that there was no overt animosity between them.

Then Aglooka spoke to one of his men, a short man with a narrow face, prominent nose. Then this man tried to talk with the Innuits. (Jo & Hannah who are my interpreters are almost certain this man was Capt. Penny's Dr. (McDonald) whom they have seen in this country – Cumberland Sound). The man who came out to meet Aglooka & Innuits was a tall man and did not laugh or smile. "Looked kind 'o ugly" as Jo expressed himself. The Innuits Ow-wer and Tuk-ke-ta think he looked so because he was afraid.

The small man that Aglooka told to speak with the Innuits could talk so that they could understand him better than they could Aglooka.

He told the names of Aglooka & the man that was with him on 1st meeting the Innuits, also asked the Innuits their names. Told these the name of one white man was Too-loo-a & another Ill-kern.

The short man had whiskers & a moustache.[7]

Again this testimony is remarkably clear. "Aglooka," the leader, is not very fluent in the Inuit language and therefore enlists another man as interpreter. This man leaves his companions and comes out to assist the first two. This may well have been (as Tookoolitoo and Ebierbing thought) Alexander Macdonald, Assistant Surgeon of the *Terror*, for he was one of the few officers on the expedition who had had, thanks to his prior whaling experience, extensive contact with the Inuit. Dr Macdonald had been known to Tookoolitoo and the natives of Baffin Island as "Ark-pik" from his whaling voyages there. Although never expressly stated, Tookoolitoo's confident identification of him may have been based on remembrances of this name by the King William Island Inuit, who may also have been told by "Doktook" of his former exploits. In other versions of this tale one of the remembered white men was called "Doktook."

The interpreter, according to Teekeeta, was short and narrowfaced. Another man, sombre and tall, also came out to meet Aglooka and the Inuit. The interpreter exchanged names with the Inuit, the other three white men being identified as "Aglooka," "Toolooah," and "Ill-kern" (according to Nourse, Hall's editor, "Tierkin").[8] "Aglooka" and "Toolooah" are common Inuit names, and the detail, garnered from another interview, that one of the men actually named himself by saying "Aglooka Wonger" ("I am Aglooka")[9] tends to favour the opinion that the white men had previously met Inuit.

"Ill-kern" may have been a simple mishearing of a European name. The second man at the ice-crack, bearer of the gun, might very reasonably have been a Royal Marine sent to protect the officer. We note that Private William Pilkington held that office aboard the *Erebus*. "Ill-kern" and "ilking," while not conclusive, are very suggestive. The identification of "Aglooka" and "Toolooah" will be dealt with later (Hall assumed that Aglooka was Crozier).

Joe now say he forgot to tell me what Ow-wer and Tuk-ke-ta said about the two men the Innuits 1st met on taking out the seal meat, of their eating a little bit of it. Aglooka eat [sic] a very small piece – a bit about as large as fore & 2nd finger to first joint as shown by Ow-wer. After tent of white men was all in complete order for sleeping in it, Aglooka went with the Innuits to their tents, which the women had erected while their husbands were absent with Aglooka. Aglooka gave Too-shoo-art-thar-u an oo-loo (woman's knife); to Tuk-ke-ta a "piece of money", as Joe says it was; to Ow-wer piece of money; to Mong-er piece of money.

Did he give the women anything?

Ans. Gave to two women some large beads.

Aglooka made picture of the Innuit men and women on paper like what I am writing on.[10]

One of the women who received the beads was Teekeeta's wife.

I ask the woman Mik-ke-em-ma if she remembers seeing Ag-loo-ka (Crozier). She answers that she remembers well. She was then about as tall as up to my neck. She saw a good many Kob-lu-nas with Ag-loo-ka. Ag-loo-ka came into the tent where she was & sat down … She says Ag-loo-ka's 1st call was for water, wh. she gave him & Ag-loo-ka made her a present of some beads. Some of the white men went to a small lake near by & one salmon was caught wh. was carried to their tent wh. was close – never saw a white man before she saw Crozier & party & none since except me. Crozier did just as I am doing while in the tent – that is, wrote much. Saw him shoot something when flying. It was a small bird of a kind that is good food.

Ag-loo-ka a man full as tall as myself, a trifle taller she says. His dress not like mine but was dark (muk-tak) & something that came down about to the knees. My dress native. This woman does not seem to remember much, for Jack has talked with her for several minutes & he says she was so young that she has forgotten most all she did know then.[11]

Aglooka's gift to Teekeeta, described as a "piece of money," was "something that had a head and a face on it."[12] This may also have been a medal or award, one of which, awarded to Dr Macdonald, was recovered by McClintock at Cape Norton. That Too-shoo-art-thariu was the only one given an oo-loo (knife) would imply that he was considered the "leader" of the Inuit by Aglooka and his party, a concept which would have been foreign to the Inuit themselves. Nevertheless, this difference in the division of goods will be seen to be a valuable clue.

Up to this point Teekeeta and Ow-wer were apparently in complete agreement as to what happened. When it came to the tricky subject of the circumstances of their departure from the white men, a note of doubt enters their story.

Saw Aglooka next morning – that is next morning after first meeting him. Aglooka came along side of Innuits tents – A CORRECTION. The

Innuits took down their tents early the next morning & as they proceeded on their journey passed by Aglooka's tent. Aglooka was standing
on the outside of his tent when the innuits passed it. *Aglooka tried to
make them stop* – put his hand to his mouth and spoke the word "Netchuk" or "Nest-chuk" (seal). But the Innuits were in a hurry – did not
know the men were starving ...

   After leaving Aglooka and party never saw anything more of them
till some were found starved to death ... Too-shoo-art-thar-u never saw
Aglooka after the time Ow-wer and Tuk-ke-ta saw him. Aglooka to their
knowledge never gave Too-shoo-art-thar-u any papers or package. (emphasis in original)[13]

   In fact this description of a departure after only one day does
not agree with Teekeeta's own testimony, given earlier, that "the
first time Aglooka came to the tents he did not come inside" but
that "the *next morning* he came to the tents & then entered one
of them & sat himself down besides Ow-werk" (emphasis
added).[14] Ow-wer also commented on Aglooka's visiting his tent,
as did Mik-ke-em-ma. Upon hearing the two versions of how the
white men and Inuit parted, Hall first started to suspect that
some information was being withheld. He noted here his own
conviction that "the Innuits feel guilty of letting white men starve
& thus their inconsistent stories. They deviate as no truth telling
men."[15]

   The final comments about Too-shoo-art-thariu and papers are
obviously Ow-wer and Teekeeta's response to questions posed
by Hall. This can be understood when we know that almost five
years earlier, in December 1864, he had been told quite a different
version of Too-shoo-art-thariu's meeting with white men.

   In September 1864 Hall had been told by some natives of the
two ships which had been frozen in the ice many years ago, and
had learned that "there were four that did not die!"[16] In December
this was seemingly corroborated when he interviewed Ouela,
Shook-she-ark-nook, and Ar-too-a (renamed by Hall Albert,
John, and Frank), and learned that one of their cousins, named
Too-shoo-art-thariu, had encountered four Franklin crewmen on
the march near Neitchille. This cousin had given the white men
some seal and cared for them throughout the following winter.
One of these men had subsequently died of an illness, but the
others had left to find their way to their own country.[17]

Hall, who had come to the Arctic with a belief that he had been called by God to find Franklin survivors, cherished this tale of Too-shoo-art-thariu's offering aid to the last four white men. Too-shoo-art-thariu's brother Nukerzhoo was one of Hall's constant companions, and in 1866, while at Pelly Bay, Hall interviewed Too-shoo-art-thariu's mother and young son, hearing again of how the hunter had met Aglooka on "the island of Oot-goo-lik." Now, in 1869, Hall heard that Too-shoo-art-thariu and his companions had "heartlessly abandoned" the white men after one or two days! His later disillusionment with the truthfulness of the stories he was told can be traced to the conflicting versions of the encounter at Teekeenu.

It must be admitted that Too-shoo-art-thariu's story, relayed by his cousins in December 1864, bears only slight resemblance to the version Hall heard in 1869 from his companions Ow-wer and Teekeeta.

When [Too-shoo-art-thariu] first found Crozier and the three men with them [sic] Crozier's face looked bad – his eyes all sunk in – looked so bad that their cousin could not bear to look at his face. Their cousin gave Crozier a bit of raw seal as quick as he could when he first saw him. Did not give any to the other three, for they were fat and had been eating the flesh of their companions. It was near Neitchille that this occurred on the ice. Their cousin is now living at Neitchille. When Too-shoo-art-thariu first saw Crozier and the men with him, he was moving, having a loaded sledge drawn by dogs; he was going from place to place, making igloos on the ice – sealing – he had with him his wife, whose name is E-laing-nur, and children.

Crozier and his men had guns and plenty of powder, shot and ball. The cousin took Crozier and his men along with him, and fed them and took good care of them all winter. Beside a high cliff Innuits saw something like Now-yers (gulls) fall down to the ground, dead, and would not touch them, for Crozier had done something to them – they (the Innuits) know not what. In the summer Crozier and his men killed with their guns a great many birds, ducks, geese and rein-deer. Crozier killed many – very many of the latter. The Innuits saw him do it. A Neitchille Innuit went with Crozier and his remaining two men when they started to go to their country. They had a kiak with which to cross rivers and lakes. They went down towards Ook-koo-seek-ka-lik (the estuary of Great Fish River).

Their cousin liked Crozier very much. Crozier wanted to give their cousin his gun, but he would not accept it, for he was afraid of it, he did not know anything about how to use it. Crozier then gave him his long knife (sword, as Tookoolitoo and Ebierbing interpret it) and nearly everything he had. He (C.) had many pretty things. Crozier told Too-shoo-art-thariu all about what had happened, but he could not understand all. This cousin is now alive, and knows all what he saw and what Crozier told him ...

They [the white men] had a small boat that had places on the sides that would hold wind (air – Ebierbing said to me). From their (our informers') description, the boat must have been an india rubber one, or something like it, with hollow places in the sides for wind (air) to hold it up when in the water ... There were sticks or holes for this boat, to keep it open (spread) when needed. This small boat was wrapped or rolled up in a bundle or pack, and carried on the shoulder of one of his men. The sides of this boat, something like Innuits' "drugs" that could be filled with air.[18]

The two versions of Too-shoo-art-thariu's meeting are so dissimilar that one is tempted to believe that they deal with different events and that perhaps there were two men named Too-shoo-art-thariu. Teekeeta and Ow-wer met about forty men dragging a sledge with a heavy boat and a smaller one with camp supplies. Too-shoo-art-thariu met four men, does not mention a sledge, and talks of a strange inflatable boat carried on the shoulders of one man. Teekeeta and Ow-wer met their party at Teekeenu, located by them as a small bay on the east side of Washington Bay on the south-west coast of King William Island. Too-shoo-art-thariu met his men near Boothia Peninsula (Neitchille). Teekeeta and Ow-wer parted from their Aglooka after one day (perhaps), while Too-shoo-art-thariu hosted his for an entire winter. There were no casualties during Teekeeta and Ow-wer's encounter, but one man died "from a sickness" during Too-shoo-art-thariu's.

Mik-ke-em-ma saw Aglooka's men hunt wildfowl and told of their fishing in the lakes, while Teekeeta and Ow-wer noted that the white men cooked "two ducks" and that they had seen "now-yers [gulls], geese and ducks hanging from the boat." Too-shoo-art-thariu also mentions Aglooka killing "a great many birds, ducks, [and] geese" but mentions "rein-deer. Crozier killed many – very many of the latter."

These strange discrepancies are matched by other correspondences. Too-shoo-art-thariu tells that he originally gave Aglooka a little piece of seal meat, Teekeeta tells that it was actually as big as two fingers put together. Too-shoo-art-thariu says that Aglooka gave him a "long knife"; in Teekeeta's version Aglooka gives "Too-shoo-art-thar-u," and only him, an "oo-loo." Finally, and most convincingly, Too-shoo-art-thariu met his white men in company with his wife "E-laing-nur." And we also have her testimony.

A decade after Hall's visit, Schwatka and Gilder met "an old woman whom we found to be another important and interesting witness. She was one of a party who met some of the survivors of the ill-fated ships on Washington Bay."[19] Since then she had seen no white man until her meeting with the Americans. This woman, then about fifty-five years of age, was named "Ahlangyah."

Ahlangyah pointed out the eastern coast of Washington Bay as the spot where she, in company with her husband, and two other men with their wives, had seen ten white men dragging a sledge with a boat on it many years ago. There was another Inuit with them who did not go near the white men.

The sledge was on the ice, and a wide crack separated them from the white men at the interview. The women went on shore, and the men awaited the white people at the crack on the ice. Five of the white men put up a tent on the shore, and five remained with the boat on the ice. The Inuits put up a tent not far from the white men, and they stayed together here five days. During this time the Inuits killed a number of seals on the ice and gave them to the white men. They gave her husband a chopping knife. He was the one who had the most intercourse with the white crew. The knife is now lost, or broken and worn out. She has not seen it for a long time.

At the end of five days they all started for Adelaide Peninsula, fearing that the ice, which was very rotten, might not let them across. They started at night, because then, the sun being low, the ice would be a little frozen. The white men followed, dragging their heavy sledge and boat, and could not cross the rotten ice as fast as the Inuits, who halted and waited for them at Gladman's Point. The Inuits could not cross to the mainland, the ice was too rotten, and they remained in King William's Land all summer. They never saw the white men again, though they waited at Gladman's Point fishing in the neighbouring lakes, going

133

back and forth between the shore and lakes nearly all summer, and then went to the eastern shore near Matty Island.[20]

We can see that E-laing-nur/Ahlangyah remembers a *third* version of events. Teekeeta and Ow-wer saw forty or more men, Too-shoo-art-thariu four, and Ahlangyah ten. Teekeeta and Ow-wer spent one day with the white men, Too-shoo-art-thariu a winter, Ahlangyah five days. In Teekeeta and Ow-wer's tale they leave the white men encamped in the morning, Too-shoo-art-thariu's white companions leave him, and Ahlangyah departs at night and sees the white men trying to keep up in the rear.

Ahlangyah continued her tale:

Some of the white men were very thin, and their mouths were dry and hard and black. They had no fur clothing on. When asked if she remembered by what names the white men were called, she said one of them was called "Agloocar," and another "Toolooah". The latter seemed to be the chief, and it was he who gave the chopping-knife to her husband ... Another one was called "Doktook" (Doctor). "Toolooah" was a little older than the others, and had a large black beard, mixed with gray. He was bigger than any of the others – "a big, broad man." "Agloocar" was smaller, and had a brown beard about four or five inches below his chin (motioning with her hand). "Doc-took" was a short man, with a big stomach and red beard, about the same length as "Agloocar's." All three wore spectacles, not snow goggles, but, as the interpreters said, all the same seko (ice).[21]

Ow-wer also described Aglooka and Toolooa.

Aglooka (Crozier) about my [Hall's] height, hair nearly like mine (auburn) but a little darker than mine & did not stand erect but with head and shoulders dropping forward a little (Something like Captain Christopher Chapel, as Ou-e-la and Jack say) – no gray hair, a scar mark across the small or indent (?) of nose.

Too-loo-a stood erect, straight up, so straight that a little bent back – that is breasted out, having slight curve inward from hands to shoulders. His hair a little gray. Aglooka's body never found among the dead. Therefore Innuits have always supposed that he got home to his country. Too-loo-a's body found on the Isle Kee-u-na & was one of the 5 found there. His skull seen there of late years with gray hair & with whiskers adhering to the skull.[22]

These descriptions too are inconclusive. Although Schwatka and Gilder both remembered Ahlangyah as indicating that it was "Doktook" who was fat and red-bearded, Klutschak's version of her testimony makes mentions only that he was "thick-set" and remembers "Aglukan" as the possessor of the "reddish-brown beard."[23] Ow-wer also remembered that it was Aglooka that had auburn hair. It seems that Ahlangyah's description of "Doktook" is mistaken and that she has mixed up the various individuals. None of Franklin's doctors were redheaded.[24]

Since Ahlangyah was not at the original meeting, at the ice crack, she does not mention "Ill-kern" at all, and, after the initial contact, neither do Teekeeta or Ow-wer. This would seemingly reinforce our conclusion that he was not an officer, and that he therefore had little further interaction with the natives.

Ahlangyah's tale corroborates the earlier versions of the encounter in some details and contradicts them in others. The same can be said of the last version of the incident at Teekeenu. It comes from the son of "Mong-er," the fourth of the Inuit hunters who met the white men.

An old man named Iggiararjuk told me [Rasmussen]: "My father Mangaq was with Tetqatsaq and Qablut on a seal hunt on the west coast of King William's Land when they heard shouts, and discovered three white men who stood on shore waving to them. This was in the spring; there was already open water along the land, and it was not possible to get in to them before low tide. The men were very thin, hollow-cheeked, and looked ill. They were dressed in white man's clothes, had no dogs and were travelling with sledges, which they drew themselves.

They bought seal meat and blubber, and paid with a knife. There was great joy on both sides at this bargain, and the white men cooked the meat at once with the aid of the blubber, and ate it. Later on the strangers went along to my father's tent camp and stayed there the night before returning to their own little tent, which was not of animal skins but of something that was all white like snow. At that time there was already caribou on King William's Land, but the strangers only seemed to hunt wildfowl; in particular there were many eider ducks and ptarmigan then. The earth was not yet alive and the swans had not come to the country.

Father and his people would willingly have helped the white men, but could not understand them; they tried to explain themselves by signs, and in fact learned to know a lot by this means. They had once been many they said; now they were only few, and they had left their

ship out in the pack-ice. They pointed to the south, and it was understood that they wanted to go home overland. They were not met again,
and no one knows where they went to.[25]

Mangaq (Mong-er) and his son once again corroborate many
of the features of the earlier tales. This time there are only "three
white men" expressly mentioned (presumably those who came
out to meet the Inuit – Aglooka, Toolooah or Doktook, and Ill-
kern), although more are implied. The crack in the ice, the exchange of seal meat for a knife, the separate tent, and the state
of the ice – breakup – are all here. The assertion that the strangers
"only appeared to hunt wildfowl" confirms Mik-ke-em-ma, while
the fact that caribou were plentiful may have led Too-shoo-art-
thariu's cousins to make the unwarranted assumption that the
white men had killed many. The white men also stayed overnight
in Mangaq's tent, a new feature which could have been exaggerated by Too-shoo-art-thariu into a winter's sojourn.

As is usual among Inuit, Iggiararjuk lent his father's tale credibility by naming those present.

For the purpose of giving his narrative an additional tinge of reliability
Iggiararjuk mentioned the names of all the people at the tent camp who
met them. There were Mangaq (the tease), and his wife Qerneq (black),
Tetqataq (flying before the wind) and his wife Ukaliaq (the leveret),
Qablut (scoop) and his wife Iliuana (point), Ukuararssuk (little snow
block – for closing the door of the snow hut) and his wife Putulik (hole),
Panatoq (long knife) and his wife Equvautsoq (crooked).[26]

We recognize Tetqataq as our friend Teekeeta, and Ukuararssuk was probably shortened by Hall to Ow-wer. We can only
identify Too-shoo-art-thariu as "Qablut" by reference to his wife
Iliuana (E-laing-nur/Ahlangyah), noting that it was usual for the
Inuit to possess many names. In fact Hall specifically mentioned
in a letter to Grinnell in 1864 that Ouela's cousin (Too-shoo-art-
thariu) had "two names."[27] We note that Teekeeta's 1869 wife
Mik-ke-em-ma either had two names as well (Iggiararjuk remembering Ukaliaq), or, as she was a young girl at the time of the
meeting with Aglooka, she may have been a junior or later wife
of Teekeeta.

Most surprising is the presence of a fifth family, Panatoq and
his wife Equvautsoq. Teekeeta and Ow-wer never mentioned

them. In this case Iggiararjuk's memory is probably playing him a little false – it must be remembered that he was an old man in 1923 when he told his tale to Rasmussen, and therefore a very young one when the events occurred. We shall identify these other individuals shortly.

The various tales of the meeting at Washington Bay (Teekeenu) offer fertile ground for speculation. Except for the one garbled hearsay account, that of Too-shoo-art-thariu, the tales of the eyewitnesses are remarkably consistent – except for two details. The amount of time that the Inuit spent with Aglooka's party, and the manner of their departure, cannot be determined.

Teekeeta and Ow-wer's testimony is internally inconsistent, asserting that they left Aglooka standing by his tent after only one night, while also telling of a visit by Aglooka to Ow-wer's tent "the next morning." Ahlangyah claimed that the white men spent five days with the small band of Inuit, and one detail of Too-shoo-art-thariu's story seems to support this. When Shook-she-ark-nook told of his cousin Too-shoo-art-thariu's meeting with Aglooka he made what Hall believed to be two contradictory statements. The first stated that Aglooka immediately ate a small piece of seal meat which was offered him upon the initial meeting (a detail corroborated by Teekeeta and Ow-wer). Another implied that Aglooka waited until one of the Inuits caught a seal before eating a small piece.

These two statements were so incongruous that Hall asked his interpreter Tookoolitoo to obtain a clarification. After a few minutes of earnest conversation with Shook-she-ark-nook, she replied that one seal "was not caught till 2 or 3 days after 1st meeting the Kob-lu-nas. It was not of this seal that the 1st and 2nd bites given to Crozier [Aglooka] were taken. The cousin had a small piece of raw seal on his sledge which he had saved for his children, & from this he cut a bit & gave it to Crozier as quick as he could for he (C.) was so poor & nearly starved."[28]

The inconsistency in time frame may have been the result of a simple misunderstanding, or it may have been a feeble attempt to minimize the impact of the Inuit "desertion" of Aglooka and his men.

The Inuit claim that they did not know that the white men were starving is disingenous, and is contradicted by their graphic descriptions of Aglooka's actions in begging for seal, and the unmistakable signs of scurvy and weakness which they noted in their descriptions. While their abandonment of these men to their fate seemed inexcusable to Hall, it was very prudent in the eyes of the native hunters, who were putting themselves and their families at risk by remaining with the white men. Perhaps because of his displeasure with the treatment of Aglooka and his men, Hall paid Ow-wer and Teekeeta very poorly for their information. Ow-wer got a brandy bottle, complete with cork but "no brandy"; Teekeeta received half of a tin can.[29]

Ten years before Hall learned the details, McClintock had been told some version of the meeting at Teekeenu.

At the time of our interview with the natives of King William Island, Petersen was inclined to think that the retreat of the crews took place in the fall of the year, some of the men in boats, and others walking along the shore; as only five bodies are said to have been found upon Montreal Island with the boat, this fact favored his opinion, because so small a number could not have dragged her there over the ice, although they could very easily have taken her there by water. Subsequently this opinion proved erroneous. I mention it because it shows how vague our information was – indeed all Esquimaux accounts are naturally so …[30]

It was not the vagueness of the native report which was to blame for McClintock's disbelief in the story of a group of survivors, "some of the men in boats, and others walking along the shore," who were encountered in the "fall of the year." McClintock was misled by slavish adherence to the information in Fitzjames's record, which stated that the abandonment had occurred in April. He could not believe that Crozier's men had marched less than five miles a day, or that 60 per cent of them had died within one hundred miles of the ships. He could not accept that the forty frail men who stumbled out of the mists at Washington Bay were the remnants of Crozier's massive party of 1848. He may have been right.

~10~

Nuvertaro

Having heard the Inuit repeatedly tell their tale of the meeting with Aglooka and his men at Teekeenu (Washington Bay), Hall wished to answer three questions. How many men were marching with Aglooka? When were they seen? Where did they go? To only the last question would he receive a completely satisfactory answer, yet all of the Inuit responses are incorporated into the "standard reconstruction" of the fate of Franklin's men.

Gilder enunciated a continual complaint of white interviewers who attempted to derive quantitative information from the Inuit. He remarked that the Inuit had "little idea of numbers beyond the number of their fingers and such as they can borrow by calling attention to their neighbor's fingers."[1] Any number greater than this was "amasuadloo" – very many. It should therefore not surprise us that uncertainty exists as to how many men were in Aglooka's party.

Too-shoo-art-thariu mentioned three white men and Mangaq four, although both may have been telling only of the initial contact at the ice edge, or of the principal participants (Aglooka, Toolooah, Ill-kern, and Doktook). Ahlangyah mentioned ten men, divided into two groups of five for sleeping, and, as she also mentions that the Inuit spent "five days" with the white men, and waited at Gladman Point for a further "five," we wonder if the recurrence of this number in her testimony is attributable to the finger method mentioned above. Gilder, ignoring his own warning, decided on the questionable basis of the presence of eyeglasses and gold watches that the "five" men who slept in the tent ashore must all have been officers.

Hall's attempt to determine the number of Aglooka's marchers is illustrative of the problem.

I now got Ow-wer & Tuk-ke-ta to try to tell me how many men were in Aglooka's party when they met it. They say they cannot tell, they were so many. One man a very short man. One man very fat all over. One man with a single upper front tooth gone. One man with very sore bleeding gums – lower gums. One man cross-eyed. Ow-wer and Tuk-ke-ta on my getting 4 men to hold up their hands, showing 40 fingers and thumbs, say that they would think perhaps 5 more – that is 4 fingers and a thumb more would represent about the number of souls in Aglook-a's party.[2]

As is obvious from the method of determination, we cannot place too much reliance in the number forty-five as an exact count. Yet Teekeeta and Ow-wer's description of the sleeping arrangements of the white men clearly shows that Ahlangyah had underestimated their number. They indicated that the tent was oval in shape and about twenty feet long, while "the men slept with their heads to the sides of the tent – that is, feet toward feet for there were 2 rows."[3]

If we allow twenty-four inches of shoulder room for each man, this would equate to twenty men in the tent. The lifeboats were all about thirty feet in length,[4] but their width would not allow double rows of sleepers and the space restrictions at each end must also be taken into account. Perhaps ten to fifteen more may have been able to sleep in the boat, making Teekeeta's estimate of forty-five a little excessive, though closer to the truth than Ahlangyah's ten.

Hall's informants were unanimous in stating that the encounter took place after the ice had begun to break up in Simpson Strait. Yet arriving at a year was a more difficult task.

I now request the whole company to take hold & see if they can make out the year – how many years ago since the 4 Innuit families met Crozier and party on the w. coast of K.W.L., which place they – Ow-wer & Tuk-ke-ta – point out on the chart as being just above Cape Herschel. The result 25 winters ago. Ow-wer & Tuk-ke-ta make out 9 to the time Dr. Rae came to Pelly Bay – the winter preceding that spring Ou-e-la and the large party from Repulse Bay spent at Pelly Bay.

I get them to try again. The result, 5 winters after seeing Aglooka, Dr. Rae came to Pelly Bay & this makes it out that the paper found by McClintock corresponds with what the Innuits of this country know. The errors of the 1st result by counting twice a summer and a winter as two years, Joe says. The 2nd result arrived at without the least intimation that the 1st calculation was wrong. The last result stated as positively so by Ow-wer & Tuk-ke-ta. (Note of mine May 19th. The last result not right by one year. So Innuits as well as myself mistaken – Hall).[5]

Once again little faith can be placed in this dating method. The first result gave 1844, a year before Franklin sailed. Although Hall states that the second was arrived at "without the least intimation that the 1st calculation was wrong," the simple fact that a second attempt was asked for would probably have been as good a clue to the Inuit as it is to any modern reader. The second attempt, based on Rae's meeting with the Pelly Bay Inuit in April 1854, gave a more amenable date – 1849. Rae himself was told that the white men had been seen "four winters past," giving 1850 as the year of meeting. At this point no conclusions can be reached from these datings as to whether Crozier's 1848 party, or a later one, is being referred to.

Having thus determined to his own satisfaction the number of Aglooka's companions (about forty-five) and the year of their encounter (1848, noting that the Inuit were "not right by one year"), Hall attempted to trace the subsequent path of Aglooka and his men after the Inuit left them in Washington Bay.

Rae had been told that "the corpses of some thirty persons and some graves were discovered on the continent, and five dead bodies on an island near it, about a long day's journey to the north-west of the mouth of a large stream, which can be no other than Back's Great Fish River."[6] McClintock and Anderson found some cached relics on Montreal Island in Chantrey Inlet, which had led some to the assumption that this was where the five dead men had found their last resting places. Presumably the graves of "thirty persons" would be found nearby "on the continent."

This is exactly what Hall learned from the natives, for he was told that the Inuit were "quite sure that the boat found on the Islet in the Inlet w. Side of Pt. Richardson was the same one that Ag-loo-ka's party had when they met the 4 Innuit families just above Cape Herschel."[7] The Inuit name for Richardson Point was "Nuvertaro," and it was here that Rae and Hall concluded most of Aglooka's men had died.

Ten years later, Gilder believed that Too-shoo-art-thariu's wife Ahlangyah had confirmed this assumption, remarking that "it would seem, from what she related today, that the party which perished in the inlet we visited yesterday [west of Richardson Point] was part of the same that Ahlangyah met on King William's Land."[8] He gave no reasons for this curious statement, and the "it would seem" implies that Ahlangyah did not expressly state that she had seen any bodies west of Richardson Point. Certainly Gilder's companions did not conclude this from Ahlangyah's testimony; although she did mention finding a place with many bodies, she invariably located this as Terror Bay on King William Island.[9]

Hall repeatedly tried to get the Inuit to estimate the number of bodies at the place where many dead men were found (which he, like Gilder, assumed was the camp near Richardson Point). Although he was again told that it would be "impossible to be precise," eventually five men held up all of their fingers. Since more men could not have died at this place than had been seen at Washington Bay, Hall arbitrarily halved this to compensate for the Inuit "overestimate" and arrive at a figure closer to Rae's "thirty persons."[10]

Hall himself never went to the inlet on the continent, as his Inuit companions were reluctant to venture farther than Todd Islet. As a further disincentive he was told that the place was so flat that everything would be covered in snow. Furthermore, although all of his informants knew of the place, only one of them had ever been there!

A careful reading of Hall's notes shows that Teekeeta and Owwer never mention having left King William Island, or having found a boat. Not surprisingly, they, like Ahlangyah, did find a tent full of bodies, but they also identified this as being on King William Island. Their testimony makes it clear that their accounts of the boat place at Nuvertaro were based on hearsay, as was their endorsement of the identification of Aglooka's boat as the one found there.

The only native to state specifically that she had visited the spot was a woman named Eveeshuk. Hall, obviously referring to Rae's report, started his interview with her by asking some leading questions.

Did you ever hear of any white men dying on Ke-ki-tuk-ju-a (Montreal Island)?

No, never.

Did you ever go to the place where the boat with many dead Koblunins was found by the Innuits?

Yes, I have been there.

Where is the place? I now show her Rae's chart – have shown it to her before – but not for the object I now have.

On ascertaining the position of Point Ogle, Macononchie Isle & Pt. Richardson, she puts her finger on the w. side of the Inlet w. side of Pt. Richardson & says that was the place where the boat was found.

Did you see any bones of white men there?

She did – the land low & muddy there – the sea-water close to. Saw pieces of the boat after the Innuits had broken it up.

Can bones – skeleton bones – be seen there now when snow and ice are gone? Ans. She thinks not, for it is so muddy there & the mud (so) soft that they have all sunk down into it. She continues – One man's body when found by the Innuits flesh all on & not mutilated except the hands sawed off at the wrists – the rest a great many had their flesh cut off as if some one or other had cut it off to eat.[11]

In fact the testimony of Eveeshuk, who visited the site "one year after it was found by Pooyetta," adds little knowledge beyond her description of the locale "on a very small island by the west coast of the inlet … half way down the inlet, where it turns sharply to the westward."[12] She never saw the boat, just pieces of it. Her account of the human remains makes it clear that she could neither confirm nor deny the number found, and as she only saw scattered bones her statements concerning mutilation and cannibalism are obviously a mere repetition of what she had been told.

More details of the remains found at Nuvertaro were relayed to Hall by In-nook-poo-zhe-jook, who again never visited the spot personally, but faithfully retold what had been repeated many times. According to Hall, the remains at Nuvertaro had originally been found by a native named Pooyetta. Pooyetta's boat was found "in complete order." Inside of it, many men with "hands sawed off at the wrists" had been found under a tent or awning, lying as if asleep under some blankets.[13] Although Hall's notes state that this boat which Pooyetta found was located "in Inlet w. side of Point Richardson," we do not know whether it was thus identified to him by In-nook-poo-zhe-jook (who himself would have been making an assumption), or whether this was Hall's own opinion.

The first explorers to actually visit the site of the continental "final resting place" were Schwatka and Gilder. After crossing Richardson Point, they camped in a small inlet and were told by the Inuit that they were within three or four miles of the "boat place" described to Hall. An old man named Seeuteetuar ("the man without ears") was indicated as one of those who had personally seen the Franklin remains, but he did not remember very much beyond "a number of skeletons near the water line."[14]

He had also seen books and papers scattered around among the rocks along the shore and back from the beach. There were also knives, forks and spoons, dishes and cans. There was no sled there, but there was a boat, which was afterward broken up and taken away by the natives, with which to manufacture wooden implements. He was shown a watch, and said he saw several like it lying around, which were also taken and broken up by the children. Some were silver and some gold. He said the bones were still there, unless carried off by foxes and wolves. He had never seen or heard of a cairn erected by white men along the coast on this side of Simpson Strait, and had never heard of any other traces of white men here.[15]

The next day Seeuteetuar escorted the white men to the spot, but they found "everything so completely covered with snow that nothing could be seen."[16]

The Americans named the place "Starvation Cove."

Schwatka's interpreter (the now-widowed Ebierbing) visited the site later, during the summer, but only "a small pewter medal, commemorative of the launch of the Steamer Great Britain, in 1843, and among the seaweed some pieces of blanket and a skull" were found.[17] The natives pointed out to him where the boat had rested, but there were no traces remaining. Such meagre relics were disappointing from this place where "thirty to forty" men had met their fate.

Seeuteetuar confirmed Eveeshuk's opinion that none of Franklin's men had ever reached Montreal Island. His comments about graves, sleds, and cairns were obviously in response to questions which tried to find elements common to the other stories Hall had been told, but the old man was as unhelpful in this regard as he was in illuminating the number of bodies found here.

That Seeuteetuar confirmed Eveeshuk's story is not really surprising. Ten years earlier Hall had encountered four native families camped on the ice east of Todd Islet. One of these families was Eveeshuk's. Another was Seeuteetuar's.

On 9 May 1869 Hall interviewed the old woman Koo-nik (or Koo-wik), who told him of the wreck of Franklin's ship on the western shore of Adelaide Peninsula and gave him a knife which came from the boat at Starvation Cove. When asked if she or her husband had personally seen the boat, she replied that they hadn't, but that they had "heard Innuits tell all about it & the many Kobluna dead bodies found there." Her husband, who said not a word, was named "See-u-ty-chu."

Hall's See-u-ty-chu was, in fact, Gilder's "Seeuteetuar." This identification is not based solely on the similarity of their names. According to Schwatka, the old man (whose name he heard as "Seetitecheing") had seen white men before; his experience, however, had "been limited to stealing a saw from Capt. McClintock during that leader's Franklin Search in 1859. He related this incident with evident gusto as the perfect joke."[18]

The incident is preserved in McClintock's narrative. On 7 May 1859 he records:

one man got hold of our saw, and tried to retain it, holding it behind his back, and presenting his knife in exchange; we might have had some trouble in getting it from him, had not one of my men mistaken his object in presenting the knife towards me, and run out of the tent with a gun in his hand; the saw was instantly returned, and these poor people seemed to think they never could do enough to convince us of their friendliness; they repeatedly tapped me gently on the breast, repeating the words "Kammik toomee" (We are friends).[19]

Hall was also told by In-nook-poo-zhe-jook that Koo-nik's husband See-u-ty-chu had met the "white men from Ik-ke-lu-suk" – Bellot Strait – and that he "playfully tried to exchange his knife for a saw this party of white men had upon the sledge."[20] In fact, according to In-nook-poo-zhe-jook, this same individual was none other than See-u-ti-chu, the man who had accompanied him when he met Rae in 1854![21]

Seeuteetuar/See-u-ti-chu/Seetitecheing had therefore met Rae, McClintock, and Hall before being interviewed by Gilder and Schwatka. As we shall see, he had also visited Ross at Felix Harbour; it seems that it was difficult for any white man to go to the central Arctic without running into this well-travelled but uncommunicative man.

The important thing to note for the present discussion is that, according to his wife, Seeuteetuar, like Eveeshuk, had not personally seen the boat at Starvation Cove. He knew of it from hearsay, and ten years later could lead Schwatka and Gilder to the spot where it was found, but as he had been present during Eveeshuk's earlier testimony we cannot know whether his statements to Schwatka were corroboration or mere repetition.

Schwatka interviewed Pooyetta's widow, named Tooktoocheer, about the boat which her husband had found.

She said she had never seen any of Franklin's men alive, but saw six skeletons on the main-land and an adjacent island ... [her son] Og-zeuckjeuwock took up the thread of the narrative here. In answer to a question which we asked his mother, he said he saw books at the boat place in a tin case, about two feet long and a foot square, which was fastened, and they broke it open. The case was full. Written and printed books were shown him, and he said they were like the printed ones. Among the books he found what was probably the needle of a compass or other magnetic instrument because he said when it touched any iron it stuck fast. The boat was right side up, and the tin case in the boat. Outside the boat he saw a number of skulls. He forgot how many, but said there were more than four. He also saw bones from legs and arms that appeared to have been sawed off. Inside the boat was a box filled with bones; the box was about the same size as the one with books in it ... In the boat he saw canvas and four sticks (a tent or sail), saw a number of watches, open-faced; a few were gold, but most were silver. They are all lost now. They were given to the children to play with, and have been broken up and lost ... His reason for thinking that they had been eating each other was because the bones were cut with a knife or saw. They found one big saw and one small one in the boat; also a large red tin case of smoking tobacco and some pipes. There was no cairn there. The bones are now covered up with sand and sea-weed, as they were lying just at high-water mark. Some of the books were taken home for the children to play with, and finally torn and lost ...[22]

Both Schwatka and Gilder assumed that this boat was the same one spoken of by Eveeshuk and Seeuteetuar as having been found at Starvation Cove. There were obvious points of similarity. Ogzeuckjeuwock noted one body that "had all the flesh on," reminiscent of Eveeshuk's completely preserved body which had only the hands removed. The books near the boat may have been the source of Seeuteetuar's many papers, while both he and Ogzeuckjeuwock mention the many watches. There can be little doubt that Eveeshuk and Seeuteetuar faithfully preserved the tale of Pooyetta's boat, or that the remains of a boat were found at Starvation Cove. What is unproven is that Pooyetta's boat and the Starvation Cove boat were the same.

Schwatka, in his account of Ogzeuckjeuwock's testimony, expressly states that "the boat and skeletons had been found in what we called 'Starvation Cove.'"[23] Yet Klutschak's version of the testimony, in all other ways entirely similar to that of his companions, does not note that Ogzeuckjeuwock specifically located the boat which he had found at all.[24]

Ogzeuckjeuwock and his mother, Tooktoocheer, both relayed another curious detail of their find. They said that one of the men, apparently the last to die, was still well preserved when found and that he was positively festooned with jewellery. According to Ogzeuckjeuwock, this man "had a gold chain fastened to gold ear-rings, and a gold hunting-case watch with engine-turned engraving attached to the chain and hanging down about the waist. He said when he pulled the chain it pulled the head up by the ears."[25] Some of the other Inuit could not agree that such a thing had ever been seen at the nearby boat, but Tooktoocheer and her son "refused to admit that they were mistaken about this latter point, and stuck firmly to their statement despite all objections."[26]

There were other discrepancies in the tales of this boat place. Schwatka assumed that the Starvation Cove boat was the one "spoken of by Rae, McClintock, and Hall, all of whom place the number of the dead at forty to fifty," yet he found that "all of the natives I interviewed and who had been eye-witnesses of the sad scene closely corroborate each other – although interviewed at different villages some distance from each other – and place the number at from six to ten."[27] Gilder also understood from the natives that relatively few men died here. He was told that "they did not remember the exact number, but thought there were about five or more."[28] Hall's collected testimony implied many more casualties than this. In 1942 the "jaw bones of three white men" and "one whole skull" were found at Starvation Cove, and while we cannot be sure that other remains had not been swept away by the tide or become submerged in the soft mud, the presence of only four individuals is suggestive.[29]

There was another feature of the Starvation Cove boat which was puzzling. Both Schwatka and Hall had been told that Pooyetta's boat was found resting on its keel. Klutschak and Gilder, surprisingly, learned from other natives that the boat at Starvation Cove had been "found upside down on the beach, and all the skeletons beneath it" and that it was "afterward broken up and taken away."[30]

Eveeshuk, who arrived the next year, had not seen the boat itself but "pieces of the boat after the Innuits had broken it up." Gilder's impression that the remains at Starvation Cove were found under an overturned boat is interesting, as it confirms what In-nook-poo-zhe-jook told Rae, that some bodies were "under the boat, which had been turned over to form a shelter."[31] As Seeuteetuar was present both when Eveeshuk told Hall, and when In-nook-poo-zhe-jook told Rae, about this boat, this is obviously what he believed as well.

Rae was told of a place "on the mainland" where thirty men had died. Hall was told of a boat which had been found to the west of Nuvertaro by Pooyetta. Schwatka interviewed Pooyetta's widow and son, who told of an upright boat surrounded by bodies. Logic demanded therefore that the boat at Nuvertaro be upright and surrounded by many bodies. But neither of these details was confirmed.

Schwatka was also told by those who had actually visited the place that the bodies of only "six to ten" men had been found at Starvation Cove. Gilder confirmed this and then added the puzzling fact that these men had been sheltered under an overturned boat. No wonder many historians doubt the usefulness of Inuit testimony! There is, of course, another explanation. The white men may have been hearing tales of different boats – at different places.

There may indeed have been more than one boat found near Nuvertaro. In 1923 Rasmussen met a native named Qaqorting-neq, who informed him of "several places in our country where we still see bones of [Franklin's] men," and together they visited one of these which the natives called "Qavdlunarsiorfik" – "the place where one seeks white men's things." Rasmussen described this as "on the east coast of the Adelaide Peninsula," and here, "exactly where the Eskimos had indicated," they found "a number of human bones that undoubtedly were the mortal remains of members of the Franklin Expedition; some pieces of cloth and stumps of leather we found at the same place showed that they were of white men ... We had been the first friends that ever visited the place."[32]

The assumption has always been that Rasmussen's "Qavdlunarsiorfik" was identical to Schwatka's "Starvation Cove," and one of the maps in Rasmussen's account shows Richardson Point as "nuverteroq – the narrow point"; an explanatory note reads "here is the so-called Qavdlunarsiorfik, where some of Franklin's men perished."[33]

But Rasmussen was quite familiar with the Schwatka expedition and therefore his statement that "we had been the *first friends* that ever visited the place" seems to indicate that he did not consider himself to be at "Starvation Cove." He built a memorial cairn over the remains that he found, and the caption to the photograph of this cairn is also suggestive. It reads: "at Qavdlunarsiorfik, on the east coast of Adelaide Peninsula, *near* Starvation Cove" (emphasis added).[34]

There actually was another white men's campsite near Starvation Cove. Confusingly, this was not on Richardson Point to the east of Starvation Cove, but about five miles north-west of it. Details of this were learned by Mr L.A. Learmonth of the Hudson's Bay Company. He remarked that an old woman named Neniook "reported having come across the skeletons of seven white men still party clothed in blue serge, and partly buried in the sand and seaweed on a small island in the vicinity. Hard boots with nails in the soles were also noted by Neniook who was a small child at the time."[35]

Another curious discovery was made to the south of Starvation

Cove. Gilder was told that "about five miles inland from Starvation Cove the natives had found during the summer the skeleton of a white man, which no one had ever seen before ... The pieces of clothing found indicated that [the] deceased was a sailor, not an officer."[36] The spot was visited by Klutschak. He describes the place as a small hill "about five miles south and somewhat east of Starvation Cove" and mentions finding the remains of clothing. He does not specifically mention a skeleton or bones of any kind, but as he mentions a "grave" this may have been an oversight.[37] With such fragmentary evidence we cannot determine whether this was a lone straggler or someone buried by companions.

The "standard reconstruction," first formulated by Hall, endorsed by Schwatka and Gilder, and largely accepted today, considered that the Washington Bay Aglooka and his forty men were the last survivors of the Crozier party which had landed at Victory Point. These men presumably travelled eastward along the southern shore of King William Island, encountered Teekeeta's band at Teekeenu, and then proceeded to the Todd Islets. After the ice completely broke up, those who survived took their boat across to the mainland where the last thirty of them died at Starvation Cove. This is what most of the Inuit themselves believed, although those who had actually visited Starvation Cove could not confirm the number. Any discrepancies in the native testimony which raised doubt about this sequence of events were ignored or attributed to Inuit inexactitude. But in 1926 physical evidence was found which further strained the credibility of this reconstruction.

In that year Peter Norberg found a skull on Adelaide Peninsula. That this came from a Franklin camp was proven when analysis by Dr H.M. Ami of the Royal Society of Canada determined it to have belonged to a young white male.[38]

Ten years later, near the same place, Learmonth and D.G. Sturrock found the remains of three men. Other relics, including a silver George IV half-crown, bearing the date 1820, and a sailor's ivory button, were conclusive. All of these finds occurred at a campsite on a point named "Tikeraniyou" (Crooked Finger) by the natives.[39]

Tikeraniyou lies on the northern shore of the Adelaide Peninsula near modern Thunder Cove; it is fifteen miles to the west of Starvation Cove.

These remains of Franklin crewmen found on the south side of Simpson Strait call into doubt the assertion that the bodies found by the Inuit at Starvation Cove were those of men who had come directly south from Todd Islets. The remains at Tikeraniyou are not on the supposed route of Aglooka and his party as envisioned by the "standard reconstruction."

It seems certain that Crozier's men did not follow the script laid out in the Victory Point record in 1848. They did not march as a single body to the Great Fish River, leaving a continuous trail of relics and remains along their route, but, as the natives told Hall, split into various detachments. There are also differing descriptions of the "final resting places" where these men died. Yet Hall's assumption that many men died at Starvation Cove, despite the difficulties with later testimony, has never been seriously questioned.

There was obviously very great mortality before Aglooka and his forty remaining men met Teekeeta and his friends at Teekeenu. We must search to the north-west of Washington Bay for the site of an earlier disaster. Perhaps then we will learn where Hall's "thirty-five to forty" bodies were actually found.

~11~

Toonoonee

Teekeeta and Ow-wer told Hall that they left Aglooka and his men in Washington Bay early in the morning because "they were in a hurry to make their journey across the land (KWL) from w side to the eastward."[1] This was confirmed by Ahlangyah, who stated that the Inuit "waited for five days at Gladman's Point for the white men. When the latter did not come, the natives moved on toward Booth Point."[2]

Gilder learned that, after leaving Booth Point, this party of Inuit "went back and forth between the shore and lakes nearly all summer, and then went to the eastern shore near Matty Island."[3] Hall was told that the Netsilingmiut (Inuit from Boothia Peninsula) often came to Simpson Strait to seal, stopping along the way at traditional camping places on or near the eastern shore of King William Island, including "Owutta," a small island near Matty Island which McClintock had searched for in 1859.[4] This is probably where Teekeeta's party wintered.

Shortly after the Inuit left them at Washington Bay, the members of Aglooka's party started dying. Less than fifteen miles east of Teekeenu McClintock found the first victim.

Shortly after midnight of the 24th May, when slowly walking along a gravel ridge near the beach, which the winds kept partially bare of snow, I came upon a human skeleton, partly exposed, with here and there a few fragments of clothing appearing through the snow. The skeleton – now perfectly bleached – was lying upon its face, the limbs and smaller bones either dissevered or gnawed away by small animals ... A pocket-book afforded strong grounds of hope that some information might be subsequently obtained respecting the unfortunate owner and the calamitous march of the lost crews, but at the time it was frozen hard ... This victim was a young man, slightly built, and perhaps above the common height; the dress appeared to be that of a steward or officer's servant, the loose bow-knot in which his neck-handkerchief was tied not being used by seamen or officers. In every particular the dress confirmed our conjectures as to his rank or office in the late expedition, – the blue jacket with slashed sleeves and braided edging, and the pilot-cloth great-coat with plain covered buttons. We found, also, a clothes-brush near, and a horn pocket-comb. This poor man seems to have selected the bare ridgetop, as affording the least tiresome walking, and to have fallen upon his face in the position in which we found him.[5]

Some of the papers found by McClintock belonged to Warrant Officer Harry Peglar, and one still finds reference to this skeleton as Peglar's in modern writings. This is almost certainly incorrect. It is difficult to know how McClintock could determine from a bleached skeleton that the man was "young"; not having been trained in medicine, he probably based this opinion on the slight build of the body. Harry Peglar was only a relatively "young" man, being between thirty-four and forty years of age in 1848. More significant was his occupation – he served in the *Terror* as Captain of the Foretop, one of the most senior seamen aboard. The Captain of the Foretop would not have been caught, even dead, with a steward's bow-knot.

Peglar had, however, been a shipmate of the *Terror*'s gunroom steward, Thomas Armitage. The two served together in HMS *Gannett* between 1834 and 1837. Armitage was not a "young" man either – he was forty-two in 1848 – but he was relatively tall (5' 9") and may have been carrying his deceased friend's possessions.[6]

The next spring after their meeting at Teekeenu, Teekeeta's party returned to southern King William Island to search for the white men and to scour the camping places for their wealth in iron and wood. They did not find the skeleton of this straggler, but they did find the remains of many of Franklin's men.

The following spring, when there was little snow on the ground, she [Ahlangyah] saw a tent standing on the shore at the head of Terror Bay. There were dead bodies in the tent, and outside were some covered over with sand. There was no flesh on them – nothing but the bones and clothes. There were a great many; she had forgotten how many ... She saw nothing to indicate any of the party she met before. The bones had the chords [sic] or sinews still attached to them. One of the bodies had the flesh on, but this one's stomach was gone. There were one or two graves outside. They did not open the graves at this time; saw a great many things lying around. There were knives, forks, spoons, watches, many books, clothing, blankets, and such things. The books were not taken notice of. This was the same party of Esquimaux who had met the white men the year before, and they were the first who saw the tent and graves. They had been in King William's Land ever since they saw the white men until they found the tent place.[7]

Hall learned from Koong-e-ou-e-lik that the tent had first been found by four "boys" who were searching the shore for drift-wood. He interviewed Teekeeta about this tenting place. Once again the correspondence with Ahlangyah's testimony is re-markable.

XI A.M. by guess time & this moment Tee-ke-ta has entered our Ig-loo & laid before me a fragment of a striped handkershief [sic] – as I suppose from its looks & a relic of Sir John Franklin's Expedition. I will now try & get the history of it.

Tee-ke-ta, where did you get this?

Ans. From Ki-ki-tung (KWL) from a tent found there.

Who got it there? Ans. "Mong-er". That is he (and) Tee-ke-ta.

Now I ask him to show me if he can by the chart (McClintock's) on what part of KWL this tent was. Having shown Dr. Rae's & McC's & Admiralty charts to this Innuit as well as others here yesterday & the preceding day, he quickly points out the place & the spot which is near the bottom of Terror Bay, a little way northerly of the point adjacent to Fitzjames Islet. The tent was on the top of some rising ground – or a very small hill – a sandy hill. The tent large & made with ridge pole resting on a perpendicular pole at either end – small ropes extended from top tent at each end to the ground where the rope ends were fast to sticks that had been driven into the ground ... the tent was partially down from the snow upon it & a fox had bitten in two one of the lines by which the tent was held upright ...

Three men saw this tent first – he, Tee-ke-ta, one of them.

How long after you saw Ag-loo-ka was it before you and the two men found this tent?

The next spring – that is, one year after.

What did you see in this tent?

Blankets, bedding & a great many skeleton bones, a great many skulls – the flesh all off, nothing except sinews attached to them – the appearance as though foxes & wolves had gnawed the flesh off the bones. Some bones had been severed with a saw. Some skulls with holes in them. On trying to get Tee-kee-ta to tell how many skulls there were in this tent, he says he cannot tell for there were so many – the tent floor seemed to be covered with bones & the tent much larger, longer, than this Ig-loo. (Our Ig-loo of oval form, the longer diameter being 25 feet.) Some of the skeletons had been completely cleaned of all flesh and sinews & [?] fastened to various portions of the dress that one might suppose to have clothed the living man.

What else in the tent?

Ans. Tin cups, spoons, forks, knives, two double barrel guns, pistol, lead balls, a great many powder flasks. If I or anybody else will go there in the summer after the snow has melted off the land will find a great many balls and see all the skeletons.[8]

Ahlangyah remarked that the books were all given to the children "for playthings." Teekeeta also remembered this.

Did you see the paper with such kind of marks or writing as you see here?

Saw a *good deal*, as you express it, what Tee-ke-ta says.

I now show Tee-kee-ta a book, Capt. Ross voyage of the Victory 8 vols. (French edition but in English) & showed him the difference between printed marks & writing marks & he says he and companions saw both kinds in tent.

What did you do with the books & papers?

Ans. As they were good for nothing for Innuits, threw them away, except one book which had pictures in it he brought home.

Where is that book?

Ans. All gone long ago. Gave it to the children & after a while all of it got torn to pieces. He says if any one goes there in summer he may find pieces of paper about there.

Any boxes in that tent?

Only one small box & something all metal, brass, inside. A sextant as Joe thinks. Now I have my large sextant (u.s.c.s. sextant) brought into igloo & he looks at the sextant and says it was not like that, it was round as one could see on opening the box. I now show him Eggert pocket chronometer & he says it was like that only much larger & the inside of it like inside my chronometer but all much bigger. Therefore this was a box chronometer. A good many watches found in the tent, found there in some of the clothes that covered some of the skeletons. Some with chains knotted around the necks of the skeletons. (emphasis in original)[9]

Hall interviewed an old lady named Ad-lark (usually identified by him as the "lady with the shaking head"), who had also seen this tent. This old lady can be identified as Teekeeta's mother: she remarked that "the 1st Innuits who saw this tent were her 2 sons, Tut-ke-ta, Ten-ne-a & Et-ker-lit a Neitch-il-ling Innuit." Ad-lark was "the old lady of the party" at that time and "after these three men found the tent they came to where they had their camping place, when all the families there, women and children, hurried to the tent."[10]

Ad-lark identified this tenting place as near a small islet called "Oo-bla-tu-ar-you." In-nook-poo-zhe-jook, who visited the place many years after Ad-lark, pointed the spot out to Hall on a chart as "at or near the head of Terror Bay,"[11] so it is probable that Ad-lark's islet is one of the two (still unnamed) in the north-west corner of the bay. Hall apparently called the islet "Fitzjames' Islet,"[12] but that name has since, confusingly, been given to another island at the south-west point of the bay.

Hall had earlier been told by Ookbarloo of an unnamed old woman (probably actually Ad-lark herself) who had visited this tent. Ookbarloo's second-hand story is one of the most powerful of all Inuit remembrances.

[An old woman] and her husband went to a big tent not very far from Neitchille, and among the frozen mass of human bones and bodies that were lying around in it she saw one Kob-lu-na body that had a bright white (probably silver) chain around the neck. She knew at once what the chain was for, as some of the other Neitchille Innuits had just come into possession of several watches and chains, which she saw.

The body of this man was lying on one side, and was half imbedded in solid ice from head to feet. The way the chain was about the neck and running down one side of the body indicated that the watch was beneath it; and therefore, to get at the watch, she found a difficult and disagreeable task before her. Neither she nor her husband had any instrument with them that they would use for any such purpose as was desired; therefore, while the husband was seeking around, she procured a heavy sharp stone, and with this chipped away the ice from all round the body till it was released …

[The woman] could never forget the dreadful, fearful feelings she had all the time while engaged doing this; for, besides the tent being filled with frozen corpses – some entire and others mutilated by some of the starving companions, who had cut off much of the flesh with their knives and hatchets and eaten it – this man who had the watch she sought seemed to her to have been the last that died, and his face was just as though he was only asleep. All the while she was at work breaking the ice near the head, especially the ice about the face, she felt very bad, and for this reason had to stop several times. She was very careful not to touch any part of the body while pounding with the sharp stone. At last, after having pounded away the ice from around and under the body, her husband helped her to lift it out of its icy bed. Still she was troubled to get the watch from the frozen garments with which the body was completely dressed.[13]

This tale clearly echoes Teekeeta's testimony. He also noted the many watches found here and especially that some of the skeletons had "chains knotted around the necks." We shall meet with this curious feature again. Too-shoo-art-thariu also told his friends that to get at the valuables in the tent they had to carry the corpses outside. This tent found at "Toonoonee" ("the back of beyond") in Terror Bay is seen to have all of the features claimed by Hall for Starvation Cove. Here was unmistakable evidence of cannibalism, here were the "thirty to forty" dead men. The fact that he had been told of two places with very similar characteristics apparently never struck Hall as anything other than an interesting coincidence.

Ad-lark's sons, Teekeeta and Ten-ne-a, gave Hall other details of the camp at Toonoonee.

The 2 sons are present & now telling what they saw in the tent – a box with one side about 6 inches high & something in it tepid, that is it smelt strong & a great many little ones each in a little part. 2 knives, a very little one; amasuadloo (a great many) watches & spoons & forks.

Close by the big tent was certain evidence by the stones that another tent had been there – but the Innuits think that Ag-loo-ka & party had had their tent at this place before the party was met with by the 4 families of the Innuits.[14]

The box which contained something "tepid" (strong smelling) and "a great many little ones each in a little part" may have been a segmented medicine chest. It seems that the many men who died in the tent were not themselves the victims of cannibalism, for Ad-lark remembered "only one skeleton that had been sawed."[15] Although many of the remains in the tent had been mutilated, both she and Teekeeta thought that this had been "as if done by foxes or wolves."[16]

As would be expected, the macabre work of dismemberment was done outside the tent. Testimony had noted that "there was & is now a pile of skulls with other bones on the outside of where the tent was – the skulls having holes in them by wh. they say the brains must have been taken out to prolong the lives of the living."[17]

Three graves were found outside the tent – "where earth was raised in mounds long & narrow."[18] This evidence of Christian burial, seemingly contrary to the "pile of skulls" and indications of cannibalism, may indicate that the site had been used for a protracted period. In the beginning the situation had not been so tragic. Alternatively, the camp may have been used at different times.

Hall, wedded to Rae's conclusion that most of Franklin's men had died on the mainland near the Great Fish River, believed that the tales he was hearing of this dreadful encampment at Toonoonee were new. When Schwatka and Gilder visited King William Island ten years later, they hoped to be able to locate and visit the site. They noted that "a month's diligent search had failed to disclose the spot," but later learned that "nature had anticipated me [Schwatka] in performing the last sad rites of burial due those dead heroes, and that some six years before the sea had obliterated the very last trace of them."[19]

Modern confirmation of the Inuit tales of the encampment at Terror Bay was obtained in 1930. In that year Burwash found a grave "which might have contained several bodies" at Terror Bay. The next year, Patsy Klengenberg found the remains of another of Franklin's crews there, and, surprisingly enough, a large mass of crumpled metal which must have been deeply covered by snowdrifts to have escaped the notice of earlier searchers. The relic was about three feet across and was "obviously the remains of a water tank from one of the life boats."[20] No other physical evidence has been obtained from this most significant place.

After finding this tent full of dead men at Toonoonee, Teekeeta and his companions followed in Aglooka's footsteps eastward along the south coast of King William Island. We do not know what remains were found by them between Terror Bay and Todd Islet, since all tales of this time were told to Hall secondhand by In-nook-poo-zhe-jook, Nu-ker-zhoo (Jack), Tukpeetoo, and his wife Eveeshuk. By their own admission, none of these individuals had been members of Teekeeta's party at the time. Although Hall did interview Teekeeta and Ow-wer, both before and after his expedition from Inglis Bay to King William Island (8–16 May 1869), according to his fieldnotes he inexplicably failed to question them about any remains except those found at Terror Bay. Nevertheless the details of at least part of the summer search had been passed on to In-nook-poo-zhe-jook.

On 12 May 1869, Hall's party had searched for graves of two white men at a place which the Inuit called "Set-tu-me-nin." Hall, very confused in his geography, described this site as "east side of the mouth of the Peffer River." Yet, as he makes it clear that this location was "in sight" of Todd Islet, and it is certain that he never proceeded west of modern James Ross Point, his "Peffer River" could not have been the stream now known by that name.

These remains had been found by a man named Nee-wik-kee-i (Nourse = "Nee-wik-tee-too"), who was now (1869) dead. This is the only mention of this individual, but as his widow was "the woman with the shaking head" (Ad-lark), Nee-wik-kee-i was evidently Tee-kee-ta's father. The graves here had been constructed by a disciplined party.

The bodies buried by placing stones around & over them – the remains facing upward & the hands had been folded in a very precise manner across the breasts of both. Clothes all on & flesh all on the bones. On back of each a suspended knife found. The bodies perfect when found but the Innuits having left the remains unburied after unearthing them, the foxes have eaten most sinews all off the bones. A tenting place (for the) whites close by where these 2 men were buried. Many needles & one nail found by the Innuits at this tenting place.[21]

Hall's guides led him to this place and, relying totally on descriptions of it which had been handed down, managed to uncover one complete skeleton under the deep snow. The other, described as being buried only ten feet away from the first, could not be found. A cairn was also erected here to mark the graves of the white men. The one complete skeleton was taken by Hall to the United States and eventually returned to England, where it created a minor sensation.

The skeleton was brought to America about 4 years ago by Mr. Hall ... He gave it to a gentleman in N. York, who last year (1872) presented it to Admiral Inglefield, by whom it was brought to England. The remains were examined & described by Professor Huxley, & the result has been all but certain identification with Mr Le Vesconte, on account of the height, the very prominent nose, & massive lower jaw, which were all remarkable characteristics of Mr. Le Vesconte. The peculiarities too of the teeth, (one of which was stopped in gold) are also identified by his family, who have, I believe, no doubt on the question. The skeleton has been placed in an oak coffin and buried [in the Painted Hall] at Greenwich.[22]

If this skeleton actually was that of Le Vesconte, and there is no reason to doubt the identification, then he must be considered a likely candidate for Aglooka. As one of the senior Lieutenants of the *Erebus* (he had been Fitzjames's second in command in HMS *Clio*), he would be quite likely to succeed to the command of a detached party. Yet we are faced with Teekeeta's direct statement, which he was eminently qualified to make, that Aglooka's body had not been found. If this is true, then Aglooka must have been a very senior officer indeed to have outranked Le Vesconte.

After leaving Set-tu-me-nin, Teekeeta's party also discovered a white man's grave on a point called "Kun-ne-ar-be-ar-nu" (of various spellings), which has usually been identified as modern Booth Point. Hall's detailed description leaves no doubt that Kun-ne-ar-be-ar-nu was actually the unnamed spit directly west of this. Hall visited this site as well, but as it was deeply covered with snow nothing could be found. A second memorial cairn was erected here as a tribute to the dead.

Either Tet-kee-ta or his father 1st found this grave. The grave & remains same perfect methodical state when found as the 2 at mouth of Peffer River. This grave on KWL about due N of Kee-u-na. The body dug up & left unburied by the Innuits. This white man very large & tall & by the state of gums of lower teeth in terrible sick (bad) state as In-nook-poo-zhe-jook described. He said that one man, a large tall man, was seen by Ow-wer & the other Innuits when they met Ag-loo-ka & the man presented a terrible sight about his lower gums & from the observation made at the grave of the one white man, the Innuits concluded he must be the same man.[23]

Beattie found the bones of one man here in 1981.[24] These bones indicated a young (early twenties) robustly built man approximately 5′5″ in height, giving some indication of the Inuit conception of "tall." While bone analysis revealed severe scurvy, it also showed that the "skull was forcibly broken" and some possible cut marks were found on the right femur which Beattie considered consistent with the Inuit stories of cannibalism, although admitting that "better quality evidence is needed before this issue can be discussed thoroughly."[25]

Gilder noted that the graves of Franklin's men found on the King William Island coast evinced "a most touching indication of their devotion to each other,"[26] and this is supported by the Inuit tales of carefully interred men with unmutilated bodies and crossed arms. As their description of the grave found here at Kun-ne-ar-be-ar-nu indicates that it was in a "perfect methodical state" and fails to note any sign of cannibalism among Aglooka's men east of Terror Bay, some other explanation of Beattie's anomalous evidence (an earlier wound or crude surgery?) is needed.

The Inuit identification of this man as one of the Washington Bay marchers, based on a description which would apply to any scurvy sufferer, may appear questionable. Yet Hall learned that a telescope was found here by Teekeeta's mother, and the fact that one was seen by Teekeeta's party in Washington Bay, and that such an instrument was definitely the property of an officer, leads to the strong suspicion that another officer was buried here.

At least one writer suggested this might have been Crozier himself,[27] although this has since been disproven by the determination by Beattie of this man's youth.

Too-shoo-art-thariu reportedly told Koong-e-ou-e-lik (who told Hall) that the remains on King William Island were found "only a few days" after the meeting with Aglooka and his men at Teekeenu.[28] This tradition, like much of the hearsay attributed to Too-shoo-art-thariu, is again contradicted by the other witnesses. Ahlangyah gave a detailed description of the Inuit party's movements, and Teekeeta specifically stated that he found these remains at Set-tu-me-nin and Kun-ne-ar-be-ar-nu "soon after he and his brother and another man had found the big tent near Too-noo-nee, that is the next summer after seeing Aglooka & men."[29] At the same time another native party was making discoveries. According to Eveeshuk, it was during this season that the white men's bodies at Keeuna, and the boat (supposed to have been found at Starvation Cove), were found by the hunter Pooyetta.

Teekeeta confirmed that "he was with Poo-yet-ta when they together found the graves of the 2 men at Set-tu-me-nin & the one grave at Kun-ne-an-be-ar-nu" but that "he was not with Poo-yet-ta when he found the 5 dead whites on Kee-u-na."[30] The last statement implies that Pooyetta and Teekeeta were in different searching parties which met in the vicinity of Keeuna. We turn our attention there.

Keeuna

Much has been written about the native hunter Pooyetta, alleged discoverer of the remains of white men at Starvation Cove and Keeuna (Todd Islet). He was held in high esteem by his Inuit acquaintances, and the story of his discovery of the white men's remains was well known. Yet we shall see that some traditions concerning him are open to revision, and some of what has been published about him is demonstrably wrong.

To eliminate outright error immediately, it should be noted that Hall's editor, Nourse, indicates in various places (pages 400–1 among others) that Pooyetta accompanied Hall to Keeuna and personally told him of the finds there. Hall's notes clearly indicate that he never met Pooyetta (not surprisingly, since he was dead), and that all of the stories concerning him were relayed by others.[1]

It will be remembered that Mangaq's son Iggiararjuk mentioned that "Panatoq" was one of the natives in Teekeeta's party at Washington Bay. Yet we have identified all of Teekeeta's original "four families" (Teekeeta, Ow-wer, Too-shoo-art-thariu, and Mangaq), and Ahlangyah confirmed that these people remained together over the winter. Another "family," provided by Teekeeta's parents Nee-wik-kee-i and Ad-lark and his brother Tenne-a, presumably joined the later searching party at the winter encampment near Matty Island. But there is no mention of Pooyetta/Panatoq in Teekeeta's testimony until the graves found north of Keeuna are mentioned.

For his part, Pooyetta also found the remains of Aglooka's men the summer after Teekeeta's meeting with them. He found the remains while "sealing with his family." This does not necessarily mean that his family was alone at the time; his wife Tooktoocheer later told Gilder that she found the remains of the whites when in company with her husband and son and "seven other In-nuits."[2]

According to Teekeeta, he and Pooyetta found some, but not all, of the remains of Aglooka's men while travelling together. The implication of his testimony is that he met Pooyetta's group at or near Keeuna (Todd Islet). Iggiararjuk correctly remembered Pooyetta as part of his father's party; he just got the year wrong.

If two separate Inuit parties wished to meet, Keeuna was a perfect rendezvous. Hall was told that hunting parties from Boothia and the Adelaide Peninsula often used to gather at Ok-e-jik-too, "the eastern Islet of Todds Isles," to "go sealing together for a while and have a grand good time."[3] Indeed, it was near that islet that Hall encountered four families of Inuit (including Eveeshuk and Seeuteetuar) camped on the ice and sealing in 1869.

Eveeshuk and her husband Tukpeetoo accompanied Hall from this encampment to Keeuna and she told him what had been found there.

Did you ever see anything of the men who died on this Island?

Ans. She has seen 5 skulls of the white men who died a long time ago here.

Did you see Too-loo-ark?

Ans. Saw the bodies of 4 men in one place on the Island & Too-loo-ark's a little way from the 4. When she 1st saw them flesh & clothing all on the bones, the bodies entire & after making tupik [tent] near the dogs devoured much of the flesh of the Kob-lu-nas (whites). It was sometime after this that she saw the 5 skulls she 1st spoke of as having seen. She saw these bodies one winter after Poo-yet-a found them. The clothes these men had on were black.[4]

In-nook-poo-zhe-jook supplied other details.

The remains were not buried but were found lying down on the high part of the island all close together & each fully dressed – flesh all on the bones & unmutilated by any animals. Next to Too-loo-a's body was one preserved meat can same as the one I [Hall] had upon the fire-(rest) thawing contents. (This of mine a 2 lb canister of preserved beef). This can found by Poo-yet-ta beside the body of Too-loo-a, unopened. The can was opened by Innuits & found to contain meat & much tood-noo [fat] with it. No bad smell to it. The contents eaten by the Innuits – the meat & fat very sweet & good. A jack-knife found in the pocket of one of the 5 men.[5]

In both Eveeshuk's and In-nook-poo-zhe-jook's testimony one of the dead men is identified as Toolooark/Toolooa, the older of the white leaders met in Washington Bay. Hall remarked in his notes that "Too-loo-a is the name given to Capt. John Ross by the natives of Neitchille & they all believe he was of the 'Forlorn Hope' [i.e.: Aglooka's] Company."[6] He questioned Eveeshuk as to why she believed that John Ross (who actually died peacefully in London in 1856) had died on Keeuna and learned that she "had heard her father tell all about Too-loo-ark, how he looked when at Ent-ev-waten-wiq (near Neitchille) & this one looked as described to her."[7] Surely Eveeshuk must have had more reason to believe it was Ross than that!

We cannot know whether Pooyetta specifically stated to Hall's informants that he had found the remains of "John Ross," or simply stated that one of the skeletons was that of a white man who had the same Inuit appellation – "Toolooa." If Pooyetta mentioned Ross's name, the body found on Keeuna would have, as Eveeshuk said, to have closely resembled him in appearance for Pooyetta to think he "recognized" his old employer. This has always struck me as being very unlikely.

The resemblance must have been uncanny, for Pooyetta had a perfect opportunity to examine the unmutilated remains closely. He also would have to make allowances for aging, for it bears remembering that when the remains on Keeuna were found John Ross was in his seventies. Although Ross was still active (in fact he had taken the yacht *Mary* to Beechey Island in search of Franklin in 1850), it would be difficult for someone to recognize him from a short acquaintance of a few days twenty years in the past – even for an observant Inuit.

Pooyetta's identification of one of the remains on the island as "Toolooa" does not require all of these assumptions. Pooyetta met Teekeeta shortly after finding the body and Teekeeta, upon visiting the spot, recognized the white man who had introduced himself as "Toolooa" the season before. According to Ow-wer, "Toolooa," the senior leader of the detachment in Washington Bay, had gray hair. Eveeshuk confirmed that the Keeuna "Too-looark" had hair that was "Kay-uk (that is gray)."[8]

Finally, Teekeeta confirmed that the man who died on Keeuna was the "Toolooa" he had seen, for "his skull [was] seen there of late years with gray hair & whiskers adhering to the skull."[9] Surely this is a much easier solution to the identification of this poor man than that Pooyetta had misidentified him as John Ross!

It is repeatedly pointed out in Hall's notes that Pooyetta was the same native of that name who had guided James Clark Ross in 1830. His identification of the body of John Ross on Keeuna is seen by Cyriax as a "curious circumstance." Yet "Pooyetta" is a common Inuit name and there is no real evidence beyond Hall's bald statement to that effect that they were the same man. Ross's Pooyetta did make a casual remark that he had relatives who lived at "O-wutta," the small islet near Matty Island near where Teekeeta and his friends had spent the winter, so it is possible that he had relocated to King William Island between 1830 and 1869, but proof is lacking.

Pooyetta's discovery of a Washington Bay marcher on Keeuna confirms that at least some of Aglooka's men followed the south coast of King William Island in Teekeeta's wake. This was also implied by the remains of the "very tall" man found at Kun-ne-ar-be-ar-nu, identified by the Inuit as one of Aglooka's party. The question arises – why?

If these men were headed for the Great Fish River, as Crozier had written in his 1848 note, they should have crossed over to the continent forty miles west of Keeuna. Here, near Eta Island, Simpson Strait is at its narrowest point – a mere two miles wide. One commentator noted that it was "quite evident" that Aglooka's men must have been "topographically confused" to have missed this obvious crossing point.[10]

This "topographical confusion" is hard to understand. Simpson had charted this strait in 1839, and Aglooka's party should have known from their charts that, from this point on, the mainland receded into the distance. Even if they did not know that this was the best crossing point, they must have realized that they were in a race with the ice, which was, by all accounts, already breaking up. Why didn't they cross?

Some of them may have. A splinter party may have broken off, as the Inuit said, and proceeded toward the mouth of the Great Fish River on their own. This group would then be responsible for the remains found during this century at Thunder Cove. They may even have supplied the bodies at Starvation Cove.

Yet the well-constructed graves found along the south coast of King William Island attest to a disciplined party. The body of Le Vesconte would indicate that senior officers were still in charge. Perhaps the crossing at Eta was simply missed in the dense summer fog attested to by Hall and others.[11]

The fact that Aglooka's party followed in the footsteps of their Inuit acquaintances may mean no more than that they tried to overtake them, or that they hoped their trail would lead to more Inuit who could offer assistance. Yet it is curious that Aglooka did not tell Teekeeta that he was heading for the Great Fish River. He did not even use a generic term like "home," or vaguely wave his arm to the southward. He was very specific. Aglooka was going to "Iwillik."

Iwillik is Repulse Bay, Rae's outpost of 1846–7 and 1854. More to the point for Franklin's men, it was a known place of resort for the Inuit. From here the white men could travel north to Parry's Winter Island and Igloolik and enlist the aid of the many Inuit there to eventually reach the whalers at Pond Inlet on Baffin Island. Alternatively, they could turn to the south in hopes of reaching the Hudson's Bay Company post at Churchill on Hudson Bay. Although, as it would turn out, both of these escape routes were much too ambitious for Aglooka's weakened men, they made eminent sense.

If no pre-abandonment party had been sent to chart the east coast of King William Island, Franklin's men may still have hoped that it was connected to Boothia "island" and that Simpson's eastward-trending strait would lead to Prince Regent Inlet and known territory. It must be remembered that this small "corner" of the Arctic south of "Poctes Bay" was still unknown in 1845 when Franklin sailed, and the shorelines here were shown as dotted lines on his charts.

We can only speculate as to why Aglooka felt compelled to stay on King William Island. The remains of his men confirm that this is what he did.

In the summer of 1931, William Gibson, a King William Island resident and part-time searcher for Franklin relics, was commissioned to search the southern coast from Gjoa Haven to Cape Herschel and to bury any remains which he could find.

Armed with the details of his predecessors, and accompanied by native guides, Gibson conducted a very thorough search. The results of his journey added more detail, and raised new questions, about the final days of Aglooka's men.

The Todd Islands are five in number: three are very small and nothing more than well-defined reefs. The two largest are about equal in size; one adjacent to the King William Island coast, the other the most southerly in the group and about 2 miles offshore. Their area would be approximately 1/2 square mile.

We began a systematic search of the islands in quest of the remains reported by the Eskimo. Hall reported finding one skeleton, which presumably he interred, and also the fact that the Eskimo had informed him that there were five skeletons in all on the islands. The first island we examined was that adjacent to the coast; presently we discovered two skulls embedded in the sand among a ridge of boulders which formed the crown of the island. By scraping in the sand over a small area a large proportion of the other remains were found. Apparently no burial had ever taken place, nor was there any cairn or other mark erected. Nothing further was found except dark disintegrated shreds mixed with the moist sand, which were believed to be traces of the navy cloth ... [12]

The remains of the two individuals found here are generally thought to be those of some of the five men described to Hall. They are not. Hall clearly describes the two major islets of the Todd group – Keeuna, "the western Isle of Todds Islets" two miles offshore, directly south of and in line with a long low point (Kun-ne-ar-be-ar-nu) and "Kookar." Kookar lies a few miles east of Keeuna, so close to King William Island itself that Hall thought it was a headland, and is separated by a narrow channel, about half a mile wide, from another islet called "Now-yarn."

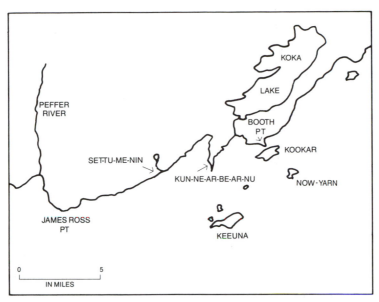

Map 4   Keeuna

Kookar, not Keeuna, is the islet that is truly south of modern Booth Point, and, as is evident from Gibson's description of it as "adjacent to the coast," it was here that he first found the two skulls. Hall, en route to Keeuna, passed between Kookar and Nowyarn and was told by In-nook-poo-zhe-jook that "at Koo-kar is the grave of one of Franklin's men & of course we shall by & by *D.V.* [God Willing] visit it," yet his notes indicate that he never did so. [13]

As two skulls were found by Gibson, it is obvious that In-nook-poo-zhe-jook was incorrect in saying that only one man had died at Kookar. When Hall did visit the grave of a single white man on the shores of King William Island, at the low point which the natives called Kun-ne-ar-be-ar-nu, he confusingly implied that Kun-ne-ar-be-ar-nu was Booth Point. This geographical inexactitude was to have later consequences.

Although In-nook-poo-zhe-jook was mistaken about the number of men who died on Kookar, we once again marvel at the accuracy of the detail in his testimony. It should be remembered that In-nook-poo-zhe-jook had not personally seen any of these remains but was operating entirely on the collected traditions of his people, yet he knew that the bodies were found "lying down on the high part of the island."[14] Since he also remarks that the bodies were found "all close together," In-nook-poo-zhe-jook's statement implied that more than one man died here, an internal inconsistency which neither he nor Hall identified. Gibson should not have been surprised to find the skulls of two men close together "on the crown of the island" sixty-two years later. It was just the wrong island.

That Hall was being told of finds on two distinct islets should have been obvious to him. Only hours before being told of the remains on the "high part," he had found a portion of a thigh bone on Keeuna, not at the "high part" but on the low flats extending to the west. He had been told of these remains by In-nook-poo-zhe-jook as well: In-nook-poo-zhe-jook said, in direct but unremarked contradiction of his earlier testimony, that "the skull of Too-loo-a & some of the other 4 men" had been found here "down on the flats." Here also he was correct.[15]

Hall was subsequently taken by Eveeshuk to the spot where, according to her, the Keeuna bodies had been found. This he described as the *eastern* end of Keeuna "within some 20 fathoms" of the shore (emphasis added).[16] This was probably a directional mistake in Hall's notes (his compass was useless, owing to the proximity of the Magnetic Pole), but could also be taken to mean that there were two distinct spots on Keeuna where bodies were found.

Either Gibson's Inuit guides were clearer in their descriptions than In-nook-poo-zhe-jook had been to Hall, or he himself distrusted the tradition that the white men were found "all close together" in one place. With characteristic thoroughness Gibson, having found the two skulls on Kookar, next moved on to search the second islet – Keeuna itself.

The smaller islands disclosed nothing of interest, and we had almost abandoned the other large one, the most southerly in the group, when we were attracted by a skull partially embedded in the sand of a low spit which ran out from the island to the westward. With the removal of a thin layer of sand an almost complete skeleton was revealed, extended in a natural position. The navy cloth was much better preserved here, and pieces could be picked up in the hand and the seams and lining of the material easily identified. The remains were apparently those of a very young man; the teeth of both jaws were intact and perfect to a remarkable degree. A short distance away one femur and some ribs and spine bones were found, evidently part of a second skeleton. We buried these also, and erected a small cairn as a mark over the grave.[17]

These were obviously the remains described to Hall "on the flats." Although they initially appeared contradictory, In-nook-poo-zhe-jook's descriptions of the various places where white men's remains were to be found had been remarkably correct. Gibson had confirmed this. Even so, Gibson himself, enslaved to the tradition that only five white men had been found in total, concluded that "four skeletons out of the five reported by the Eskimo to Hall were accounted for" on the two islets.[18]

In fact the five bodies reported to Hall had all been found by the Inuit on Keeuna; the two (or more) from Kookar, only one of which was known to In-nook-poo-zhe-jook, had never before been investigated.

The single body found by Hall at Kun-ne-ar-be-ar-nu, commonly thought to have been found at modern Booth Point, was actually found to the west of there. Adjacent to Booth Point is Kookar, where In-nook-poo-zhe-jook knew of one body (there were actually two), but which Hall never visited. The confusion in this case is quite understandable, and as the spots are in fact less than a mile apart the error in location is inconsequential. The same cannot be said of the similar confusion created by the two bodies found near the eastern mouth of a stream on the mainland – called by the Inuit Set-tu-me-nin and by Hall "Peffer River."

On 9 May 1869, while still to the east of Todd Islet, Hall had mistakenly identified a point on the King William Island shore as James Ross Point. He later realized his error when the "real" James Ross Point was seen from Keeuna. The next day he camped on the ice between King William Island and a small low islet called Ook-soo-too which he thought might be "the w. Islet of Todd's – if so, then Kee-u-na which we are bound for is an Islet not shown on the chart."[19] Again, he later learned that he had been wrong. Shortly after leaving this islet his party passed the "mouth of a small river (Peffer?) of KWLand." This stream, according to In-nook-poo-zhe-jook also called Ook-soo-too, was later also found not to be Peffer River.

Hall's geographical confusion can be partly explained by the fact that for much of his trip to the Todd Islets he blindly followed In-nook-poo-zhe-jook through impenetrable fog. This led In-nook-poo-zhe-jook to make at least one mistake himself (he mis-identified the high ground near Gjoa Haven as "Kookar" before arriving at the real place), but it is also apparent from Hall's notebooks that his grasp of the local geography was shaky. We have already seen that Hall was confused when he visited the King William Island shore "within sight" of Keeuna and visited the gravesite of Aglooka's men at the mouth of a stream called "Set-tu-me-nin." He still had not arrived at the mouth of the modern Peffer River, as he thought.[20]

This led to confusion when Schwatka and Gilder arrived on the scene, for they were told of a white man's cairn near the mouth of the "Peffer River," but were assured by Ebierbing and "Ishoowark" (In-nook-poo-zhe-jook?), who "both had accom-panied Hall on his last search," that they were certain that Hall had never visited this part of King William Island.[21] In this they were correct, for Hall never passed (modern) James Ross Point to visit (modern) Peffer River.

Schwatka and Gilder therefore became very excited to learn of a previously undiscovered cairn near a stream on King William Island. They were to be subsequently disappointed when the native Ahdlekok led them to this cairn, which they positively identified as Hall's. They do not mention having taken any ob-servations here to determine whether this cairn was actually at Peffer River, but they assumed that it was, and thus firmly en-trenched this misconception that Hall had actually proceeded further west than his notebooks indicate. True, the chart of their discoveries did show that Hall's cairn was definitely east of the river, between it and the Todd Islets, but the scale was such as to make the true location uncertain.

The next person to visit the site was Lieutenant Hansen of Amundsen's party. During a 1904 excursion from Gjoa Haven to Victoria Island, his small detachment visited "Point C.F. Hall" and found the skulls and bones of two white men. This was definitely Set-tu-me-nin, as Hansen found the stone which Hall had inscribed nearby.[22] Unfortunately, Hansen does not describe the location either, and his map of the excursion is also imprecise; although it implies that "Hall Point" is to the east of James Ross Point, it does not prove this to be so.

Hall himself may have had a later inkling that he had been incorrect in attributing these finds to the "Peffer River." Perhaps, at his leisure, he compared his field-notes with a chart. The site is unequivocally described in his notes (and by the Inuit) as having been on the eastern bank of a stream, yet Hall wrote to his patron Grinnell on 20 June 1869, after his return from King William Island, of "a camping place on the sea shore of K.W.L. about 3 miles Eastward of Peffer river where 2 men died & received Christian burial. At this place fish bones were found by the natives ... the next trace ... occurs some 5 or 6 miles further eastward, on a long low point of King William's Land where one man died & received a Christian burial: then, about SSE 2 1/2 miles distant from there the next trace occurs on Todd's Islet where the remains of 5 men lie."[23]

Here is a clear description of the various sites. It indicates that the remains Hall found at "Set-tu-me-nin" were located on the bank of a stream located roughly halfway between modern Peffer River and Booth Point. Now we can locate it.

After visiting (modern) Booth Point to search for the remains of the one man falsely reported by Hall to have been buried there (finding nothing), Gibson in 1931 "crossed to a low gravel beach separating the sea from a large freshwater lake."[24] This, echoing the name of the nearby islet, is now called "Koka Lake" and takes its name from a famous Inuit fishing spot nearby.[25] According to modern maps, this lake now empties into the ocean at this beach between Booth Point and "Kun-ne-ar-be-ar-nu," but the coast of King William Island is almost a foot higher now than it was in Franklin's day, and the drainage from the lake may have changed. In 1931 Gibson described the outlet as "some four miles to the west" of Booth Point. Here he found a "beautiful little stream, swollen to a freshet" which "tumbled down to the sea-ice."[26] This was probably the site of Set-tu-me-nin. The significance of this somewhat lengthy geographical digression will appear shortly.

Gibson, unaware of all this, continued his 1931 search of King William Island. He remained "on the look-out for traces of the graves in which Hall had interred three other members [two at Set-tu-me-nin and one at Kun-ne-ar-be-ar-nu] of the Franklin party between the Todd Islands and Piffer [sic] River,"[27] not knowing that he had already passed the spots he was seeking. He, of course, found nothing.

He next searched the banks of the modern Peffer River for remains which Hall had never seen. Amazingly enough, he found them anyway!

> On the left bank of the stream, at its entrance to the ocean, the remains of Lieutenant Le Vesconte, of HMS *Erebus*, were found by Hall in 1866 … We had an Eskimo report that another skeleton remained, and after some time spent in searching the high ground we were rewarded by the discovery, on the low beach about 3 yards from the juncture of ice and the shore, of one femur and several smaller bones. The femur was of unusual length. From the position in which these remains were found it is very probable the greater part of the skeleton was washed away by high tides.[28]

As at Keeuna, Gibson thought that he was merely confirming Hall's finds. Yet, if the preceding is true, he did not find one of the two remains "found by Hall in 1866" (actually Hall only found one of the two reported – in 1869) at Set-tu-me-nin but made an original discovery of remains of which Hall was unaware.

Gibson continued westward. Ten miles west of the Peffer River, in Douglas Bay, he had been told by the Inuit that further human remains would be found on a small islet, "although we did not know the exact location from the vague description of the Eskimo."[29] No white man, before 1931, had ever heard of these remains.

> On proceeding down the bay the following day we encountered further low-lying islets; about 2 miles from the head, and off the eastern shore, was the largest: it was approximately 500 yards long by 150 yards wide and rose to a central ridge of about 30 feet in height. On wading through the shore water and gaining the beach the first object which attracted our attention was a human skull lying above the high-water mark. On circling the island three more skulls and a large collection of human bones were found, while among the boulders on the elevation three further skulls and many bones were also located. There was no doubt in our minds that these remains were those of seven Europeans …[30]

An isolated grave had been found earlier by Schwatka and Gilder on Tullock Point, the western point of Douglas Bay, but no one had expected to find a large encampment between Washington Bay and Keeuna. Aglooka's men, as the Inuit descriptions indicated, were in a pitiful state. Gilder noted that the grave "had been made of small stones, while larger and more appropriate abounded in the vicinity, showing the reduced physical condition of the party at the time."[31] A hundred years later Beattie found only Inuit bones at Tullock Point[32] but, although some scattering and mixing of bones may have occurred, the description of the grave is undoubtedly that of a white man.

The remains found at Douglas Bay are much more significant than most historians indicate. Hall was unaware of them, either because his informants had not yet found them, or because the stories he heard about this place had been mistakenly attributed by him to another location. Presumably the human remains found here would have had many of the same features of similar finds at Terror Bay, Erebus Bay, and Starvation Cove.

And here lies the problem. Any site where the remains of dead white men were found would of necessity have many of the same features. Some of these sites are positively identified, owing to concrete geographical clues, or were pointed out on a chart, yet others are not. How can one differentiate between these places? One modern writer noted that "Starvation Cove has a great deal in common with [the camp at] Terror Bay"[33] but accepted that the similarities of the descriptions of these places were coincidental. Another idea, that these similarities are "echoes" of only one find which were mistakenly attributed to another, should be investigated.

The relatively minor geographical errors Hall made can be forgiven, as can his misleading information about the numbers and locations of the remains at Todd's Islets. He assumed the forty men in Aglooka's party had been reduced by ten members – 1 found by McClintock north of Gladman Point, + 2 at "Set-tu-me-nin," + 1 at "Kun-ne-ar-be-ar-nu," + 1 (reported) on Kookar, + 5 on Keeuna. The remainder presumably took their boat south to Starvation Cove and became Hall's "thirty bodies" on the continent.

Even if we accept Hall's original count of Aglooka's party, we find that he had significantly underestimated the number of bodies found on the south shore of King William Island. At least ten more of Aglooka's men died on the march – 1 at Tullock Point + 7 in Douglas Bay + 1 at "real" Peffer River + 1 more, found by Gibson, on Kookar. These extra bodies would have reduced Aglooka's forty men by half by the time they left Keeuna. As eight more men died near, but not at Starvation Cove (see table 2), this would leave twelve survivors, consistent with Schwatka's estimate of "six to ten" bodies at Starvation Cove, but at odds with Hall's figure of "thirty."

Such mathematical gymnastics do not prove that the bodies found at Starvation Cove were Aglooka's men; indeed, for reasons that will appear shortly, I doubt whether this was the case. What they do show is that Hall greatly overestimated the number of men who reached Starvation Cove, and that his "thirty bodies" were found elsewhere – probably at Terror Bay.

Table 2
Disposition of Aglooka's Men

Hall's Count		
Seen at Washington Bay	40	(estimate)
Gladman Point straggler	− 1	(McClintock)
Set-tu-me-nin	− 2	
Kun-ne-ar-be-ar-nu	− 1	
Kookar	− 1	
Keeuna	− 5	
	———	
Supposed to arrive Starvation C.	30	
Missed by Hall (King William Island)		
Tullock Point	− 1	(Schwatka)
Douglas Bay	− 7	(Gibson)
Peffer River (modern)	− 1	(Gibson)
Kookar	− 1	(1 reported above, 2 skulls found)
	———	
Left Keeuna (revised)	20	
Found Near Starvation Cove		
On small islet to NW	− 7	(Learmonth, Neniook testimony)
5 miles inland	− 1	(Gilder)
	———	
Remaining men	12	
Qavdlunarsiorfik	− ?	(Rasmussen, may = Starvation C.)
	———	
	6–10	bodies reported to Schwatka (Gilder: "about five")

Note: The above does not prove that Aglooka's men died at Starvation Cove, but does show that Schwatka's estimate of the number of bodies found there was more accurate than Hall's.

More significant than the number of Aglooka's detachment who died on the south coast of King William Island is the spacing and location of their graves. Only one skeleton, that of the "steward" (mistakenly identified as Peglar), was found on the thirty miles of shore between Washington Bay and Tullock Point. This man was unburied and the details of his discovery make it apparent that he was a solitary straggler who had wandered away from the main party. As his body was undiscovered for at least a decade, it is possible that he had become lost in one of the sudden summer blizzards common to King William Island and his remains hidden in a drift both from his searching friends and the Inuit.

At Tullock Point the story changes. Here at least one man was carefully buried under small stones. A mere three and a half miles further at least seven died at the campsite in Douglas Bay. Because of their late discovery we do not know if they were buried, but as their comrades both before and after were so treated we can reasonably expect that they were.

Ten miles further another camp was established at the Peffer River, and at least one more man died. A further five miles and two men died and were buried at the campsite at Set-tu-me-nin. A mile and a half eastward is Kun-ne-ar-be-ar-nu where the man in a "terrible state" was buried. Another mile to Kookar, two more casualties and the last burial. Two miles south of Kun-ne-ar-be-ar-nu is Keeuna, where the last five men lay unburied on the western spit. The camps are closer together, the men dying at an increasing rate.

The party was also losing its leaders. Le Vesconte died at Set-tu-me-nin. The body at Kun-ne-ar-be-ar-nu, found with a telescope, was also probably that of an officer. And the senior officer, Toolooa, was found on Keeuna, a short distance from the bodies of four of his men. The fact that he was unburied tells a tale in itself. In light of the care taken with the others only a few miles away, it seems unlikely that any survivors would have abandoned their commander on the snow and callously taken their departure by boat to Starvation Cove. It is much more probable that the men on Keeuna were themselves the last survivors.

We have seen that there is no physical evidence that specifically supports the Inuit view that Aglooka and his remaining men crossed over from Keeuna to Starvation Cove. Yet the undeniable presence of the boat there is a powerful argument. Aglooka's men were dragging a heavy boat on a sledge. We have found many of their bodies on the south coast of King William Island but, until now, no trace of their boat. The "standard reconstruction" explains this by asserting that Aglooka's boat was found at Starvation Cove. There are other possibilities. Aglooka's boat may have drifted or been taken to some other location on the mainland (Qavdlunarsiorfik), or he might have left it on the King William Island shore. Gibson continues:

On a close examination for any relics remaining [on the islet in Douglas Bay] we were rewarded by the discovery of several small pieces of oak and numerous shavings of oak, and what we believed to be Norwegian pine, were also picked up, and one of these contained nail holes.

The Eskimo of the present day speak decidedly of a boat which was discovered, broken up, and used by the people after the Franklin disaster. This was said to have been found on the Todd Islands, though some disagreed with this location as the place of the find. No wood or shavings were found on the Todd Islands, and it is probable that we had here in Douglas Bay evidence of the breaking up of a lifeboat, a number of which we know accompanied the retreat; on the other hand, an oak sled would have accounted for the remnants found, which were undoubtedly caused by the Eskimo fashioning the material to their own uses. [34]

Only in Douglas Bay and at Keeuna was there any evidence that more than two members of Aglooka's party died at one camp. The remains of "seven Europeans" found in Douglas Bay by Gibson indicate, as he remarked, that "this island marked a halt in the march of the retreating crews, and was the site of one of their camps: a camp from which many never rose to pursue the terrible march."[35] It is not unreasonable to suspect that both Aglooka's boat and sledge were left here and that the last few men stumbled on to the east, finally succumbing on Keeuna.

If the traditions concerning Starvation Cove are actually a mixture of real elements and transplanted details from Toonoonee (where many bodies were definitely found), then we should be able to trace how the confusion came about. Most of the details concerning the "boat place" were told to Schwatka and Gilder by Pooyetta's wife Tooktoocheer and her son. They apparently did not specifically state where this "boat place" was, but Inuit tradition definitely ascribed the boat at Starvation Cove to Pooyetta.

If Pooyetta's boat was found elsewhere, then Eveeshuk, who actually saw pieces of the boat at Starvation Cove, must have been mistaken in stating that it was the same one that Pooyetta found. Teekeeta as well would need to be similarly misguided in asserting that this was the same boat he had seen in Washington Bay. Clearly we must re-examine the traditions concerning Pooyetta and his boat.

~13~

Pooyetta's Search

The provenance of the wood found by Gibson in Douglas Bay is uncertain. The chips and shavings which he found, almost a hundred years after Franklin's men had passed, could as easily have come from Aglooka's sledge as his boat. The "standard reconstruction" assumes this, locating Aglooka's boat at Starvation Cove, and there is strong evidence for this assumption in that the Inuit repeatedly remarked that they believed that this was so – Aglooka's boat was found by Pooyetta, and Pooyetta found his boat on the "continent." At least this is what Hall thought they said.

Teekeeta, who apparently never visited Starvation Cove, nevertheless told Hall that Aglooka's boat was found there by Pooyetta "the next year" after Teekeeta's encounter with Aglooka. We do not have Teekeeta's exact words to this effect, but we do have Hall's account of what he heard. In a letter to Henry Grinnell, Hall remarked that the "next certain trace" of the party which perished on Keeuna "is on the West side of the Inlet west side of Point Richardson on some low land that is an island or part of the main just as the tide is low or high."[1]

This is an interesting statement. It is at best ambiguous. It is obvious that the description relayed to Hall of the boat place had elements both of "main" (mainland) and "island." As Eveeshuk had earlier told that the boat which she found was near a little islet in Starvation Cove, itself part of the "mainland" of North America, Hall invoked the somewhat forced explanation about the tides. Unfortunately, his supporting statement that "the tide is high on the west side of inlet of [sic] Point Richardson" appears to be false, for in fact there is only a slight tidal range in the waters of this area.[2]

Hall can be easily forgiven for assuming that the boat place "on the main land" was actually at Starvation Cove, for we must keep in mind the circumstances under which he learned of it. In May 1869 he had interviewed Teekeeta and Ow-wer, who told of the encounter at Teekeenu in Washington Bay. They also mentioned that Aglooka's boat had been found the next season by Pooyetta. Later that month, Hall camped with several Inuit families on Todd Islet, including Eveeshuk and In-nook-poo-zhe-jook, looking for the remains of white men. In-nook-poo-zhe-jook told him of the tent place at Toonoonee, while Eveeshuk told of the boat which she had found on Adelaide Peninsula, originally found "by Pooyetta" the season after the Washington Bay encounter.

Hall quite naturally saw these stories as a connected series of events, the Teekeenu marchers being survivors of the large camp at Toonoonee who had eventually succumbed to their weakness at Starvation Cove. The capstone of this reconstruction seemed to be the Inuit assertion that the same boat seen by Teekeeta in Washington Bay was found by Pooyetta on the "mainland."

But where was the Inuit "mainland/island" combination? Although in English "mainland" and "continent" are synonyms, the same was not true to the Inuit, who had less definite ideas about geography. It is interesting to note that Hall's editor, Nourse, remarks that "the next day Hall crossed over to the mainland" from Todd Islet to search for remains "near the mouth of the Peffer River."[3] Here he uses the term "mainland" to refer to King William Island, the "main island" which was large enough to warrant such a description. Is this a clue?

Hall's idea that many men died at Starvation Cove was probably largely due to the information which had been given, at second hand, to Rae. Rae believed that the Inuit "found a number of white men, at least 40 ... scattered about dead, close to the water's edge, on a low, flat part of the coast, which I believe to have been in the neighbourhood of Point Ogle, as the native description agreed very closely with that of Sir George B[ack]."[4] In the light of hindsight we can see that, although this testimony was remarkably accurate, either In-nook-poo-zhe-jook or Rae had misinterpreted it: we have already seen that the most likely location of the "thirty bodies" was the large camp in Terror Bay.

Rae had been told that "the corpses of some thirty persons and some graves were discovered on the continent, and five dead bodies on an island near it, about a long day's journey to the north-west of the mouth of a large stream, which can be no other that Back's Great Fish River."[5] Reading "continent" as Adelaide Peninsula, many had assumed that the "island near it" where five dead bodies were found must be Montreal Island. Yet Hall himself, while camped on Keeuna and learning of the five men who had died there, could see the error in this. He wrote, "how mistaken the ideas in the civilized world of *Montreal* Island being the one on wh. *the 5* men of Franklin's Expedition died" (emphasis in original).[6]

Rae's informant went on to tell of the remains of one man seen "on the island" who had a telescope strapped over his shoulders – an obvious reference to the man found at Kun-ne-ar-be-ar-nu north of Keeuna. Indeed the reference to the place where the "thirty bodies" was found as a long day's journey north-west of the mouth of the Great Fish River is a tolerable pointer to Toon-oonee; it is certainly incompatible with Starvation Cove, which was only a few miles from the river and could be visited in a matter of hours.

The whole source of the confusion here is the Inuit word or phrase which Rae translated as "continent" and Hall translated as "mainland," but which actually referred to King William Island. In one case it led Hall to conclude wrongly that the bodies found at Terror Bay had been located at Starvation Cove. It could easily have led to confusion of two "boat places" as well.

The Inuit tradition that a boat was found on Keeuna is interesting. No evidence of such a find has reached us, and it seems inconceivable that Pooyetta, Teekeeta, and company could have missed a boat had one been left here. What we have here is a probable linkage of stories of Pooyetta finding a boat "on an island" with the recollection that he also found bodies on Keeuna. In many ways Keeuna (islet) and King William Island (mainland) more closely matches the Inuit description of an "island near the

mainland" than does the unnamed islet in the inlet west of Richardson Point. Reducing the Inuit statement about Pooyetta's boat
to its barest element of "island"/"west"/"inlet"/"mainland" seems
to remove any evidentiary value from it; there are very many
places in the Franklin area where these elements can be made to
fit. We require some further clue.

In only one place does Teekeeta name the locale where Pooyetta's boat was found. Hall noted in passing that "Ow-wer and
Tut-ke-ta say that the boat that was found by Poo-yet-ta and his
party near Kiny-nuk-shane (Richardson Point) on the west side
of the inlet that is on the west side of said Point was the same
boat that Aglooka & party had when they met them."[7] This ill-
constructed sentence could easily be read as Teekeeta's statement
"the boat that was found by Poo-yet-ta and his party near Kiny-
nuk-shane ... was the same boat that Aglooka & party had when
they met them" and Hall's explanatory insertion "Kiny-nuk-
shane (Richardson Point) on the west side of the inlet that is on
the west side of said Point."

Hall assumed that Richardson Point was called "Kiny-nuk-
shane." It was not. In all Inuit stories Richardson Point appears
as "Nuvertaro" (Hall: Noo-oo-tee-now; Gibson: Nu-oo-tar-ro;
Rasmussen: nuvertaroq), which means "the narrow point" and
is an apt description. As far as I have been able to determine,
there are no locations on Adelaide Peninsula with an Inuit name
even remotely like Kinynukshane. There are, in fact, only two
similarly named places in the whole Franklin area, and one of
them, "Kanerlukjuaq," is "the big fjord" – Douglas Bay.[8]

Gibson found the bodies in Douglas Bay on a small islet. Ow-
wer and Teekeeta apparently never visited Starvation Cove or
saw the boat there. They also fail to mention either finding a boat
at Douglas Bay or Keeuna, or having been told of one by Pooyetta
while he accompanied their party. The implication is that Pooyetta found his boat after his meeting with them on Todd Islet
and that they learned of it at a subsequent meeting. How then
did they come to identify Pooyetta's boat place with Starvation
Cove? Immediately after their mention of Kiny-nuk-shane they
give the standard Inuit reasoning for thinking so.

It is sure, say Ow-wer and Tut-keta, that Aglooka did not pass further
eastward that Kee-u-na (Todd's Island) & Kun-nee-an-be-ar-u ... for the

party of four (4) Innuit families had made deposits of seal meat & blubber at various places near the shore of King W. Land, commencing at or near Ok-Bar (Matheson Isle of Rae) & thence along the south shore of said KWL as the families moved from time to time, and none of these deposits had been found & disturbed by Aglooka (Crozier) & party. Therefore, it was concluded Aglooka and his people had crossed over from Kee-u-na to the place where the boat was found.[9]

It is hard to follow this line of reasoning. Untouched caches of meat along the south shore of King William Island to the west of Ok-Bar (Mount Matheson) would prove that Aglooka's party were either excessively honest or unobservant, but little else. Only if the caches had been untouched to the *north-east* of Ok-Bar would this serve as evidence that Aglooka's party had not travelled beyond Keeuna. Even so, this would not necessarily imply that they had crossed to the continent – perhaps the last man died on the western spit of Keeuna itself, perhaps they manned the boat and went somewhere else. If this evidence was the basis of the belief held by the Inuit that Aglooka's boat was found at Starvation Cove, it is very flimsy indeed.

Pooyetta's widow, Tooktoocheer, could have confirmed where the boat initially discovered by her husband was found. Klutschak's record of her testimony records her exact words in describing the location "near the beach in a small inlet," but it is left for a later commentator to conclude that this inlet was Starvation Cove. The description could easily refer to Douglas Bay – the inlet that is west of the island of Keeuna (where the five bodies were found), rather than the inlet that is west of Montreal Island (where the five bodies were *thought* to have been found). Gibson remarked that most of the remains here were found "close to the high water mark."[10]

Schwatka described Pooyetta's widow as "decrepit and wrinkled with age," but admitted that "her memory seemed to have survived the general wreck with the least impairment." He told that she related a tale of "a central place, or last resting place, in which the vital records of the Franklin Expedition had been placed by the last survivors,"[11] but he offered no opinion as to where that place actually was.

What Tooktoocheer actually said was both ambiguous and interesting. She spoke of "six skeletons on the main-land and two on the island. This she pointed out on the southern coast near ninety-five degrees west longitude."[12] Here she is undoubtedly speaking of Keeuna and the "main-land" of King William Island. But her story abruptly changes locale. In the next sentence but one she remarks "this was when she was at the boat place west of Richardson Point. In fact, she seemed to have the two places somewhat mixed up in her mind."[13]

Certainly someone had these two places "mixed up," but whether it was Tooktoocheer or the white men has yet to be shown. Hall apparently could not make entire sense of the stories which he had been told about Pooyetta's boat either, for he wrote that "there is something mysterious connected with the history of this boat & the many dead men found in it that needs to be solved."[14]

Tooktoocheer's testimony was so confusing that her son, Ogzeuckjewock, who had been a mere lad at the time, was interviewed in preference. According to Schwatka, "he gave a concise report, speaking with no hesitation ... There were ten in the party of Eskimos and they were the first (as they afterward learned) to come upon the scene."[15] Ogzeuckjeuwock's memories of this boat place were detailed. One of the most dramatic of these was the fact that he had been injured there when he and a friend caused an explosion!

The Boat on the w side of the Inlet that is w. side of Pt. Richardson found same season ... A keg of powder found at the Boat & much of its contents emptied on the ground, a gun or 2 found there. The nature and use of these things not known to Innuits till they saw Dr. Rae in 1854 at Pelly Bay. Poo-yet-ta had seen guns of Ag-loo-ka at Neitchille but didn't know the nature of the black sand stuff (powder). An igloo was blown to atoms by a little son of Poo-yet-ta & another lad who were afterward playing with the powder canister having some of the black stuff in it. They dropped some fire into the canister through the vent or opening – their faces awfully burned & blackened with the explosion – no one killed – Igloo completely demolished.[16]

Once again we cannot know whether the description of the site as "the w side of the Inlet that is w. side of Pt. Richardson" was expressly stated in Ogzeuckjeuwock's testimony or was a later explanatory insertion. An interesting feature of this story is its context. Immediately preceding it, the Inuit are talking about the remains found at Keeuna. Immediately following it, they talk about the remains found at Set-tu-me-nin and Kun-ne-ar-be-ar-nu. The "jump" across Simpson Strait from the south shore of King William Island to Richardson Point is suspicious.

The most dominant theme of Ogzeuckjeuwock's tale was his evidence of cannibalism. If the Inuit assertion that the boat at Starvation Cove was Aglooka's is correct, and if Ogzeuckjeuwock is describing this boat, then the party which carefully buried the remains of their comrades at Tullock Point, Peffer River, Set-tu-me-nin, and Kun-ne-ar-be-ar-nu, and left the unmutilated bodies of others of their comrades on Keeuna, finally lost all discipline and restraint at Starvation Cove. This is not impossible; it actually happened at Toonoonee. And it actually happened at another "boat place."

In-nook-poo-zhe-jook accompanied Hall to King William Island in 1869. Like Rae, Hall found In-nook-poo-zhe-jook to be a very intelligent man, "very finicky to tell all the facts."[17] In-nook-poo-zhe-jook told Hall that he had searched King William Island after McClintock's visit and that during this investigation he visited the "tent place" found by Teekeeta and his party. However, unlike Teekeeta, In-nook-poo-zhe-jook realized that the white men had left things all along the west coast of the island, and he continued his search to the northward.

On showing In-nook-poo-zhe-jook the large Admiralty chart, he pointed out the place of this big tent wh. is at or near the head of Terror Bay. He says that when he & party had visited this tenting place they followed the coast around to the northward & westward till they arrived at the Extreme w Point & then turned to the Eastward where they finally found the boat ... Farther on about 1/2 a mile ... they found the other boat ... To go from the aforesaid tenting place to the Boats following the coast line, *as Innuits travel*, it takes 2 to 2 1/2 days – but to cut across direct the distance can be made easily travelled in one day. The distance can be made by a smart walk throughout a long day by coast line from the tent place Head of Terror Bay, to the 2 Boats says In-k [In-nook-poo-zhe-jook]. (emphasis in original)[18]

In-nook-poo-zhe-jook found that "somebody had been to one of the Boats for everything are [sic] gone out of it."[19] Hall concluded that "somebody" must refer to Hobson and McClintock, who had found a boat nearby in 1859, and In-nook-poo-zhe-jook, who knew of their visit, did not contradict him. Yet the testimony makes it clear that In-nook-poo-zhe-jook did not know who had first found the boat, only that, as he said, "somebody" had.

In-nook-poo-zhe-jook said that he found "several skulls," a jack-knife, file, and small axe in the pillaged boat as well as five paddles, a roll of sheet lead, drag ropes, and some canvas. He also mentioned that after clearing the bottom of the pillaged boat of ice he found a dozen silver tablespoons and a quantity of manuscript papers (although Hall mysteriously noted in his margin that he found this "to be untrue by In-nook-poo-zhe-jook's own double statement").[20]

When Hall tried to match these items with what McClintock had left behind, he ran into some trouble.

With McClintock's list before me of things he left at the Boat I ask Did you see box with tools in it? No.
Any leather boots? No.
3 Small axes? No.
Broken saw? No.
Clothing? No.
Saw nothing more than what he has told me above! I tell Hannah [Tookoolitoo] that some one must have been there after Mc was there & taken away many things. She says from what In-k says no Innuit had been there before him (In-k).[21]

In-nook-poo-zhe-jook's opinion that he was the first Inuit to find the boat was undoubtedly based on the fact that he had never heard of anyone else's finding it. That does not prove that no one had. Perhaps he had heard a story of this boat but mis-identified it.

A thousand yards from this "pillaged" boat was another that had apparently escaped detection. In-nook-poo-zhe-jook told of finding "one whole skeleton with clothes on – this with flesh all on but dried," three skulls, and "many skeleton bones."[22] In-nook-poo-zhe-jook, like Ogzeuckjeuwock, found gruesome evidence that near these boats the weakened members of the retreat party had resorted to the last recourse. He found "a big pile of skeleton bones near the fire place & skulls among them." There were so many of these bones that In-nook-poo-zhe-jook could not count them. They had been "broken up for the marrow in them" and piled "close to the cooking place."[23] In addition, In-nook-poo-zhe-jook had found some "long boots" which "came up high as the knees & that in some was cooked human flesh – that is human flesh that had been boiled."[24]

The men found in and around these two boats on the Erebus Bay shore have usually been thought to have been a small party. According to tradition, a few weak men were left here in the boats while their strong comrades continued on to the ships. In-nook-poo-zhe-jook's evidence tells a different story. Although we do not know how many individuals contributed to the "big pile" of bones, we should not conclude that, as only four skulls were found, only a handful of men stayed here. The fireplace and elaborate preparation of the cooked remains indicate that the site was occupied for a considerable period of time, and In-nook-poo-zhe-jook's mention of "a tent near this boat" shows that the two abandoned boats were not the only shelter used.[25]

The first of In-nook-poo-zhe-jook's boats could have been found by a member of another Inuit party. Pooyetta's son Ogzeuckjeuwock's description of what was found, and presumably removed, from his boat – spectacles, watches, jewellery, books and boxes – are all missing from In-nook-poo-zhe-jook's "pillaged" one. The only things remaining were some canvas (sail or awning according to Ogzeuckjeuwock), paddles, and overlooked items (one each – file, axe, and jack-knife). Also left behind were the white men's remains.

The similarity of the human remains found outside Ogzeuckjeuwock's boat ("a number of skulls ... more than four. He also saw bones from legs and arms that appeared to have been sawed off") to those seen by In-nook-poo-zhe-jook outside his boats ("several skulls ... human bones that had been broken up for the marrow") is suggestive. But In-nook-poo-zhe-jook found his boats in Erebus Bay on the west coast of King William Island, not on the Adelaide Peninsula at Starvation Cove. Could Pooyetta's party have found this boat instead?

Tooktoocheer confused Schwatka by talking of the remains found by her husband as if they were all on King William Island. We have already seen the confusion between "continent" (Adelaide Peninsula) and "main land" (King William Island) in relation to the finds at Keeuna. Ogzeuckjeuwock had been only about ten years old at the time and may have been confused; at any rate he never unequivocally locates where he found the "boat place" with his father.

When Teekeeta met Pooyetta on Todd Islet he had already searched the south coast of King William Island eastward from Terror Bay. He undoubtedly related the tale of the large tent full of bodies which had been found there. Yet he makes no mention of Pooyetta's telling him about finding a boat, and certainly never crosses over to Starvation Cove to see it. Presumably he would have invested the few hours necessary to detour to visit this boat if he had heard of it. On the other hand, we know that Pooyetta must have been told of the white men's camp at Toonoonee which had been earlier seen by Teekeeta. Did his group continue west to visit it and then carry on to Erebus Bay?

There are few places on the west coast of King William Island which the Inuit bothered to name – it was a poor hunting ground and not normally visited. One place that did have a name was modern Cape Franklin, the northern point of Erebus Bay. It is the only spot, besides Douglas Bay, which had a name reminiscent of Teekeeta's "Kiny-nuk-shane" where Pooyetta found his boat. It was called "Kani-lugjuaq" (the big headland), surprisingly similar to "Kaner-lukjuaq" (the big fjord).[26]

This again is very interesting. Ogzeuckjeuwock's description of his boat, upright and surrounded by mutilated human remains, is very reminiscent of In-nook-poo-zhe-jook's description of a boat place near "Kani-lugjuaq." There is no way that this boat could be the same one seen by Teekeeta the year before, but Aglooka's boat could have been found at the similarly named "Kaner-lukjuaq." The potential for a misunderstanding is obvious.

Is there any evidence that Pooyetta and his family actually visited Toonoonee and In-nook-poo-zhe-jook's boat place? Took-toocheer and Ogzeuckjeuwock never mention a "tent place" as such. Ogzeuckjeuwock's tale of the body with the chain attached to his ears is, however, reminiscent of Teekeeta's remark about Toonoonee that there was something "fastened to various portions of the dress" of the white men and "chains knotted around the necks of the skeletons."[27] There were papers and unmistakable evidence of cannibalism at both the tent place (Terror Bay) and the boat place (Erebus Bay), which, although separated by a day's journey, are almost invariably described together, and Ogzeuckjeuwock also had vivid memories of mutilated remains.

Some of the phrases used to describe Toonoonee are also suggestive of phrases used by Ogzeuckjeuwock to describe his "boat place." Teekeeta said that the papers at Toonoonee were "given to the children as playthings." Ogzeuckjeuwock also remembered that "some of the books were taken home for the children to play with."[28] Ahlangyah said that the tent at Toonoonee was full of mutilated bodies "with the exception of one body that had the flesh on,"[29] Ogzeuckjeuwock remembered "one body had all the flesh on" at his boat,[30] and In-nook-poo-zhe-jook remembered one body "with flesh all on but dried."

Rae interestingly remarked that "there appears to have been an abundant store of ammunition, as the Gunpowder was emptied by the Natives in a heap on the ground out of the kegs or cases containing it and a quantity of shot and ball was found below high water mark, having probably been left on the ice close to the beach before the spring thaw commenced."[31] Gilder laconically noted that "some shot, bullets and wire cartidges" were found near the boat in Erebus Bay, but Klutschak considered that among the articles found "the most striking" were "some pieces of sacking in which bullets and shot, as well as some percussion caps, were tied up."[32]

A similar consideration applies to the gunpowder which was emptied onto the ground. The event which most impressed young Ogzeuckjeuwock was undoubtedly the explosion which injured him at the boat place. According to the natives, this happened when Ogzeuckjeuwock and a young friend were playing with powder which came from a "can." Teekeeta mentioned that there were many powder cans at Toonoonee; the only ones actually recovered were found by Schwatka and Gilder near the boat in Erebus Bay.[33]

Where did this explosion take place? Traditional wisdom indicates Starvation Cove on the north coast of Adelaide Peninsula. Hall was told that the igloo was blown up at Ootgoolik, which, admittedly, is on Adelaide Peninsula.[34] This is not as conclusive as it sounds, for the Inuit had quite definite and specific names for different parts of the peninsula. While the whole peninsula was called "Ilivileq,"[35] "Ootgoolik" was always used to refer to the west coast – far from Starvation Cove. But Ootgoolik is the coast opposite which one of Franklin's ships sank, and it would therefore be quite easy for the Inuit to say simply "the place where the ship sank" and for Hall to give it a name – Ootgoolik. The problem with this would be that Franklin had two ships, and the evidence is that the other one sank off the west coast of King William Island – near Erebus Bay.

Tooktoocheer offered another vague clue when she indicated to Schwatka that the boat had been found near "a central place, or last resting place, in which the vital records of the Franklin Expedition had been placed."[36] Owing to a garbled translation and general misconceptions about what he was being told, Schwatka could make no guess as to where this was, and assumed that the white men had carried their valuable records to the "last resting place" at Starvation Cove. But a case can be made for leaving records behind where the ship was abandoned rather than taking them on an uncertain retreat. And there is, as we shall see, another tradition of records being deposited, on the west coast of King William Island – in Erebus Bay.

One of the most curious parts of Ogzeuckjeuwock's testimony about the "boat place" which his family had visited concerned a case full of books.

In answer to a question which we asked his mother, he said he saw books at the boat place in a tin case, about two feet long and a foot square, which was fastened, and they broke it open. The case was full. Written and printed books were shown him, and he said they were like the printed ones. Among the books he found what was probably the needle of a compass or other magnetic instrument, because he said when it touched any iron it stuck fast. The boat was right side up, and the tin case in the boat.[37]

Ogzeuckjeuwock's party broke open a case full of printed books near an upright boat. When In-nook-poo-zhe-jook visited the upright boats in Erebus Bay he found many loose papers scattered carelessly about. Hall specifically asked whether these papers had "marks on them same as I am now making in either of the boats? No but saw a good many like the paper of the book beside me (McClintock's Voyage of the Fox)." Interestingly, In-nook-poo-zhe-jook also recovered "something like my [Hall's] compass, but no glass about it."[38] Had Ogzeuckjeuwock removed the compass needle?

According to traditions concerning Too-shoo-art-thariu, he had also seen a "long box" – at Terror Bay. Too-shoo-art-thariu, who was with Teekeeta's party when the tent at Toonoonee was first found, told his friends that the box "was not opened by this party of Innuits first visiting these tents as they did not know the nature or use of such things: but *the next party that went to the tents opened the box* & found in it a great many fine things silver forks, spoons" (emphasis added).[39] Were Pooyetta and his family the "next party" that broke open the box?

If Pooyetta and his family extended their search of King William Island from Keeuna to the westward and originally discovered one of the boats left in Erebus Bay, the evidence of cannibalism makes more sense. Here, and nearby at Terror Bay, we have independent corroboration of this dread recourse, and, except for the anomalous case of "Pooyetta's boat in Starvation Cove," this detail is nowhere else evident along the line of the survivors' march.

The preponderance of evidence, all of it admittedly circumstantial, indicates that it is likely that Pooyetta confined his search to King William Island, never crossed over to Starvation Cove, and could not have found the boat there. The boat which he did find at "Kinynukshane" was probably one of those later rediscovered by In-nook-poo-zhe-jook near the similarly named "Kanilugjuaq" – Erebus Bay.

Of course, the boat found in Erebus Bay could not have been the same one seen further south in Washington Bay by Teekeeta. This "same boat" was probably found later on the islet in Douglas Bay (again similarly named "Kanerlukjuaq"), and this detail was incorporated into the tradition concerning Pooyetta's boat. The islet in Douglas Bay, near the "main land" (King William Island), wrongly led the investigators into thinking that Pooyetta had found his boat at Starvation Cove, and further confused them as to what had been found – thirty bodies near an upright boat, or six to ten bodies under an overturned one.

This reconstruction is supported by some curious "echoes" in the Inuit testimony, but mostly by the fact that it was early in the march – at Toonoonee and the "boat place" in Erebus Bay – that we have solid evidence that cannibalism occurred. It was here that there was a major crisis. The great tragedy of the expedition did not come at the end of the march but in the middle – north of Washington Bay. Something significant happened before Aglooka and his men met Teekeeta, long before anyone arrived at Keeuna or Starvation Cove.

~14~

Toolooa and Aglooka

In our previous discussions concerning the party seen at Washington Bay and the remains found at Keeuna, we have largely ignored the recurring names "Toolooa" and "Aglooka," which we have heard used by the Inuit. These names might prove to be clues, but ones which we must use with caution.

European names were difficult for the Inuit to pronounce, and vice versa. It is not surprising that each tended to "rename" the other. Hall called Tookoolitoo and Ebierbing by the names "Hannah" and "Joe." He was himself called "Artungnun" after exchanging names with a native of that name at Igloolik, who was henceforth known as "Mitter Hall."[1]

Exchange was the most common way of acquiring an Inuit nickname. Another way was to have some identifiable physical characteristic. Schwatka was known to the natives as "Igearktooaloo" or "big spectacles."[2] A third method was due to phonetic similarity. The Inuit heard little difference between "Misser Geeter" (Mr Gilder) and "mosquito," and Gilder was henceforth known as "Keektooyakaloo" or "big mosquito."[3]

The Inuit delighted in bestowing new names on the white men. Steward Light of Ross's *Victory* remarked that the Inuit had a peculiar habit "in which some humour is exhibited, and that is in the aptitude in which they applied their nicknames to the officers of the ship, according to the different characters which they exhibited."[4]

As we have seen, John Ross was known to the natives as "Toolooark." Light unkindly supposed that this name, which means "raven," was given to Ross in recognition of his beaklike nose, his large size, or his gluttony. It is much more likely that the name was acquired by name-transference with a native ("Tul-luhiu") for whom a wooden leg was made by the *Victory's* carpenter.

This name, in its more common form of "Toolooa," was also that of the elderly Franklin survivor met by the four hunters at the ice crack in Washington Bay. We remember that this man was later confusingly identified as John Ross by the Inuit. We also recall that Adam Beck had told that "Tolloit" had died in connection with the "two ships encompassed by ice."

Although no other explorer is definitely known to have been called Toolooa, it was a very common Inuit name. In addition to Ross's wooden-legged friend, we know that one of Hall's informants was called this, as was the native guide who travelled to King William Island with Schwatka and Gilder ten years later. While at Winter Island and Igloolik, Parry met with no less than four Inuit who shared the name.[5]

Parry also encounted a ten-year-old boy named "Aglooka" at Igloolik, and the same person, now middle-aged, met Hall over forty years later. This name, meaning "he who takes long strides," could legitimately be given to any tall, purposeful white man – and was. One of those so named was James Clark Ross;[6] another was one of his best friends – Francis Rawdon Moira Crozier.

The Inuit remembered that "Cro-zhar" had been "Esh-e-mut-ta-nar (mate or some officer not so great as captain on Parry's ship)" and that he "was called Ag-loo-ka by the Innuits. Crozier's name was given to old Ook-bar-loo's son, whose name was Ag-loo-ka, and Ag-loo-ka's name was given to Crozier."[7]

Hall reported that the Repulse Bay natives remembered that Crozier, with the brashness of youth, "told the Innuits at Igloolik that he purposed to come in to the Innuits country sometime as *Esh-e-mut-ta* (Captain) with a ship or ships & he wished them to tell all Innuits they should meet, that his name was *Ag-loo-ka* &

of what he expected to do" (emphasis in original).[8] As only one of many midshipmen (the lowest rank of officer), this was quite a prediction for Crozier to make. It was not entirely in character either; in 1845, when friends remarked that he rather than Franklin should have been put in command of the Arctic expedition, Crozier remarked privately that he was quite happy to go as second, and that he truthfully did not feel up to the rigours of command.

There is evidence that Parry and John Rae were also known as "Aglooka," or at least that stories attributed to "Aglooka" refer to them. Cyriax rightly remarked that "the mere fact of an explorer's being called "Aglooka" by Eskimos affords slender evidence of his identity."[9]

Hall invariably translated "Aglooka" as "Crozier" in most of the stories which he heard from his companions, and steadfastly insisted that the "Aglooka" of the Washington Bay encounter was the Captain of the *Terror*. Hall based this identification on information which he derived from Koong-e-ou-e-lik (Too-shoo-art-thariu's brother-in-law). Koong-e-ou-e-lik informed Hall that Too-shoo-art-thariu had learned that the "Kob-lu-na name" of the white man (Aglooka) who had been seen at Teekeenu was "Oo-li-zhen."[10]

Hall remarked that "Oolizhen" was a name which he knew "to mean *Crozier* from what has many times been communicated to me by the Repulse Bay natives."[11] Hall undoubtedly based this idea on the fact that Ookbarloo's son Aglooka, who had exchanged names with Crozier at Igloolik in the 1820s, was, according to other natives, "now called Oo-li-zhum."[12]

This all seems quite convincingly straightforward. Crozier exchanged names with a native named Aglooka/Oolizhum. The elderly leader at Washington Bay, Aglooka, had another name as well, not, as Too-shoo-art-thariu thought, his "kobluna" name, but the other name of his native friend of many years before – "Oo-li-zhen." Hall knew that, of all those known to have been called "Aglooka," only Crozier could possibly have been seen on the march in Washington Bay.

For reasons which will appear shortly, I do not believe that Crozier was among the survivors of the Washington Bay detachment. How then can I explain the "Oolizhen" coincidence? The clue lies in the one discordant element in the above explanation, the fact that Too-shoo-art-thariu identified "Oolizhen" not as a second name acquired by the white man from an Inuit host, but as a "kobluna" name. The ending "zhen" is very unusual for an Inuit name, but as "son" would be quite common to the white men.

The young boy Aglooka exchanged names with Crozier, whose "kobluna name" was accurately preserved as "Cro-zhar." Perhaps the young Inuit also exchanged names with another of Parry's crewmen and, preferring this second name, used it in later life. If so it is almost certain that the original "Oolizhen" was not Crozier at all. The best candidate for "Oolizhen" was John Allison, the "Greenland Mate" of the *Fury*. [13]

John Allison served Parry as his ice-master, a job which was given only to experienced whalers. These men, usually captains in their own right, were hired by the navy to advise the naval officers on Arctic conditions. It is much more likely that the "Aglooka" who bragged to the Inuit of Igloolik that he would one day return with a ship of his own was the experienced Allison rather than the neophyte Crozier.

Allison did not sail with the Franklin expedition, and could not have been seen at Washington Bay, but, as we shall see, there was a tradition among the Inuit that, in addition to Crozier, three other men from Parry's earlier expedition had served on the *Erebus* and *Terror*. In any case Hall's identification of the Washington Bay "Aglooka" as Crozier, based on the name "Oolizhen," is not justified.

It is interesting that the men seen on the march at Teekeenu had common native names – indeed, it is surprising that they had any native names at all. The leaders Toolooa and Aglooka could have acquired their Inuit names on previous voyages, but most of Franklin's officers had no experience in the north. Gilder concluded that it was probable that the names which the white men used phonetically resembled the Inuit names. [14] If we look at the crew lists of the *Erebus* and *Terror* (appendix 1), it is hard to verify this. No men with names that sound like Aglooka or Toolooa leap from the page in the manner of "Ill-kern"/Pilkington or "Oolizhen"/Allison. However, it should be remembered that Stefansson found that even after repeated coaching the Inuit pronounced "Jim" as "Perk" or "Zerk" and that to them "Rae" sounded just like "Nerk"! [15]

It is doubtful that in the case of Toolooa and Aglooka the Inuit were phonetically copying the white men's real names, for the natives told that the Washington Bay Aglooka, while sitting in Ow-wer's tent, introduced himself by saying "Ag-loo-ka wonger" – "I am Aglooka" while "patting his own breast."[16] Any officer familiar enough with the Inuit language to know that "wonger" (oo-wunga) meant "me/I am" would probably know that "Aglooka" was a name which had been given to officers in the past, although he may have mistakenly thought that it was a title rather than a given name.

Teekeeta's story of Washington Bay marchers named Toolooa and Aglooka, and tales about similarly named remains found at Keeuna by Pooyetta and Eveeshuk, can apply only to members of the Franklin expedition. But there is one more story which involved the duo Toolooa-Aglooka, which, owing to its content, must predate the meeting in Washington Bay. Hall was told of a visit by the Inuit to some ships locked in the ice.

Kok-lee-arng-nun, their head man, showed two spoons which had been given to him by Ag-loo-ka (Crozier), one of them having the initials F.R.M.C. stamped upon it. His wife Koo-narng, had a silver watch-case. This opened up the way for immediate inquiries. Through Too-koo-li-too who as usual soon proved a good interpreter, it was learned that these Innuits had been at one time on board of the ships of Too-loo-ark, (the great Esh-e-muta, Sir John Franklin), and had their tupiks on the ice alongside of him during the spring and summer. They spoke of one ship not far from Ook-kee-bee-jee-lua (Pelly Bay), and two to the westward of Neit-tee-lik, near Ook-goo-lik. Kok-lee-arng-nun was "a big boy when very many men from the ships hunted took-too [caribou]. They had guns, and knives with long handles, and some of the party hunted the took-too on the ice; killing so many that they made a line across the whole bay of Ook-goo-lik." The Pelly Bay men described the esh-e-muta as an old man with broad shoulders, thick and heavier set than Hall, with gray hair, full face, and bald head. He was always wearing something over his eyes (spectacles, as Too-koo-li-too inter-preted it), was quite lame, and appeared sick when they last saw him. He was very kind to the Innuits; – always wanting them to eat some-thing. Ag-loo-ka (Crozier) and another man would go and do everything that Too-loo-ark told them, just like boys; he was a very cheerful man, always laughing; everybody liked him – all the kob-lu-nas and all the Innuits.

Kok-lee-arng-nun showed how Too-loo-ark and Ag-loo-ka used to meet him. They would take hold of his hand, giving it a few warm and friendly shakes, and Too-loo-ark would say, "Ma-my-too-mig-tey-ma."[17]

After the loss of one of these ships, Kokleearngnun stated that Aglooka later attempted to go home overland. He was accompanied by a "pee-e-tu" (steward or non-seaman) who was named "Nar-tar." Hall noted that Inuit attempts to pronounce the word "doctor" invariably resulted in "nar-tar."[18] Ahlangyah remembered one of the men at Teekeenu as "Doktook." Kokleearngnun's identification of one of Aglooka's companions as a "pee-e-tu" reminds us that McClintock found the body of one of the Washington Bay marchers near Gladman Point, and that he was, by his dress, a steward.

Kokleearngnun's tale of a visit to Toolooa's ship has long been the subject of intense debate. Many ingenious theories have been proposed to account for its seeming inconsistencies. Hall initially believed that he was hearing a tale about Franklin (Toolooa) and Crozier (Aglooka). After thinking it over he changed his mind about Kokleearngnun's testimony.

I may note the fact that in every interview I have with the Innuits on the subject of the last expedition more or less is mixed in that has reference to Ross's expedition in the *Victory* ... In fact, after hearing the story of old Kokleearngnun and that of his wife's [sic] about *Ag-loo-ka* and his chief Too-loo-a ... I really was overwhelmed with joyous emotions for I believed they had visited many times Sir John Franklin's ships while beset in the ice near King William's Land and there met him, Crozier and all their Company. It took something like three days while encamped on the ice ... to find out the fact that all the old man and wife had told me was of Captain and Commander Ross. (emphasis in original)[19]

Without further reasons, we cannot know why Hall eventually rejected Kokleearngnun's tale. In any case there is no doubt that he was wrong in stating that everything the old man and his wife had told him concerned the Ross expedition. Even Cyriax, who considered Kokleearngnun's tale to be "clearly of no value as regards the Franklin expedition,"[20] felt that it was "probably a mixture of boyhood recollections of John and James Clark Ross and of their ships ... of hearsay information about the Franklin expedition; and of a misunderstanding concerning Rae."[21]

Most of the modern comment on Kokleearngnun's story has been that, since the Victory Point record mentioned no Inuit visit to the *Erebus* and *Terror* before the 1848 abandonment, Kokleearngnun's tale must refer to a visit to some other explorer's vessels. Like Hall, most have decided that the Ross expedition of 1829–34 is the most likely candidate, and that Kokleearngnun and his wife must have visited the *Victory* at some time while she was beset in Lord Mayor Bay. As we saw earlier, Cyriax cleverly found a way around the problem that the *Victory* was not "two ships" by invoking the small sixteen-ton tender *Krusenstern* as a second ship.

Considering the *Krusenstern* to have been a second "ship" is not entirely unjustified. The Inuit possessed two types of watercraft – the hunter's "kayak" and the larger "umiak" used to transport supplies and personnel. As we have seen, they used the word "umiak" to describe both the white men's ships and their boats. Yet it is curious that they would call two such dissimilar vessels as the *Victory* and *Krusenstern*, one of which was ten times the size of the other, "two ships." In contrast, the much larger *Erebus* and *Terror* were almost identical in size.

In-nook-poo-zhe-jook told Hall that the *Victory* was "very small compared to that [ship] wh. came from the North down to Ookjoo-lik" and that "there was something curious about the *Victory* – describes its peculiarities so that Pa-pa says that it was a propeller like See-bee-leri (Chapel's St. John's steamer)."[22] The *Victory* was indeed a very small ship, originally a mere 85 tons. Even when modified for Arctic service, she was less than half the tonnage of the *Erebus* or the *Terror*. She was thus in many ways a hybrid vessel, quite different from Franklin's ponderous 340-ton bomb ketches. In-nook-poo-zhe-jook's mention of a "peculiarity" concerning the "propellors" may have referred to the fact that the *Victory* had paddlewheels – the only Arctic exploration ship to be so equipped.[23] In any case, it is obvious that the Inuit were quite capable of distinguishing between different vessels.

Cyriax went on to compare the description of "Toolooark" with that of John Ross. He noted that "John Ross was 52 years old; he wore spectacles, at least occasionally, and the Eskimo name for him was 'Toolooa'. He usually offered the natives something to eat, and his relations with them, except for a few quickly rectified misunderstandings, were mostly friendly."[24]

Cyriax's assertion that Ross's relationship with the Inuit was "mostly friendly" leaves much unsaid. Of course there is no hint of any discord in Ross's official Narrative, but a second account of the voyage, based on the remembrances of Ross's steward, William Light, gives a very different view.

Initially the natives were welcomed on board the *Victory*, even if they were denied handsaws. They were invited into the ship and offered "civilized" food (which they consistently refused), and they traded their implements for such trifling articles as were usual. After some pilfering occurred, and with the increasing familiarity of the Inuit women with his crew, Ross's attitude changed and the Inuit were then not generally allowed aboard. Light maintained that the natives were often turned away hungry.[25] According to Light, once the Inuit had delivered their geographical information and such articles as were wanted, "a treatment was adopted towards them, which did not stop at mere unkindness and incivility, but it degenerated at last into downright cruelty and inhumanity."[26]

Light frequently alluded to John Ross's later ill treatment of the natives, which was "very different to that which was shown towards them on their first acquaintance," remarking that Ross "carried that treatment to an unjustifiable length, and thereby exposed himself to the charge of great ingratitude ... treating them literally as if they were but a degree removed from the bears of their native land."[27]

Ross's steward admittedly had no love for his Captain (he was the only crewman "Not Recommended" for future service on Ross's return), but, even taking into account personal animosity, some of the documented events aboard the *Victory* are hard to reconcile with Kokleearngnun's description of Toolooark as "a very cheerful man, always laughing."

On one occasion John Ross pretended to possess magical medical powers in order to repossess some stolen goods. The thief, told that unless he returned the articles he would sicken and die, understandably returned them to the ship and was then preemptorily dismissed, "very much displeased indeed with those who could act so unjustly and dishonourably."[28]

Even Pooyetta, who was the most favoured of the natives and

given the "run of the ship," ran afoul of the Captain. Having innocently made free with John Ross's intended dinner and then lain down in a flour tub for a nap, Pooyetta was unceremoniously hauled out and beaten in punishment. Unable to understand what was happening, and seeing the cloud of flour which rose from his garments on every stroke, Pooyetta kindly concluded that the white men were dusting him off![29]

The next "favored guest," Takkeelikkeeta, was frightened by a discharge of the ship's guns, and took refuge under the desk in the Captain's cabin. Ross, angry at his interrupted solitude, exploded into profanity and berated the crew.[30] On another occasion the Inuit moved their snow houses near the ship, and Ross, sensing a challenge to his having taken possession of the land for England, seriously considered removing them by using violence![31]

Ross, again according to Light, was hardly more friendly with his own crew. There seems little doubt that Ross was "not a sociable character" or that he was steeped in "reserve and haughtiness" and "the starch of official dignity."[32] Light often mentions the sailors' disdain for their Captain and on at least one occasion said that the feeling against Ross ran "little short of direct mutiny."[33] Ross himself hints at a near-mutiny shortly after the *Victory* was abandoned.[34]

For his part, Ross maintained himself in virtual isolation in his cabin and, as confirmed by later testimony, even had repeated quarrels with his nephew, James. There was such bad feeling between the two men that they would remain estranged for the rest of their lives. During a later official inquiry, James remarked that he had not felt himself to be under John Ross's command at all but considered himself a "co-commander."[35] None of these incidents are mentioned in Ross's own published account of the expedition, but many widely different versions of Ross's Journal exist, only the most sanitized of which reached print.[36]

The obvious rancour and ill feeling between Ross and his crew are hardly reminiscent of Kokleearngnun's description of the relationship between Toolooa and his men, where "Ag-loo-ka and another man would go and do everything that Too-loo-ark told them, just like boys ... everybody liked him – all the kob-lu-nas and all the Innuits."

Ross's ship(s) differed from Franklin's, and his conduct was not always as described by the Inuit. Cyriax, despite his own belief that Kokleearngnun had visited Ross, was too honest a scholar not to note other problems with his theory. He noted that "Ross' ships were never on the west coast of Boothia; his narrative contains nothing to suggest that he was either lame or ill for any length of time during his second expedition; and he was not bald in 1834. Moreover, he did not carry out a reindeer hunt like the one described by Kokleearngnun; indeed, he and his companions killed only one reindeer during their entire stay in the Arctic. Lastly, though his narrative gives the names of many adult Eskimos and children whom he met, it does not mention Kokleearngnun; but the list is admittedly incomplete."[37]

That Ross's ships "were never on the west coast of Boothia" was very well known to the natives. Kokleearngnun specifically stated that there were "three ships in all – that is one they know about not far from Ook-kee-bee-jee-lua (Pelly Bay) just beyond Cape Barens & 2 beyond the westward of Neit-tee-lik, near Ook-goo-lik." That the old man was referring respectively to the *Victory* and the *Erebus* and *Terror* is beyond question.[38]

The fact that Ross "was not bald in 1834" is more significant than Cyriax would imply. Ross's portraits show that he had a luxuriant head of hair. The curious incident of "Ross's" body being found on Keeuna confirms that the Inuit knew quite well what John Ross looked like. John Rae once remarked that the natives "described so perfectly the personal appearance of Sir John Ross and Sir James Ross – although the men spoken with had not seen those gentlemen – that any one acquainted with these officers would have recognized them."[39]

Cyriax also tried to show that Kokleearngnun was too old to have been a visitor to the *Erebus* and *Terror*, for "he was a 'big boy' when he saw 'Toolooark', and Nourse's narrative explicitly states several times that he was an old man when Hall met him in 1866 ... if he was right in describing himself as a 'big boy' when he visited 'Toolooark's' ships, these cannot have been Franklin's, and must have been those of some earlier explorer."[40]

Leaving aside the problem of determination of Inuit ages from physical appearances, the argument about chronology based on the relative merits of subjective terms like "big boy" and "old man" is hardly conclusive. We do not know how old Kokleearngnun was in 1866. As he then had a grown son and grandchildren, presumably he was born near the turn of the century. By 1866, when Hall interviewed him, Kokleearngnun was blind and crippled. Shortly thereafter, Kokleearngnun requested that his son Koong-e-ou-e-lik release both himself and his wife Koo-narg from pain by hanging, a sorrowful but customary duty which, when performed by the obedient son, both shocked and saddened Hall.[41] Presumably Kokleearngnun had been about thirty years old when Ross visited Neitchille, and about forty-five when Franklin's ships arrived at King William Island. Neither of these ages is accurately reflected by the English phrase "big boy."

Other details of Kokleearngnun's remembrance are interesting. One of Toolooark's men was very tall, "much taller than any of the rest," so tall in fact that "one could see the sky by looking between his legs" – a curious statement which made Tookoolitoo and Ebierbing conclude that the man had been walking on stilts.[42] This is an inconclusive clue, for to the usually diminutive Inuit most white men were tall, but we shall see that there is another tradition concerning a giant, and this one definitely relates to Franklin's expedition.

According to Ross, he gave the visiting Inuit pieces of barrel hoop, a useful if not very expensive gift. Light stated that none of the *Victory*'s guests ever received anything worthwhile in exchange for their skins and curiosities. Yet Kokleearngnun's wife Koo-narg told of being given an "ood-loo" (knife) by Toolooark, remarking that she was not the only recipient of such largesse. Toolooark apparently had a joking ritual when giving out knives to the women, where he would "hold [the knife] in his hand [and] draw it back to his body" as if he would not give it up after all.[43] This good-natured teasing was not characteristic of the dour Ross.

Ookbarloo told Hall that her husband, Seegar, had three cousins who "belonged to Neitch-il-lee," and that they knew all about the ship or ships which were "in the ice near a large island not far from Neitch-il-lee." She remarked that these three cousins had visited the ship or ships "several times." She then related the story of another native who had come across the ship while travelling alone, and who had been the guest of a great Captain.

There was one Neitch-il-lee Innuit that visited the ship alone, she (O) did not recollect his name. He went with dogs & sledge on the ice to the ship. The *Kob-lu-na Esh-e-mut-ta* (the white chief or Captain) of ship was very kind to him (the Innuit) & gave him many things. The Captain took him down into the Cabin & gave him something to eat & drink &

then he went home. Some time after, when the sun was high, that is it was well into spring or summer, the same Innuit visited the ship again & the Captain took him down into the Cabin & gave him *see-qu-la* (Bread – Crackers) to eat & he (the Captain) gave him a *long big piece of something that was white – a good deal of ook-sook* [blubber] *to it with a little thin bit of meat with bone in it.* And this Innuit thought something bad about this & did not wish to take it. He thought perhaps it was a piece of the side of an *Ek-er-lin* [Indian] or perhaps of a *Kob-lu-na*! He never saw anything like it. He knew it was not of a Ni-noo (Polar Bear) though it looked something like – in fact he never saw anything like it, & could not help thinking *it must be a piece of the side of an Indian or Kob-lu-na*; it would bend so: it was so white: – it had such thick ook-sook; & had so little meat & bone to it![44]

Tookoolitoo told Hall that this was undoubtedly a piece of pork rib. The interesting thing about this encounter is that Ross's Narrative makes it clear that the first natives who visited the *Victory* were offered bread and other "civilized" food, which they politely accepted, but it soon became apparent that they did not like it. If Ross was this unnamed Captain, it is strange that he would continue to offer his own food to a solitary native visitor. There was something else strange about this encounter.

Bye & bye he [the Inuit] went again to the ship all alone with his dogs & sledge. He went on deck, & a great many men – *black men* – came right up out of the hatch-way & the first thing he (the Innuit) knew, he couldn't get away. These men who were then all around him, had *black faces, black hands, black clothes* on – *were black all over!* They had little *black noses*, only so big: [the old lady here put her hand on the bridge of her nose showing that the noses were not more than half the length & size of common ones] & this Innuit was very much alarmed because he could not get away from these black men but especially was he frightened when they made three great noises [three rounds of cheers as Too-koo-li-too thinks these great noises were]. When three great noises were made, the Esh-e-mut-ta (Captain) came up out of the Cabin & put a stop to it, when all the black men went down the same way they had come up. This Innuit believed these men belonged down among the coals & that they lived there.

Then the Captain took this Innuit down with him into his Cabin & made him many presents, for he (the Innuit) had been frightened so. Before the Captain took him down into his Cabin he told this Innuit to take a look over to the land, the Captain pointing out to him the exact spot where was a big Tupik (tent). The Captain asked him if he saw the tent, & the Innuit told him he did. Then the Captain told him that *black men, such as he had just seen, lived there*, & that neither he (this Innuit) nor any of his people must ever go there. After the Innuit had received the presents that the Captain made him, he left the ship & went home; & he would never go to the ship again because of the *frightful looking black men that lived there down in the Coal hole.* (emphasis in original)[45]

Hall was mystified by the detail of the black features, musing that perhaps the native had interrupted some kind of pantomine or entertainment. More likely the men were simply covered in coal dust. But the story has disquieting features. The fact that the men were blackened is itself curious, and betokens a lack of the normal naval discipline one would expect. This is supported by their seizure of the poor visitor, and their behaviour when ordered to release him. The "Captain" was apparently the only officer to meet the native.

Then there is the detail of the men living on shore in a big tent, men who posed some kind of threat to the Inuit and his people. None of Ross's men lived in a big tent ashore within sight of the ship. The *Erebus* and *Terror* were never within easy sight of King William Island before 1848 either; if this story deals with them we are hearing of later events.

The last argument against Kokleearngnun's having confused a visit to Ross's ships with later tales about the *Erebus* and *Terror* is that, as Cyriax stated, "though [Ross's] narrative gives the names of many adult Eskimos and children whom he met, it does not mention Kokleearngnun." Ross, unaware that a complete list of his native visitors would later be useful for historians, wrote that it could not "much interest any one, who was the wife, son, nephew, granddaughter, or bethrothed, of whom."[46] Nevertheless, he kept excellent records of his encounters with the natives and these subsequently formed the nucleus of an extended listing which he published in the Appendix to his best-selling account.

In this Appendix, Ross relates that he met with "about 160 souls," and he gives drawings and brief biographies of twenty-two of these – presumably those with whom he had most contact. He further mentions another twenty-three individuals by name and gives their interrelationships. He later names seven other

Inuit, remarking of them only that "as the rest of the natives have nothing remarkable or peculiar to them, I shall only mention a few of their names."[47]

If Kokleearngnun was an important visitor to the *Victory*, we should find him somewhere in Ross's list.

The remembrance of names was very important in Inuit oral history and was often cited as a proof of reliability. In the case of Teekeeta's companions, the recollections of their names was a very helpful feature. Yet, as seen in the case of Too-shoo-art-thariu/Qablut, the Inuit usually possessed many names. It was felt that "men must have as many names as possible, as every name will presumably protect them and hold them up," and it was also common for Inuit to address each other not by their real names but by "nicknames" denoting their relationships.[48] In addition to these difficulties, the white men were quite often misled by the strange (to them) Inuit phonetic system: native names were often hard for the white men to transcribe. For all of these reasons the value to be placed on the non-appearance of the specific name "Kokleearngnun" on Ross's list of native visitors is questionable.

Nevertheless, there is very good correspondence between the names of natives whom we know to have visited Ross's winter quarters and the names in his records. Hall was told by Teekeeta's mother Ad-lark that she and her husband Neeweekeei had visited "Aglooka and Toolooa" at "Satu-wa-tu-wig" (Eveeshuk – E-tow-tow-wig, Rasmussen – Icuartorfik), now know as Sheriff Harbour.[49] The mention of the location gives unmistakable notice that we are hearing of a visit to the *Victory*, and Teekeeta's parents probably appear in Ross's list as the couple "Neeweetioke and Udlia." Hall was told by others of the visit to that ship of Ooblooria (Ross – Ooblooria), Toolooa (Ross – Tulluahiu), and Pooyetta (Ross – Poyettak), all of whom are easily recognizable.

Ross's list has no such approximation to "Kokleearngnun" – there is little similarity between the four male names which start with a "K" (Kawalua, Kunana, Kannayoke, and Konyaroklik) and Hall's version of his old informant's name.

Light, as Ross's steward, was ideally situated by his job to meet the visitors to the *Victory*. In his book he mentions thirty-one individual visitors by name, eleven of whom can be easily recognized in Ross's account. The other twenty names attest to the difficulty involved when transcribing Inuit names, although they may also confirm Light's claim that the seamen had much contact with the Inuit unbeknown to the officers. Neither Kokleearngnun nor his wife Koo-narg is recognizable in Light's account either.

The lists of visitors to the *Victory* are, as Cyriax stated, "admittedly incomplete," yet we find that in most cases we can tentatively cross-identify individuals. It is impossible to identify even an approximate correlation with "Kokleearngnun." It is always possible that Kokleearngnun appears under another name, or that "Kokleearngnun" itself is such a poor rendering of his real name that he is unrecognizable. There are, of course, two other possible explanations. Either Kokleearngnun much overrated his status as a visitor, or it was not the *Victory* which played host to him, and "Toolooark" was not John Ross.

~15~

Toolooark's Ships

Kokleearngnun's story of a visit to the ships of "Toolooark" and Aglooka had elements which could apply to almost any Arctic expedition. Certainly, if we rely solely on physical descriptions of the ships and officers, or on details of the hospitality received, we will find little to differentiate Parry from Ross, or Ross from Franklin. But Kokleearngnun did not tell only of a visit to the white men's ships. He told of the wreck of one.

After the first summer and first winter, they saw no more of Too-loo-ark; then Ag-loo-ka (Crozier) was the Esh-e-muta.

The old man and his wife agreed in saying that the ship on board of which they had often seen Too-loo-ark was overwhelmed with heavy ice in the spring of the year. While the ice was slowly crushing it, the men all worked for their lives in getting out provisions; but, before they could save much, the ice turned the vessel down on its side, crushing the masts and breaking a hole in her bottom and so overwhelming her that she sank at once, and had never been seen again. Several men at work in her could not get out in time, and were carried down with her and drowned. "On this account Ag-loo-ka's company had died of starvation, for they had not had time to get provisions out of her."[1]

It is this element of Kokleearngnun's story which causes the most controversy. It also may account for Hall's later disbelief, for he assumed that "Toolooark" was Franklin and that Aglooka was Crozier. This required Kokleearngnun to have visited the *Erebus* and *Terror* before Franklin's death on 11 June 1847, which in turn called into doubt the incident of the sinking ship, for Fitzjames's Victory Point record of April 1848 implies that both of the ships were intact when abandoned.

The most serious objection to seeing Kokleearngnun's story as a remembrance of Franklin is the curious lack of corroboration. If Kokleearngnun and other natives visited Franklin's ships over an extended period of time, socialized, and conducted at least one major hunt together, we would expect to find other traditions to that effect. Where are they?

There is an echo, however faint, of Kokleearngnun's story in Adam Beck's tale of the wreck of a ship near Omanek. Beck had told of two ships "encompassed by the ice" near Omanek, and that "the men [Inuit?] went to them." Beck further stated that the two ships "were broken up by the ice" and "that a part of the crews were drowned," a remarkable correlation with Kokleearngnun's tale. In what could be a remembrance of the white men's camps at Erebus and Terror Bays, he said that "the remainder were some time in huts or tents apart from the natives." Beck's story of the ships being "afterward burnt by a fierce and numerous tribe of natives" may have had the same source as the offhand comment to McClintock about the natives "burning through the masts."[2]

If, as most historians conclude, the Inuit never visited the *Erebus* and *Terror*, it is difficult to account for their detailed knowledge of the two ships. One of Schwatka's main informants, Puhtoorak, lived his whole life on Adelaide Peninsula, and was therefore unaware of the white men's presence until his people found the one ship which the natives reported to have been driven ashore at Ootgoolik. Not surprisingly, he never spoke of Franklin having more than one vessel.

Teekeeta had been told by Aglooka that he had left two ships in the ice, but, owing to language difficulties, did not obtain a detailed description of them. McClintock's Boothian informants were more knowledgeable. They remarked that "two ships had been seen by the natives of King William's Land," and that one of these "was seen to sink in deep water."[3] One man indicated that the ship had "three masts" and that it "had been crushed by the ice out in the sea west of King William's Island." He told Petersen that "he was not one of those who were eye-witnesses

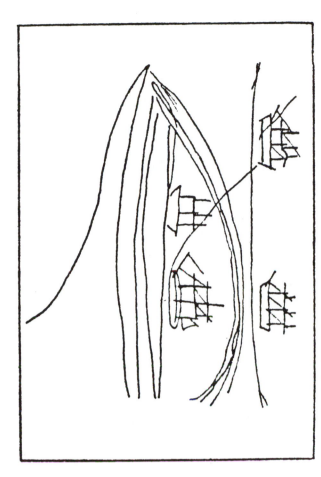

Figure 2 The *Chieftain* Drawing. The two ships on the left may indicate the *Erebus* and *Terror*. One of these appears to lie on its side and have its sails rigged. The line from one set of ships to the other crosses intervening land (Boothia?) and may represent the travels of the Inuit informant.

of it" and that "the ship sunk, so nothing was obtained by the natives from her."[4]

McClintock's informant was not one of the "eye-witnesses." Was Kokleearngnun?

The testimony of the "liar" Adam Beck and the few cryptic comments recorded by McClintock cannot serve as solid corroboration of Kokleearngnun's visit. There was, however, another Inuit tale which told of a visit to icebound ships.

In the late summer of 1849 the Master of the whaler *Chieftain*, then lying in Pond's Bay, was visited by a strange Eskimo, who, of his own volition and without previous questioning, handed him a remarkable drawing. It depicted a long narrow strip of land. On the right were shown two three-masted ships, on the left two more three-masted ships, one of which was on her beam-ends. The Eskimo then explained, mainly by signs, for no interpreter was present, that two of the ships had been frozen up for four years on the west side of Prince Regent Inlet, and the other two on the eastern side for one year. That second pair was probably the *Enterprise* and *Investigator*, then on their first relief expedition under the command of Sir James Ross; they had been ice-bound for nearly a year at Leopold Island off the western entrance to Prince Regent Inlet ... [The Inuit] and some companions had been on board all four ships the previous spring and they were safe.[5]

Captain Ker of the *Chieftain* thought that the story indicated that the two sets of ships were on opposite sides of Prince Regent Inlet. Yet it seems obvious from the native drawing that the ships were separated by intervening land, and that this land was wide at both ends and narrowed to an isthmus in the center – a tolerable description of the Boothia Peninsula.

That an Inuit story which was conveyed largely by sign language was misinterpreted should not surprise us. The report which has been handed down from the *Chieftain* may not have been the best. There apparently were several variants of the tale, and Dr Goodsir, brother of Franklin's naturalist (then surgeon of the whaler *Advice*), "complained that it was distorted and embroidered as it passed from ship to ship." One version indicated that Aglooka "had travelled between the two pairs of ships, which explained the connecting line [on the drawing]."[6]

The opinion that two of the ships were the *Enterprise* and *Investigator* seems unassailable, for they had passed the winter of 1848–9 at Port Leopold in Prince Regent Inlet. This in itself is remarkable, for at the time the whalers themselves did not know where these two ships were. That the other two ships were the *Erebus* and *Terror* seems less certain. Most historians either ignored this evidence completely or concluded that the *Chieftain*'s informant, like Kokleearngnun before him, had been telling of a visit to John Ross's *Victory*.

The *Victory* had been abandoned on the west side of Prince Regent Inlet, while the native drawing indicated the ships were to the west of Boothia, but this was seen as a minor discrepancy. The *Victory* had also been visited by the Inuit, admittedly not a few months ago but nineteen years earlier. Finally, Ross had indeed wintered for four years, although the last of these had not been in his ship but in a makeshift shelter at Fury Beach. Nevertheless, these difficulties were easier to explain away than the idea of a visit to the *Erebus* and *Terror* in 1849 was to support.

This Inuit story initially caused quite a sensation among the whalers, but the story was soon "disproven" when James Clark Ross's ships emerged from Port Leopold without having had any Inuit visits during their entire stay. This discredited the statement that the unnamed native had been on board all four ships, and the *Chieftain* story was placed on the trash-heap of useless Inuit remembrances. Nevertheless, while the natives may not have actually been aboard Ross's vessels, they certainly saw them and kept track of their movements.

These objections to this tale seem to focus on trees while missing the forest. Whether the story was embroidered or simply misunderstood by the whalers, the fact that the native knew of the two sets of ships is in itself significant. The fact that he professed to have visited them only a few months previously during the spring of 1849 is even more so, for it would support the idea that some of Franklin's men had remanned their vessels after an abortive 1848 abandonment.

If the *Chieftain* story and Kokleearngnun's testimony both related to Ross's expedition, it was necessary to explain the fact that one pictured a vessel on its beam-ends and the other told of a dramatic wreck. The *Victory* was leaky but upright when abandoned. Once again, Cyriax invokes the *Krusenstern*.

During the first winter (1829–30) the *Krusenstern* sank, but the exact date is not mentioned in Ross' narrative. She was brought ashore in July 1830; the damage was repaired, and she does not appear to have sunk again. No Eskimo visited Ross after the summer of 1831. He abandoned the *Victory* in Victoria Harbour, and left the *Krusenstern* on the beach there, in May 1832. The Eskimos appear neither to have known that he intended to leave nor to have seen him depart; when they afterwards found the *Victory*, or what was left of her, he and his entire command had vanished. It would have been most natural for them to conclude that he had suffered a disaster there.[7]

The most dramatic aspect of Kokleearngnun's tale is the sinking of one of "Toolooark's" ships with a crushed side and loss of life. The misfortune which overtook the tiny *Krusenstern* had none of these features. In fact, Ross's small tender seems to have been a perpetual nuisance. Ross rarely mentions it in his published account, but Light, possibly because he was more involved with the actual labour of rescuing it, repeatedly tells of the trials in-

volved. On 13 January 1830, four days after the arrival of the first
Inuit, Light records that "an unfortunate accident this day befel
[sic] the launch, which got completely under the ice and the crew
were occupied the whole of the following day in the extrication
of it."[8] It must have been especially galling that on the very next
day the launch sank again.[9] It was again recovered, only to be
overwhelmed on 24 March.[10]

On the 14th of July the *Victory* was threatened by an upwelling
of ice. Ross's journal records that "at this time a piece of ice came
up to the surface from beneath the ship, so forcibly as to lift her
up on one side and cause her to heel, to the temporary alarm of
those who were below." The *Victory*'s trial was temporary and
Ross makes no mention of the *Krusenstern* at all, going on to
remark on the irritations caused by the mosquitoes.[11] But this
disruption, which is the only one chronicled during that month,
was apparently responsible for a problem with the smaller vessel,
for later, without any reference to a sinking, Ross remarks on
26 July that "the *Krusenstern* was cleared out, and launched off
the ice to the beach, that she might be repaired and caulked."[12]

In his end-month summary, Ross laconically stated that "having frequently spoken of the *Krusenstern*, I have now to observe,
that when the ice had overflowed it had sunk her, carrying her
with it to the bottom. On the thaw she was at last relieved and
brought on shore; but she had sustained more damage from the
pressure than we had suspected. Many of her timbers were broken; but these and all other defects had been at last repaired."[13]

It is hard to reconcile Ross's report of an occurrence which he
himself apparently considered trivial with the dramatic events
recounted by Kokleearngnun. While Kokleearngnun's ship had
been crushed in the ice, the *Krusenstern* had had some planks
broken. Kokleearngnun's ship had sunk and "never been seen
again"; the *Krusenstern* was taken to the beach, repaired, and left
there "en cache" to be later found by the Inuit.

The most telling discrepancy is the reported loss of life. Cyriax's
idea that the Inuit would assume that Ross had suffered a disaster
at Victoria Harbour appears unfounded. The natives knew quite
well that Ross and his party safely abandoned their ship and
"went away"; they had no tradition of any disaster overtaking
them.[14] In fact they seemed to know the details at least as well
as John Rae, who later interviewed them, for they ventured to

correct him when they thought that he had made a mistake. Rae told them that the "two chiefs (Sir J. and Sir J.C. Ross) and their men had all got home safe to their own country," but the Inuit remarked "that this was not true, for some of the men had died at the place where the vessel was left." Rae understood this contradiction to refer to the death of James Dixon, whose grave had been built on the western shore of Victoria Harbour. Rae had forgotten about this and assumed that the natives had not.[15]

This may have been the case. However, it is interesting that the natives did not remark that "one" of the crew of the "two chiefs" had died, but that "some" of them had. Could they have been speaking of Franklin's and Crozier's men who died at the place where one of their ships sank? Perhaps Rae was close to a major discovery, but did not realize that he was hearing new information and did not know the proper questions to ask.

Although Kokleearngnun's story of a visit to the ships can best be compared to the Ross expedition, it is possible that the story of the sinking of a ship had another, even earlier, source. During Parry's second expedition the Inuit told him of the recent wreck of two ships (the whalers *Dexterity* and *Aurora* on 28 August 1821). The natives remarked that "at a place called Arkoodneak, a single day's journey beyond Toonoonek, two ships like ours had been driven on shore by the ice, and that the people had gone away in boats equipped for the purpose, leaving one ship on her beam ends and the other upright."[16]

The story of one ship on her beam-ends and another upright is reminiscent of the *Chieftain* drawing. In this case, "Toonoonek" refers not to Terror Bay but to northern Baffin Island in the vicinity of Pond Inlet, yet it would be easy for this story to be confused with the tale of Franklin's ships near the identically named Toonoonee many years later.

McClintock also heard of these wrecks while at Ponds Bay in 1858. One old woman there told of a wreck which had been driven ashore "without masts and very much crushed" when she was a little girl.[17] Other natives, whose sledges were made from wood taken from the wreck, told McClintock that there had been two ships. These wrecks were "a short day's journey apart," the northern one "a few miles east of Cape Hay," but the one to the south "in an inlet or strait which contains several islands" – another curious coincidence with the *Erebus* and *Terror*.[18]

The physical evidence offered by Kokleearngnun in support of his story included a spoon stamped with Crozier's initials. Cyriax, convinced that the visit described could not have been to the *Erebus* and *Terror*, attempted to sidestep this tangible link between the native and Franklin's ships. He concluded that "Kokleearngnun's possession of a spoon which had unquestionably belonged to Crozier, and his statement that 'Aglooka' had given it to him, do not prove that 'Aglooka' was Crozier, nor that 'Aglooka' in person had given him the spoon. Hall found relics of the lost expedition widely distributed among the Eskimos, and Kokleearngnun, who was blind, may have confused the spoon with another given him by someone else."[19]

It does seem improbable that Crozier or anyone else "gave" two silver spoons to Kokleearngnun; white men were never that generous in their trades with the Inuit. Kokleearngnun's wife, it will be remembered, had a silver watch case, again a very valuable relic to have been acquired as a "gift." Yet, however they were obtained, it would have been quite remarkable for Kokleearngnun to have mistaken where these valuable things had come from.

Relics of the Franklin expedition were widespread among the Inuit and in many cases these were mixed in with things which had been obtained from other expeditions. What Cyriax fails to mention is that there was usually little difficulty in sorting out where every item had come from, for, as Hall said, the Inuit knew "the distinct history of even minute things they possess."[20]

Like all explorers, Hall paid for Franklin relics and certainly encouraged the Inuit to bring some to him. On many occasions he assumed that some item had come from Franklin's ships, only to be told that it had not come from King William Island. Once, when given a string of seventy-three beads, he was told that only two of these, easily identifiable by their singular shape, were from the Franklin expedition. The others had been received as presents from Dr Rae.[21] At another time he was told the exact source of such insignificant items as a wooden button, a single white bead, and individual bolts, hinges, and pieces of chain.[22]

Gilder also noted that the Inuit "never attempted to deceive us in regard to relics, though perhaps it would seem easy and profitable. In many instances what appeared to us to be interesting relics they told us came from the natives of Repulse Bay and elsewhere."[23] Kokleearngnun may not have received the

Crozier spoon from Crozier himself, but it is highly unlikely that he would have mistaken which ship it came from.

What must be realized when assessing the many objections to Inuit visitors to the *Erebus* and *Terror* is that many of these objections are "time-related." The *Chieftain* native was disbelieved not only because he had not set foot on the *Enterprise* and *Investigator* but because he told of a visit to Franklin's ships in 1849 – a year after Fitzjames's record had told of their abandonment. Similarly, Kokleearngnun's tale of a visit to Toolooark/Franklin and of two years spent camped on the ice by his ships admittedly has no place in the period (1846–8) when Franklin was alive. But it must be realized that, while this argues against identification of Franklin with "Toolooark," it does not necessarily follow that the two ships visited by the Inuit were not the *Erebus* and *Terror*. In one of his last statements concerning Kokleearngnun's story, Cyriax seems to realize this when he remarks that some of the officers and men may have returned to the ships after the 1848 attempt to reach the Great Fish River, and "a catastrophe like the one described by Kokleearngnun may have taken place afterwards," although he concluded that "nothing in his statement warrants so free an interpretation."[24]

With the lack of any certain post-1848 records from the men of the *Erebus* and *Terror* we cannot be sure whether one of the ships sank in later years in the manner described by Kokleearngnun. The only information surviving from Franklin's men themselves comes from the reported words of the Washington Bay commander, Aglooka. We should not place too much reliance on such a source, suffering as it does from obvious translational difficulties. What is surprising is that while Aglooka's words do not necessarily corroborate Kokleearngnun's story, they are certainly not incompatible with it.

The Washington Bay leader was not completely fluent in the native tongue. According to Hall's editor, Nourse, "Ag-loo-ka tried very hard to talk to the Innuits but did not say much to them ... The full meaning of what he said about the ice *destroying the ship* and his men dying was afterward understood" (emphasis added).[25]

Teekeeta could "afterward understand" Aglooka's men dying, for he later visited Toonoonee and saw their bodies. But Cyriax wondered how he could have known that the ships had been "destroyed."

The officers commanding the main body are most unlikely to have known what happened to the ships since their departure from them. It thus seems evident that if the natives did conclude, in consequence of what the white men tried to explain, that a ship had sunk, they misunderstood what their informants tried to describe. *I admit that more than one attempt to escape may have been made and that Eskimos may have met white men after a ship had sunk*, but there is no evidence for such an occurrence. (emphasis added)[26]

Armed with Hall's original notebooks, as Cyriax was not, we can understand how Teekeeta came to the opinion that the ship had been destroyed. Aglooka told him so! As Aglooka pointed to the north he moved his arm from that direction and "slowly moved his body in a falling direction and all at once dropped his head side ways into his hand, at the same time making a kind of combination of whirring, buzzing & wind blowing noise. This the pantomimic representation of ships being crushed in the ice."[27]

This wordless testimony by Aglooka does not prove that Kokleearngnun witnessed the destruction of the *Erebus* and *Terror*. Fitzjames's Victory Point record states that the ships were abandoned but makes no reference to their condition, and it is entirely possible that one or both of them may have been overwhelmed by the ice and left broken. Indeed some writers have concluded that no other circumstance could have made Crozier abandon his vessels so early in the season. In this view Kokleearngnun's story of a ship crushed by the ice is mere coincidence.

Kokleearngnun and his wife expressly indicated that they had visited the ships, but their testimony makes it unclear whether they themselves had seen the actual sinking of one of them or were repeating what they had been told. Certain facts tend to indicate that the details of the "sinking" were, if not incorrect, premature. When McClintock was told of the sinking of one ship in deep water the Inuit made it clear that this had occurred after the white men had abandoned it and that "all the people had landed safely."[28]

The strongest evidence against the kind of sudden sinking described by Kokleearngnun is that in addition to the ship cast ashore at Ootgoolik, another was apparently discovered, abandoned, further north. Amundsen, while wintering at Gjoa Haven on King William Island, had interviewed the natives concerning

Franklin's ships. One man named Uchyunciu, a native of "Ogluli" (Ootgoolik), told him that one of the ships had been found by the natives "when they were seal fishing on the south coast of Cape Crozier, the most westerly point of King William's Land."[29]

Uchyunciu went on to give details of the wreck at Ootgoolik as if it was the same ship, but the discovery of a vessel near Cape Crozier was probably not related to the one found further south except by later tradition which combined the remembrances. As McClintock had been told, there were two different ships – one found far out in the ice which sank quickly, and one which was driven ashore and pillaged by the Inuit. Amundsen, not realizing this, concluded that the Inuit "knew nothing of the other vessel; in all probability it had been crushed by the ice on the north side of the Royal Geographical Society Islands."[30]

A native named Qaqortingneq also told Rasmussen of the discovery of an abandoned ship far out in the ice to the west of King William Island.

Two brothers were once out sealing northwest of Qeqertaq (King William's Land). It was in spring, at the time when the snow melts away round the breathing holes of the seals. Far out on the ice they saw something black, a large black mass that could be no animal. They looked more closely and found that it was a great ship. They ran home at once and told their fellow-villagers of it, and next day they all went out to it. They saw nobody, the ship was deserted, and so they made up their minds to plunder it of everything they could get hold of. But none of them had ever met white men, and they had no idea what all the things they saw could be used for ... At first they dared not go down into the ship itself, but soon they became bolder and even ventured into the houses that were under the deck. There they found many dead men lying in their beds. At last they also risked going down into the enormous room in the middle of the ship. It was dark there. But soon they found tools and would make a hole in order to let light in. And the foolish people, not understanding white man's [sic] things, hewed a hole just on the water-line so that the water poured in and the ship sank. And it went to the bottom with all the valuable things, of which they barely rescued any.[31]

Rasmussen remarked that Qaqortingneq, in the typical Inuit manner, gave the names of all of the natives who had been involved in finding this ship. Rasmussen, much to the annoyance of later historians, declined to record them. This information would have been valuable, for Rasmussen elsewhere reported that Iggiararjuk's father, Mangaq, who had met Aglooka on the march, had "afterwards, at another time" found Aglooka's ship. Perhaps Mangaq had been one of the two brothers spoken of by Qaqortingneq (we shall see that the other was named Nukeecheuk). Iggiararjuk said that his father's ship had been located "out in the ice between King William Island and Victoria Land" and, in apparent corroboration of Qaqortingneq's story, that "many dead men were on the ship" who had "died of a sickness."[32]

These traditional tales told to Rasmussen long after the event are in many ways similar to Kokleearngnun's. The differences in the two traditions are more apparent than real. Kokleearngnun thought that many men "drowned" in the ship (or at least that is what Hall understood him to say) while Qaqortingneq told of "many dead men" in the ship. These are not exactly the same thing, but upon hearing one it would be easy to assume the other. Kokleearngnun thought that the ship was crushed and immediately sank, Qaqortingneq confirmed that the ship, once damaged, sank quickly. Qaqortingneq asserted that the natives "barely rescued any" of the valuable things; in Kokleearngnun's version the ship sank before the white men, labouring to save their provisions, "could save much." In Kokleearngnun's story it was the ice which broke a "hole in her bottom" while Qaqortingneq blamed the Inuit for making the hole.

These same elements can be traced in testimony which Hall received from the old woman named Ookbarloo at Repulse Bay in 1864. As she had never been personally involved with the tragedy, her stories were also based on hearsay and had assumed the status of tradition. Ookbarloo's story also contained elements of the discovery and destruction of both of Franklin's ships and she was obviously confused about this. She remarked that the Inuit "visited the ship or ships (the old lady could not recollect whether there was one or two)." Ookbarloo also remembered that the Inuit recovered "a great many things and carried them ashore" from one of these ships and that "no Kob-lu-na's dead body was about the ship" – elements from the second vessel found at Ootgoolik. Other details of her remembrances, however, seem to echo Kokleearngnun.

Kokleearngnun thought that the ice had made the hole in the ship, Qaqortingneq blamed the natives. Ookbarloo was unsure, remarking that "the Kob-lu-nas, or the Innuits, made a big hole in the bottom of the ship, as if they wanted to sink it." Like Kokleearngnun, Ookbarloo noted that "nearly the whole of one side of the vessel had been crushed in by the heavy ice that was about it," and she thought that this was why "the Kob-lu-nas had left it and gone to the land and lived in tents."[33]

The fact that the men went ashore and "lived in tents" is reminiscent of the camp at Terror Bay, and curiously similar to Beck's statement that after the men drowned in the ship near Omanek "they lived apart in tents."

It is difficult to determine which parts of Kokleearngnun's tale are represented by him to have been his own experiences, and which, like the sinking, may have been modified versions of hearsay. Hall's editor, Nourse, mentions that the testimony ascribed to Kokleearngnun was from "several interviews" which had been "collated" by Hall, so that we cannot even be sure that all of the traditions were relayed by Kokleearngnun himself. Other Pelly Bay natives may have told parts of the tale which Hall included in Kokleearngnun's story, or Kokleearngnun may have told of a visit to Ross's ships, relayed a tradition of the sinking of the *Dexterity* and *Aurora*, and possessed spoons taken from the white men's camp where they had "lived apart in tents." The difficulty comes not in finding a plausible origin for the various elements in the native tales – as with the Omanek stories, the permutations are almost endless – but in attributing elements of the tales to their proper source.

We do not require verifiable eyewitness details of the visit and the wreck to confirm that some of the traditions which Hall "collated" from the Pelly Bay natives do not readily apply to any known exploratory expedition. That they concern the only expedition for which we do not have records, the Franklin expedition, cannot be ruled out.

If we accept Kokleearngnun's story, we are forced to revise the standard reconstruction of what happened to the crews of the *Erebus* and *Terror*. This acceptance leads logically to certain assumptions. If we remember our earlier supposition that the 1848 abandonment was primarily intended as a hunting excursion, it is tempting to suppose that Crozier's southbound party encountered the Inuit in their traditional caribou hunting grounds near Simpson Strait and that the great communal hunt described by Kokleearngnun took place in late 1848.

Beck said that when the Inuit visited the white men's ships "they said they had been here four winters." As noted earlier, only the Ross expedition spent four winters in the Arctic, and only three of these in their ship(s). Yet if natives visited the *Erebus* and *Terror* in 1849 the crew could legitimately claim to have spent four winters (including Beechey) in the Arctic. If "here" is taken more literally to mean in the vicinity of King William Island then the fourth winter would have been 1849–50.

In 1849 the *Chieftain*'s informant told of a visit to the ships a few months previously "in the spring," and, according to his drawing, one of the vessels had already been forced on her side. We might suppose that the surviving crews therefore abandoned the ships for the second time in 1849 and that Teekeeta and Ow-wer met Aglooka during that year. Indeed it will be remembered that when Hall tried to get the natives to date this event they eventually arrived at 1849, which he assumed was "mistaken" by one year.[34]

Alternatively, the ship may have righted herself without much damage, an occurrence not unknown in the records of other expeditions, and survived for another year. Kokleearngnun mentioned "the first summer and first winter," a phrase which would imply that there had been at least two "winters" of contact before the ships were abandoned, i.e.: 1848–9 and 1849–50. Presumably the forty men encountered by Teekeeta and Ow-wer would then have been sent to Repulse Bay (Iwillik) in an effort to direct aid to those who remained behind in the camp at Toonoonee. This encounter would then reasonably have been in 1850.

John Rae was told in April 1854 that the forty men had been seen on the march "four winters ago." This led most historians to reiterate the complaint that the Inuit had no conception of numbers, for Fitzjames's record proved that the abandonment had occurred in 1848. I have always been doubtful of this ethnocentric assessment of the ability of the natives to remember chronology. While admitting that higher mathematics, of which they had no need, was beyond their capabilities, I believe that an error of two years over a span of six cannot be so blithely ignored. If we believe in Kokleearngnun's story we can conclude that Rae's informants were exactly right in their reckoning, and that it was the "experts" who had "no conception" of the true course of events.

Since the ships were whole when abandoned in 1848, Kokleearngnun's tale of one of them sinking was similarly "disproved" by reference to Fitzjames's record. Yet, by concluding that the initial abandonment was only a temporary hunting excursion, or that in any case some men were forced to return to the ice-bound ships, we can remove both difficulties.

Having been led to the conclusion that the *Erebus* and *Terror* were first seen by the Inuit after the 1848 retreat, we must next determine where this took place. McClintock was told of the wreck which occurred in deep water as having taken place to the west of King William Island. This is, of course, too general a description to be very useful as positive evidence. However, McClintock also collected "negative evidence," for he noticed that "no part of the coast between Cape Felix and Cape Crozier has been visited by Esquimaux since the fatal march of the lost crews ... none of the cairns or numerous articles strewed about – which would be invaluable to the natives – or even drift-wood we noticed, had been touched by them."[35]

This curious fact has been used to discredit Kokleearngnun's story of a visit to the *Erebus* and *Terror*. As Cyriax remarked, "had any Eskimos visited the ships near that coast before the retreat to the Great Fish River ... they would almost certainly have returned to the north-west coast during the next few years to see whether the white men had left behind anything worth taking away."[36] Again, this does not prove that Kokleearngnun did not visit the *Erebus* and *Terror*; what it does show is that, if he did, the ships were no longer near the north-west coast of King William Island.

The natives' lack of interest in the north-west coast of King William Island is remarkable. Teekeeta's party apparently never searched for relics of Aglooka's party further west than the head of Terror Bay. Perhaps Pooyetta's group extended their search to the "boat place" in Erebus Bay; if so, the confusion which surrounded the location of his boat kept any other Inuit from searching for this place for many years.

McClintock concluded that the Inuit knowledge of the Franklin expedition "must be limited to the shore-line southward and

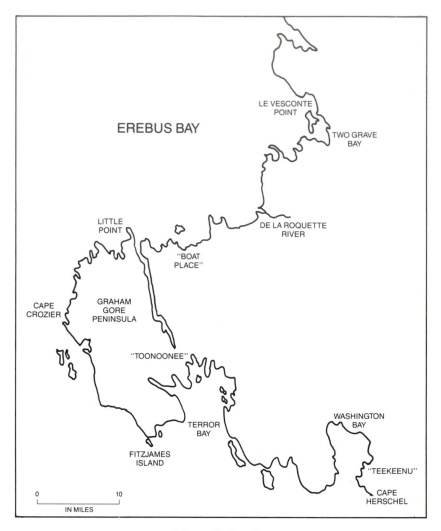

Map 5 Erebus Bay

eastward of Cape Crozier."[37] Interestingly, Uchyunciu (Amundsen's informant) located the wreck of one of Franklin's ships nearby. Kokleearngnun's story of a visit, if it applies to the *Erebus* and *Terror* at all, would obviously predate the discovery of this abandoned wreck. This would lead us to conclude that Franklin's ships were likely located to the north of Cape Crozier when the visit occurred, probably in the vicinity of Erebus Bay.

We are faced with a pivotal question in the Franklin saga. Basing their theories on the fact that McClintock found the boat in Erebus Bay to be pointing to the north in a way which indicated a return to the ships, and supporting them by the strange find of Lieutenant Irving's grave at Victory Point and some references to traces of living white men associated with the final wreck at Ootgoolik, most commentators have allowed that the ships were probably remanned by some remnant of the 1848 crew. Beyond that they have universally declined to speculate. Yet in Kokleearngnun's tale we seemingly have a coherent account of the next phase of the tragedy. We can only disregard it as an indecipherable mix of the Franklin and Ross traditions if we do some violence to the facts. If it is true that a sizeable part of the crews survived until the vessels were found by the Inuit near Cape Crozier, then a world of possibilities opens up.

It is beyond doubt that Kokleearngnun's visit with "Toolooark" and "Aglooka" details a real visit to the ships of some explorer. The tale probably refers in most of its particulars to a visit to the *Erebus* and *Terror* or to Ross's *Victory*. And it must be admitted that, owing to some unlikely coincidences, both the Franklin and Ross expeditions satisfy many of its requirements. James Clark Ross and Crozier were both known as "Aglooka," each was second in command to an older commander, each expedition came with two ships which wintered over near Boothia, and each group abandoned its vessels after one of them was "wrecked."

On its own strength, it is impossible to determine whether Kokleearngnun's story was a recitation of a visit to the *Victory* and *Krusenstern*, the *Erebus* and *Terror*, or, as Cyriax believed, a mixture of the two. Similarly, the story of the wreck may refer to the 1821 sinking of the two whalers, the problems with Ross's launch, or the wreck of one of Franklin's ships.

By allowing that at least some of the details collected from Kokleearngnun by Hall may refer to the lost Franklin expedition, we can begin to account for some of the problems which we have identified in our treatment of the Washington Bay Aglooka. The great loss of life which has always been assumed to have occurred to the north of Terror Bay is explained by Kokleearngnun's story as a result of the sudden destruction of the first ship. Such a sinking would also neatly account for the lack of human remains on the shores of northern King William Island, as would Qaqortingneq's description of the ship "far out in the ice" with "many dead men in their beds."

Similarly, the slow pace of Aglooka's detachment, which only reached Washington Bay by July, is seen to have been more apparent than real, for the men need not have departed the ships in April as was the case with the single-retreat thesis.

Kokleearngnun made one statement which we have yet to investigate. He remarked that after the first summer and first winter "they saw no more of Too-loo-ark; then Ag-loo-ka was the Eshe-muta." "Eshemuta" was as close as the native language could come to "Commander" (Rasmussen translated "isumataq" as "the one who thinks for others").[38]

Kokleearngnun linked the drowning of the white men to "Toolooark's" disappearance. He remarked that "3 men once drowned in a small boat near the ship," which may have been garbled into the account of many men drowning when the ship was nipped. He also stated that the superstitious Inuit, to whom the concept of "accident" was unknown, believed that "the old man (Tooloo-ark) designed it to be so." If these men had died while carrying out the Commander's orders, it is possible that the natives would have interpreted his remorse as guilt. Then, "a little while after," Toolooark was seen no more, and the natives "supposed he had died because he had as they thought caused the other men to be drowned."[39]

This disappearance of the "eshemuta" and the accession to command of a junior at first convinced Hall that he was hearing about Franklin and Crozier, though, as we have seen, he later changed his mind. Although a case can be made that the sinking could have referred to the *Krusenstern*, there is no doubt that on only the Franklin expedition did one "eshemuta" die – a dramatic event which could hardly go unremarked by natives in the area. Perhaps we can find an Inuit story of this as well.

"Then Aglooka Was the Eshemuta"

Whether Kokleearngnun's story is a true eyewitness account of a visit to the *Erebus* and *Terror* or a garbled melding of traditions of the Parry, Ross, and Franklin expeditions will probably never be completely determined. It doesn't really matter. Even if we grant that all of the elements of Kokleearngnun's story which could possibly relate to the *Victory* were actually inspired by Ross, we are left with certain features which are completely incompatible with his voyage. As these elements do not correspond with what is known of any other expedition to the Arctic, they must be seen either as pure fabrications or as remembrances of the one expedition for which we have no records – Franklin's.

One of these anomalous incidents was Kokleearngnun's description of a great hunt, jointly conducted by the natives and white men. He remembered that "very many men from the ships hunted took-too [caribou]" and that they were so successful that they "made a line across the whole bay of Oot-goo-lik." Yet no great hunt was conducted by the men of the *Victory*; Ross's men were singularly unsuccessful in killing caribou. There is no mention of such an event in Parry's journals either.

It is difficult to understand why Kokleearngnun insisted that the white men and Inuit had hunted caribou at Ootgoolik. Perhaps he made no such identification but simply indicated that the hunt occurred near "where the ship sank." As we noted in the last chapter, there were two places where a Franklin ship was reported to have sunk – one at Ootgoolik and one near Cape Crozier. Kokleearngnun's story, if it refers to Franklin at all, must refer to the latter place. Erebus Bay itself is largely inhospitable and is not very productive of game, but, as the expeditions of Gore in 1847 and Crozier in 1848 may have confirmed, across the thirteen-mile-wide expanse of the intervening peninsula, in Terror Bay, lay the best hunting ground on King William Island. Klutschak confirmed this.

During the crossing from the north side to the south side of the large Graham Gore Peninsula a significant difference became discernible. The sharp mudstones ceased, to be replaced as we penetrated farther by meadow areas and numerous lakes. The immediate vicinity of Terror Bay is a true paradise compared to the northern part of King William's Land and possesses a great abundance of caribou. With regard to the quality and tenderness of their meat these animals left nothing to be desired. The good grazing and the relatively small area within which they could move resulted in considerable quantities of fat accumulating on the animal's backs and ribs, and once again we could eat caribou steaks ... During those few days in Terror Bay we enjoyed by far the best food of the entire expedition ... But these rich hunting grounds extended east only to around Cape Herschel; from there on, despite the fine mossy meadows, caribou were only rarely sighted. This transition was an astounding one ...[1]

If Kokleearngnun, Ookbarloo, and Adam Beck are correct, the men of the sunken ship moved ashore to live in tents. If their ship was locked in the ice of Erebus Bay a question arises: where did they go? The camp at Toonoonee consisted of at least two tents, one large and another smaller, so it seems reasonable to conclude that the "great hunt" may have taken place in Terror Bay as well. Perhaps the hunters set up the encampment which would later be used by a more desperate company. It is interesting to note that among the gruesome evidence of cannibalism at Toonoonee there were three graves, two close together and another about fifty yards away. These were reported to have been set somewhat back from the beach on a small sandy hill. These features will be seen to be significant.

If there was interaction between the natives and Franklin's crews before the final tragedy occurred, we would expect some traces of it to be evident in other testimony. The apparent lack of such corroboration is the main support for the critics who condemn Kokleearngnun's tale as fantasy or unintelligibly garbled half-truth.

One of the most famous, and most bitterly disputed, of the Inuit tales came to light in the present century. In 1930, T.W. ("Judge") Jackson of Vancouver attempted to sell the Canadian government a document which he claimed would solve the Franklin mystery. He asked twenty-five thousand dollars for what has since become known as the "Jamme document."

Mr George Jamme had befriended an old man named Peter Bayne. As a young man Bayne had been an able seaman on the whaler *Ansel Gibbs*, and had been hired by Hall for a period of one year between 1867–8 as a hunter. Before his death, Bayne told Jamme "secret information" concerning the Franklin expedition which he had obtained years before and hoped to be able to investigate personally. Although the government was unsure of the reliability of Jackson/Jamme's information, the Department of the Interior did pay a thousand dollars for the "Bayne story."[2]

From such unlikely sources came one of the most interesting tales to emerge from the north. Because of its late emergence and the obvious financial motive, many have disputed its relevance; others, however, have accepted it as one of the most detailed and informative accounts in our possession.

Bayne had been quite popular with the Inuit, often accompanying them on their hunts and acquiring "much of the Eskimo language in the usual way." During these hunting trips the subject of earlier white explorers would often come up, and Bayne soon learned some details, which he believed concerned the Franklin expedition, from his new friends. He heard that "during the first summer," many of Franklin's men had come ashore, and that they "caught seals like the natives, and shot geese and ducks of which there was a great number; that there was one big tent and some small ones; and many men camped there ..."[3]

This may have been a slightly garbled account of the meeting with Aglooka in Washington Bay. But there are interesting discrepancies, namely the "big tent and some smaller ones" which is reminiscent of Toonoonee (Aglooka had only one tent), and the "first summer," which echoes Kokleearngnun's tale of a "first summer and first winter" and implies a longer interaction.

Bayne arrived back from this hunting trip in early March 1868 to find that Hall had decided to delay his own trip to King William Island in order to follow up a questionable story of Franklin survivors on the Melville Peninsula. After Hall left on this abortive quest, Bayne again set out on a hunting expedition accompanied by another whaler named Pat Coleman and his old native friends. The two white men stayed with the Inuit from late March until early May. We let Bayne (through Jamme) tell his story. Like Hall, he appears to have accepted that Aglooka was Crozier.

Late in April the camp was visited by a Pelly Bay native who had with him his wife and three children, the latter fairly well grown. A few days later, two men and a woman from Boothia peninsula came in. Both the Pelly Bay natives and the Boothia natives had been to King William Island. The former declared he had seen Crozier [Aglooka] at Pelly Bay, but was not sure of the date. The Boothia natives said that their people frequently went to King William Island to hunt seal, they considered it their own particular hunting ground ... The older man did most of the talking and related that he and his wife were at the north end of the island during the spring and summer of the first year, and the summer of the second year, the two ships were fast in the ice. The couple had a baby boy then that was "two winters old"; the boy was now married and had a child "one winter old". The couple would, therefore, probably be in the twenties at the time they described, and capable of making correct observations. [4]

Of course, Crozier had never visited Pelly Bay. In this case "Aglooka" was probably Dr Rae, who passed Pelly Bay repeatedly on his journeys of 1847 and 1854. The details of the two ships "fast in the ice" from the second informant seemingly must refer to the *Erebus* and *Terror*. Their location near an island (which Bayne assumed to be King William Island) could apply to Parry's ships at either Winter Island or Igloolik, but could not apply to any of the wintering places used by the *Victory* and *Krusenstern*. Parry's expedition is contraindicated by the assertion that the events had occurred when the Inuit's now-grown son (and new father) had been a baby himself. The old man's son was "fairly well grown" in 1868; if he had been a two-year-old when his parents visited Parry in 1823 (or even Ross in 1830), he would have been quite well grown indeed! Despite the difficulty in ascertaining Inuit ages, it is probable that Bayne was correct in ascribing the described events to about twenty years in the past – 1848.

Once again we note the similarities between this story and Kokleearngnun's tale. Bayne was told of events during "spring and summer of the first year, and the summer of the second year," while Kokleearngnun used almost the same words to describe the time of his visit, "during the spring and summer ... After the first summer and first winter, they saw no more of Too-loo-ark; then Aglooka was the Esh-e-muta."

The extreme uniformity of the two remembrances might make us suspect that Bayne's unnamed informant was possibly Kokleearngnun himself. Yet Kokleearngnun had died shortly after meeting Hall in 1864, three years before Bayne was hired.[5] Moreover, Kokleearngnun asserted that he himself had visited "Toolooark's" ships, while Bayne's native confided that "he had not gone out to the ships but other natives had, and had camped alongside for several days, and had seen and talked with Franklin [Toolooark]."[6]

We recognize that the story told to Bayne is independent corroboration of Kokleearngnun's testimony. The timing and major events are identical, as are the words used to describe them. There is one other point of similarity. Kokleearngnun remarked that during the second year "they saw no more of Too-loo-ark; then Aglooka was the Esh-e-muta"; Bayne may have heard details of Toolooark's funeral.

In relating the events that took place [the Boothian native remarked that] ... many of the white men came ashore and camped there during the summer; that the camp had one big tent and several smaller ones; that Crozier (Aglookna) came there some times, and he had seen and talked with him; that seal were plentiful the first year, and sometimes the white men went with the natives and shot seal with their guns; that ducks and geese were also plentiful, and the white men shot many; that some of the white men were sick in the big tent; and died there, and were buried on the hill back of the camp; that one man died on the ships and was brought ashore and buried on the hill near where the others were buried; that this man was not buried in the ground like the others, but in an opening in the rock, and his body covered over with something that, "after a while was all same stone"; that he was out hunting seal when this man was buried, but other natives were there, and saw, and told him about it, and the other natives said that "many guns were fired."[7]

Bayne and his companion Coleman were very excited by this tale of a military funeral and continued to question the natives and to extract details.

He got the Boothia native to give a description of the tenting ground and of the place where the men who died were buried. From the description given, Bayne figured the camp to have been about a fourth of a mile back from the beach, and about the same distance south of where the ship's boats usually landed; that it was situated on a flat-topped mound near the base of a low ridge; that the crest of the ridge was not very wide and was formed of projecting rocks; and that the slope on the other side faced the south-east.[8]

When Bayne and Coleman returned to their camp at Repulse Bay, they brought these natives with them and endeavoured to convince them to stay until Hall returned from Melville Peninsula. The Boothians were eager to get back to their own territory, however, so the whalers arranged for them to retell their stories to other natives so as to impress all of the events in their collective memory and have their friends act as group interpreters.

The only thing new that developed out of these recitals, other than what Bayne had already learned, was that there were several cemented vaults – one large one, and a number of small ones; that the natives thought that these latter contained only papers, for many papers were brought ashore – some blew away in the wind, but others were buried. These natives had seen a number of the dead white men since that time, whose bodies lay as they had died, now frozen in the snow. Bayne and Spearman drew maps and got the natives to try and locate the camp and the graves and the ridge with respect to the beach. The sketch attached is made by the writer (Jamme) from memory from a map Captain Bayne had among his papers, but which cannot be located now.[9]

When Hall returned from his trip, his men eagerly approached him with what they had learned, but "he rather resented their acts" and, at least on the surface, discounted the story as worth-

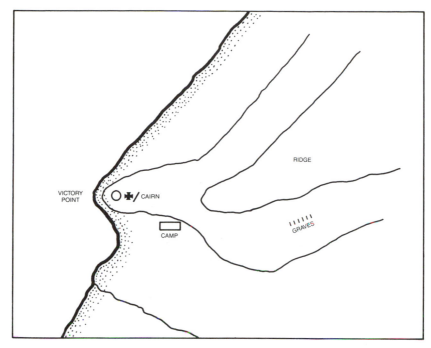

Figure 3 The Bayne Map as redrawn by Jamme. The identification of the location as Victory Point is patently wrong, and may have been a later element.

less. Shortly afterwards, Hall put down what he felt was an incipient mutiny by fatally shooting Coleman, and, understandably, the remaining men returned to the whalers and left Hall alone with his Inuit companions. Bayne accounted for Hall's attitude "as one of pique; and his action in withholding the information from his records, as the stand of a strong-willed man. The great ambition of the old Captain was that he might be able to go himself, and prove to the world the existence of the 'Cemented Vaults.'"[10]

When the Bayne story emerged, reaction to it was almost universally negative. Some considered that "it is scarcely credible that Franklin was buried on the island, since the Crozier record [at Victory Point] does not mention it,"[11] while others based their disbelief on the supposed fact that no other explorer had heard of any "cemented vaults" until Bayne made his belated disclosure.

The first objection – that no burial was mentioned in the 1848 record – vanishes if we conclude that the burial did not take place until at least a year after this record was written. The second objection, also, is weak. Although direct references are unknown, there is ample indirect evidence that knowledge of the cemented vaults was widespread. It apparently remained largely unpublished and unremarked, for each person who heard the story felt that he had a key to the mystery and, like the old Captain himself, dreamed of "proving to the world" that Franklin had been buried ashore. Noel Wright commented that "there seems to have been a conspiracy of silence about the matter."[12]

That Bayne did pass some version of his story to Hall in 1868 is certain, for Hall later wrote that "from information I had gained from the natives, I had reason to suppose [I] would be rewarded by the discovery of the whole of the manuscript records that had been accumulated in that great expedition, and had been deposited in a vault a little way inland or eastward of Cape Victory."[13]

Hall must have passed some mention of "cement" to his other patron as well, for "in October 1869 Lady Franklin wrote to Mr Grinnell asking for further information on this subject, and saying that McClintock thought the Eskimos might have found a paved spot which had been the site of a magnetic observatory."[14]

There is other evidence that the Bayne story was widely circulated soon after Hall's return to the United States. In 1875 Sir Allen Young, a veteran of McClintock's expedition, made an unsuccessful attempt to take the yacht *Pandora* through the North-West Passage. One of his declared purposes was, "if successful in reaching the locality of King William's Land in the summer season when the snow was off the lands, to make a search for further records and for the journals of the ships *Erebus* and *Terror*."[15] It is hard to believe that after the passage of thirty years Young could expect to find the perishable records and journals unless he had heard that they had been carefully deposited in such a manner that McClintock had missed them – underground.

A careful reading of Schwatka's and Gilder's accounts of their explorations in 1879 also reveals that they may have known of the story, even though they do not specifically mention it. After meticulously searching the north-west coast of King William Island, Schwatka somewhat disappointedly remarked, "I confidently expected to find their graves [i.e. those of Franklin, Gore, and the other casualties from the ships] between Cape Felix and Victory Point, but the most unremitting search of days, embracing miles along this short coastline of fifteen miles revealed nothing that could be supposed to be their resting places."[16]

One must wonder why Schwatka so confidently thought he would find their graves here after such a passage of time. He certainly had not heard a full account of Bayne's story, for Hall's Narrative was not published until after the Schwatka party had left for the Arctic, and it contained only vague references to buried records. Nevertheless Schwatka must have heard something, for he noted that the diligent scouring of the north-west coast was inspired by Hall, who "had published the belief that the records and other valuables were probably stored some distance inland from the scene of the two year's [sic] imprisonment."[17]

Bayne's account is remarkable in its detail and accuracy and contains too much internal consistency to be dismissed out of hand just because it poses problems for a traditional reconstruction of the Franklin disaster, a version which has no place for an Inuit visitation to the ships or a burial ashore. Noel Wright, who passionately embraced the Bayne story and used it as the key to a reconstruction of his own, thought that it was eminently trustworthy.

It seems to me that the proper tests of any Eskimo story of this nature should be: is it likely? Does it ring true? Does it contain any corroborative touch that could hardly be imagined? Bayne's story stands up to all three. It is eminently likely, except to diehard believers in the theory of the burial in the ice; and that sentence "many guns were fired" in itself tells a story – the story of a naval funeral. And it certainly contains a corroborative touch; the Eskimos could hardly have imagined that substance "which after a time became all stone". At some time, in some place, before the year 1868, they must have come upon a cemented patch or patches, and it almost seemed as though they must have meddled with the cement immediately after it had been laid down; otherwise how did they know it altered its condition from soft to hard?[18]

Wright is correct that at some time before 1868 the Inuit must have witnessed a naval funeral and encountered cement. This does not, of course, prove that this occurred on the Franklin expedition, for Bayne's Pelly Bay informants could as easily be relaying tales of other parties of white men. Once again the Ross expedition and the earlier sojourn by Parry in 1821–3 on the east coast of the Melville Peninsula seem to be the only likely alternatives.

Ross lost three of his men during his expedition with the *Victory* – James Marslin, James Dixon, and Chibham Thomas. The last two of these can probably be discounted as sources for Bayne's tale, for they died after the Inuit had left Lord Mayor Bay in quest of better hunting – Dixon at Victoria Harbour on 10 January 1832 and Thomas at Fury Beach on 22 February 1833.

Marslin, on the other hand, died on 20 January 1830, and although he was specifically buried early in the morning the next Sunday (the 24th) so that the ceremony would not be interrupted by the natives, they arrived at the ship a few hours later. Ross's journal notes only that the burial was "performed with the usual forms and solemnity,"[19] but Light described Marslin's burial, in a shallow grave only thirty inches deep, in more detail. At ten in the morning the corpse was carried to the spot, accompanied by the whole crew, and they "beheld the partner of their toils laid in his last resting place – no coffin enclosed his remains – no gilt escutcheon told his name and age, his hammock was his shroud, his pillow a piece of granite; the latter part of the funeral service was read, the grave was filled up with coarse gravel, and the crew retraced their steps to the vessel."[20] There is no mention of a gun salute; perhaps this military flourish was not considered appropriate for a privately financed non-military expedition.

Another problem with the idea that the Inuit saw Marslin's funeral is the element of contact between the ship and shore by boats, "where the boats usually landed," for the *Victory* was solidly frozen in only a few hundred yards from shore.

Dixon's funeral at Victoria Harbour, as mentioned, could not have been witnessed. It took a week to cut his shallow grave in the permafrost and once again there is no mention of a vault. Of the funeral itself, Ross gives no details except that the "usual solemnities" were observed.[21] Thomas was similarly buried in a "shallow grave" at Fury Beach, and no Inuit were in the vicinity.[22]

The winters spent by Parry's *Fury* and *Hecla* at Winter Island (1821–2) and Igloolik (1822–3) offer more likely comparisons with Bayne's testimony. Three of Parry's men died at Winter Island – James Pringle on 15 May 1822, John Reid on the 26th of that month, and William Souter on 25 June. Pringle was buried on 21 May. No details of the ceremony are given in Parry's account, but Lyon mentioned that "a volley was fired over him."[23] The other two men were buried on Friday 28 June.

The remains of our deceased shipmates were committed to the earth, with every solemnity that so mournful an occasion demanded. They were interred in one grave, on a rising ground a few hundred yards from the sea to the northeastward of the ships. A handsome tomb of stone and mortar was built over the spot, having at one end a stone let in, with the usual information engraved on it. The sides were plaistered [sic] with a kind of viscous clay found in one of the ponds, and the top covered with tufts of the purple saxifrage. The duties of the ship now permitting it, Captain Lyon employed his men in building a similar tomb over the grave of Pringle.[24]

This account of a grave on "rising ground a few hundred yards from the sea" echoes Bayne's "flat-topped mound" which was "about a fourth of a mile back from the beach." Neither commander notes a gun salute at this ceremony, but there almost certainly was one. The hardened clay might have corresponded to something which changed from soft to "all same stone."

One of Parry's boats had been briefly launched on 1 June to take soundings in the nearest open water in preparation for cutting out of the ice, although this was an isolated event, there being no regular waterborne traffic between the ships and a place where they "usually landed."[25] This feature of boats working near the ships is entirely missing from most Arctic expeditions for which we have records. It is, however, reminiscent of Kokleearngnun's tale of the boat accident in which three of Toolooark's men drowned.

Another potential occasion on which the Inuit could have witnessed a funeral similar to that described to Bayne occured at the interment of Alex Elder, who died on 15 April 1823 while Parry's ships were at Igloolik. At Ponds Bay, McClintock was told (by the same woman who relayed the information about the *Dexterity* and *Aurora*) of the burial of a white man at Igloolik. She even remembered that his name was "Al-lah or El-leh."[26]

According to Lyon, Elder was buried in a shallow grave less than three feet deep, and two volleys were fired.[27] Parry mentions that a "tomb of stones," possibly similar to that used to honour his earlier comrades, was built over his grave.[28]

This poses a problem. If we cannot legitimately differentiate between Parry's two funerals, how can we conclude that Crozier, who had been present at them, did not take them as precedent and later adopt similar methods to bury his own dead men? On the details of the funeral itself we can conclude no more than that the Inuit were witnesses of a typical military ceremony which occured somewhere in the Arctic. Where?

At least one writer has assumed that the funeral which is being spoken of was that of Franklin himself, and in any case Bayne's vault has usually been sought on the north-west coast of King William Island between Cape Felix and Victory Point. But all the reasons used to show that Kokleearngnun could not have visited the *Erebus* and *Terror* while Franklin was alive likewise argue against this, and these arguments have occasionally been used to invalidate the story as a whole. Yet invalidation of a wrong assumption derived from the testimony does not constitute disproof of the testimony itself. The fact that the funeral was not Franklin's does not automatically show that the story does not involve the men from the *Erebus* and *Terror*. Indeed, there is no internal reason contained in the story to indicate that the funeral was that of an officer at all.

Closely related to this is the assertion that, since the coast from Victory Point to Cape Felix has been repeatedly and thoroughly searched without any sign of a "cemented vault" being found, and since there was apparently no open water between Franklin's ships and the shore before 1848 which would allow the boats to "usually land" anywhere, the Bayne story has been shown to be useless. Once again, the conclusion is not justified by the evidence – the absence of a grave on the north-west coast of King William Island does not mean that it does not exist, simply that it must be searched for elsewhere.

We have no proof that Bayne ever identified the point where the cairn and vault were located. It is certain that the natives would not have been able to ascribe any name to it which the untutored whalers-turned-explorers would have understood. Bayne indicated only that it was to be found on King William Island, and the small map drawn to accompany Jamme's report does label the site as "Victory Point," but whether this was Bayne's work or that of another we do not know. If Bayne did name the locale he may have identified it as Victory Point solely because that was the only named geographical feature on King William Island with which he was familiar.

Cyriax based his distrust of Hall's belief in the vault on his opinion that the story of a vault was based entirely on previously mentioned testimony given to Hall by Seepunger.[29] It will be remembered that Seepunger had visited the north-west coast of King William Island in the early 1860s and mentioned finding an Enookshooyer (tall monument – presumably one of those near Cape Felix), and a cairn and white man's grave near a pile of clothes (Victory Point). A careful review of his testimony shows that Seepunger made no mention of a vault, but this did not stop Hall from making some unwarranted conclusions. Hall's notebook of 8 May 1866 confirms that he had persuaded himself that Seepunger's "monument" was the "vault" of which he had heard.

Hall had heard from Seepunger of an Enookshooyer and cairn associated with a sealed tin cup and a box which contained papers, and assumed that the vault must be at Victory Point. It seems likely that when Bayne told Hall of "cemented vaults" two years later, Hall considered it "old news" concerning Seepunger's monument at Victory Point. Bayne may have believed this as well. But they were wrong.

Regardless of how "worthless" Hall told Bayne the Inuit remembrance was, he certainly believed in the existence of a vault which contained Franklin records. His letters show that he was not only confident of finding such a cache when he set out for King William Island, but, as late as 1871, he was still confident that a search of King William Island would result in the discovery of the records of Sir John's expedition.[30] It is hard to believe that Bayne's story did not have something to do with that attitude.

If Bayne's informant did witness a military funeral on the west shore of King William Island, it must have occurred after the supposed visit of Kokleearngnun, in 1849 or 1850. Kokleearngnun mentioned that after the "first summer and first winter" the commander or "eshemuta" was replaced by "Aglooka" and the implication is that the former died. This did not happen on the Ross or Parry expeditions. It can only be a remembrance of the *Erebus* and *Terror*.

If we are correct in assuming that the first native interaction with the *Erebus* and *Terror* occurred in 1849, then it is obvious that Kokleearngnun's "Toolooark" cannot have been Franklin.

Fitzjames's record revealed that Franklin died on 11 June 1847. Who, then, was "Toolooark"?

The physical description of "Toolooark" was quite specific. According to Kokleearngnun, the leader was "an old man with broad shoulders, thick and heavier set than Hall [who carried over two hundred pounds on a five-foot eight-inch frame], with gray hair, full face, and bald head." In 1840 Crozier had been described by McCormick, the surgeon on the *Erebus* at the time, as "a somewhat heavy man," while another acquaintance at Hobart had noted that he was "tall, stout, and middle aged" and mentioned that even then his hair had been prematurely white.[31]

Of the officers aboard Franklin's ships, most were not "old men" but contemporaries or juniors of Fitzjames. Fitzjames's age is uncertain (he was a foundling), but most estimates make him about thirty-seven in 1849. The other officers who could have taken over command – Le Vesconte, Fairholme, Hodgson, and Little – were all relatively young. The elderly purser, Osmer, and the two ice-masters, Reid and Blanky, need not be considered, for none of these were in the normal chain of command. In 1849 Crozier would have been fifty-three years of age.

If Kokleearngnun's visit really was to the *Erebus* and *Terror* in 1849, then the "Eshemuta" when Franklin's ships were first seen must almost certainly have been Crozier. Since he was the leader of the expedition he was given the name which was traditionally given to such a person, "Toolooa," although he sometimes appears in other stories as "Aglooka" – the name of his youth. Or perhaps the Inuit assumed that the elderly Toolooa who was with Aglooka in Washington Bay must have been the same individual who had been in command of the ships in the ice and therefore applied the same name to both.

It seems certain that the Inuit met Crozier himself, probably on the ships, for although they never mention Franklin they knew of Crozier and his role quite well. Kokleearngnun was from Pelly Bay, so we should expect that the other natives from this area would have known about the two ships caught in the ice near King William Island, and their commander. And they did.

When Hall interviewed Artooa at Repulse Bay in 1864 he was told that Artooa "had heard of Crozier when at Pelly Bay, that he (C) was one of the Koblunas belonging to the two ships that were in the ice near Neitch-il-le for two years before the white men left them."[32] All of the Pelly Bay Inuit knew of "Cro-zhar," who had been an "Esh-e-mut-ta-nar (mate or some officer not so great as captain on Parry's ship)."[33] They were also aware that the "same man, Crozier, who was at Igloo-lik when Parry and Lyon were there, was Esh-e-mu-ta (meaning captain in this case, the literal chief) of the two ships lost in the ice at Neitchille."[34] How could they know this unless some Inuit had visited the ship?

It could be argued that the large man with grey hair seen at Washington Bay (Toolooa) was Crozier himself, and that this is where the Inuit learned that their old acquaintance from Igloolik had sailed aboard the *Erebus* and *Terror* as well. The physical descriptions are not incompatible, and we have seen that Le Vesconte was, in the opinion of the Inuit, no better than third in seniority among the marchers, implying that both Aglooka and Toolooa were senior officers. This does not entirely ring true in light of some of the details of the meeting at Teekeenu. The dominant role among the white men was taken by Aglooka, the younger man, and it is hard to see why Crozier would allow this. In addition, Toolooa had difficulty with the Inuit dialect and had, once again, to defer to Aglooka and Doktook. Yet Crozier was the most experienced officer on board, the veteran of three previous Arctic voyages. It is apparent from the memories retained of him at Igloolik that he was quite familiar with the natives, and able to interact with them.

One of the most curious pieces of evidence in our possession unequivocally states that the Inuit learned of Crozier's identity before the ships were abandoned. Unfortunately, the source was none other than Too-shoo-art-thariu's cousins, who also told Hall the garbled story of Too-shoo-art-thariu's meeting with Aglooka and his three men.

Crozier told this cousin that he was once at Iwillik (Repulse Bay), at Winter Island and Igloolik, many years before, and that at the two last-named places he saw many Innuits, and got acquainted with them. This cousin had heard of Parry, Lyon, and Crozier, from his Innuit friends at Repulse Bay, some years previous, and therefore when Crozier gave him his name he recollected it. The cousin saw Crozier one year before he found him and the three men, where the two ships were in the ice. It was there that he found out that Crozier had been to Igloolik.[35]

Since Teekeeta and Ow-wer both confirmed that Too-shoo-art-thariu first met white men in Washington Bay, and that he had never seen them before this or encountered them later, this statement has obvious difficulties. Perhaps it was not Too-shoo-art-thariu but some other "cousin" who was here being spoken of. But it seems that this accurate thumbnail biographical sketch could only have come from Crozier himself! The fact that the natives knew that Crozier had served with both Parry and Franklin is remarkable enough; the fact that they learned this from Crozier's own lips, while he served as "eshemuta" of the two ships in the ice, is, according to the standard reconstruction, inexplicable.

On 15 April 1868, three years after his interviews with Too-shoo-art-thariu's cousins, Hall interviewed the adult Aglooka who was now known as Crozier. This native had gained his new name as a boy at Igloolik through name-transference with the young Crozier. According to Aglooka/Crozier, he had learned from the natives of Pelly Bay that "there were three (3) men of the number [of men who had starved at Neitchille] that had formerly been to Ig-loo-lik with Parry: Their names: – 'Aglooka (Crozier), Par-kee & ——'" (blanks in Hall's notes).[36]

This potentially significant but incomplete clue is puzzling. Parry himself or Lieutenant Charles Palmer may have been the source of the name "Par-kee"; Erktua remembered the latter as "Par-mee". Another candidate for "Park-ee" could have been the *Fury*'s Jonathan Sparks. None of these men sailed with the *Erebus* and *Terror*.

James Clark Ross, known to the Inuit as "Aglooka," had, like Crozier, visited all of the enumerated places. A seaman named Park also sailed in the *Victory* and may have been "Parkee," but he had not sailed with Parry. The only other name common to both the *Victory*'s and Parry's muster sheets is Taylor – George Taylor being third mate of Ross's ship and Henry Taylor having sailed in *Hecla*.

We cannot identify three of Parry's men among the 129 crewmen of the *Erebus* and *Terror* either – although some curious linkages occur. Crozier, like James Clark Ross, fits the bill as "Aglooka." There were two men named Hammond, John (*Terror*) and James? (*Fury*); interestingly, both were marines. William Smith was Blacksmith of the *Erebus*, and the name also occurs on the earlier lists, one on each of Parry's ships. Unfortunately Franklin's man was, according to his description book, only six years old when the *Fury* and *Hecla* entered the Arctic.

Other surnames found on both Franklin's and Parry's lists are Thompson, Johnson, and Reed, but none of the first names match. Less common correlations exist with the names Dunn, Lloyd, Berry, Best, and Aylmer (Aylmore). Once again the given names are at variance in the lists, although these are often barely legible shortened forms, and it is not inconceivable that one or more of Franklin's men were related to Parry's.[37]

If "Toolooark" was Crozier, then Kokleearngnun's statement that "after the first summer and first winter, they saw no more of Toolooark" implies that he must have died before the spring of 1850. After this there was another "Eshemuta," a younger man, who was, in turn, called "Aglooka." This second "Aglooka" was presumably the man in charge at Washington Bay, assisted by another elderly "Toolooa," who was probably one of the ice-masters (Blanky or Reid).

Historians discount Bayne's story of a burial ashore because they do not believe that Franklin would be taken over the many miles of rough ice to the shores of King William Island for burial, and because no significant grave has ever been found to the north of Victory Point. If "Toolooark" was Crozier, and if he died after the "first winter" (1848–9), then the ships were relatively near to shore in Erebus Bay. Later, he could easily have been buried "where the ship's boats usually landed."

As previously noted, no explorer has ever found any hint of cemented vaults or an orderly cemetery on the west coast of King William Island. When we review the literature we find that McClintock found no graves at all north of Cape Crozier. Nevertheless Schwatka and Gilder, perhaps inspired by Bayne's story, conducted a much more thorough search – with better results. Schwatka mentioned finding the remains of two Franklin crewmen near Point Le Vesconte in what is now called Two-Grave Bay (part of Erebus Bay). Admittedly the scattered remains which he described were a far cry from Bayne's description of the neatly arranged line of graves on his ridge of shingle.[38] Klutschak described a grave found here as well. He noted that "the builders of this grave no longer had the strength to build an above-ground grave out of large rocks" and that "a few stones were all that they used to cover the corpse."[39] Yet this grave at Le Vesconte Point was in some ways unique. Almost all of the dozen graves found on King William Island were simple piles of small stones which were placed over the bodies, which were, in turn, arranged on the surface of the ground. As such they had no adornment, and were subsequently difficult to distinguish from the grey-brown background. There was only one exception to this rule. Gilder supplemented his companions' somewhat colourless accounts of it.

It was a beautiful though saddening spectacle that met our eyes at the only grave upon King William's Land, where the dead had been buried beneath the surface of the ground. Near Point le Vesconte some scattered human bones led to the discovery of the tomb of an officer who had received most careful sepulture at the hands of his surviving friends. A little hillock of sand and gravel – a most rare occurrence upon that forbidding island of clay-stones – afforded an opportunity for Christian-like interment.

The dirt had been neatly rounded up, as could be plainly seen, though it had been torn open and robbed by the sacrilegious hands of the savages; and everywhere, amid the debris and mould of the grave, the little wild flowers were thickly spread as if to hide the desecration of unfriendly hands. The fine texture of the cloth and linen and several gilt buttons showed the deceased to have been an officer, but there was nothing to be seen anywhere that would identify the remains to a stranger. Every stone that marked the outline of the tomb was closely scrutinized for a name or initials, but nothing was found.[40]

Klutschak's opinion that the absence of large stones at this grave was caused by the debility of Franklin's men curiously contrasts to Gilder's opinion that the grave (dug into the earth and therefore not requiring large stones) was a testimonial to their care for their comrade.

Bayne had been told that the white men had been buried on a "hill" or "flat-topped mound" and that the "vault" was located nearby. The three graves found at Terror Bay were also near a "small sandy hill." Here again we find the same description, a "little hillock of sand and gravel" in the depths of Erebus Bay. Perhaps the sailors had established a tent-camp here as well.

There are other clues. Tooktoocheer told Schwatka of a location where the records had been buried. Bayne was told that some smaller "vaults" contained papers and books. We earlier concluded that Tooktoocheer, her husband Pooyetta, and her son Ogzeuckjeuwock may have visited the boat place in Erebus Bay, and that this was mistakenly assumed to have been at Ootgoolik owing to the ambiguity of the description as "near where the ship sank."

We also recall that, while at this boat place, Ogzeuckjeuwock had injured himself by playing with gunpowder. Gunpowder was carried aboard Arctic vessels to allow them to blast their way through the ice. In small quantities it was also used for firearms. Because of the inherent danger, the normal procedure was to store it in a specially built "powder-house" ashore as soon as the ships were firmly frozen in. Ross had done this at Felix Harbour, and Parry had similarly cached the powder from the wrecked *Fury* at Fury Beach, later instructing Ross to destroy it lest it harm any unsuspecting natives.[41] Had the powder which injured Ogzeuckjeuwock been similarly placed ashore when the *Erebus* and *Terror* were beset in Erebus Bay? Was that why the officer on the ship with the "black men" did not want the natives to go to the place ashore near the tent?

If the grave described by Gilder was the one spoken of to Bayne, it would support our earlier conclusion that the ships were first encountered nearby. We should remember that the grave was near the place "where the ship's boats usually *landed*." This phrase implies a regular waterborne commerce between ships and shore which is incompatible with the Parry and Ross expeditions, and with Franklin's expedition before 1848. The tent where the "black men" lived was within sight of the ship, only a few miles away at most. During the summers the broad lane of open water along the shore would require boats to ferry men from the tent place to the nearby ship.

One other fact reinforces our conclusion that Erebus Bay was where the *Erebus* and *Terror* were beset in 1849–50. McClintock found a boat with two skeletons along the southern shores of this bay and concluded that "the boat was returning to the ships: and in no other way can I account for two men having been left in her."[42]

This seemed to be a reasonable assumption, that when the weight of the sledge became too oppressive the weaker men were left with a store of provisions while the stronger carried on to the ships with plans to return soon with help. The main problem was that McClintock's boat was, by his reckoning, "50 miles – as a sledge would travel – from Point Victory, and therefore 65 miles from the position of the ships."[43] This seemed to be a long way for men to go to secure assistance (which unfortunately never arrived).

But if the party from Toonoonee was returning to the ships in their later position in Erebus Bay, then the abandonment of two of their comrades, which at first seems heartless and hardly justifiable, may have originally been intended to last for only a few hours until the men could reach the nearby ship and return. In fact, the two boats, which McClintock felt were too heavy to have been sensibly dragged along the coast, may never have left the beach at Erebus Bay. They may have been taken ashore (presumably from the "wreck") to serve as a way to return to the ships once the ice broke up, to take to the south if needed, or to provide temporary shelter for any men caught halfway between the ships and the camp at Toonoonee.

We have seen, based on a chain of interconnected evidence and testimony, that it is likely that the *Erebus* and *Terror* were remanned by a portion of their crews after the abortive march of 1848. We have demonstrated that it is highly probable that they were subsequently visited by the Inuit, and that the natives were quite familiar with their location and the activities of the white men during 1849. A few men died and were buried ashore "where the boats usually landed." In the first summer the white men and Inuit hunted caribou, probably in Terror Bay, and three men who died here were decently buried. Then Crozier ("Toolooark") died and was buried ashore in Erebus Bay, and some journals were preserved nearby in some "cemented vaults."

Disaster struck. One ship was thrown on her side by the ice, and the men moved ashore to tents on the shore of Erebus Bay and at Toonoonee. Thoughts turned once again to an attempt at self-help. Led by the new commander, Aglooka, the strongest forty men set out from Toonoonee in an attempt to reach Repulse Bay in 1850. They met Teekeeta's party in Washington Bay, and their own fate at Keeuna.

Discipline broke down among those left behind. Some preferred to return to the ships, others to remain in camp. Those who remained at Toonoonee would all eventually die after being reduced to the last extremity. Of those who retraced their steps many could not proceed beyond the boats and the large tent in Erebus Bay. These men were also reluctantly left behind to die. Perhaps cannibalism was already being practised, and that, not the presence of gunpowder, is the reason why the officer on the ship with the "black men" did not want the Inuit to mix with these outcasts.

The final few men did manage to reach the ship(s). While living in the intact one they suffered further casualties. Perhaps rather than invest the effort to cut graves in the ice these men were taken the short distance to the "wreck" and placed in bunks. This broken ship full of dead men would be found out in the ice near Cape Crozier, would sink quickly, and would give rise to Kok- leearngnun's tale. As discipline further deteriorated the men stopped washing, became "black," and may have tried to capture an Inuit visitor as a potential meal. The few remaining officers were losing any control over events, retiring to their cabins and awaiting the inevitable end.

Then, miraculously, the ice broke up. The surviving ship, and its pathetic crew, was again made ready for sea. This second ship, with a very few survivors on board, would eventually be- come beset many miles to the south at Ootgoolik. The Inuit will tell us what happened to it as well.

~17~

Aglooka's Ship

At one time both the *Erebus* and *Terror* were intact off the coast of King William Island. While here they may have been visited by the Inuit. One ship, crushed and perhaps on her side, was found far out in the ice of Victoria Strait near Cape Crozier. She sank quickly and little wealth was obtained from her. In 1859 McClintock was told by some natives that the other ship was driven ashore by the ice at a place called "Oot-loo-lik"[1] and that all of the relics which he could see had come from this other ship.

McClintock thought that Ootgoolik referred to the west coast of King William Island, but we have seen that this term applies to the west coast of the Adelaide Peninsula. Hall was told that the natives found this second ship "in the ice of the sea between Dease Strait and Simpson Strait" – modern Queen Maud Gulf. From descriptions of the actual wreck site, Hall concluded that the ship came to rest near O'Reilly Island. He was told that the ship, "sank some time after they [the Inuit] found it but not so bad what the topmasts were above water – ultimatley [sic] the ice broke the vessel that masts, timbers etc. drifted to the land south side of Ook-joo-lik sea & there found in abundance by Ook-joo-lik natives."[2]

Hall was later given more detail about this wreck by an Ootgoolik native named Ek-kee-pee-ree-a.

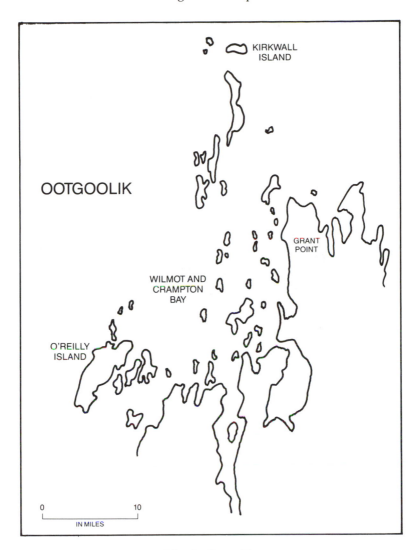

Map 6   Ootgoolik

This ship 1st seen he said by Nuk-kee-che-uk an Ook-joo-lik Innuit who is now dead, having been killed by his (Ek-kee-pee-ree-a's) father. This he told me with a smile. This ship had 4 boats hanging at the sides and 1 of them was above the quarter deck. The ice about the *ship one winter's make*, all a smooth flow [sic] & a plank was found extending from the ship down on to the ice. The Innuits were sure some white men must have lived there through the winter. Heard of tracks of 4 strangers, not

Innuits, being seen on the land adjacent to the ship. (emphasis in original)[3]

The traditions concerning the ship which arrived in the south were remarkably consistent. Seeuteetuar's wife, Koo-nik, had part of a glass jar in her possession which "came from a large cask filled with glass jars near where the great ship was seen & was finally sunk at Ook-joo-lik."[4] This opened the way for further conversation with Hall.

She says that Nuk-kee-che-uk & other Ook-joo-lik Innuits were out sealing when they saw a large ship – all very much afraid but Nuk-kee-che-uk who went to the vessel while the others went to their Ig-loo. Nuk-kee-che-uk looked all around and saw nobody & finally *Lik-lee-poo-nik-kee-look-oo-loo* (stole a very little or few things) & then made for the Ig-loos. Then all the Innuits went to the ship & stole a good deal – broke into a place that was fastened up & there found a very large white man who was dead, very tall man. There was flesh about this dead man, that is, his remains quite perfect – it took 5 men to lift him. The place smelt very bad. His clothes all on. Found dead on the floor – not in a sleeping place or birth [sic] … The vessel covered over with *see-loon*, that is housed in with sails or that material, not boards, but as Jack [Hall's guide Nu-ker-zhoo] says like Capt. Potter's vessel when at Ship's Harbour Isles in the winter quarters.
The Ig-loos or cabins down below as "Ansel Gibbs" not on deck like "Black Eagle." (emphasis in original)[5]

One of the most striking and significant elements of this re-membrance was the fact that one dead man was found aboard the Ootgoolik ship. This body understandably made quite an impression on the natives. Earlier, McClintock had been told that a dead man had been found on the second ship, and that he "must have been a very large man, and had long teeth."[6] Hall was repeatedly told of the "very large man" whose teeth "were long as an Innuit finger & of very great stature."[7]
This is apparently unequivocal proof that we are hearing of either the *Erebus* or *Terror*. No other known exploratory ship was abandoned with a dead body still aboard. We remember Kok-leearngnun's story of the very tall companion of "Toolooark" who was a veritable giant to the short Inuit. Was his body aboard the wrecked ship? The presence of this body poses a problem for the

traditional reconstruction, for Crozier and Fitzjames specifically mention that they had abandoned the ships in 1848 with all "105 souls" remaining at that time. Some of those men apparently returned. If Kokleearngnun is to be believed, most of them did.

In a letter to his patron, Grinnell, Hall included other details of the find.

The party on getting aboard tried to find out if any one was there, and not seeing or hearing any one, began ransacking the ship. To get into the igloo (cabin), they knocked a hole through because it was locked … one place in the ship, where a great many things were found, was very dark; they had to find things there by feeling around. Guns were there and a great many very good buckets and boxes.

On my asking if they saw anything to eat on board, the reply was there was meat and tood-noo in cans, the meat fat and like pemmican. The sails, rigging, and boats – everything about the ship – was in complete order.

From time to time the Neitchilles went to get out of her whatever they could; they made their plunder into piles on board, intending to sledge it to their igloos some time after; but on going again they found her sunk, except the top of the masts. They said they had made a hole in her bottom by getting out one of her timbers or planks. The ship was afterward much broken up by the ice, and then masts, timbers, boxes, casks, &c., drifted on shore …[8]

Hall's informant Ek-kee-pee-ree-a was an Ootgoolik native, and therefore a reliable source for the wreck which had occurred there. But as he prefaced his remarks by telling Hall that he had "heard" the natives tell of this ship, he was probably not personally involved. Koo-nik had never visited the site either. In 1879 Schwatka and Gilder interviewed Puhtoorak (Ikinnelikpatolok), who specifically stated that he himself had been aboard.

Puhtoorak had seen white men twice in his long life before encountering the Americans. The first time had been when, as a boy, he had seen some white men in a boat on the Great Fish River. This was probably the Back expedition, which had descended the river in 1834 with one boat, although it should be noted that while both Schwatka and Gilder heard Puhtoorak say "one boat," Klutschak heard "two boats," which, if true, would indicate the Anderson party of 1855 which used two canoes in their travels.[9]

The other kobluna of Puhtoorak's acquaintance was a corpse found by him "in a bunk inside the ship" at Ootgoolik.[10]

When his people saw the ship so long without any one around, they used to go on board and steal pieces of wood and iron. They did not know how to get inside by the doors, and cut a hole in the side of the ship, on a level with the ice, so that when the ice broke up during the following summer the ship filled and sank. No tracks were seen in the salt-water ice or on the ship, which also was covered with snow, but they saw scrapings and sweepings alongside, which seemed to have been brushed off by people who had been living on board. They found some red cans of fresh meat, with plenty of what looked like tallow mixed with it. A great many had been opened, and four were still unopened. They saw no bread. They found plenty of knives, forks, spoons, pans, cups, and plates on board, and afterward found a few such things on shore after the vessel had gone down. They also saw books on board, and left them there. They only took knives, forks, spoons, and pans; the other things they had no use for.[11]

We can see that many of the details of the Ootgoolik ship are identical to those told to Rasmussen about the ship which we earlier concluded sank near Cape Crozier. In both cases the traditions about the original discovery (in one case by "two brothers," in the other by "Nuk-kee-che-uk and other Innuits") are strikingly similar. In both cases the Inuit broke into the interior, where it was very dark, and found similar things. In both traditions the ship sank as a result of a hole made in the side by the natives. Even Rasmussen's "many dead men" found in their bunks may have been an exaggeration of the single body which was found at Ootgoolik.

We should not be surprised at these similarities. In the first case some of them would naturally result from the constraints of the event itself. Any white man's ship was bound to be locked and dark inside. The food, guns, ammunition, and utensils found would also be common to different ships. It is even possible that in both cases the Inuit would gain entry by breaking through the hull, although this element, confirmed by the eyewitness Puhtoorak, probably occurred only at Ootgoolik (there being little need to break into a vessel whose side was crushed in by the ice).

The main reason for the echoes which we clearly hear in the traditions of the two ships is the simple fact that the native informants were operating on hearsay, and that the white listeners tended to amalgamate all stories concerning wrecked ships into one, only semi-coherent, account. This can be clearly seen in Hall's notes. While interviewing the natives in their igloos, surrounded by relics from the wreck at Ootgoolik, he heard both of repeated and fruitful looting of the wreck over a protacted period, and of very little being obtained from her owing to the rapidity of her sinking. Still he failed to see that these diametrically opposed traditions concerned different wrecks, the location of each of which he had been told. Hall, and many of those who followed, attributed all stories of a wreck to the Ootgoolik ship, and this has led to an almost indecipherable mixing of elements which can be only tentatively unravelled.

Whatever the confusion between the two Franklin ships, it is certain that the body of one white man was found on the Ootgoolik vessel. Yet there have been attempts to ignore or explain away the troublesome presence of this body.

In 1851 the passengers and crew of the *Renovation*, while crossing the Grand Banks off Newfoundland, saw what they believed to be two abandoned vessels locked in the ice of a passing iceberg.[12] Some nineteenth-century historians believed these icebound wrecks to have been the *Erebus* and *Terror*, and Admiral Noel Wright has more recently resurrected this view in two imaginative books. He claimed that the vessel found at Ootgoolik was in fact the *Investigator*, a Franklin search ship which had been beset and abandoned on the north coast of Banks Island in 1853.[13]

As no body was left aboard the *Investigator* when she was abandoned, Wright theorized that the one "dead man" was actually the ship's figurehead. This was described by Lieutenant Cresswell as a large animal, which was intended, according to one officer, to have represented a walrus.[14] Ignoring the fact that the Inuit were quite unlikely to mistake a carving of a walrus for a dead white man, Wright thought that this would explain why the man was so heavy and why his teeth were remarked to have been so "big" (the Inuit actually said "long").

Wright also noted details of the Inuit description of the wreck which, while being consistent with the *Investigator*, he felt could not apply to the *Erebus* or *Terror*. These included the fact that the former carried four boats over her quarters "whaler fashion" while presumably the latter did not, that copper sheeting was found among the natives (presumed to have come from the ship's bottom sheathing – the *Investigator* was so sheathed, the *Erebus* and *Terror* apparently not).

Wright's idea has never gained much acceptance among historians. Cyriax devoted considerable time, skill, and energy to refuting his arguments in scathing (but unpublished) reviews of the Admiral's books.[15] Most of Wright's assumptions concerning the carrying of boats, the source of the copper sheeting, and so on can be easily questioned, but only two facts are really necessary to explode his hypothesis. The Inuit told that the ship which came to Ootgoolik had four quarter-boats hanging from the davits, yet the *Investigator*'s boats had all been landed ashore when she was abandoned.[16] And only real corpses, not figureheads, "smell bad."

We can confidently assert that the Ootgoolik wreck was one of Franklin's vessels. One of the relics which the Schwatka expedition recovered, said by the Inuit to have come from the wreck, implies she was the *Terror*. Gilder described "a piece of ship's block" which was recovered from this ship. It was "marked with the number 10 or the letter OR, the letter R being imperfect," and he concluded that, if the block had been marked with the vessel's name, this would prove the Ootgoolik wreck to have been Crozier's ship.[17]

Another curious relic obtained from this ship has largely defied explanation.

This was a black-painted board "which had been in the head of a bunk or top of a box or locker." Schwatka remarked that it had "been covered with heavy black oil cloth in which were driven brass-headed tacks forming the initials I.F." (Gilder and Klutschak read "L.F."). The natives had indicated that it was "torn from the interior of the ship," but all efforts to identify the vessel by means of it were fruitless.[18]

Cyriax, assuming that the letters were some crewman's initials, found that they did not match any individual who served with Franklin. With his customary thoroughness he also noted that "no person with these initials served in H.M.S. *Terror* when Sir George Back tried to reach Repulse Bay, in the *Erebus* or *Terror* during the Antarctic expedition, in the *Investigator*, or the *Victory*."[19]

The irrepressible Admiral Wright had an opinion as to this relic as well. He considered the entire question to be "a mare's nest originated by a non-seafaring man." Noting that the Royal Navy did not usually designate berths by individual but by rank, he concluded that "L.F." was short for "Lieutenant" (in the Royal Navy, Lieutenants were known as "Luffs"). As the use of tacks was a "clear sign of extemporization," he felt that this confirmed the wreck as the *Investigator*, which had recently been purchased by the Navy. The *Erebus* and *Terror*, being purpose-built vessels, would have used "standard metal tallies."[20]

In 1987 William Barr, like Wright, considered that this relic had not come from the *Erebus* and *Terror* at all. He felt that it could have come from a third source – the abandoned ships of the Belcher expedition. Barr reasoned that the "L.F." might stand for "Lady Franklin," the name of one of the sledges which operated from the *Assistance* and *Pioneer* in 1852. He asked, "could one of these ships (with the sledge Lady Franklin still on board) have drifted to the northeast coast of O'Reilly Island?"[21] Well, of course, the answer is yes. If the *Investigator* could drift from Mercy Bay then Belcher's ships could come from Wellington Channel. But, for many of the same reasons bedevilling the *Investigator* scenario (the dead man, etc.), this is highly unlikely. The Inuit clearly stated that the board was "torn from the interior of the ship" at the "head of a bunk or top of a locker" which showed it "to be a permanent fixture of the vessel."[22]

I may here be allowed to put forth a theory of my own. Since the letters were formed of brass tacks pushed into a board covered in black oil cloth it is impossible to say whether the "L.F." were the only letters, or if, in fact, these were the original letters at all. Schwatka read them as "I.F." (although the "I" may have been Schwatka's typesetter's rendition of a lowercase "l"). In any case a few well-placed tacks would close the F into a P. We would then have a black-painted, black-draped board, possibly taken from the head of a bunk which contained the body of a dead man, containing a message. Two of those letters would have been I.P. Is it possible that there was originally a third letter which, before the valuable tacks were stolen, had preceded the others? If so, it is probable that it was an "R."

Assuming we have been correct in our conclusions about the fate of the survivors in 1849–50, this lone seaman or officer (the big kobluna was found in the "back part" of the ship in a cabin

– "officer country") must have been one of a party which returned to the ship a second time after the débâcle at Terror Bay. He was not alone. The Inuit gave other details which imply that the vessel contained a living crew when it arrived at Adelaide Peninsula.

The natives all believed that the white men had been living aboard during the winter previous to the vessel's discovery. Ek-kee-pee-ree-a had noted that a plank was set down from the ship to the ice. That this had been done recently is attested to by the fact that the ship was enclosed in "new ice" (one winter old). According to Puhtoorak, "on their first visit the people thought they saw whites on board"[23] and that "when he went on board the ship he saw a pile of dirt on one side of the cabin door showing that some white man had recently swept out the cabin."[24]

There is another slight clue that the Inuit saw signs of life on the vessel. When McClintock first asked the natives for details about the southerly wreck "without masts," his question "gave rise to some laughter amongst them, and they spoke to each other about fire." McClintock's interpreter did not fully understand what had been said but "thought they had burnt the masts through close to the deck in order to get them down."[25]

This is unlikely, for the detailed nature of the Inuit recollections of the wreck shows that they would surely have perpetuated knowledge of such an event. But the story must have some kernel of truth.

Once again Admiral Wright jumps into the breach by noting that "the *Erebus* and *Terror*, although actually sailing ships, were equipped with auxiliary steam power" and that "the sight of the smoke pouring from their (collapsible) funnels caused the Eskimos to think – not unnaturally – that they had caught fire. Similar misconceptions were frequent in English coastal towns in the early days of steamships."[26]

This time Wright may be correct. The story of steam exhaust need not have originated with the *Erebus* and *Terror*, however. The *Victory* was also steam-assisted and may have provided the inspiration for the "burning masts." But this solution is improbable on two counts. The *Victory*'s "execrable machinery" was almost useless, and Ross used it so infrequently that he eventually (and joyfully) tore it out and heaved it onto the beach. Also, Ross tells us that the fires were fed air by bellows and therefore "a smoke stack was unnecessary."[27]

On the other hand, the engines on the *Erebus* and *Terror* came complete with stacks. Before leaving England, Lieutenant Irving wrote of the engine that "it has a funnel the same size and height as it had on the railway and makes the same dreadful puffings and screamings, and will astound the Esquimaux not a little."[28]

Of course, the inspiration for the native remark may not have been the main machinery at all, but simply the steam exhaust of the central heating system installed in the *Erebus* and *Terror*, or the common cooking smoke which issued out of the short chimneys of all Arctic ships. Regardless of the source, if the Inuit saw steam issuing from the "mast" of the ship at Ootgoolik it would be a sure indicator of habitation.

There was another interesting detail concerning the Ootgoolik ship. Hall was told that the ship was covered in canvas awnings, as was usual among vessels prepared for the winter. He may have misunderstood, however, for Puhtoorak told that no tracks were seen on the deck, which was "covered with snow." Schwatka heard of canvas as well, but this was not in the form of an awning. He was told that "some of the ship's sails were set."[29] Klutschak confirmed that this is what was said, but thought that the Inuit report "that the ship had many sails spread may be erroneous; at best the sails may have been loosened from the yards by storms, leaving them hanging in rags."[30]

The crew which brought the ship to Ootgoolik may have attempted to sail out of the ice when they found themselves in the "polnya," or lane of open water, which later froze over to form "a smooth floe" of one-year ice. If steam power had been used in an attempt to free the ship this could be the source of the "burning mast" story as well. Significantly, since the Ootgoolik ship was already immobilized when found, such efforts could only have been observed by the Inuit prior to that ship's arrival. If the Ootgoolik Inuit were correct in identifying the canvas as "sails" rather than awnings, the traditions concerning a ship under canvas that Hall heard, like those of a ship trying to steam out of the ice, could only refer to events further north.

The strongest evidence that the ship had been remanned before it arrived on the west coast of the Adelaide Peninsula is provided by traces which were found on the nearby shore. While accompanying a native hunting party, Puhtoorak came across the tracks of four white men and "judged they were hunting for deer." He later found the tracks of three men in the snow, but it is unclear whether this indicated the same party of hunters or not. Puhtoorak thought "that the white men lived in this ship until the fall and then moved onto the mainland."[31]

Once again Puhtoorak was confirming testimony which had earlier been given to Hall by Koo-nik.

Do you know anything about tracks of strangers seen at Ook-joo-lik?

The Innuits at *Ook-soo-see-too* saw when walking along the tracks of 3 men Kob-loo-nas & those of a dog with them ... [Koo-nik] say she has never seen the exact place not having ever been further w or w & south than Point C. Grant wh is the Pt. NE of O'Rialy [sic] Island. She indicates on Rae's chart the places, recognizing them readily.

Ook-soo-see-too the land E of O'Reilly Isle as she shows on chart.

The vessel seen 1st & then little while after the tracks of the 3 Kob-lu-nans & dog seen on the land.

The vessel seen in the spring about the time of the next moon or it may have been as moon now is, that is about the middle of May or 1st of June ...

Koo-nik, when did Ook-joo-lik Innuits first see the large ship? Was it before or after the Innuits saw Ag-loo-ka & his men on Ki-ki-tung [at Washington Bay]? The time was about the same, either same year or next after, one or the other – is sure not 2 years after." (emphasis in original)[32]

According to In-nook-poo-zhe-jook, "one man, from his running steps, was a very great runner – very long steps. The natives tracked the men a long distance, and found where they had killed and eaten a young deer."[33]

That these tracks were actually those of white men is almost beyond doubt. The impression left by the white men's hard-soled boots was quite distinctive; In-nook-poo-zhe-jook described these "foot-marks" as "long, narrow in the middle, and the prints like as if of the boots found in the two boats."[34] The Inuit, in their soft-soled boots and with their characteristic pigeon-toed gait, were understandably alarmed by such strange-looking footprints. Hall, based on his own experience, was certain that the Inuit could not have been mistaken.

There is no such thing as their being mistaken when they come across strange tracks & pronounce them not to be Innuits. Not only can they unmistakably determine White men's tracks from Innuits but to a most remarkable degree they can distinguish characteristics in tracks of their own people which enable them to tell the *individual* who made them. This remarkable skill in this matter has often caused me to greatly wonder. A case in point: on my last spring sledge journey on reaching Am-i-toke we found fresh foot prints in the snow of 2 men & a dog & these led from Am-i-toke to the northward. Pa-pa on our first seeing the tracks said they were of Innuits who had been adrift on the ice & had escaped therefrom & were making their return to Oo-glit Isles or in that direction & furthermore said that the tracks of the men were as he thought of *Too-goo-lat* & *Nood-loo*. On arriving at the N. Ooglit Isles we found it to have been just as Pa-pa had told me ... (emphasis in original)[35]

Modern comment upon these tracks has been almost non-existent. Cyriax admitted that the stories were internally consistent, and that if the location could be believed they must refer to Franklin crewmen who had remanned the ship. He did, however, include the caveat that "neither the *Erebus* nor the *Terror* seems to have had a dog on board when she left the Whalefish Islands."[36] We now know from Fairholme's letters (which Cyriax never saw) that there were in fact many animals on the ships. These included a monkey, a dog named "Old Neptune," another unnamed "Newfoundland" dog, and one cat.[37]

Puhtoorak also mentioned finding more concrete evidence that the white men had come ashore, for "after the ship sank, they found a small boat on the mainland,"[38] presumably in Wilmot Bay. Klutschak thought that this boat "might have drifted to the spot after the ship sank."[39]

When the ship was first seen by the Inuit it had four boats hanging on davits over the quarters and another over the stern. Puhtoorak stated that when he saw the ship "there was one small boat hanging from the davits which the natives cut down," but failed to mention whether any of the others were missing. More than seventy years after the event, the attempted salvage of this boat was graphically described to Rasmussen: "One man, who saw a boat hanging up over the gunwale, shouted: 'A trough, a gigantic trough! I am going to have that!' He had never seen a boat and so he thought that it was a meat trough. He cut through the lines that held the boat, and it crashed down on to the ice bottom upward and was smashed."[40]

Puhtoorak also stated that the first time the Inuit saw the Ootgoolik ship was "in the fall" and that "the following spring they visited the spot again and found the ship in the same position."[41] As noted, Puhtoorak was sure that the white men had spent the winter aboard, and as the tracks ashore were seen, according to Koo-nik, in late May or early June, and the vessel had already been visited and pillaged by the time of breakup in late July, this tells us that the white men left the ship in the early summer.

The native stories are consistent in stating that the white men abandoned the ship after its arrival. But there is some doubt as to when the ship finally sank. Puhtoorak's assertion that this occurred at breakup "the following summer" is probably correct. As the only admitted eyewitness, he should be trusted. Yet there are stories implying that the natives pillaged the ship for a much longer period. It would seem that the careful looting also took considerable time, for the Inuit visited the ship "from time to time" to make their pillage into piles "intending to sledge it to their igloos some time after," although this may only refer to the months spent aboard the ship between the first visitation in the spring and the breakup of the ice.

McClintock certainly expected to be able to visit the wreck in 1859. The natives of Boothia told him of the wreck that was "forced on shore by the ice, where they suppose she still remains,"[42] while Inuit encountered near Cape Norton on the east coast of King William Island indicated that "but little now remained of the wreck which was accessible." They informed McClintock that an old woman and a boy had been the last visitors to the wreck, and stated that "they had been at it during the winter of 1857–8."[43]

Ookbarloo stated that In-nook-poo-zhe-jook and his companions "went with others of his people aboard Aglooka's ship after the Neitchille Innuits heard that the Kob-lu-nas had left it,"[44] yet In-nook-poo-zhe-jook himself never mentioned having visited Ootgoolik, or having seen a wrecked ship. We know from his own testimony that he did not travel west until after his meeting with Rae in 1854. We have, however, seen that Ookbarloo was not the most reliable of witnesses.

These later visits may not have been to the ship itself but to the adjacent shores. The Inuit all mentioned that debris had collected on the beach after the ship sank. As late as 1879 a native named Toolooah told of finding traces of white men in the Ootgoolik country, and that "as late as last summer [he] had picked up pieces of bottles, iron, wood and tin cans" near where the ship had been wrecked.[45]

We have added another piece of the puzzle. It seems reasonable that when the white men found that the first ship was in danger they had launched all of her boats onto the ice and subsequently took them to shore. One of these was taken by Aglooka to Washington Bay (and left in Douglas Bay?), and two others were found on the shores of Erebus Bay by In-nook-poo-zhe-jook. After the disaster at Toonoonee, the retreating men had no reason to take these latter boats back to their nearby, second, ship, for all of her boats, as the Ootgoolik natives confirmed, were still in their davits. When the ice broke up these men attempted to sail or power their way to the south. Eventually they arrived at Ootgoolik and were frozen into new one-year ice. They were not starving, for they left full cans of food aboard, and they hunted caribou ashore. The men abandoned the body of one of their comrades (perhaps an officer) in a locked cabin before leaving the ship. Perhaps they took one or more of the ship's boats with them when they left, and they may have abandoned one of these on a nearby island.

It is interesting to note that the boats found in Erebus Bay all contained relics of the *Erebus* and her officers, while the boat found in Wilmot Bay was identified by Schwatka as having probably come from the *Terror*. This would support the tenuous thread of evidence that it was the latter ship which survived to reach Ootgoolik.

Only two major questions remain. Exactly where did the Ootgoolik ship come to rest? And where did the men who abandoned her go?

Keeweewoo

The copious and consistent Inuit testimony has allowed us to reconstruct the main events associated with the wreck of the vessel at Ootgoolik. There is little mystery attached to it. The arrival of the ship among the Inuit was such a significant occurrence in their lives that they faithfully and vividly remembered and retold all of the details. The only issues which are left for historians to resolve are the exact place and date of the sinking, and the eventual fate of the few white men who abandoned the vessel "in the spring."

The date of the sinking, as we have seen, will probably never be determined. Puhtoorak said that the year after its arrival at Ootgoolik the natives cut a hole in the ship's side and that it went to the bottom with the next ice breakup. Koo-nik thought that this occurred within one or two years of the encounter at Teekeenu. A more exact date is probably unattainable.

It would seem that the location of the much-visited wreck would be more straightforward. Yet even this is a matter of some dispute. We have seen that "Ootgoolik" (of various spellings) was used by the natives to describe the entire west shore of the Adelaide Peninsula, but Hall thought that he had localized the wreck site to a specific part of that coast. In-nook-poo-zhe-jook drew a chart which indicated the location of the wreck as an island in the southern reaches of Queen Maud Gulf. The name given to this island by In-nook-poo-zhe-jook, "Keeweewoo," may have been more description than name, for "keeweewook" was translated by Gilder as "sunk."[1]

This island, which appears to be opposite the entrance of Sherman Inlet, has been traditionally associated with O'Reilly Island. Modern testimony confirms that "a small island to the west of O'Reilly Island is still confidently indicated by the present generation of Eskimos as the spot near which the ship sank."[2]

The fact that the Franklin ship arrived at Ootgoolik at all testifies to the presence of a crew aboard and argues against an aimless drift. The *Erebus* and *Terror* were heavily built vessels, drawing, when they left Greenland, seventeen feet of water. And, as McClintock noted, there was a "gauntlet" of islands to be run to the south-west before the ship could reach Ootgoolik.[3]

The first obstacles to be bypassed were the Royal Geographical Society Islands, which lie to the west of Cape Crozier. Covering over one thousand square miles, these islands and surrounding reefs lay directly in the drift path of Franklin's ships. A modern description noted that "even before the group was sighted from the deck many reefs similarly formed were crossed, some rising to within six feet of the surface. The islands themselves appear to have only shallow channels between them, no channel for a boat drawing more than six feet having yet been located."[4]

If it successfully avoided the Royal Geographical Society Islands, the ship next had to contend with the many hazards further south. Queen Maud Gulf is also liberally strewn with reefs. A Canadian reconnaissance survey carried out in 1962 indicated that "several isolated shoals, with depths of from 6 feet to 24 feet (1m 8 to 7m 3) over them, exist within a 15 mile radius northward and westward of O'Reilly Island."[5] These shoals lie directly in the path of the ship from King William Island.

The wreck of the Ootgoolik ship has never been located, which is surprising when the clues about its location are reviewed. In a letter to Henry Grinnell, Hall remarked that "it was found by the Ootgoolik natives near O'Reilly Island, lat. 68 30' N., long. 99 W."[6] This is a somewhat confusing statement. O'Reilly Island is the largest single member of a numerous group of islands west of the Adelaide Peninsula and is one of the few which have been named. It is not, however, at the position given by Hall.

Hall described elsewhere how In-nook-poo-zhe-jook, using McClintock's chart, had "readily pointed out the place where the Franklin ship sank. It was very near O'Reilly Island, a little eastward of the north end of said island, between it and Wilmot and Crampton Bay."[7] We do not have a copy of McClintock's chart and do not know its accuracy or scale. Nor can we know the exact placement of In-nook-poo-zhe-jook's finger, so it is impossible to better Hall's description. We also do not know which island in Queen Maud Gulf was named O'Reilly during the late 1800s on the admittedly inaccurate and incomplete charts of the time.

But Hall gave us another clue in his latitude and longitude. He was one of the most accurate of the Victorian explorers in determining his true position, and we know that he learned of the location of the wreck while encamped at Keeuna. Hall recorded the position of Keeuna as 68° 23' N, 96° 33' W,[8] and this is remarkably accurate, being only about seven miles from its true position. Moreover, most of this error was in longitude (i.e. east-west), which was difficult to determine with the rudimentary navigation equipment available.

The latitude (north-south) co-ordinates which Hall gave for the wreck indicate that he thought that it was seven miles to the north of his Keeuna position and about forty-five miles to the west. This would bring him to the western entrance of Simpson Strait in the southern part of what is now Storis Passage. Modern O'Reilly Island is actually about thirty miles to the south of this.

If we ignore Hall's identification of "O'Reilly Island" and note simply that he felt that the wreck was located to the west of Keeuna/Todd Islets, as noted by his estimate of latitude and longitude, this would place the ship about seven miles to the north-west of modern Grant Point. Where did later explorers think the ship had come to rest?

The definitive description was given by the eyewitness Puhtoorak, who "told Ebierbing that the next time he saw a white man was a dead one in a large ship about eight miles off Grant Point."[9] Gilder's account of Puhtoorak's description was the most specific. Gilder recorded that the ship "was frozen in the ice near an island about five miles due west of Grant Point" and that "they [the Inuit] had to walk out about three miles on smooth ice to reach the ship."[10]

A recent Canadian map (67A Simpson Strait, scale 1:250,000) indicates that there are two islets directly west of Grant Point, one at two miles and one about seven miles distant. These are only two of a group of about ten islands and as many reefs which clutter the area to the south and west of Grant Point and fill Wilmot and Crampton Bay. The northernmost of these is named Kirkwall Island, and, interestingly enough, it is located at 68° 30′ N 99° 07′ W, which is Hall's exact latitude for the wreck, and only two and a half miles further to the west than he indicated.

According to Hall's informants, when the ship sank her mastheads were visible extending out of the water. We do not know the exact height of the *Erebus* and *Terror* from keel to truck (and topmasts were usually struck down when in winter quarters), but contemporary drawings allow us to make a reasonable estimate of from 120 to 150 feet – certainly not more than the latter figure.

The Ootgoolik coast is still imperfectly charted, but the admittedly incomplete soundings available indicate that the area has average depths on the order of 15–30 fathoms (90–180 feet).[11] This would fit in well with the story of the exposure of the ship's masts. Significantly, water depths increase to the west of O'Reilly Island, usually varying between 120 and 180 feet, which is too deep to allow the mast-tops to have been visible above the surface.

The water depths are more suitable near Kirkwall Island. Here there are also many reefs which would have arrested any southbound vessel. Major L.T. Burwash, who lived on King William Island for many years and was entirely familiar with the surrounding geography, undertook a journey by small coastal vessel from Cambridge Bay to King William Island in 1930. He remarked that the waters of Queen Maud Gulf "appear to present a difficult problem in navigation … as at no point was any great depth of water found, while even when out of sight of land two fathoms was not uncommon."[12]

Most major traffic takes the route to the north of Kirkwall Island, using Requisite and Storis Channels to transit through the Gulf, but it is interesting to note that in 1955 a supply ship grounded near the island in 2 fathoms (12 feet) of water. Modern research gives more information about the vicinity.

There is deep water right up to the beach on the eastern side … and to within a few hundred yards of the southern side, but the water is shoal off the western and northern sides ... Two islands of similar height and appearance to Kirkwall Island lie 1 1/2 and 3 1/2 miles respectively westward of its southwestern extremity; ... A shoal, awash, was sighted in 1963, five cables [1000 yards] southwestward from the southern end of this [outer] island. A depth of 31 feet (9m 4) was found 5 cables westward of this shoal, which may indicate that it may be of considerable extent. Another shoal, with a depth of 19 feet (5m 8), exists about 4 cables northwestward of the northwestward end of this island ...

An islet, 7 cables southeastward of the island west of Kirkwall Island, rises sharply from comparatively deep water. The bottom off the southern side of these islands is very uneven with depths varying from 25 fathoms to 4 fathoms. [13]

It is easy to imagine the dilemma faced by any ship which drifted into this area. The hazards are seen to extend to the north and west, precisely the direction from which the Franklin vessel must have come, and yet it is clear that the ship did not immediately run aground, for she was found encased in smooth ice and only sank when released. Since first-year ice forms in place, it then becomes obvious that something must have halted the progress of the ship in deep water before freeze-up. The only explanation seems to be that she was anchored by her crew.

The question then arises why Franklin survivors would choose to anchor near Kirkwall Island. The answer is immediately apparent. In coming south from King William Island the crews would face two choices as to route. They could attempt to navigate to the west through the narrow straits discovered by Dease and Simpson, a route which would ultimately take them to the trading posts of Alaska; or they could attempt to sail eastward through Simpson Strait in the hope that it did in fact connect with Prince Regent Inlet or Repulse Bay where assistance might be obtainable. The second of these alternatives, if less certain, was much shorter.

Simpson Strait has a narrow entrance which would not be easy to find. Kirkwall Island is only a few miles to the south of it, and it is quite possible that the ship was brought to anchor here by the crew while a search was made for the opening which they had obviously missed. Equally obviously, the mouth of the strait was not found in time.

The waters around Kirkwall Island must remain the primary

area of search for the missing ship. Perhaps it has already been unwittingly found in the form of one of the many shoals which rise abruptly from the bottom in the area. Nevertheless the idea that the wreck is to be found near O'Reilly Island, based largely on Hall's misidentification, is still current.

In the 1960s O'Reilly Island was apparently vindicated as the site of the wreck. A small magnetic anomaly was recorded during a magnetometer survey of the area, and proponents of the theory that this was caused by one of Franklin's ships pointed out that the iron contained in the ship's fifteen-ton engine and her protective bow sheathing could have been the source. The results of further search were inconclusive, but the geologists concluded that it was "highly unlikely" that one of Franklin's ships could have caused the reading, and that there was "a very good chance that the anomaly discovered near O'Reilly Island is a meteorite."[14]

A more detailed survey of the area was done by Dr E.F. Roots of the Canadian Department of Mines and Technical Surveys in 1965. Using a sledge-drawn magnetometer, he conducted long traverses at three-hundred-meter intervals to localize the anomaly and then a comprehensive set at one-hundred-meter spacing around the strongest area. Dr Roots was convinced that the anomaly was "purely geological – too big and deep to be man-made" and was probably caused by "iron and manganese deposits in serpentine." The search was conducted approximately five miles to the north "and a little to the west" of O'Reilly Island, in the vicinity of a small islet which was called "Nail Island" because of a find of "a nail with the navy broad arrow and chips of wood."[15] The Canadian geologists did find some shore debris that suggested that some ship or ships may have been destroyed in the vicinity, but the O'Reilly anomaly was simply a red herring.

Undaunted by these conclusions, modern searchers have continually attempted to locate the wreck in the waters near O'Reilly Island. An ambitious undertaking was "Project Franklin," which was organized by the Canadian Armed Forces in 1967 as one of the projects in support of the centennial of Canada's Confederation. Fifty-two men from various military units undertook an air, land, and sea search of most of the significant locales associated with the Franklin story in an effort to find any relics which still remained. As part of the search, divers explored the sea-bed near O'Reilly Island.

The diving teams found nothing underwater, but they recovered some copper sheeting, spice tins, a block, a belaying pin, an oar, and other minor items in beach searches of the northern end of O'Reilly Island and concluded that the pattern of the shore debris suggested a wreck might lie nearby. Overlooked was the possibility that the boat which the natives reported to have been found on an island in the Ootgoolik sea may also have been the source of these things.[16]

The question remains unresolved to this day. The finding of the ship, either near Kirkwall Island or near O'Reilly Island to the south, would be a source of incalculable benefit in unravelling the Franklin mystery – especially if, as seems likely, some protected record was left with the vessel to tell subsequent searchers of the history of the expedition.

If the ship sank in about one hundred feet of water, as the natives said, then she should have been deep enough to survive the ravages of surface ice, which forms to a depth of six to seven feet in this area. The ship should also have been protected from any incursions of heavy ice from Victoria Strait by the shoals of Queen Maud Gulf.

If Aglooka's ship was brought to anchor near Kirkwall or O'Reilly Islands, it seems unthinkable that some record would not have been left ashore. O'Reilly Island has been meticulously searched for any remnants of a cairn without success, but Kirkwall Island has been ignored. Yet the *Arctic Pilot* notes that "three stone cairns are situated on the top of the [central] ridge ... one cairn is located at each end of the ridge, while the other is near the middle. These landmarks are visible from Storis Passage to the northward."[17]

These cairns may be modern. However, it is unlikely that natives would build three such cairns on top of a ridge which has a "height of between 60 and 80 feet," for their meat-storage cairns are almost invariably built near campsites at sea level. It is also certain that the three cairns were not recently erected by white men to serve as navigational marks, for a modern beacon serves that purpose only a few hundred yards away. These three stone markers may have a tale to tell.

One other piece of evidence favours Kirkwall Island as the location of the wreck. Rasmussen had the native Qaqortingneq label a sketch map of the King William Island area. This map is a very faithful representation of the geography of the region, and Qaqortingneq's identification of the various landmarks is quite reliable. Unfortunately, he does not corroborate In-nook-poo-zhe-jook's identification of "Keeweewoo." Smith and Grant Points are labelled "tikerqat – the small forefingers. Two long peninsulas, one on each side of a narrow bay," which is an excellent description. The large island which is now named O'Reilly was called "tajarnerjuaq – the big forearm" by the Inuit as its shape resembled "the flipper of a seal."[18]

To the north of this last island and to the west of Grant Point/ Tikerqat lies an island which Qaqortingneq labelled "umiartalik – the place where there are umiaq." Rasmussen considers this to be "Crenchel Island," but this identification is uncertain since this name does not appear on any modern charts or in any gazetteer. It occupies the position, and may have been the original name, of Kirkwall Island. The last word of the native designation is the clue, for as we have seen "umiaq" is the word which the natives commonly used to designate a white man's ship.

~19~

The Trail to Shartoo

We do not know how many men were aboard the Ootgoolik ship when she arrived at Kirkwall Island. Hall concluded that there were five (four tracks ashore + one body aboard), but admitted that this was circumstantial. The dead man could, earlier, have been a member of the four-man hunting party, or the tracks seen might have been of only one such group among many.

The Inuit did not know what happened to these men. Apart from the tracks and the boat found in Wilmot Bay, there were no traces of them on the west coast of the Adelaide Peninsula. McClintock's Boothian informants remarked that the men from the wrecked ship "went away to the large river, taking a boat or boats with them, and that in the following winter their bones were found there,"[1] but this was probably a (faulty) remembrance of the party seen at Washington Bay. In either case it was an assumption.

Similarly, we do not know when these men abandoned the Ootgoolik ship. The natives finally boarded the abandoned ship in the "spring" (May/June/July) before breakup, and Puhtoorak thought that the white men had abandoned it "in the fall" of the year preceding. Koo-nik thought that this occurred the same year as the Teekeenu encounter, or maybe a year after.

That so few traces were found ashore, and no footprints at all on the ship or nearby ice, might indicate that the men departed by boat before the freeze-up which imprisoned their vessel in one-year ice. Having survived the harrowing ordeals at Too-noonee and Erebus Bay, these men would presumably be well aware that their strength was inadequate for another march. A boat voyage, under sail, might have been their last hope.

The fact that the boat which was later found by the natives in Wilmot Bay was not on a sledge might support this. Klutschak stated that "it could not be determined with any certainty whether the boat ... had come ashore with men in it or whether it had drifted there."[2] The details of deck sweepings on the ice, however, imply continued habitation after freeze-up, as does the fact that the Inuit believed that there were still men aboard when the ship, already beset, was first seen. The white men might have abandoned their ship after it itself had become beset but before all of the nearby leads of open water had closed.

Another fact which might argue against a last water-borne attempt at escape is the testimony of the natives about the boats of the Ootgoolik ship. When first seen the ship was in a perfect state, with four boats hanging on davits and one over the stern. Puhtoorak told of a native cutting down the latter. In-nook-poo-zhe-jook told Hall that three boats, presumably including the one found in Wilmot Bay, were found "much broken & these three thought by the Inuits to have come from the ship that drifted down to Ook-joo-lik, which had 4 at cranes & one over the quarter deck."[3] As the *Erebus* and *Terror* each carried nine boats, nothing definite can be concluded from the native testimony as to whether one or more were "missing."

The assumption that the survivors departed by boat during the short open season is largely due to the fact that the Ootgoolik natives found no traces of a retreating party on the shores nearby. A boat party would explain this, for such a group leaves few traces of its passage. On the other hand, boat transport reduces the field of search: to men of the Franklin expedition, there was only one water route which would lead to safety – Simpson Strait.

It must be remembered that when Franklin sailed from England in 1845 there was no certain knowledge of where this strait led. In 1839 Simpson had thought that it connected to the southern part of Prince Regent Inlet, which in turn was thought to connect with Repulse Bay. The Inuit had earlier told Ross that this was not so, and Rae surveyed most of the southern reaches of Prince

Regent Inlet in 1847, but it was not until his second journey in 1854 that he finally proved the non-insularity of Boothia. Franklin's men would have been operating on Simpson's earlier, incorrect, information.

If the men from the Ootgoolik ship did attempt a boat passage to the east this would explain the only remains which we have not yet accounted for – those found on the north coast of the Adelaide Peninsula at Thunder Cove and near Starvation Cove.

As was mentioned earlier, the campsite at Thunder Cove does not tie in with the supposed retreat of a single party travelling directly from Todd Islets to Starvation Cove. There seem to be only two reasonable explanations for this anomalously placed encampment: that the Washington Bay Aglooka's party divided at Eta Island, one detachment proceeding along the King William Island shore to Keeuna while the other chose the Adelaide Peninsula coast, or that a party from the Ootgoolik ship was eastbound in Simpson Strait. The same can be said of the other Adelaide campsite found by Neniook about five miles north-west of Starvation Cove.[4]

The next certain trace of Europeans along the north Adelaide shore is at Starvation Cove itself. We remember that "no sled" was found here. This would seem to indicate that the boat must have arrived by sea when it was ice free – i.e. in late autumn. William Gibson disagreed with this assessment, feeling that the evidence at both Thunder Cove and Starvation Cove strongly indicated that the men "reached there before the summer had set in or the snow had melted from the beaches."[5] This is almost certainly incorrect, for it would place the arrival at Starvation Cove before the meeting at Washington Bay, and long before the time when Aglooka's men fished for salmon at Set-tu-me-nin. This difficulty could be overcome by concluding, as we do, that the men at Starvation Cove arrived the year after Aglooka's fateful march, yet the absence of a sledge at Starvation Cove still poses a problem if a pre-breakup arrival is required.

Curiously, Gibson based his opinion on the fact that the remains on the Adelaide Peninsula "were found on or just above the high water mark."[6] Yet this is precisely the point. If the Thunder Cove and Starvation Cove parties had arrived before the ice breakup, then they would probably have camped on the level shore ice. Had they done so, their remains would not have been found at all but would have been cleansed from the beaches by the first high tide. The fact that their camp was established above the tide mark would seem to argue strongly that they arrived when the sea was free of ice.

Seeuteetuar reported that there were no graves or cairns at Starvation Cove. This shows the temporary nature of the encampment at this traditional "final resting place." The fact that the bodies were found under an overturned boat (according to Rae and Gilder) would also indicate that the boat had not merely drifted ashore, and that someone must have survived this encampment. Dead men cannot pull a boat over themselves.

Of course, more concrete evidence exists for our supposition that Starvation Cove was simply another in a series of retreat encampments. This was provided by the remains of the man found five miles south-east of the boat place. This solitary crewman, who apparently was walking to the south in an attempt to find the Great Fish River, was obviously a survivor of Starvation Cove. Gilder and Klutschak were very imprecise in locating this body, but their descriptions would place it quite near the western verge of Barrow Inlet. The proposed searching party might have confused this inlet with Chantrey Inlet further east, and other remains might yet be found to the south.

The most interesting thing about Starvation Cove, and the one least remarked on, is its singular location. It is difficult to explain why any eastbound boat-crew would proceed down the narrow inlet rather than follow the coast from headland to headland. One could conclude that they were simply seeking a sheltered campsite, but then why was at least one man wandering five miles further inland?

It seems that, although both Aglooka's men and our hypothetical boat-crew from Ootgoolik had Iwillik (Repulse Bay) as a final destination, the men in the boat at Starvation Cove were looking for the mouth of the Great Fish River. Perhaps they hoped to meet with the native band described by Back as living near the Franklin Rapids, to obtain food or a guide.

In any case, Chantrey Inlet, which was the apparent intended route, had been described by both Back and Simpson in their journals. Unfortunately, its position was at variance in the two accounts – Back's calculation being more accurate. His given longitude of Montreal Island (in Chantrey Inlet) was four miles to

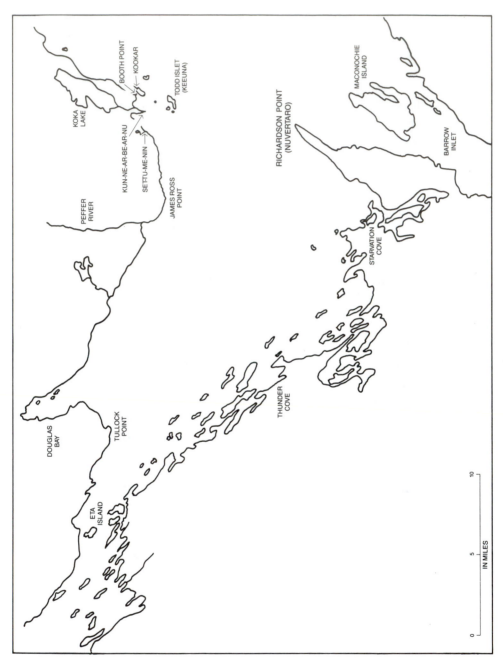

Map 7   Simpson Strait to Starvation Cove

the east of its true position, whereas Simpson's later position was mistakenly twenty-five miles further west!

Using Simpson's figures, which, as the more recent, they may have thought more accurate, a party advancing from the west could have concluded that the entrance to the Great Fish River was closer (further west) than it actually is. In any event, confusion as to its position would have been unavoidable.

This geographical confusion can be clearly seen in Hall's notes. While encamped at Keeuna he could see Maconochie Island and Richardson Point to the south. Yet he seems to have been somewhat confused by this, repeatedly thinking that the point due south of Keeuna, called by the natives "Noo-oo-tar-oo" (Richardson Point), was Point Ogle. Hall found that "Pt Ogle," to his surprise, was "nearly 2 Points [22 degrees] to the westward of our meridian wh. is 117 – 30' w. This confirms what In-nook-poo[-zhe-jook] & (wife) have said that Noo-woo-tee-roo (Pt. Ogle) was to the westward of south from here; therefore Maconochie [sic] Isle & Point Richardson must be very much to the westward when by Chart they are about due south."[7] Assuming Aglooka's party to have crossed from Keeuna to Starvation Cove, Hall remarked that "the party of Franklin's men must have felt like *lost men* to find Points & Islands so far to the westward of what their charts showed" (emphasis in original).[8] The same comment would apply equally well to men coming from the west.

Despite their geographical inaccuracies, both Back and Simpson described Chantrey Inlet, the route to the river's mouth, as lying between two headlands – Ogle Point and Cape Britannia (called "Ripon Island" by Back). Franklin's men were therefore undoubtedly searching for a deep inlet lying between two obvious headlands, and, indeed, this is what they found. But it was the wrong inlet.

There are four main points which extend to the northward from the Adelaide Peninsula, and all lie within a few miles of each other. Coming through Simpson Strait from the west the first to be encountered is the small unnamed point which forms the western shore of Starvation Cove. Next is the eastern boundary – Richardson Point – about seven miles distant. This in turn is separated from Ogle Point by twelve-mile-wide Barrow Inlet, which is itself neatly subdivided by Maconochie Island. The most easterly headlands, Ogle Point and Cape Britannia, actually form the outer limits of Chantrey Inlet. Apparently the error made by the commander of the boat party was in thinking that the first inlet that he encountered was the route to the Great Fish River.

If the survivors were led into this "false" inlet by Simpson's erroneous longitude they would soon have discovered their mistake. It would appear that some of them made camp while others detached to search for the entrance to the great river. Here, at Starvation Cove, six to ten of them died. The number of the searching party who succumbed is unknown; only one of them has been found to bear witness to their reconnaissance.

Gilder was told by the guides who escorted him there that when the natives found the boat at Starvation Cove it was "upside down on the beach, and all the skeletons beneath it." Later, as we have seen, he was told by Ogzeuckjeuwock of a boat that was found "right side up," and that a number of skulls were found "outside the boat," but ignored the discrepancy and concluded that this was the same boat. We have concluded that the tales of this upright boat, the one found by Pooyetta, may refer to a boat found on King William Island. But another possibility exists – that there actually were two boats found near Starvation Cove.

Beyond Starvation Cove we enter the realm of almost complete speculation as to the final days of Franklin's men. No body or relic which can be shown to have been deposited by the final survivors has been found to the east. It is not that there is no evidence of white men travelling in the area, but that what evidence there is can be attributed to other parties. Simpson and Dease travelled along this coast in 1839, leaving campsites and cairns in their wake. John Rae again approached the area, in the reverse direction, in 1847 and 1854. The evidence of their passage could later be attributed to the movements of a small group of Franklin survivors – or vice versa. Such difficulties do not prove that Franklin's men did not travel east beyond Starvation Cove, only that it is impossible to state conclusively that they did. As always there are, however, faint clues.

The first questionable site, attributable only to the Franklin expedition, is Qavdlunarsiorfik. Unfortunately Rasmussen did not tell us exactly where Qavdlunarsiorfik was. In our discussion of Nuvertaro we remarked in passing that doubt existed as to whether the spot visited by Rasmussen in 1923 was the same as that which the Americans had called Starvation Cove in 1879. Were there two distinct places with a boat at each?

We recall that Qaqortingneq located Qavdlunarsiorfik as a point "on Adelaide Peninsula, almost opposite the place where Amundsen wintered," and that Rasmussen described the location (which he visited) as on "the east coast of the Adelaide Peninsula near Starvation Cove." Rasmussen's curious remark that "we had been the first friends that ever visited the place" also implies that Qavdlunarsiorfik was distinct from Starvation Cove, as he was well aware that Schwatka's party had visited the latter place.[9]

In 1949 Captain Larsen conducted another survey. He visited the "coast around Starvation Cove" and "some of the islands nearby." Larsen reported finding "a leather boot sole and the remains of old camps on a low point of land jutting out from the south end of Point Richardson," and, while noting that "most of the camps seemed to be of Eskimo origin," he concluded that "some came from the Franklin expedition."[10]

The significance here is the fact that remains were not found at a single place, and that Larsen concluded that "some" camps had been established nearby. The description of where the boot sole was found is too vague to be of use (and the boot may have been dropped there by Inuit), but the idea of any white man's camp to the east of Starvation Cove, not envisaged in the standard reconstruction, is very interesting.

Associated with the description of Qavdlunarsiorfik, Rasmussen was also told of another find. He learned that in the same year that the ship at Ootgoolik sank, but "later on in the spring," three hunters travelled south from King William Island to hunt caribou. These men "found a boat with the dead bodies of six men. There were knives and guns in the boat, and much food also, so the men must have died of disease."[11]

A boat with six bodies to the south of King William Island is a perfect description of the remains found at Starvation Cove. As we have concluded that Pooyetta's boat was found on the "mainland" of King William Island itself, we might here be hearing of the true discovery of the remains at Nuvertaro. Unfortunately the lack of detail in this story makes the identification of this boat uncertain.

Another curious story involves a boat, or rather a ship and a boat, on the northern shore of Adelaide Peninsula to the east of

Starvation Cove. On 2 August 1855 Anderson's men found items which appeared to have been taken from a white man's boat. These were found in some native caches which had been discovered on a small unnamed islet "divided by a channel from Montreal Island" and lying between it and the mainland shore. As Rae had indicated that five men had died on an island near the "mainland" – an island which we take to be Keeuna – Anderson had assiduously searched for the graves but could find no trace that white men had ever passed this way.[12]

Although many writers state that Anderson found a boat on this islet (usually mistakenly said to be Montreal Island itself), this is imprecise and misleading; what he found were cached articles taken from a boat. The most interesting of these relics were two small pieces of wood, one of which was marked "*Erebus*" while the other had "Mr. Stanley" (Surgeon of that ship) carved on it. Also found were various boat's fittings, some ironwork, blacksmith tools, and other small items (one of which, a piece of leather, was later identified by Jane Franklin as part of a backgammon board presented by her to the officers of the *Erebus*). Anderson's journal makes it clear that these items were taken out of caches, and the boat from which they had been taken was not found.

Six days after finding these relics, while camped at Ogle Point, Anderson noted in his journal that "4 of the best men were ferried across in the Halkett boat, and the whole of Maconochie's Island was minutely examined without success."[13] But apparently the report received by Anderson from his subordinates was not exactly candid.

In 1890, thirty-five years later, J.B. Tyrrell met one of Anderson's men, Joseph Boucher, who said that, after the return of the party who had been sent to the west, he had learned that a ship had been seen far out in the ice. Nothing had been said to the officers about this, as the men knew that Anderson would attempt to reach the ship, and they were unwilling to run the risk of traversing the heavy ice or of delaying their return home.

In 1893 Tyrrell checked this story by arranging for the other principals to be interviewed. Edward Kipling, Paulet Papanakies, and Thomas Mustagan were all contacted (the fourth man was Henry Fidler), and their stories, with a few minor discrepancies, supported Boucher. Kipling said that the party divided, he and

Fidler going to the west while Mustagan and Papanakies went east, and that when they returned to camp Papanakies reported having seen a ship far out to sea.[14]

Thomas Mustagan was interviewed by J.A. Campbell in 1893. He remembered only three men – himself, Kipling, and Papanakies – and told that they "found something on one of the islands," but he did not remember what. At the last island he, "being the heaviest man in the party," had been left behind to make more room in the small boat, and when Kipling and Papanakies returned from the furthest island they reported having seen nothing. After the expedition had returned to Norway House he was told by Papanakies that he had seen a ship.[15]

Paulet Papanakies was, according to all accounts, the one who actually saw the "ship." According to his statement, he had encountered one native "fishing at the mouth of a river" who said that "a ship had been 'ruined' and plenty people dead." The native then showed him by signs that the ship had been all "broken." Whether this had occurred at the Great Fish River or later near Maconochie Island was unclear. Papanakies was insistent that he alone had climbed to the highest point of the big island and seen "what he still believes to have been two masts of a ship."

Papanakies remarked that "had there been more sticks standing around it would have been easy to have made a mistake. But there was nothing but rocks and ice as far as he could see." When his comrades later taunted him about the sighting he told them that "it was a very clear day and I have seen the ship at York [Factory] too often to be deceived." J.B. Johnson, who interviewed Paulet on behalf of Tyrrell, considered that there was "no room whatever to doubt his veracity or the sincerity of his belief" and remarked on the keenness of the native eyesight which "will detect objects at a distance which you or I would overlook twenty times."[16]

This story, even though told by an admitted eyewitness, has been almost completely ignored on the seemingly reasonable grounds that it is almost impossible that either of Franklin's ships could have been seen in Simpson Strait at this late date. The wrecks of both the *Erebus* and *Terror* had been accounted for, and the treacherous shallows of Simpson Strait were probably impassable to such large ships in any case.

But Papanakies did not see a "ship"; what he saw were "two masts" (actually two "sticks"). The only explanation which would seem to fit his testimony would be that he saw the masts (mast and bowsprit?) of a ship's boat which was standing on its keel, and that he was fooled by perspective into thinking that the small nearby boat was a large more distant ship.

Convinced that Papanakies had seen what he so earnestly claimed to have seen, Tyrrell concluded that the "sticks" might have belonged to the boat at Starvation Cove. This is doubtful. In addition to the fact that the Inuit testified that the Starvation Cove boat was overturned, the masts seen in 1855 were viewed "far out in the ice" from the north-east point of Maconochie Island. The boat place at Starvation Cove is nine miles to the south-west of there, beyond the intervening land which extends to Richardson Point. Papanakies's testimony seems inexplicable unless we conclude that a boat, on its keel, was seen to the north-east of Maconochie Island, itself north-east of Starvation Cove.

Papanakies's "sticks" were not the only thing of which Anderson was unaware. Kipling also remarked that the next day he and Fidler, while searching near the west side of Montreal Island, "found the mark of the keel of a small boat that had been dragged across the island, and found the boat broken in small pieces on the eastern side ... nothing was reported about what we had seen."[17]

The exact location of this boat is also in doubt. If Kipling was correct in saying the boat was found the "next day," then it must have been seen during the return trip from Ogle Point to "Pechell Point," a prior camp on the mainland well to the north-west of Montreal Island.[18] On the following day the party proceeded from their camp at Pechell Point to another old campsite at Backhouse Point, passing along the south shore of Montreal Island but not stopping to search it.[19]

Kipling probably found his boat not one but two days after the excursion to Maconochie Island, for on the 10th Anderson noted that "we arrived at the Strait separating Montreal Island from the w. Main the Halkett boat was launched and a small island examined on which were some old Esq. encampments."[20] From his description of the place, this was quite near the islet where the relics had been found in the native caches eight days before.

The significance of Kipling's "unreported" boat, found between Ogle Point and Montreal Island, is uncertain. The native stories seemed to indicate that the boat at Starvation Cove had been broken up where it was found, but perhaps it had been taken by the Inuit to this more convenient place to be broken up. However, Kipling's boat can also be seen as corroboration of Rasmussen's "Qavdlunarsiorfik" campsite, complete with "many bones" and other relics of the white men, and as vindication of his description of it as being on the "east coast" of the Adelaide Peninsula.

Thunder Cove, Starvation Cove, Richardson Point, Maconochie Island, Qavdlunarsiorfik, and Montreal Island are all associated with the remains of white men. These places seem to form a continuous chain of evidence, a testament to an eastbound party which paused, but did not stop, at Starvation Cove. As in other cases when the physical evidence has been confusing, we look to Inuit testimony for clarification. The traditions are admittedly uncertain, yet tantalizing stories do exist.

Beyond Chantrey Inlet the coast turns to the north-east. In 1839 Simpson and Dease left cairns on this coast at Cape Britannia and the Castor and Pollux River. Rae had come from the east in 1847, and he also visited the cairn at the latter place. Did some of Franklin's men cover this ground in the time between these expeditions?

The cairn at Cape Britannia was massive and well built. Like those at Trap Point on Victoria Island and at Cape Herschel on King William Island, also built by the Simpson party, it still exists. It was built on a high elevation and probably had a horizontal cross-piece to render it more conspicuous.[21] The cairn was originally fourteen feet high and the customary record of Simpson's discoveries was deposited in a bottle.[22] The Inuit knew it well. In-nook-poo-zhe-jook told Hall that a "monument very large & high was found a year or two ago [1867–8] at Cape Brittania [sic] (as he In-k pointed out) by a native of Oot-ka-ish-e-lik mouth of Great Fish or Back River. In it he found a single bottle – but there was nothing in it."[23]

Hall was in fact told of two cairns, this one with the bottle found at "King-ark" one year before, and another found at Ke-ark-che-wai-chen-wig many years before. He concluded that the first was the cairn at Castor and Pollux River and the latter was that at Cape Britannia.[24] As other sources unequivocally indicate that Kingark ("two mountains") was the name for the Cape,[25] Hall had these two cairns confused.

The fact that Simpson's record was missing might imply that the Cape Britannia cairn had been taken down and rebuilt. If a Franklin party passed this way it is conceivable that they might use this well-known cairn as a post-box, perhaps removing the record from the bottle and redepositing it underground – perhaps, as other explorers did, ten feet north of the cairn. It is even possible that there were two cairns at Cape Britannia, for in 1955 a native tale emerged of a large cairn which had been discovered and completely demolished, and that "two pieces of paper had been found inside which they [the natives] eventually destroyed."[26]

Noel Wright was the foremost proponent of the view that this cairn (Simpson's "Beacon Six") might hold the last records of the Franklin expedition. Inspired by his book *Quest for Franklin* (1959), a small overland party led by Robert Cundy descended the Great Fish River in 1962 and inspected the cairn. They found only a "small yellow film can, wrapped in polythene" in which a short note had been deposited by some predecessors of "Operation Back River 1960." Mindful that a record might be buried nearby, Cundy was prepared to dig for one, but noted that "there was not a scrap of soil on that windswept bluff, merely an irregular pattern of cracks, which revealed nothing."[27]

The next landmark on this forbidding coast was at the mouth of the Castor and Pollux River where the discoveries of Simpson and Rae met. Rae found a white man's cairn here, which he partially demolished, in 1854. The Inuit again knew the details of this cairn.

In-nook-poo-zhe-jook located this monument on the chart by pointing to "the coast south side of Inglis Bay, into wh. Murchison River empties to that particular part of the coast s. of a long narrow Island" – a perfect description of the site. Although Hall, confused, thought that In-nook-poo-zhe-jook was again describing the cairn at Cape Britannia, it is probable that the native was describing this second cairn when he noted that "no bottle found in this but a pair of shears & some beads were found suspended by a string that encircled the top of the cairn." Characteristically, In-nook-poo-zhe-jook gave the name of the discoverer of this cairn (In-now-me-ta). He did not think that this cairn was very old, for "there was no moss on the stones in a way indicating time long ago";[28] he further remarked that there was a "long stone on the top the stone pointing in the direction of

Ki-ki-tuk," and, apparently referring to Rae's visit, that "this monument has all been destroyed by some white man or men."[29]

Like that at Cape Britannia, this cairn had been built by Simpson.[30] At first Hall doubted this, and, believing it to have been the work of Franklin survivors, he questioned In-nook-poo-zhe-jook very closely. It was not until his return to the United States that Hall learned that Simpson had built the cairn, and he was therefore forced to modify his views. He nevertheless still believed that Franklin's people had visited it, a belief which was based on some remembered details of this find which he found very suggestive.

With the English Admiralty Chart (Large Arctic Chart) before us. I asked In-k to tell me again where the monument had been erected that had the long stone on the top pointing toward Ki-ki-tuk (KWL) wh. he told me about yesterday? He then pointed to the same place as yesterday, to wit, on the coast south side of Inglis Bay. S. of the long narrow Island wh. is but a little way E. of the mouth of Castor & Pollux River discovered by Dease and Simpson in 1839 ... In-nook-poo-zhe-jook then placed a board nail wh. I had in my hand directly over the spot of the monument the same nail pointing to Shar-too & thence on to Point Victory where another monument had been erected by white men & found by the Innuits. I was not only deeply interested in this particular description of In-k but greatly surprised for he particularly said that the long stone on the top of that monument not only pointed in the direction of *Shartoo* (*Cape Colville* low land opposite the SE extreme of KWL) but to the place of the monument that had been erected North side of the Inlet at the NW extreme of KWL, – that is at Point Victory. He said that Innuits who saw the said monument S. side of Inglis Bay noted what he states.

After seeing the direction in wh. this nail pointed to the northward & westward I drew a line in the opposite direction, to the southward & eastward to see if it might not if prolonged, come near to Repulse Bay & found such to be the fact, – therefore the pointing stone may have been intended by those who placed it there, to indicate whence they had come & to what place they were bound. But this latter is of my own conjecture founded upon what In-k has told & upon what information has been derived from some of the Repulse Bay & Igloolik natives. (emphasis in original)[31]

Hall freely admits that this idea, that Franklin's men had rearranged the cross-piece on the Simpson cairn to indicate both their past path and their future destination, is pure speculation. His reference to other information derived from Repulse Bay and Igloolik presumably refers to the stories of white men on the Melville Peninsula (usually attributed to Parry and Rae), and to other sightings of white men near Pelly Bay and Repulse Bay (probably memories of Rae). But Hall, with his tenacious belief in far-ranging survivors, could not entirely discount these tales as remembrances of Franklin's men. It must be admitted, however, that if Hall was confused about these cairns, In-nook-poo-zhe-jook was hardly less so.

In-nook-poo-zhe-jook, while telling Hall about the cairn whose cross-piece pointed to Shartoo, continually referred back to another cairn which he had found to the east of Pelly Bay shortly after Rae's second visit. Hall's notes show that he had difficulty in sorting out the details of these different cairns.

In-nook-poo-zhe-jook saw the cairn at Castor and Pollux River, near Shartoo, on his return from his search of King William Island. Years before, shortly after meeting with Rae in 1854, In-nook-poo-zhe-jook had found an almost identical monument at "E-te-u." This was pointed out to Hall as a location on the Simpson Peninsula near Cape Barclay.[32] In another interview In-nook-poo-zhe-jook was more specific.

He said it was at *Shar-too*, at the same time putting his finger on the Chart & moving it along down the East Coast of Simpson's Peninsula, till his finger rested on Point Anderson & Cape Barclay wh. are at the entrance N. side of Keith Bay – & then he said "that is E-to-uki", meaning the projections Point Anderson & Cape Barclay. Then he moved his finger carefully along up the coast till he got to Points J. & R. Clouston or Clouston Pts as they are called in Admiralty Chart when he said that is where that monument was & the stone on top was pointing directly toward a small island that is far out to the Eastward & northward of where the monument was. (emphasis in original)[33]

When Rae travelled up the east coast of the Simpson Peninsula (between Pelly and Committee Bays), he passed a point on 11 April 1847 which he named Point Silveright. This was a few miles north of Colvile Bay, and the natives called it "E-to-uke."[34] The next day he left a "deposit" a few miles to the north of this.[35] In a letter to the New York *Herald*, in which he expressed little respect for Hall, or trust in his collected Inuit stories, Rae explained the monument with the pointing stone.

The monument with the stone on top pointing in a certain direction is easily accounted for without bringing any of Franklin's crew such a very long way to built it. By I-vit-chuk's advice we were to cross over land here, as he said the doing so would save us many day's journey. A depot of provisions was to be made for our return, but as we were to follow the coast line on our way back and would not necessarily pass by our "cache" a man was sent to the eastward across Keith Bay with orders to build a conspicuous cairn on Cape Barclay as a guide to our food depot, which was on the low flat western shore of the bay, as a precaution in the event of foggy weather or a change in the aspect of the coast, by snow drift or other cause. [36]

Rae therefore concluded that the "Shartoo" to which In-nook-poo-zhe-jook referred was Cape Barclay. He apparently did not remember that he had earlier been told of another nearby Shartoo, the large island called by him Prince of Wales (now simply Wales) Island which lay directly to the east and which Rae had learned was called "Sha-took." [37] In fact the Simpson Peninsula itself was also accurately described as "the flat one" and called "Shartoo" by the Inuit. The name was frustratingly common. [38]

We therefore see that In-nook-poo-zhe-jook found two similar white men's cairns, one built by Simpson at Castor and Pollux River (near Cape Colville/Shartoo) and another, probably built by Rae, on Simpson Peninsula (Colvile Bay/Shartoo). Shartoo, "the flat one," like Omanek, "the heart-shaped one," was bound to lead to difficulties. As in this case each "Shartoo" was associated with a "Colville" there is no wonder Hall was confused!

The fact that there were widely separated places called "Shartoo" may have caused confusion even before Hall's arrival. In 1854, one day before meeting In-nook-poo-zhe-jook and Seeu-teetuar, Rae had had a less than satisfactory encounter with some Pelly Bay Inuit. They had tried to prevent him continuing west, had told confusing stories, and had attempted to "mislead" Ouligbuck. Rae felt that the Inuit were trying to protect their favoured hunting grounds and the caches of meat which they had established to the west. Many years later, Hall thought that he had found a more convincing motive.

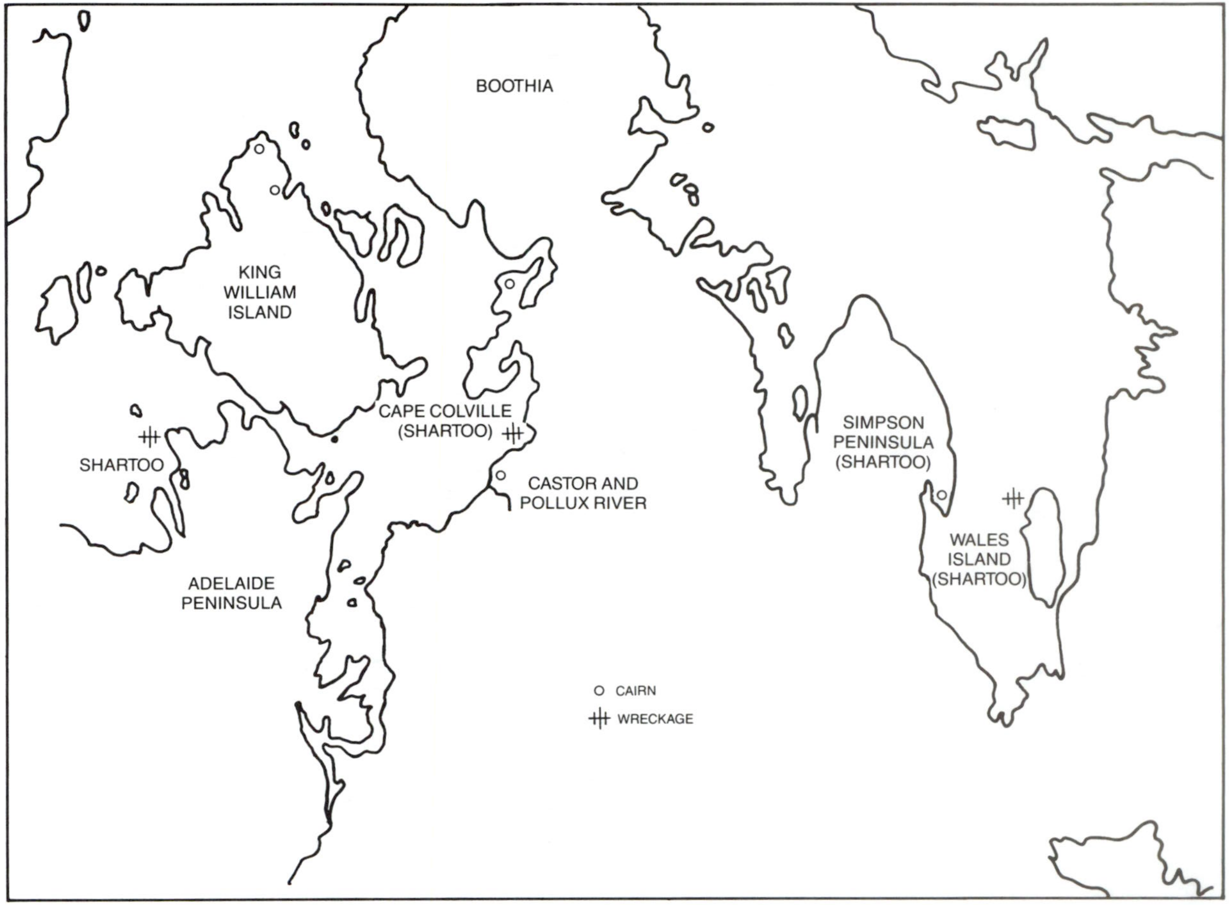

BOOTHIA

SIMPSON
PENINSULA
(SHARTOO)

WALES
ISLAND
(SHARTOO)

○ CAIRN

╫ WRECKAGE

CASTOR AND
POLLUX RIVER

CAPE COLVILLE
(SHARTOO) ╫

KING
WILLIAM
ISLAND

ADELAIDE
PENINSULA

SHARTOO

Map 8   Shartoo

Hall was told that "some of the Innuits with whom he was wintering, had tried, together with others from Pelly Bay, to persuade Dr. Rae to go to Shartoo, an island in Akkoolee Bay (the island called Prince of Wales Island, and the bay, Committee Bay, in Dr. Rae's chart), where he would find spars, rigging, casks, and boxes, and perhaps the hulk of a vessel. They understood from him that these were the very things he was looking for." The Innuits, therefore, professed that the objections referred to had been made in good faith, and in order to lead Rae's party to the best locality.[39]

When Rae heard of Hall's explanation of the native conduct he responded that "nothing was said to me in 1854 about this wreckage."[40] In-nook-poo-zhe-jook, one of Rae's informants, told that the real reason that Rae's party was warned against proceeding to the west was because the natives in that direction were acting particularly violent. This rings true, for the next day Ouligbuck/Mar-ko tried to desert, and In-nook-poo-zhe-jook confirmed "the reason Mar-ko ran away from Dr Rae was because the Innuits of Pelly Bay told him the party was liable to get killed."[41]

How then did the Inuit tradition about wreckage at "Shartoo" emerge? The natives told Rae that "large trees grew" on Wales Island, although he thought that they had been misled by the peculiarities of the refractive atmosphere and ice formations. There may have been a fossilized forest here (as elsewhere in the Arctic), or the natives might simply have been referring to driftwood which collected in the depths of Committee Bay. Some of this driftwood had lately been of a curious character.

In 1847, while travelling around the southern reaches of Committee and Pelly Bays, Rae had repeatedly come across relics from the wreck of some ship. He found a large sledge made of "the planks of some vessel (probably of the *Fury* or Sir John Ross's steamer the *Victory*)."[42] He was told that on the western shore of Melville Peninsula "some round sticks, probably spars belonging to one of the two vessels left in Prince Regent Inlet" had been found by the Inuit,[43] and he later saw "a large and heavy hoop of iron" which he concluded had at "one time been round the rudder head, bowsprit end, or mast head of a vessel" since the native who tried to sell it to him said it had been "taken off a large stick."[44] Hall and Rasmussen would each later conclude from the testimony gathered that most if not all of the wood used by the Pelly Bay Inuit had come from Ross's ship.

By the time of Hall's visit this tradition made even more sense. Hall was told that "a ship's beam, painted black on one side, and a long and large mast, had been seen on the east shore near the southern terminus of Committee Bay." This wreckage was found on or near Wales Island – the eastern Shartoo – but as it had been found, according to Hall's informants, "four years after Rae's last visit," it might not have been that mentioned to Rae in 1847.[45]

Even more confusingly, the late tradition of wreckage at Shartoo might not have referred to this wreckage at all! Amazingly, there was another place named Shartoo which both muddied the water and tied everything together. In an offhand remark about a relic from the Ootgoolik ship, Hall mentioned that it came from a purchase block "that was attached to one of the masts which In-nook-poo-zhe-jook found on the shore of Ook-joo-lik not far from O'Riley [sic] Island – Shar-too as called by the natives."[46]

This is very interesting. According to the later Inuit rationalization, Rae was told about a place called Shartoo where there were certain relics – "spars, rigging, casks, and boxes, and perhaps the hulk of a vessel." This "Shartoo," near where the Ootgoolik ship sank, had all of these features. In-nook-poo-zhe-jook himself had a sledge whose runner was made out of a mast which had been found there,[47] while the other things which the Pelly Bay Inuit described – boxes, casks, etc. – had been found ashore after the Ootgoolik ship sank.

The wreckage from this ship had also been accumulated near the "central" Shartoo, in Inglis Bay. In 1869 Hall found that much of the wood from the Franklin wreck had been cached nearby, including a piece of ship's mast fourteen feet long, a box used for rope, two new native boats which had been made from the ship's masts, and parts of ship's blocks.[48]

As if the confusion concerning the various places named Shartoo was not enough, there was one more story where this name was mentioned. It will be remembered that in 1863 the Pelly Bay native Seepunger, accompanied by his uncle, had crossed the Boothian isthmus and searched northern King William Island. As we have already seen, he was one of the first natives to visit the cairn and pile of clothes at Victory Point, and, as he mentions a skeleton there, he may have disinterred Irving.[49]

Three years before hearing of In-nook-poo-zhe-jook's monument at Shartoo, Hall had interviewed Seepunger and determined that the E-nook-shoo-yer which the latter had found was "near Shar-too" which Hall initially determined was "not far from Pelly Bay."[50] At this time the only places called Shartoo of which Hall had knowledge were the Simpson Peninsula and Wales Island, both of which were indeed near Pelly Bay. As Seepunger became more specific about his route to and from his monument it became apparent that he was speaking of King William Island, and its environs.

Seepunger's cairn was not In-nook-poo-zhe-jook's. While the one at the Castor and Pollux River had a pointing stone, Seepunger's had a piece of wood which had been carved into the shape of a pointing finger. In addition, Seepunger's indicated route never took him to the south of Cape Colville. It is interesting to note that according to Rasmussen the entire peninsula separating Spence Bay from Inglis Bay was called Shartoo. Cape Colville is the south-western extreme of this peninsula; the north-western point was called "Naparutalik" – "the place where there is something standing upright."[51] Was this upright thing the tall monument with the wooden finger?

The monument described by Seepunger is more reminiscent of those found by Hobson and Schwatka near Cape Felix, in one of which the latter also found a piece of paper with a pointing finger. When we remember the "direction posts" of Beechey Island, we can see that such a pointing finger is a trademark of sorts for the crew of the *Erebus* and *Terror*.

We also recall that Seepunger found a document inside a tin cup which resembled the Victory Point record. As he found many cairns (Victory Point, Cape Felix, Port Parry, and Shartoo), the location of this record (which was thrown away) is uncertain. If it was found in a cairn north of Cape Colville, it would still be an ambiguous clue, more likely a relic of some 1847 exploration party sent from the ships to delineate "Poctes Bay" than a final note from the last survivors northbound from the Great Fish River.

Various Inuit stories concerning many different places called "Shartoo" managed to convince Hall that the Franklin survivors in which he fervently believed had realigned Simpson's cairn at Castor and Pollux River in a significant direction. Most of these places were associated with wreckage from ships, and there were white men's cairns near others. As with the beginning of the expedition near "Omanek," the ending of the expedition near "Shartoo" is a confused medley of interweaving elements, all or none of which might apply to Franklin.

"Two sticks" seen out in the ice by a reluctant witness, some wood chips left on Montreal Island with "*Erebus*" and "Mr. Stanley" scratched on them, a missing record from a bottle at Cape Britannia, a curiously aligned cross-piece on a cairn and another with a wooden board carved into the shape of a pointing finger – such faint clues, if they are clues, can prove nothing. The trail of the last few Franklin crewmen, perhaps fittingly, eventually fades into the Arctic mists.

In-nook-poo-zhe-jook's
Boats

Teekeeta met Aglooka on the march between 1848 and 1850. The following year his party of ten combed the southern shore of King William Island to search for valuables. They apparently did not know that the white men had come down the west coast of the island; at any rate they did not search north of Terror Bay. Pooyetta's party may also have visited Toonoonee, and may have extended the search as far north as the boat place on Erebus Bay. After Pooyetta's and Teekeeta's experiences, it would seem natural for swarms of Inuit to have congregated at King William Island as knowledge of the enormous wealth in white men's relics spread. But apparently this did not occur. No Inuit searched the northern or western shores of King William Island until after McClintock's visit of 1859. Inexplicable as this may seem to us, there were some very good reasons why this should be so.

King William Island was a virtual no-man's-land among the Inuit. By the time that McClintock arrived it was only sparingly used as a hunting ground by the natives from Boothia. It had not always been thus; in 1869 In-nook-poo-zhe-jook told Hall that no natives then lived there but that "once – a long time ago when he was a boy, there were natives there, but they all died off – starved to death in the winter. Men, women & children starved."[1] This must have occurred within a few years of the Franklin expedition. Did the great tuktoo hunt described by Kokleearngnun denude the island and indirectly cause a famine?

For whatever reason, there apparently was a dearth of game. The Inuit recalled that "the two winters the two ships were at Neitch-ille were very cold. The Innuits never knew such very cold weather – there was no summer between the two winters – could catch no seals or kill any rein-deer at most of the usual places where they were most accustomed to find them."[2]

Probably for this reason, the presence of the white men was not universally welcomed. Ookbarloo told Hall, "very reservedly – in a way of letting me know a matter that is a great secret among the Innuits," that two of the Boothian angekos had cast spells so "that no animal, no game whatsoever would go near the locality of the two ships, which were in the ice near Neitchille many years ago. The Innuits wished to live near that place ... but could not kill anything for their food. They (the Innuits) really believed that the presence of the Koblunas (whites) in that part of the country was the cause of all their (the Innuits') trouble."[3]

Ookbarloo did not elaborate on the nature of the Inuit "trouble." In 1859 McClintock was told that "formerly many natives lived there [Ootgoolik], now very few remain."[4] As King William Island was a traditional hunting ground for the Ukjulingmiut, this testimony once again points to the immediate post-Franklin years as the time of native hardship.

In 1923 Rasmussen also heard how these natives had experienced a great famine, a "year of horror." Although periodic famine was almost routine among the Inuit, this must have been a very severe occurrence. The Ukjulingmiut were almost wiped out, and the few survivors permanently abandoned their former country and relocated near the mouth of the Back River.[5] Rasmussen was told that the Ootgoolik natives had "mixed with the Utkuhikjalingmiut" (Back River Inuit), and that "the oldest men alive to day [1923] personally experienced this change from coast dweller to inland dweller."[6]

Again this last detail strongly implies that the famine was soon after the visit of the *Erebus* and *Terror*. This might explain the lack of corroboration of Kokleearngnun's story – most of the natives who could have been visitors to Franklin's ships were soon after claimed by the famine.

It must also be noted that there were different, often mutually hostile, bands of Inuit involved in witnessing the Franklin saga. The natives who actually met the white men on their retreat (Ow-wer, Teekeeta, Too-shoo-art-thariu, Mangaq, and Ahlangyah) were all Netsilingmiut. Their usual hunting grounds were on the Boothia Peninsula, and in 1879 Klutschak noted that "only occasionally would the odd family, responding to the nomadic urge, undertake a journey to ... King William's Land. Even so, they visit it only in the fall, and even then only the southeastern part."[7]

The Netsilingmiut were considered to be warlike and barbarous by most of their native neighbours, and apparently with reason. By 1880 the northern Netsilingmiut had spread over the entire Franklin area, moving south into Pelly Bay, acquiring the favoured hunting grounds along Simpson Strait, and occupying the west coast of the Adelaide Peninsula which had been abandoned by the Ukjulingmiut. By Rasmussen's time the whole area was firmly dominated by the Netsilingmiut.

The Utkuhikhalingmiut (now combined with the Ukjulingmiut refugees) were encountered by Schwatka's party in 1879. Klutschak described them as the "remnant of a once large tribe"[8] and indicated that famine was not the only force at work during this great mid-century migration.

As a result of prolonged fighting with the Ugjulimmiut and Netsilingmiut now occupying that area [Ootgoolik], the number of Utkuhikhalingmiut had been greatly reduced, and they found themselves obliged to abandon their hunting grounds and to drag out their lives in this quiet corner. The entire tribe now consisted of only sixteen families ... only a few years would suffice to entirely expunge this once powerful tribe from the face of the earth.[9]

Rasmussen confirmed that the Utkuhikjalingmiut had once been "a great nation, so numerous that all the hills looking over Lake Franklin were sometimes enveloped with smoke from the many camp fires," and they admitted that once they had been "an arrogant, warlike people, on bad terms with all their neighbours."[10]

These movements and exterminations of Inuit would have direct relevance to the later unravelling of the Franklin stories. Most of the natives interviewed by the white explorers were Netsilingmiut, who, except for isolated sealing parties like Teekeeta's, had not been directly involved with the white men. The original inhabitants of King William Island had either died or been displaced by the time the stories came to light. Schwatka's party found only two old Ugjulingmiut (Puhtoorak and Toolooah) who had survived to tell of the sinking of Franklin's ship at Ootgoolik. Seeuteetuar and his wife Koo-nik had lived for a time at Ootgoolik and had traditions to tell Hall, but they were probably Netsilingmiut newcomers who, like Ek-kee-pee-ree-a, had "heard the natives tell" of the ship, but had not personally been involved.[11]

Many of the Franklin tales came from even further afield. Most of Hall's informants (Kokleearngnun, Seepunger, Kobbig) were Arviligjuarmiut who inhabited the areas south of Pelly Bay and near Repulse Bay. These natives were quite familiar with white men, having met with the Rosses and Rae. Some of the older individuals even remembered Parry at Igloolik. Of all of the Inuit bands the Arviligjuarmiut were the most wide-ranging, having generally amicable relations with other natives, and whalers, as far away as Igloolik and Pond Inlet.

The Arviligjuarmiut were the "middlemen" of the central Arctic. Rasmussen learned that they had originally lived at the crossroads of two trade routes, one crossing Rae Isthmus to Hudson Bay and another which led via Back River to the interior of the Barren Lands. He remarked that "they were a hardy people who thought nothing of starting out on long sledge journeys, which might last years," to obtain the wood and iron which their country lacked.[12]

The Pelly Bay Inuit were "connected with the Netsilingmiut tribal group by relationship and intermarrying" but preferred to "isolate themselves from them" because of the latter's propensities for violence.[13] This was apparently a long-standing complaint, and was attested to by the explorers who visited the area.

When approaching the Boothia Peninsula in 1846, Rae was apprehensive when he met strange natives, for he had been told by the Arviligjuarmiut of Pelly Bay that the Netsilingmiut had a "very bad character." They were consequently "much feared" by his guide, Ivitchuk, who refused to hunt seal at night for fear of them.[14] Ouligbuck in 1854, and Hall in 1866, were again warned by the Pelly Bay natives that to the north and west lived the "Seeneemeutes," a branch of the Netsilingmiut who seemed to be on violent terms with all of their neighbours.[15] Matters had reached such a state by 1866 that Kokleearngnun took his people from Pelly Bay to live with their south-eastern kin of Repulse Bay (Seegar, his wife Ookbarloo, and their sons). He did this despite long-standing personal disagreements with these relatives, some of whom threatened violence.[16]

We can see then that the Arviligjuarmiut, although not directly involved with Franklin, heard all of the standard stories from their own travellers and from their relatives to the west. Because the Arviligjuarmiut were centrally located and had had extensive contact with earlier white visitors, the potential for confusion in their stories was great. We have seen that many elements of the "Franklin" stories told by these natives contain "echoes" of the Ross and Parry expeditions, and that they were occasionally confused about details.

These divisions of Inuit were by no means totally exclusive. We have seen that Seeuteetuar visited Ross at Felix Harbour and saw Rae at Pelly Bay, McClintock on Boothia, Hall at Keeuna, and Schwatka near Starvation Cove. In-nook-poo-zhe-jook (a Netsilingmiut) first met Rae when travelling from Boothia to Pelly Bay, and often visited Repulse Bay.[17] Pooyetta (Netsilingmiut) had an Arviligjuarmiut wife (Tooktoocheer).[18] Too-shoo-art-thariu (Netsilingmiut) was a cousin of Ouela and his brothers at Repulse Bay, and his mother lived at Pelly Bay.[19] Eek-choo-ar-choo ("Jerry"), a native of Pelly Bay,[20] was a cousin of Teekeeta (Netsilingmiut),[21] and met Hall while living at Igloolik! Indeed, a careful reading of the journals and notes of the various investigators reveals that very few individual Inuit were involved with the Franklin story, and that most of these were, in some complex way, related. (See appendix 3.)

We concluded in an earlier chapter that the woman who acquired a watch by chipping the ice away from a body in the tent at Toonoonee was probably Ad-lark, Teekeeta's mother. Old Ookbarloo, who recounted this tale to Hall, identified this woman as the "mother-in-law of In-nook-poo-zhe-jook."[22] This would make In-nook-poo-zhe-jook and Teekeeta brothers-in-law!

In-nook-poo-zhe-jook was instrumental in spreading the word of the Franklin disaster among the Inuit. When Hall asked how he had come to learn of it, In-nook-poo-zhe-jook replied that "before leaving Neitchille he saw Tut-ke-ta & his mother & had the story from them."[23] He also said that before this time "the Pelly Bay natives didn't know anything about the white men's starving."[24]

It seems that Pelly Bay became the clearing-house for Franklin information among the Inuit. Hall was repeatedly told of the great meeting of the Inuit which had occurred there the winter before Rae arrived. Most of the natives who would later tell of Franklin had been present – Too-shoo-art-thariu[25] told his story of the meeting with Aglooka to his uncle Seegar and his aunt Ookbarloo.[26] Their sons Ouela, Artooa, and Shookshearknook, then mere boys, would later tell Hall garbled stories of their cousin's adventures.[27] Seeuteetuar and his wife Koo-nik were there, as were Ad-lark and her husband Neeweekeei (and possibly their son Teekeeta).[28] Also present were Hall's future companions Eek-choo-ar-choo ("Jerry")[29] and Nukerzhoo ("Jack").[30] Presumably Kokleearngnun and Seepunger attended as well, probably acting as hosts. A few months after this "conference," Rae and In-nook-poo-zhe-jook arrived, and the tales were told again, many of the various threads of the story becoming intermingled, and in some cases, confused.

It might be thought that, now that the news of the white men dying had filtered out from the Boothia Peninsula by way of Too-shoo-art-thariu and In-nook-poo-zhe-jook, Inuit parties would finally venture to King William Island to investigate and search for relics. Again there was apparent indifference. Some of the natives from Igloolik remained near Repulse Bay for "seven winters and a half" and then returned home.[31]

In-nook-poo-zhe-jook himself did not immediately follow up the story, first spending five winters hunting between Repulse and Pelly Bays, returning to Boothia in 1859 and finally going to King William Island in the spring of 1861.[32] This visit to King William Island was not inspired by the stories he had earlier told and heard at Pelly Bay in 1854, but by McClintock's expedition five years later, of which In-nook-poo-zhe-jook had learned from his old friend Seeuteetuar.[33]

It seems that only at this late date did the realization emerge that white men's relics were scattered along the north-west coast of King William Island. Until McClintock's expedition in 1859, the Inuit apparently believed that Aglooka and his men had come ashore at or near Cape Crozier, leaving their ships far out in the ice, and that the relics which had been left behind from their retreat had all been discovered.

This can be clearly seen when we review what Rae was told in 1854. In this testimony we note the fact that the Inuit knew of all of the places visited by Teekeeta and Pooyetta, but of little else. As Rae's informant was In-nook-poo-zhe-jook, who had derived his information from his brother-in-law Teekeeta, we should not be surprised to learn from Rae about "forty white men" who were seen "dragging a boat and sledges," or that these men "purchased a small seal, or piece of seal" and told "that the ship or ships had been crushed by the ice" (Teekeenu). Rae also learned about "the corpses of some thirty persons and some graves" (Toonoonee), which, as we have seen, he thought had been discovered "on the continent." In-nook-poo-zhe-jook also accurately told of "five dead bodies on an island" (Keeuna) which Rae thought was Montreal Island. One of the bodies "had a telescope strapped over his shoulders," a slightly garbled account of Ad-lark's discovery of a body lying on a telescope at Kun-ne-ar-be-ar-nu, and the mention of "fish-bones and feathers of geese" at one encampment probably refers to Set-tu-me-nin, the only place where evidence of fishing was reported by the Inuit.

The remains at Starvation Cove may also have been found, by someone, before 1854. Rae was told that some of the bodies were discovered under a boat which had been turned over to form a shelter, and many of his informants remarked that there was no sledge found with this boat.[34] As the boats found in Erebus Bay were definitely upright and sledge-borne, this detail must be from a boat found further south, at either Douglas Bay or Starvation Cove.

Significantly, except for a repetition of Aglooka's statement concerning the ice destroying his ships far out in the ice, no mention was made to Rae of the wreck of a ship on the Ootgoolik shore. Rae noted that all of the wooden relics in Inuit hands at this time came from Ross's *Victory*. Apparently the information from the Ootgoolik natives had not filtered to Pelly Bay before 1854, although the Netsilingmiut native On-na-lee would tell McClintock of the Ootgoolik wreck five years later.

The fact that McClintock's party found relics on the north-west coast of King William Island apparently came as a great surprise to the Inuit. They had told him of the wreck at Ootgoolik, and of the relics which had been found "on the island in the river" (Montreal Island?), but had no knowledge of relics on the west coast, a coast that they had not visited in eleven years. One of the first to venture to Kikertak after McClintock was In-nook-poo-zhe-jook.

In-nook-poo-zhe-jook, accompanied by his son Neer-kood-loo, his nephew Oo-ar-zhoo, and two other hunters (Ook-pik and Ekke-pe-re-a), decided in 1861 to make "a tour on purpose to search after such things as they could find that belonged to the white men that had died on K.W.L."[35] They apparently travelled westward along the south coast, but did not know of, or at any rate did not stop at, Keeuna and the nearby graves, for when In-nook-poo-zhe-jook led Hall there in 1869 he was visiting the places for the first time.

In-nook-poo-zhe-jook did find the encampment at Terror Bay. It was still essentially the same as when Teekeeta's party had seen it. During the intervening decade the bodies had decomposed and the tent blown away, but there were still plenty of relics available to reward their effort. Proceeding northward along the coast this party next arrived at the boat place in Erebus Bay. McClintock and Hobson had found one boat here; In-nook-poo-zhe-jook, who may have heard of it, found two.

One of the boats which In-nook-poo-zhe-jook found in 1861 had been cleared of relics; the other, slightly farther inland, had apparently once been hidden from view, for it remained untouched. Hall believed, and In-nook-poo-zhe-jook did not contradict him, that the "pillaged" boat was the one found by McClintock in 1859. Yet we earlier noted that Ogzeuckjeuwock described a boat with remains very similar to those found by In-nook-poo-zhe-jook, and we concluded that the former's father, Pooyetta, might have been the original discoverer of this boat in Erebus Bay.

Pooyetta found a boat, and emptied it, the year after Teekeeta and the four families met with Aglooka in Washington Bay. Pooyetta's boat at "Kinynukshane," usually thought to be Starvation Cove, would necessarily have most of the features associated with the boats in Erebus Bay. Like Pooyetta, McClintock removed everything of value from the boat which he found, yet there were numerous discrepancies between what In-nook-poo-zhe-jook found at his boat and what McClintock left behind. Could In-nook-poo-zhe-jook's empty boat have been that found by Pooyetta?

This would require us to assume that McClintock must have found a *third* boat. This is quite an assumption, and one which it would seem is almost impossible to verify. Yet it is interesting to note a reference by Hall that "according to information of numerous natives" the remains of Franklin crewmen "lie about the place of the 3 boats".[36]

McClintock found his boat "early in the morning," having en-camped at Cape Crozier the previous night, and gave its latitude and longitude as 69° 08′ 43″ N, 99° 24′ 42″ W. If accurate, this would place his boat between Cape Crozier and Little Point, about ten miles in a direct line from his night camp, a healthy morning walk indeed![37] The boat was found on the beach of "a wide bay,"[38] which is a good description of this part of the coast, and it was "barely, if at all, above the reach of occasional tides."[39]

In-nook-poo-zhe-jook and his party demolished one of the two boats which they found in 1861, leaving the other (the previously visited, empty one) behind. This second boat was found, by Schwatka, not in a "wide bay," but "at the bottom of one of the deepest inlets or bays" in 1879.[40] Was this McClintock's boat? Although both Schwatka and Gilder believed so, the latter re-marked "if this is the boat seen by him [McClintock], it is certainly a long way from the position represented on the maps."[41]

The boat found by the Americans was definitely one of the two found by In-nook-poo-zhe-jook. Schwatka remarked that "a most diligent search was made to discover the whereabouts of the second boat spoken of by Captain Hall ... and also frequently alluded to by the Netchilluk natives who had described the spot to me. But we met with no success. I afterwards learned from the Netchilluks that they had removed one boat and sled so completely that no trace of it could probably be seen."[42]

The standard reconstruction states that only two boats were found in Erebus Bay, one of which was originally discovered by McClintock (actually Hobson), visited and found empty by In-nook-poo-zhe-jook two years later, and subsequently rediscov-ered by Schwatka. This is inherently logical and, as it requires no assumption about "extra" boats, elegantly simple. To prove it all one needs to do is to show that the boat found by Schwatka was the same one seen by McClintock twenty years earlier.

Schwatka felt that the boat which he had found was "no doubt the one referred to by McClintock,"[43] but he never stated his reasons for this belief. Gilder agreed with his companion's as-sessment, and in the introduction to his book he stated that "among the relics that were brought home was the prow of the boat seen by Sir Leopold McClintock in Erebus Bay."[44]

This should effectively resolve the argument, for McClintock gave a detailed description of the boat and sledge which he found and this can be compared to the relic recovered by the Americans.

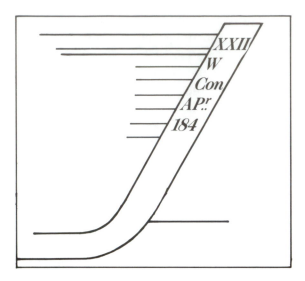

Figure 4 The markings seen by McClintock on the boat which he found in Erebus Bay. The stem recovered by Schwatka, usually thought to be from the same boat, has no such marks.

The easiest and most obvious way to confirm the identity of McClintock's boat would have been to compare the distinctive markings carved into the prow. McClintock's book contained a drawing which clearly showed these markings, markings which indicated "that she was built by contract, was received into Woolwich Dockyard in April, 184?, and was numbered 61. There may have been a fourth figure to the right hand, as the stem had been reduced in order to lighten the boat."[45]

Both Schwatka and Gilder specifically mention that the prow and stern-post of the boat which they found were in good condition. Yet they apparently did not have McClintock's book with them for reference, for Gilder remarked that "whether or not this is the same boat seen by McClintock is a matter that can be ascertained, for we have brought home the prow containing the inscription spoken of by him."[46] This is a rather confusing statement, for if the inscription had been verified the phrase "can be ascertained" would have been unnecessary.

McClintock himself was certain that his boat had been found. In the fifth edition of his book (1881), published shortly after the return of Schwatka and Gilder, he states that "the prow (or stem) of this boat is now in England ... The letters and numbers deeply

cut into the stem are identical with my description ... and therefore prove her to be the same boat."[47] This too is curious.
McClintock must have derived this information through correspondence with someone in England rather than by personal
observation, for between 1879 and 1883 Admiral McClintock was
living in Bermuda, where he was serving as the Commander in
Chief of the North America and West Indies station.[48] The
amendments which he made to his own book were apparently
based on a study of the published accounts of Schwatka's discoveries – Schwatka had assumed the boats were the same,
McClintock, based on Schwatka's assumption, confirmed it.

Gilder remarked that the Franklin relics, including the boat's
stem, were "added to the relics already deposited at the Museum
in Greenwich Hospital," now the National Maritime Museum in
Greenwich.[49] It is still there. According to the curator, it is "in
rather fragmentary condition" but "does not appear to bear the
markings, as described by McClintock."[50]

The prow of the boat which Schwatka and Gilder recovered in
1879 was from the empty boat found by In-nook-poo-zhe-jook,
but it was not McClintock's. In-nook-poo-zhe-jook's boat must
have been visited prior to 1861 by another Inuit. As the only
other native description of a boat with similar features to that
found by In-nook-poo-zhe-jook was provided by Pooyetta's wife
and son, this strengthens our earlier supposition that Pooyetta's
searching party had come as far as Erebus Bay. Here, as In-nook-
poo-zhe-jook would later confirm, was the evidence of cannibalism. Here, not in Starvation Cove, tragedy had overtaken most
of Franklin's men. Most significantly, here, at the "boat place,"
Tooktoocheer had told Schwatka of a "central place, or last resting
place, in which the vital records of the Franklin expedition had
been placed." If this was also the place where Bayne's informants
told of vaults containing records having been deposited, it would
be a most important spot.

It should be easy to locate In-nook-poo-zhe-jook's boat place.
McClintock found his boat to the east of Cape Crozier "early in
the morning" after leaving his campsite there. In-nook-poo-zhe-
jook described his route to the boats which he found as well,
and it is obvious from his testimony that the site was likewise to
the east of "the extreme west point" of King William Island –
Cape Crozier – but he gives no indication of how far to the

eastward. Hall thought that In-nook-poo-zhe-jook's boat was actually "a little way westward of the one found by Hobson"[51] but gives no reason for this belief.

Schwatka remarked on the discrepancy in location between his boat and that of McClintock. According to him the boat was "some ten or fifteen miles southeast from [McClintock's] point as noted on the Admiralty Chart."[52] This, like Gilder's surprise at the inaccuracy of McClintock's map, was suggestive, but, owing to the inherent difficulty of ascertaining position, hardly conclusive. Schwatka noted that "mistakes of from five to twenty miles are not infrequent in the hurried exploration of Arctic countries, and from my two years of Arctic surveying, I could write a volume descriptive of mistakes I encountered."[53]

Gilder helpfully mentioned that there was a small island to the north of the inlet where the boat was found, a feature which exists only to the east of Little Point. This confirms that the two boats were found in one of the many closely spaced inlets between Little Point and the De La Roquette River, where, in 1982, Beattie's searching party also found scattered remains. McClintock found only two skeletons in his boat. In-nook-poo-zhe-jook described "very many" bones, and Beattie confirmed that the remains of "six to fourteen individuals" were grouped around the few remaining pieces of the boat and in the three bays immediately to the north-eastward.[54]

The map which accompanied Gilder's account also showed the position of their find as being between Little Point and the De La Roquette River. The text verifies this, for it is remarked that on their southbound route the explorers "had to go a long distance inland to find a place where we could ford a wide and deep river" that emptied into Erebus Bay. The next day the boat was found, and it was only after another day's fruitless search that they came upon a "deep inlet entering near Pt. Little."[55]

This locale in the depths of Erebus Bay would be a suitable place for boats from a nearby ship to "usually" come ashore. Little Point, a few miles to the west, is itself the western point of a narrow but very deep inlet which almost completely cuts through the Graham Gore Peninsula at its narrowest point. The southern end of this inlet comes within four miles of the head of Terror Bay – quite near where the large camp was established. Even when frozen this inlet would have offered an excellent route between Erebus and Terror Bays.

McClintock's remarks about the "mere accumulation of dead weight" associated with this boat has usually called into question the decision-making ability of Crozier and Fitzjames – why did they allow their weakened men to transport such a mass of scarcely useful items? Even more inexplicable is the idea that the scurvy-ridden and starving survivors of the Toonoonee débâcle would bother to burden themselves with such junk while making an obviously desperate return to distant ships.

The combined testimony of Kokleearngnun, Bayne, Tooktoocheer, and In-nook-poo-zhe-jook paints a radically different picture. These stories imply that Erebus Bay was the true focus of the post-abandonment story. In this scenario In-nook-poo-zhe-jook's two boats were not sixty-five but probably less than fifteen miles from the vessels. They were admirably positioned to provide temporary shelter, halfway between the ships and the hunting station at Terror Bay. When the survivors of Terror Bay stumbled northward across the Graham Gore Peninsula in an attempt to regain the ships these boats would have provided a natural, and for many a final, campsite.

These boats may have come from Kokleearngnun's "wrecked" ship, been loaded with supplies, and "cached" on the beach in case of future need. The sledges and their heavy loads had not come ashore at Victory Point at all, but had been brought over a few miles of rough ice between the ships and shore. They had not been modified for the ascent of the Great Fish River, but simply to reduce their weight. Crozier and Fitzjames were not fools.

In-nook-poo-zhe-jook's 1861 search of King William Island was not the last undertaken by the Inuit, but it was the last for which we have much evidence. He apparently stayed on King William Island during the winter, for he stated that "in 1861 the ice between Cape Crozier & Amiralty [sic] Inlet was very rugged & heavy but the next year (1862) when he visited the boats all smooth ice between those places."[56]

Surprisingly, In-nook-poo-zhe-jook never mentions having searched north of Erebus Bay. Perhaps the traditions that this was where the ships had first been seen still restricted the field of search. As we have seen, it was not until 1863 that Seepunger and his uncle arrived from Pelly Bay and discovered the cairns at Cape Felix and Victory Point, as In-nook-poo-zhe-jook indicated by pointing out these places on Hall's map. Even then their visit was not inspired by the hunt for white men's relics but by a quest for seals.

The physical remains became less attractive and harder to find with the passage of the years. When Adlekok visited Hall's cairn at Set-tu-me-nin between 1869 and 1879 he recovered only one pair of snow-goggles.[57] When returning from Cape Felix with Schwatka a boy named Awanak found a native cairn near Cape Maria Louisa which contained minor Franklin relics. Gilder noted that one of the natives of Adelaide Peninsula had told him that he had "cached just such articles somewhere along the coast, and had afterward forgotten the place."[58]

Eventually everything of value was taken, and King William Island was again deserted. In this century, the arrival of the white traders of the Hudson's Bay Company at Gjoa Haven on the south coast, and of the military who established a radar station near Gladman Point, began the process of "civilizing" the island. As always, the southern and eastern coasts were utilized, and the scene of the Franklin disaster, except for brief visits, lay quiet. There are still traces of the major sites at Cape Felix, Victory Point, and Erebus Bay, but nothing can be learned from the odd piece of wood or cord. Only the stories remain.

Too-shoo-art-thariu

When Hall first interviewed the natives at Repulse Bay, he heard a story which led him to believe that four of the men from the *Erebus* and *Terror* survived under the care of the Inuit. As we have seen, the stories concerning their supposed benefactor Too-shoo-art-thariu, told by his aunt Ookbarloo and his cousin Ouela, were incorrect. Too-shoo-art-thariu, husband of Ahlangyah, and companion of Teekeeta, Ow-wer, and Mangaq, had, by the collective testimony of these four people, never seen white men before encountering Aglooka at Teekeenu, and, according to his friends, "never saw Aglooka after the time Ow-wer and Tut-ke-ta saw him."[1] It should be noted that this last statement does not preclude a later meeting with another white man, although Too-shoo-art-thariu's wife in later testimony mentioned only one encounter.

Unfortunately, Hall did not interview Too-shoo-art-thariu himself at this time; his cousins stated that he was then living at Neitchille. Five years later he was told at Pelly Bay that Too-shoo-art-thariu had moved to King William Island, but upon his arrival there Hall learned that the elusive native was "now at Wollaston Land opposite Coronation Gulf" (modern Victoria Island).[2] Schwatka and Gilder were unaware that Ahlangyah-Elaingnur was his widow when she was interviewed in 1879.

Too-shoo-art-thariu's Repulse Bay relatives were not the only ones to have heard of his tale. In 1869 Kokleearngnun's brother

Kob-big stated that "all of the white men except two who were a long time ago at Ki-ki-tuk had perished. One of the two was Ag-loo-ka (Crozier), and both of these had certainly been seen by some of his (Kob-big's) friends."[3] Kob-big had apparently learned this during the great conference (1853–4) "when Ou-e-la (Albert) and his brothers ... saw this cousin that had been so good to Crozier and his men, at Pelly Bay which is not far from Neitchille." At that time "the cousin had not heard whether Crozier and the two men and Neitchille Inuit had ever come back or not. The Innuits never think they are dead – do not believe they are."[4]

Seegar, another attendee at the Pelly Bay meeting, endorsed this view.

Tookoolitoo had just made the sympathetic remark – "What a pity it is that Ag-loo-ka and the two men who started together from Neitchille for the purpose of getting to the Kob-lu-nas country had never arrived." Old See-gar listened ... to all that Tookoolitoo said, and when she made the last remark, See-gar sprang from his seat, quick as a flash, and looking staringly at Tookoolitoo, exclaimed with great force and surprise, "What! Ag-loo-ka not get back! Why the Kin-na-pa-toos (Innuits who belong to Chesterfield Inlet), told me several years ago that Ag-loo-ka and one man with him arrived among their people, and that they (Ag-loo-ka and his men) had gone to where the Kob-lu-nas live further down the Big Bay (to Churchill or York Factory, as Tookoolitoo thinks See-gar tried to explain it) ... Ag-loo-ka, of whom he (See-gar) had heard Too-shoo-art-thariu tell all about at the same time that Ou-ela and his brother saw him, arrived among the Kin-na-pa-toos, having one man with him, and his powder and shot were nearly all gone ... Too-shoo-art-thariu told him (See-gar) (this was in the winter of 1853–4 at Pelly Bay) that Ag-loo-ka would probably get home to where the Kob-lu-nas live, unless somebody killed him, for he (Ag-loo-ka) knew all about how to hunt and kill took-too (rein-deer) and nearly everything else that the Innuits could kill; knew how to keep himself warm, how to live, just as the Innuits do; as he (E.) [Aglooka; Hall occasionally spelled this name "Eglooka"] had lived and hunted with him (Too-shoo-art-thariu) and with many others of the Neitchille Innuits. Ag-loo-ka knew all about everything that the Innuits knew. The Kin-na-pa-too Innuits told him (See-gar) about Ag-loo-ka and his men; did not see them; but said that they had their information from others of their people, who did.[5]

The fact that none of Franklin's men ever reached home, and the later discovery that the tradition of Too-shoo-art-thariu's offering aid to Ag-loo-ka after the Teekeenu encounter was untrue, ultimately led to Hall's disillusionment with Inuit testimony in general. This verdict has been often endorsed. Yet so much of what we have heard in the preceding pages has turned out to be accurate; how can we explain the glaring discrepancies in Seegar's and Too-shoo-art-thariu's stories?

There are various ways around the problem. One would be to invoke two different natives named Too-shoo-art-thariu. More reasonably, we could assume that Ouela had two different cousins (Too-shoo-art-thariu and "Cousin 2"), each of whom met a white man named Aglooka, and that either the Repulse Bay natives had melded the experiences or Hall had misunderstood what he had been told. Hall did note in a letter that Ouela's cousin "had two names (but I cannot stop to get them now),"[6] and that the tradition was confused is shown in another place where it is Ouela's brothers Artooa and Shookshearknook who fed Crozier and his companions.[7] Kob-big further confused the picture by identifying Too-shoo-art-thariu and In-nook-poo-zhe-jook as those who had seen the white men, a perfectly true statement (Too-shoo-art-thariu saw Aglooka, In-nook-poo-zhe-jook saw Rae), but of little use in sorting out the confusing stories.

The third and most probably solution is that here, once again, we have confusion between different Aglookas.

There are actually three different traditions concerning Too-shoo-art-thariu, all controversial, and all intriguing. The first, embedded in the accurate detail of the meeting at Teekeenu, was that four white men, one of whom was Crozier (Aglooka), were found wandering on the ice. They looked bad, "very thin and almost starved" with sunken eyes. This was especially true of the leader, who, unlike his companions, had not been practising cannibalism. Too-shoo-art-thariu (or Cousin 2) "took Crozier [Aglooka] and his men along with him, and fed them and took good care of them all winter," but one man, who was sick, died shortly after the meeting. The others recovered and "in the summer Crozier and his men killed with their guns a great many birds, ducks, geese and rein-deer. Crozier killed many – very many of the latter. The Innuits saw him do it. A Neitchille Inuit went with Crozier and his remaining two men when they started to go to their country. They had a kiak with which to cross rivers and lakes. They went down toward Ook-koo-seek-ka-lik (the estuary of Great Fish or Back's River)."[8]

This account, contradicted by the other participants in the Tee-keenu meeting, could conceivably be explained as exaggeration or invention on Too-shoo-art-thariu's part. There is, unfortunately, one problem with any attempt to completely ignore this account of three white men being offered aid. Another participant remembered it as well.

In 1881, Captain Adams of the Dundee whaler *Arctic*, while engaged in searching for whales in Prince Regent Inlet, received on board a "very intelligent Esquimaux" who told him an interesting story.

The native stated that when he was a young man in his father's hut three men came over the land towards Repulse Bay and that one of them was a great Captain. The other two lived some little time in his father's hut, and he showed Captain Adams the spot on the chart where they were buried. The Esquimaux, continuing his narrative, said that seventeen persons started from two vessels which had been lost far to the westward but only three were able to survive the journey to his father's hut.

From all the information furnished by the Esquimaux Captain Adams has no doubt that the vessels referred to were those of the Franklin expedition and that the great captain mentioned was no other than Lieutenant Crozier. Assuming that what the Esquimaux stated was correct it would seem that the members of the Franklin expedition were attempting to reach Hudson Bay Territory. Judging from the present age of the native, Captain Adams is of the opinion that his allusion to having seen the men when he was a young man must refer to a period some thirty five years ago.[9]

This late tale, like so many others, has been largely ignored. Yet apparently we have here an eyewitness account of the meeting with the three white men which has been preserved under Too-shoo-art-thariu's name. Perhaps this visitor to the *Arctic* was the son of "Cousin 2"; in any event it is a valuable corroboration of the "Too-shoo-art-thariu" testimony.

Admittedly, the details of the story told to Captain Adams do not exactly match those told to Hall about Too-shoo-art-thariu.

Adams's informant stated that the great Captain had two companions, whereas Too-shoo-art-thariu mentioned three (one of whom soon died). Although the younger informant stated that "they were buried," which implied that all of the whites in his father's care died, Too-shoo-art-thariu told that Aglooka and his remaining two comrades carried on toward their own country. Even so, the tales seem remarkably consistent, and these minor discrepancies may have been the result of poor translation or the younger man's imperfect memory.

Captain Adams was extremely excited by this story and intended to bring the young native back to England; "circumstances occurred which prevented this resolution being carried out, but he is in a position to furnish information of a very detailed nature and calculated, he thinks, to throw considerable light on the movements and ultimate fate of the members of the Franklin expedition." Captain Adams also returned with "a few papers found in the vicinity of Fury and Hecla Straits" which he forwarded to the Admiralty.[10] As nothing further was heard of these "few papers," it must be assumed that they held little of interest. Nevertheless their mere existence lends credence to Adams's tale.

In addition to the endorsement by this unnamed native, the tradition preserved under Too-shoo-art-thariu's name has a detail which is a strongly corroborative touch. This lies in the description of one of the items Aglooka had with him, a "boat that had places on the sides that would hold wind ... with hollow places in the sides for wind (air) to hold it up when in the water ... There were sticks or holes for this boat, to keep it open (spread) when needed. This small boat was wrapped or rolled up in a bundle or pack, and carried on the shoulder of one of his men."[11] Such detail could not have been invented.

Hall realized that this description of an inflatable boat was a pivotal piece of evidence. He concluded that "Franklin must have had in his vessels a boat or boats called Halkett's air-boats, or its equivalent. But I do not recollect of ever reading or hearing about this particular."[12] And he was right.

The *Erebus* and *Terror* were indeed supplied with Halkett boats, forerunners of the modern inflatable dinghy. In 1845 these were being taken to the Arctic for the first time.[13] Considering the fact that even in England this new-patent type of boat was largely unknown, there can be no doubt that some Inuit must have seen one to be able to describe it so accurately.

If the Franklin expedition had been the only one to use a Halkett boat in the area, there would be strong support for Too-shoo-art-thariu's questionable story. Unfortunately it wasn't. In 1846–7 Rae made use of "one of Halkett's air boats, large enough to carry three persons," at Repulse Bay, for setting and examining the fishing nets in the nearby lakes.[14] In fact this particular boat had been intended for Franklin, but he felt that the Hudson's Bay Company's land expedition would have more use for it and graciously surrendered the boat to Sir George Simpson for Rae's use. Another was made for the *Erebus* and *Terror*.[15]

Rae used this boat on his second expedition of 1854 as well, although he noted that another such boat which he was given failed to reach the north owing to "some irregularity in the railway baggage trains between London and Liverpool."[16] This second boat (named *James Fitzjames*) eventually did reach its destination, and was given to the 1855 Anderson expedition for its use on the descent of the Great Fish River.[17]

The tradition about the boat which would "hold wind" was based on fact. At some time a member of the Anderson, Rae, or Franklin expeditions was seen using it. The problem is to sort out which expedition is being spoken of.

The mention of a Halkett boat used by Anderson in Chantrey Inlet ties in nicely with the native insistence that Aglooka and his men departed toward the Great Fish River. Similarly, it evokes memories of a second questionable story attributed to Too-shoo-art-thariu. According to Ouela, Too-shoo-art-thariu had been told by the man he helped that "before the other men from the two ships had died, they had battled with Indians (Etkerlins). One day Crozier had been out hunting: 'Suddenly one Indian very near him jumped up from behind a big stone & threw his lance at him, hitting him in the forehead. The lance passed right across the forehead just above the eyebrows & cut a long ugly gash in it.' Crozier shot and killed the Indian. The next day he and his men were attacked by others but succeeded in driving them off with their guns. It was after this fight that so many koblunas froze and starved to death."[18]

This incident did not occur during Anderson's expedition, but, as we have seen, something similar had happened nearby. A fight with natives (actually Inuit – but they not surprisingly changed that) had actually taken place "before the other men from the two ships had died," long before, during Back's expedition.[19]

Anderson may have provided the inspiration for another element of the "Too-shoo-art-thariu" tale, for during his descent of the Great Fish River he met Inuit who may have been "Kinnepatoo." On 20 July 1855 he encountered six natives standing on the bank who indicated by signs that "they came down McKinley's R. and most probably belong to the Chesterfield Inlet tribe."[20] A later editor concluded that these were Sangnianajormiut, "an inland tribe that obtained its iron, glass beads, and other European objects by trading with Qaernermiut Eskimo around Chesterfield Inlet,"[21] which would endorse Seegar's detail that the Kinnepatoo had not themselves seen Aglooka, but had heard of it from others. Anderson's natives knew nothing of the Franklin expedition, but he concluded that they had had contact with the Inuit at Churchill "as there were 2 tin kettles in the Lodges."[22]

There are, of course, objections to Anderson as the incarnation of Aglooka. He only very briefly met Inuit and did not winter over in the Arctic. He had no interpreter with him and therefore could not exchange much information. None of his men died, and although he was a proficient hunter, and had much opportunity during the traverse of the Barren Lands, the natives did not witness this.

In addition Anderson apparently did not make very extensive use of his Halkett boat. After leaving his canoes at Point Pechell on the Chantrey Inlet shore (7 August), his party set off to search Ogle Point. They definitely took the Halkett boat with them, for the next day the party was ferried over to Maconochie Island in it. They used it again briefly on the 10th near Montreal Island, but after this no other mention of the inflatable boat is made. During the period 7–10 August no Inuit or traces of recent native habitation were seen, although the white men may have been secretly observed.[23]

As with many of the Inuit stories we can see that the Anderson expedition of 1855, if mixed with memories of Back, can be a possible source of one of the traditions ascribed to Too-shoo-art-thariu. Memories of Anderson, skilfully integrated into the encounter at Teekeenu and attributed to the hero of that encounter, could provide a factual basis for the confused tradition.

Other elements could have been provided by the other white man to come to the Arctic with a Halkett boat.

In 1880 Dr. Rae declared that in all probability he himself had been this "Aglooka", and the correctness of his opinion, based upon careful comparison between his own actions and those attributed to "Aglooka", can scarcely be questioned, although, as will shortly appear, his statement does not fully elucidate the source of some of the Eskimos' stories.

In May 1847, Dr Rae with four of his men and an Eskimo guide, named Ivitchuk, travelled from his winter quarters at Repulse Bay along the west coast of the Gulf of Boothia, and himself reached Lord Mayor Bay. During the return journey he bought seal-meat and blubber from some Eskimos on Helen Island. In 1854, again after wintering at Repulse Bay, he travelled with three men and his Eskimo interpreter Ouligbuck along the west coast of Committee Bay and thence across the Boothian Isthmus to Rae Strait. He met many Eskimos, on both journeys had a Halkett boat with him, and shot much game. He thoroughly understood Eskimo ways. During both expeditions he travelled in boats past Chesterfield Inlet to and from Repulse Bay and thus visited all the places on the route which "Aglooka" was definitely stated to have followed.[24]

Rae himself was convinced that the Too-shoo-art-thariu story was based on his own explorations. He even identified two of "Aglooka's" companions as described to Hall, the man who was "cross-eyed or squinted" and the other "with one of his upper teeth gone." Rae noted that these descriptions fitted his own men from 1847 – Adamson had a squint, and "either Foster or Matheson had a front tooth out or broken, which his companions used to remark upon as convenient for holding his pipe."[25] It must be admitted that Rae's first expedition (1846–7) does compare very well with many of the preserved traditions.

Of course, neither Rae nor his companions were ever reduced to cannibalism. But they did on occasion "look bad." Rae and his exploring detachments were almost continually on short rations; upon his return from Pelly Bay he described their appearance as "so black and scarred on the face from the combined effects of oil, smoke, and frost bites, that our friends would not believe but that some serious accident from the explosion of gunpowder had happened to us" and so famished that "we were as ravenous as wolves."[26] Later in the season, after a second extended and fatiguing march to Melville Peninsula, he remarked that "a limited allowance of food had reduced the whole party"[27] and that "although not very stout when I set out, I had to tighten my belt six inches before my return."[28]

Rae did not lose one of his companions either, but his interpreter Ouligbuck did seriously wound himself. On his trip to Pelly Bay his companion Flett had also been injured – snowblinded and partially crippled – and had to be assisted as he walked along. While here, the party briefly met four Inuit hunters, and a tradition of the stumbling, injured Flett might have been preserved.[29]

The remarks about Aglooka's proficiency in hunting and his ability to live like the Inuit certainly applied to John Rae. In two days of hunting in September 1846, Rae and his party shot twenty-seven caribou, and their total tally for the month was "63 deer, 5 hares, one seal, 172 partridges, and 116 salmon and trout."[30] Indeed Rae was such an efficient hunter that he not only did not require assistance from the Inuit but rendered it to them!

The tradition recalled that a native accompanied Aglooka and his remaining two men when he went south. This could be a remembrance of Ouligbuck, Rae's native interpreter, although, as a native of Churchill he was not a "Neitchille" and there were actually two natives who went south – Ouligbuck and his son William Jr ("Mar-ko").

Alternatively, the tradition could refer to Ivitchuk, a Repulse Bay native who took Oulibuck's place on the trip to Pelly Bay (after the injury to the former), although he remained behind with his people when the white men left. The tradition stated that the benefactor had been offered a gun by Aglooka but refused it out of fear; Ivitchuk was indeed offered a gun by Rae (a very rare occurrence), but he, unlike the traditional native, avidly accepted it.[31]

Rae, as noted, also had a Halkett boat with him at Repulse Bay. Its only specifically mentioned use was for tending the fishing nets near his winter quarters, and he does not refer to its being taken or used on any of his foot travels. Finally, Rae met with Kinnepatoo from Chesterfield Inlet each time that he passed Cape Fullerton (13 July 1846 and 16 August 1847).[32]

With a few minor modifications the history and details of Rae's first expedition can be matched with the obscure testimony. But problems remain. As Cyriax remarked, "Rae was wholly unconnected with the ships lost near Boothia," and the traditions were clear that the starving men had come from there. He never came closer to the Great Fish River than the Castor and Pollux River, and then only on his second expedition.

Moreover, and most seriously, he and his activities were extremely well known to the Repulse Bay natives – the very natives who perpetuated the story of their cousin's encounter. Ouela, Artooa, and Ookbarloo had all met Rae. So had In-nook-poo-zhe-jook. They well knew that he had come to the Arctic twice, they knew the exact routes which he had followed, and they were quite familiar with the Ouligbucks (father and son) and Ivitchuk, pointing out his grave to Hall many years later.[33] They even knew that Rae was a non-smoker! How likely were they to confuse the activities of "Aglooka" with those of the man who had spent the winter of 1846 camped alongside them?

There is another detail to the story of the sheltered white men which is difficult to reconcile with Anderson or Rae. Ouela and his brothers remarked that Aglooka had tried to give his benefactor a gun, but the native was understandably wary of it and therefore was given a "long knife" (which was interpreted to mean a sword), "and nearly everything he had."[34] Upon leaving Repulse Bay, Rae did distribute "our spare kettles, some hoop iron, &c.," but this was hardly the outpouring of gratitude described by the tradition – indeed neither he nor Anderson had a reason to be so generous as to give away everything. Rae did give Ivitchuk a gun, but neither he nor Anderson, as traders with the Hudson's Bay Company, would have had a naval sword. Yet a complete sword and scabbard were "given to Chief Factor Roderick MacFarlane in 1857 by a very old Eskimo, who claimed it to be a Franklin relic."[35]

Rae and/or Anderson, with some juggling, can be made to fit the Inuit testimony in some of its particulars. By referring the "fight with the Indians" to Back's expedition, we can eliminate that source of confusion as well. Unfortunately, the third element of the Inuit tradition is impossible to reconcile with any of these men. According to this element the native who offered the white men aid met Aglooka twice. The first time "Crozier [Aglooka] told this cousin that he was once at Iwillik (Repulse Bay), at Winter Island and Igloolik, many years before." The same native had learned this "one year before he found him and the three men, where the two ships were in the ice."[36]

Cyriax recognized that this could not apply to Rae, noting "there are adequate grounds for doubting whether he was the sole source of the Eskimo stories, and for believing, on the contrary, that some Eskimos confused him with another 'Aglooka', probably James Clark Ross."[37]

As with the stories of the visit to the ships, it must be admitted that the invocation of the Ross expedition solves some problems. Cyriax noted that J.C. Ross had visited all of the enumerated places during Parry's second voyage (as had Crozier), and supposed that the reference to Aglooka's one companion who died may have been to the death of James Dixon, whose grave the natives presumably found at Victory Harbour. He explained the intrusion of details from the Ross expedition (the *Victory* and *Krusenstern* again supplying the part of the "two ships in the ice") by remarking that In-nook-poo-zhe-jook had visited Ross before seeing Rae.[38]

In-nook-poo-zhe-jook definitely met Rae in 1854, but I have been unable to determine where Cyriax got the impression that he had ever visited the *Victory*. Except for a brief description of Ross's ship, which he may have learned from others, there is no indication in any of Hall's notes, or his many interviews with In-nook-poo-zhe-jook, that this was so.[39] In-nook-poo-zhe-jook had a grown son in 1869, but he was by no means an old man, and would have been a veritable child forty years earlier when Ross came north – hardly likely to converse with one of the officers about his prior Arctic experience. Furthermore, when Rae met Seeuteetuar and In-nook-poo-zhe-jook in 1854 and asked his primary informant "the usual questions as to his having seen white men before, or any ships or boats, he replied in the negative."[40] Confusion exists in Hall's notes as to which of the two natives supplied Rae with his information, but as he later learned that Seeuteetuar and his wife Koo-nik had indeed seen Ross,[41] Rae's question was presumably posed to In-nook-poo-zhe-jook (whose statement that it was he that told Mar-ko the news is thus confirmed).

Except for the one troubling detail of Aglooka's former travels, the Ross expedition of 1829–32 has few parallels to the native tradition. The small party seen on the ice could possibly refer to James Clark Ross and his travelling companions en route to King William Island or the North Magnetic Pole. The native accompanying them would then be Ooblooria or Pooyetta. But these parties never received aid from the Inuit, had poor success in hunting, and, like Rae, never went near the Great Fish River. The white men in distress could be the Ross crew marching north from their ship(s) to Lancaster Sound, although there were more than three (actually eighteen) of them, and no Inuit were encountered. Finally, as with Rae, the activities of these men were so well known to the Inuit that the probability of their being confused with a non-existent Aglooka seems remote.

There are enough ways to make the Too-shoo-art-thariu story fit the various known expeditions to make us certain that it was not a simple fabrication. The corroboration from Captain Adams and the evidence about the Halkett boat confirm that there was a real source behind it. By picking and choosing among the various expeditions and accepting slight discrepancies, we can explain how the story might have come about. But, as always, there is another explanation. The story, although wrongly attributed to Too-shoo-art-thariu, may have been strictly and literally true, and it might be a remembrance of survivors of the *Erebus* and *Terror*.

We have followed the proposed path of Aglooka and his companions from Ootgoolik to Starvation Cove, and possibly beyond. From Starvation Cove at least one man, and probably more, walked to the south. Others from Qavdlunarsiorfik, or from the boat found near Montreal Island, may have finally reached the Great Fish River. If the tradition about the last three men leaving after a winter of assistance is true, we must accept that they too went where the Inuit said they did – "toward the Ook-koo-seek-a-lik."

The Anderson party descended the Back River in 1855, but, with the exception of the two tin kettles already described, and a few curious stones which his men did not think resembled Inuit marks, they found no trace that any white men had ever passed.[42] Due to the nature and vastness of the area, and the small size of any surviving party, this is to be expected. Nevertheless, others have attempted to find some trace of the Franklin men.

The Back River Eskimos may well have suggested that Crozier follow one of the well-used overland routes to the Baker Lake-Thelon system, where the two white men would be in the country of the Caribou Eskimos who traded regularly with the Hudson's Bay post at Churchill. That this is what Crozier actually attempted seems fairly certain, for there were subsequent Eskimo reports of Crozier and one other white man having been seen in the Baker Lake area sometimes between 1852 and 1858. From this point in space and time, there is no further certain trace of these last two survivors of the southern party. However, in 1948 a very ancient cairn, not of normal Eskimo construction, and containing fragments of a hardwood box with dove-tailed corners, was found by myself [Farley Mowat] and a companion at Angikuni Lake on the Kazan River in central Keewatin, near a famous junction where the Eskimo trade routes between Churchill and the Arctic coasts converge. Considerable research has failed to identify the builder of this cairn. Only one white man, Samuel Hearne, is known to have visited this place at a reasonably distant date, in 1770, and the assumption is that the cairn may have been built by him. But since he makes no mention of it in his journals, the possibility remains that this mute monument was built by Crozier, before he vanished utterly.[43]

The "subsequent Eskimo reports" of the white men "in the Baker Lake area" have eluded me, unless Seegar's testimony is being referred to. As for the mysterious cairn which was found, it is impossible to identify its builder for certain. It is unlikely to have been built by Hearne. J.W. Tyrrell crossed the Barren Lands in 1893 and, while he makes no mention of a cairn at Angikuni Lake, he did note building cairns at nearby Dubawnt and Carey Lakes. A record was placed in the cairn at Carey Lake, while on the rocks used at Dubawnt Lake "the latitude of the spot and the date and name of the expedition" were painted with red enamel paint. Neither Tyrrell's narrative nor his chart indicates that he approached Angikuni Lake, and no mention of a dovetailed wooden box is made in association with either of the cairns which he built.[44]

Tyrrell must nevertheless be considered a more probable builder of this distant cairn than Aglooka. Yet, among Franklin aficionados, hope of finding some trace of the last of the doomed crew dies hard. For those who search, probably in vain, for a final answer to the tragedy, I include this last piece of evidence. On an island near the east side of Selwyn Lake, a hundred miles to the south of the old cairn, Tyrrell found a "lonely grave ... at the head of which stood a plain wooden cross. It was, doubtless, the grave of some Christian Indian who had been taught by the priests at Fond-du-Lac, and who, when out on a hunting expedition, had been stricken down by the great reaper, and by his companions had been laid to rest."[45]

In speaking of the Franklin expedition, as we have seen, the word "doubtless" should be used with care.

~22~

The Verdict

What secrets may be hidden within those wrecked or stranded ships we know not – what may be buried in the graves of our unhappy countrymen or in caches not yet discovered we have yet to learn. The bodies and graves which we were told of have not yet been found; the books (journals) ... have not been recovered, and thus left in ignorance and darkness with so little obtained and so much yet to learn, can it be said and is it fitting to pronounce that the fate of the expedition is ascertained?[1]

These words of Lady Franklin, written in an attempt to have the British government continue its efforts, have led many in the intervening century and a half to take up the tale of the Franklin tragedy anew. Unfortunately, my attempt, like its predecessors, cannot claim to have reached any incontrovertible conclusions.

The Franklin saga provides a challenge akin to a complex jigsaw puzzle. Some of the pieces are missing, others mangled. Pieces from other puzzles have been mistakenly mixed in. By a little judicious cropping with the scissors we can make almost all of the pieces fit together, but whether they form a true picture is less certain. Even the picture thus formed is incomplete, a corner here, a bit of coherent background there. These too can be arranged in other patterns to reach quite different results.

Owing to the nature of the physical evidence, the most significant pieces of the puzzle are the traditions which the Inuit preserved of white men in their country. The general tendency has been to ignore this source of information, and many reasons for this attitude have been advanced. It has been noted that much of what the Inuit recalled is at variance with the account preserved in the Victory Point record, and that their statements have therefore been considered to be useless. By concluding that the Inuit did not encounter the *Erebus* and *Terror* until after April 1848, we can accept the first half of this statement (which is fact), while challenging the conclusion based on it (which is opinion). It is claimed that the Inuit would say anything they thought the white interviewers wanted to hear, an unproven assertion which fails to account for macabre and distressing details of mutilated bodies and cannibalism.

A more reasonable justification for ignoring the Inuit traditions of white men, and one which we have shown to be at least partly valid, is that these can be ascribed to specific expeditions only with some difficulty. Some historians correctly point out that most of the features of any expedition were essentially identical – the white men came in similar ships, wore the same clothes, and followed the same routines. This argument echoes Humpty Dumpty, who complained to Alice that all human faces look the same – they all have two eyes, one nose, and a mouth. According to Humpty what was needed to identify individuals better was a distinctive rearrangement of these features; "if you had the two eyes on the same side of the nose, for instance – or the mouth at the top – that would be some help."[2]

When it comes to the Arctic expeditions, the details are there. The natives knew that the *Victory* was a small ship with something strange about its propellors, and that the *Erebus* and *Terror* had three masts. They described the physical appearance of all of the white men they met. They preserved the origin of even the most insignificant relic and perpetuated the names of the people involved and the places where events occurred. Some of these details allow us to conclude that traditions have no connection with Franklin. Others leave us wondering.

From the first time I read Rae's testimony that he had heard of "40 white men" travelling "four winters ago," I found it hard to believe that the natives, no matter how poor their conception of numbers and time, could have been talking of Crozier and his 105 companions travelling overland six years before. It seemed more reasonable that they were describing a separate event. I concluded that the natives probably knew what had occurred in their land more accurately than the historians who tried to reconstruct the events from a meagre 138-word record and a broken trail of remains.

Likewise I could not accept the conclusion that Kokleearngnun had not visited the *Erebus* and *Terror* despite his detailed story – just because the record failed to mention it – or that the Beck, Bayne, and Too-shoo-art-thariu testimonies were all lies. There is no difficulty in finding actual events which could have inspired each of the questionable stories (Beck describing the *William Torr*, Bayne a burial at Winter Island, and Too-shoo-art-thariu a meeting with Rae). Or they might, after all, be remembrances of Franklin. The charm of the puzzle lies in its uncertainty.

The problem with Inuit traditions does not in the end have much to do with whether they are "true" in the historical sense. We cannot even remotely approach a verdict on any of them "beyond a reasonable doubt." The difficulty lies only in determining which truth we are hearing – whether Kokleearngnun visited Parry, Ross, or Franklin – and in deciphering testimony concerning identically named places like "Omanek" or "Shartoo." The natives were exceedingly reliable witnesses. The problem is to determine which events they were witnessing.

How much of the Inuit testimony relates to actual occurrences of the Franklin expedition will ultimately be decided by the reader's tolerance for coincidence or inexactitude. Amundsen tossed his crates overboard, the Inuit found some neatly stacked hundreds of yards from the water – are they the same crates? Kokleearngnun tells us that "Toolooark" was bald and friendly, while John Ross's own portraits show him with a wealth of hair and his crew (even his nephew) paint a less flattering picture of him – was John Ross "Toolooark"? Aglooka lived through a winter with the Inuit and one of his men died of a sickness, Rae never lost a man – was Rae "Aglooka"?

Other elements cannot conceivably be explained by reference to other expeditions. Who engaged in the great caribou hunt with the Inuit? How did they know that "Cro-zhar" was Captain of the *Terror*? Who was the big dead man found in his bunk at Ootgoolik? Who were the four men with the dog? Why was Aglooka going to Iwillik when Crozier's record indicated the

Great Fish River? What was Aglooka trying to indicate by his pantomime of a ship being crushed? Who camped and died at Thunder Cove? Who built Seepunger's monument with the wooden pointing finger, and what did that finger point to?

There are no adequate answers to any of these questions.

Historians have tried to justify their intense interest in the Franklin expedition in many ways. After all, the mystery was adequately resolved a decade later, and the loss of 130 men, however tragic, was soon eclipsed by the horrors of the Crimean War and the ill-fated Charge of the Light Brigade. Except for Franklin, none of the participants was remotely famous, and today most people associate the name Franklin itself more with Benjamin than with John.

Initially the story was maintained by its natural features of adventure and tragedy. Present-day historians have changed the tone of the inquiry. They have endeavoured to discover what went wrong, why a well-equipped and resolute group of fine Victorian sailors came to grief in an area which, while admittedly hostile, supported "primitive" people well. We have already seen the areas where the blame has traditionally been attributed – faulty provisions, murderous natives, unwieldy ships, and incompetent leadership. More recently the still-unproven lead poisoning theory has emerged.

But reading backwards from effect to cause is always a difficult task. The fact that the expedition failed does not necessarily imply that it was poorly planned or executed. The general tone has been to ask the "why didn't" questions. Why didn't Franklin try to go down James Ross Strait and avoid the "heavy masses of ice" which had been noted in Victoria Strait? Why didn't Crozier lead his men to Fury Beach and Lancaster Sound? Why didn't the Europeans learn the lessons of survival in that harsh land from the natives?

These may be inappropriate questions. If the *Erebus* and *Terror* first came to grief in Poctes Bay, then Victoria Strait was the only alternative. If Crozier led his men in search of fresh meat, then he also went the right way. The stories of the final survivors living with Too-shoo-art-thariu could indicate that at least some of the men absorbed as much of the native ways as they could, and to good effect.

The fact that Rae, Hall, and Stefansson, among others, could survive and thrive while wearing Inuit clothing and adopting native ways has often been used as an example of how the cultural blindness of the Royal Navy caused the disaster, poisoning the men with canned or salted food, providing them with inadequate woollen clothing, cumbersome ships, and inappropriate traditions.

What is missing from these considerations is a sense of scale. Hall, Rae, and Stefansson did not have over a hundred travelling companions. Rasmussen's 1923 census showed only 259 Netsilingmiut inhabiting the entire area from Bellot Strait to Adelaide Peninsula, and most of these were concentrated at Pelly Bay, Boothia, and the Adelaide Peninsula itself.[3] Only 150 of these were male, half of these again were of hunting age. There were no permanent inhabitants of King William Island itself, the surrounding natives using it only for seasonal hunting. Even when armed with modern weapons, Rasmussen's native companions lived a tenuous existence.

Based on Rasmussen's observations, it had probably taken several months for a small band of Inuit without rifles to kill fifty caribou. This would have provided food for Crozier's men for no more than a week. It took seven caribou skins to make one suit of clothing. Even if every caribou skin was devoted to making clothing for the men of the *Erebus* and *Terror*, it would have taken years of hunting before the last man could shed his woollen suit. Despite Hall's condemnation of Teekeeta, Ow-wer, Too-shoo-art-thariu, and Mangaq for abandoning Aglooka and his forty men in Washington Bay, it was undoubtedly the logical decision. Had every Netsilingmiut hunter miraculously gathered at King William Island with the express purpose of aiding Franklin's 105 men, the result would probably have been the demise of both populations.

The crews of the *Erebus* and *Terror* were simply in a "no win" situation. They found an open passage which was unknown to their contemporaries, and which treacherously froze solid behind them. Those sent to their aid incorrectly concluded that this passage was non-existent. The *Erebus* and *Terror* became trapped in what was possibly the least favoured spot in the Canadian Arctic, about as far from possible help as they could get, yet so tantalizingly close to the achievement of their goal that an early retreat was unthinkable. A similarly equipped modern group, knowing what we do today, might not fare any better without outside assistance.

Incrementally the story moves on. Recently, the Beechey graves have been excavated and thorough autopsies conducted. Eventually one or both of the wrecked ships will be found, and be found to contain valuable evidence. Perhaps some future explorer will uncover an overlooked cairn, or stumble upon Baynes's "vaults."

That an account of the Franklin retreat could have survived for over a century is by no means far-fetched. In 1973 a perfectly legible note was recovered from a cairn in the interior of Cornwallis Island which had been deposited by Commander Phillips in June 1851. Even more remarkably, a letter written by Willem Barents, the intrepid Dutch explorer who spent the winter of 1595 at Ice Haven on Novaya Zemlya, was recovered intact in 1871, 276 years later! I have little doubt that somewhere, probably ten feet from the remains of a once prominent marker, a Franklin record was similarly buried in the permafrost. When discovered it will instantly render all speculative books, this one included, obsolete. Even then, the drama of the story will keep it alive, and until then the unanswered questions will keep it compelling.

Appendices

APPENDIX 1

Erebus and Terror Crew List

In command of expedition – Sir John Franklin (sailed in *Erebus*)

HMS *EREBUS*

OFFICERS

Captain – Commander James Fitzjames

Lieutenants – Graham Gore, Henry Thomas Dundas Le Vesconte, James Walter Fairholme

Mates – Robert Orme Sargent, Charles Frederick Des Voeux, Edward Couch

Second Master – Henry Collins

Surgeon – Stephen Samuel Stanley

Assistant Surgeon – Harry D.S. Goodsir

Purser – Charles Hamilton Osmer

Ice-Master – James Reid

WARRANT OFFICERS

Boatswain – Thomas Terry

Carpenter – John Weekes

Engineer – John Gregory

PETTY OFFICERS

Boatswain's Mate – Samuel Brown

Carpenter's Mate – Thomas Watson

Appendices

Captain of the Fo'c's'le – Philip Reddington
Quartermasters – Daniel Arthur, William Bell, John Downing
Sailmaker – John Murray
Caulker – James W. Brown
Blacksmith – William Smith
Leading Stoker – James Hart
Cook – Richard Wall
Captain's Coxswain – James Rigden
Captain of the Maintop – John Sullivan
Captain of the Foretop – Robert Sinclair
Captain of the Hold – Joseph Andrews
Caulker's Mate – Francis Dunn
Captain's Steward – Edmund Hoar
Gun-room Steward – Richard Aylmore
Paymaster and Purser's Clerk – William Fowler
Subordinate Officers' Steward – John Bridgens
Stokers – John Cowie, Thomas Plater

ABLE SEAMEN

Charles Best	Thomas McConvey
William Clossan*	John Morfin
Charles Coombs	William Orren
Robert Ferrier	Francis Pocock
Josephus Geater†	Abraham Seeley
John Hartnell	John Stickland
Thomas Hartnell	Thomas Tadman
Robert Johns	George Thompson
Henry Lloyd	George Williams
William Mark	Thomas Work

ROYAL MARINES

Sergeant – Daniel Bryant‡
Corporal – Alexander Paterson

---

* Written with the first "s" as an "f" in Victorian manner i.e.: "Clofsan"; Cyriax reads "Closson."
† This name appears twice in the original list.
‡ First name read as "David" in Cyriax crewlist.

Privates – William Braine, Joseph Healey, Robert Hopcraft, William
  Pilkington, William Reed

BOYS
George Chambers, David Young

HMS *TERROR*

OFFICERS
Captain – Francis Rawdon Moira Crozier
Lieutenants – Edward Little, George Henry Hodgson, John Irving
Mates – Frederick John Hornby, Robert Thomas
Second Master – Gillies Alexander MacBean
Surgeon – John Smart Peddie
Assistant Surgeon – Alexander Macdonald
Clerk – Edwin James Howard Helpman
Ice-Master – Thomas Blanky

WARRANT OFFICERS
Boatswain – John Lane
Carpenter – Thomas Honey
Engineer – James Thompson

PETTY OFFICERS
Boatswain's Mate – Thomas Johnson
Carpenter's Mate – Alexander Wilson
Captain of the Fo'c's'le – Reuben Male
Quartermasters – David Macdonald, John Kenley, William Rhodes
Caulker – Thomas Darlington
Blacksmith – Samuel Honey
Leading Stoker – John Torrington
Cook – John Diggle
Captain's Coxswain – John Wilson
Captain of the Maintop – Thomas R. Farr
Captain of the Foretop – Harry Peglar
Captain of the Hold – William Goddard
Caulker's Mate – Cornelius Hickey
Captain's Steward – Thomas Jopson
Gun-room Steward – Thomas Armitage
Subordinate Officers' Stewards – William Gibson, Edward Genge
Stokers – Luke Smith, William Johnson

Appendices

ABLE SEAMEN

John Bailey
John Bates
Alexander Berry
George J. Cann
Samuel Crispe
John Handford
William Jerry
Charles Johnson
George Kinnaird
Edwin Lawrence

David Leys
Magnus Manson
Henry Sait
William Shanks
William Sims*
William Sinclair
William Strong
James Walker
William Wentzall

ROYAL MARINES

Sergeant – Solomon Tozer
Corporal – William Hedges
Privates – James Daly,[†] John Hammond, William Heather, Henry
   Wilkes

BOYS

Thomas Evans, Robert Golding

The following men were returned to England from the Whalefish Islands in the *Barretto Junior*:

HMS *Terror*: William Aitken, Marine; John Brown, Able Seaman;
   Robert Carr, Armourer; James Elliot, Sailmaker
HMS *Erebus*: Thomas Burt, Armourer[‡]

---

* First name read as "David" in Cyriax crewlist.
† This name is not in the Muster Books but is taken from Cyriax.
‡ McClintock spells this as "Birt."

APPENDIX 2

Inuit Place Names

The following Inuit place names follow the text. Variations of names
are indicated in parentheses.

Akkoolee (Akule) "the delta bay, the bay into which many rivers
empty" – Committee Bay

Alraruheq "the one like an afterbirth" – Maconochie Island

Amitoke (Amitsoq) "the narrow one" – lake in the center of King William Island, famous fishing spot

Arviligjuaq "the big one with whales" – Pelly Bay

E-te-u (E-tee-u-oki) "?" – Cape Barclay on Simpson Peninsula

Igloolik (Igluligarjuk) "the place where there are many igloos" – island
off the east coast of Melville Peninsula. Traditional habitation of Inuit. Parry and Lyon wintered here with the *Fury* and *Hecla* in 1822–
3. A similarly named place was near Cape Norton on the east coast
of King William Island.

E-tow-tow-wig (Ent-ev-waten-wig) "?" – probably Rasmussen's "Icuartorfik," a place in Lord Mayor Bay. This and "sakfiorfik" were
names for Sheriff Harbour, Ross's second wintering place in Lord
Mayor Bay.

Ilivileq "?" Adelaide Peninsula

Iwillik "?" – Repulse Bay

Kaklerfik "the place where it once thundered" – Thunder Cove. This
received its English name from Thomas Simpson, whose party

camped here during a rare and severe thunderstorm in 1839. That
it had the same name in Inuit seems a wildly improbable coincidence, unless the name was derived from the white men between
1839 and 1923 when Rasmussen learned it. The nearby Franklin
campsite was called "two fingers" – Tikerkaniyou (Tikerqat).

Kanerarwikjuak "the big point" – Gladman Point

Kaner-lukjuaq "the big fjord" – Douglas Bay

Kani-lugjuaq "the big headland" – Cape Franklin

Keeuna (Qiunaq) "where one can starve to death" – barren southern
islet of the Todd group. Although some of Franklin's men died
here, the "ones" referred to are stranded caribou. Other islets in
the group were named Koo-o-kok, Ook-soo-too, and Now-yarn
(see Kookar).

Kikertak (Kikituk, Kikertung, Ki-ki-tung, Qeqertarjuaq) "the big island"
– King William Island

Kil-lee-nuk-oo "?" – Felix Harbour. Near the old ruins of Sarfak.

Kinak "the two mountains" – Cape Britannia

Kingak "the mountain" – Matty Island

Kinynukshane "?" – the unidentified place where Pooyetta found his
boat

Kok "the river" – Castor and Pollux River

Konajuk "the big river" – Back or Great Fish River. According to
Hall, the mouth of the river was called Oot-koo-ish-ee-lee (Rae –
Oot-koo-hi-ca-lik).

Konuaq "the little river" – Hayes River

Kookar northernmost islet of Todd group. It is possible that the islet
itself was not being indicated but the large lake which lies a short
distance inland (now called Koka Lake). Rasmussen was told that
"Qoqa" was a favourite fishing spot on the south King William Island coast.

Kun-ne-ar-be-ar-nu "?" – Franklin campsite on spit to the west of
Booth Point

Naparutalik "the place where there is something standing upright" –
possible location of Seepunger's cairn

Neitchille (Nacilik, Netsilik) "the one with seals" – Willerstedt Lake in
the Boothian Isthmus. Used by explorers for the entire Boothian
Peninsula. The Netsilingmiut or "seal people" took their name from
this lake in the center of their hunting grounds.

Nuvertaro (Nuvuteroq, Noo-oo-tee-roo) "the long point" – Richardson
Point.

Ogbuk (Agvaq) "the halved one" – Mount Matheson near the south-east coast of King William Island. This is the highest point of the island and was a certain landmark for Inuit coming from the east.

Omanek (Omenak, Umana, Ommanate, Omanaq) "the heart-shaped one" – King Island. Also an island in Lord Mayor Bay near Ross's Victory Harbour, and Taylor Island in Victoria Strait.

Ooblatuaryou "?" – small islet in Terror Bay near Franklin camp

Ootgoolik (Ujulik) "the one abounding in bearded seals" – Queen Maud Gulf. Also used for the facing (west) coast of the Adelaide Peninsula, whose specific name was "Ook-soo-see-too," according to Koo-nik.

Orsotoq (Ojortoq, Ooksootoo) "the blubber abounding one" – Gjoa Haven

Owutta small island near Matty Island, popular Inuit meeting place

Qablorsertorjuaq "the one that looks white from a distance" – Montreal Island.

Qavdlunarsiorfik "the place where one meets white men." Both Ross's Felix Harbour and a spot near Starvation Cove were called this.

Qilanartot "joyful beach, or the sample bite of joyous expectation" – Victory (later Victoria) Harbour, where Ross wintered and his ship the *Victory* was abandoned.

Satiumaneq "the projecting one" – Cape Crozier

Set-tu-me-nin "?" – Franklin campsite near Cape James Ross

Shartoo (Satoq) "the flat one" – name given to many localities, including a place on the west coast of the Adelaide Peninsula, the peninsula dividing Spence Bay and Inglis Bay (especially Cape Colville), Simpson Peninsula, and Prince of Wales Island (now called Wales Island; see chapter 19).

Siorartoq (See-er-ark-tu) "the sandy one" – Ogle Point

Tajarnerjuaq "the big forearm (seal flipper)" – O'Reilly Island

Teekeenu "?" – location on the east shore of Washington Bay

Tikerqat "two forefingers" – Grant Point

Toonoonee (tununeq) "the back of beyond" – name generally given to the entire north-west coast of King William Island from Cape Felix to Cape Crozier; In-nook-poo-zhe-jook used it to indicate both the tent place at Terror Bay and the boat place at Erebus Bay.

Tunornup-nuna "the land behind" – Cape Felix (see Toonoonee).

Umiartalik "the place where there are umiaq (boats or ships)" – Kirkwall Island.

Netsilingmiut (Boothia)   *Arvilingmiut (Pelly Bay)*

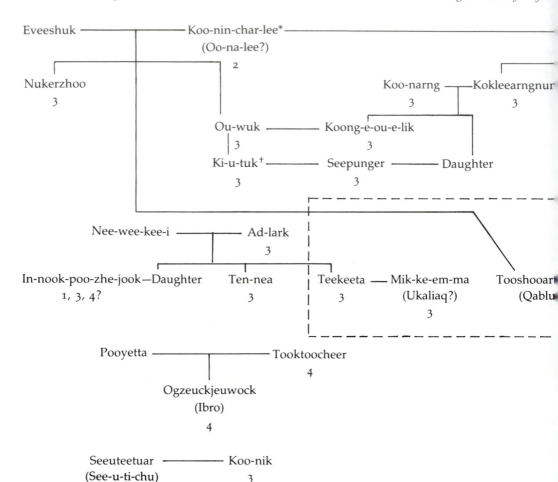

Interviewed by:

1. Rae (1854)
2. McClintock (1859)
3. Hall (1864–9)
4. Schwatka (1879)
5. Rasmussen (1923)

334

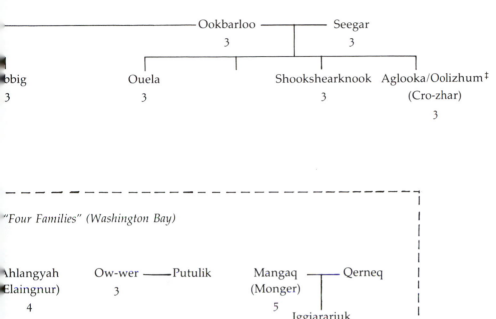

Arvilingmiut (Repulse Bay)

```
                              ┌──── Ookbarloo ──────┬──── Seegar
                              │         3           │        3
                    ┌─────────┴──┐           ┌──────┴────┐
  bbig          Ouela         Shookshearknook   Aglooka/Oolizhum‡
   3              3                  3              (Cro-zhar)
                                                       3
```

"*Four Families" (Washington Bay)*

```
 hlangyah      Ow-wer ──── Putulik    Mangaq ──┬── Qerneq
 Elaingnur)        3                  (Monger)  │
    4                                     5     │
                                           Iggiararjuk
                                                5
```

liaq (father saw Aglooka)
        5

At one time Koo-nin-char-lee, Kokleearngnun, and Seegar had been friends. All originally lived at Neitchille (Boothia). Koo-nin-char-lee and Kokleearngnun were so close that they vowed that if one should die the other would care for both families. They cemented this vow through intermarriage of their children. After Koo-nin-char-lee's death, Seegar and Kokleearngnun fell out, and Seegar took his wife and sons and moved to Iwillik (Repulse Bay).

In addition to the family relationships shown here, most of these Inuit were friends and acquaintances. Ookbarloo's unnamed female friend was probably Ad-lark. In-nook-poo-zhe-jook and Seeuteetuar were hunting companions. The "four families" who met Franklin's men on the march at Washington Bay were joined in their search the following year by Nee-wee-kee-i and his family, and by Pooyetta and his.

---

* Koo-nin-char-lee was probably the unnamed "uncle" who accompanied Seepunger to King William Island. Ookbarloo was also married to him, and upon his death she married Seegar. Koo-nin-char-lee's wife Eveeshuk was probably not the woman of the same name who later met Hall at Keeuna.

† Ki-u-tuk was the granddaughter of Koo-nin-char-lee through his daughter. Whether that daughter was Ou-wuk or an unnamed sister is uncertain.

‡ One source indicates that Aglooka/Oolizhum was Ookbarloo's nephew rather than son.

APPENDIX 4

Lead Poisoning

This book deals primarily with the Inuit testimony concerning the Franklin expedition in an attempt to derive clues as to the course of events. The Inuit descriptions of the Franklin men and their bodies, with hard black mouths and emaciated limbs, afford graphic evidence that the primary cause of death for many of them was scurvy – vitamin c deficiency. Yet any book written about Franklin at this time would be incomplete without at least a brief discussion of the recent work of Dr Owen Beattie and his colleagues, work which suggests that the crew of the *Erebus* and *Terror* were suffering from chronic lead poisoning as well.

Dr Beattie is a forensic anthropologist, and his interest in Franklin led him to conduct two surveys, in 1981 and 1982, in which he recovered bones from King William Island. When these bone samples were analysed a surprising result emerged. Bone recovered from the southern King William Island shore (Kun-ne-ar-be-ar-nu) showed a very high bone-lead content (224 ppm as compared to three Inuit skeletons ranging from 22 to 36 ppm). This led Beattie to conclude that lead poisoning may have contributed to the outcome of the expedition. As bone lead levels could be attributed to long-term exposure, Beattie proposed to exhume the bodies from the three graves at Beechey in an effort to analyse the soft tissues and more accurately assess exposure during the expedition itself.

Lead Poisoning

In 1984 the perfectly preserved remains of John Torrington were exhumed in the interest of science and history. His 90-pound, 5′ 2″ corpse was exposed and a thorough autopsy performed. Beattie found, after laboratory analysis of recovered tissue, that Torrington presented "a picture of a young man wracked with serious medical problems." No specific cause of death could be established, although the young man's blackened lungs, undoubtedly caused by his occupation as a chief stoker, when combined with signs of previous lung disease, emphysema, and tuberculosis, showed that the engine-rooms of the early steam-assisted ships were not healthy places to work.[1]

Although it was concluded that the immediate cause of death was pneumonia complicated by tuberculosis, trace element analysis showed that Torrington had been suffering from lead poisoning as well. His bone lead levels of 110–51 ppm were lower than those from the Kun-ne-ar-be-ar-nu skeleton, which might have been the result of less time of exposure owing to his earlier death, but were still ten to twenty times the normal current averages.

In 1986 Beattie and his team returned to Beechey Island to fully excavate the graves of John Hartnell and William Braine (Hartnell's coffin had been briefly exposed in 1984). Hartnell had been the subject of a brief autopsy in 1846, and, although both bodies were remarkably well preserved, no conclusions could be reached at the gravesite as to their cause of death. As with Torrington, some tissue samples which were taken for later analysis revealed high lead levels.

Beattie felt that the hair lead levels were the most significant, for they showed the effects of contamination to which the crewmen had been exposed during the weeks immediately preceding their deaths. Torrington's hair lead levels ranged from 413 to 657 ppm, while Hartnell's hair samples showed 138–313 ppm lead and Braine's hair yielded 145–280 ppm. In Torrington's case Beattie found that "only over the last few centimetres did the level of exposure drop, and then only slightly."[2]

It was concluded that the hair lead levels were a good indicator that the lead source had been the expedition's tinned food supply, caused by the leaching of lead from the solder used to seal the tins. This was later confirmed when the lead isotope ratios from the bones were compared to those obtained from analysis of the solder.[3]

These high lead levels were not of themselves fatal, and Torrington's autopsy report concluded that "the significance of the elevated lead levels in determining the course of the expedition remains uncertain."[4]

Although Beattie's work has been imaginative and skilful, it nevertheless casts little light on the fate of Franklin's expedition. One reviewer remarked that "the hypothesis that lead poisoning played anything other than a minor role in the ultimate outcome of the Franklin expedition is clearly unsubstantiated by the currently available evidence."[5] Although lead poisoning may have been an overall contributing factor in the debility of Franklin's men, we must agree with the autopsy report's opinion that the "findings do not illuminate the events that led to the loss of the remaining members of the expedition in 1847 and 1848."[6]

APPENDIX 5

Glossary of Terms

Variations are indicated in parentheses.

Aglooka (aklukaq)   "the one who takes long strides"; name commonly given to white explorers

Amasuedloo   very many

Angeko (angatkut, anatkoq)   shaman or medicine man

Chimo (teyma)   friend

Enookshooyer (Innookshooyer)   cairn, tall marker

Eshemuta (isumataq, Ishumatar)   "the one who thinks for others," a leader

Etkerlin (Itqilik, Ik-kil-lin)   Indians

Igloo   snow hut, house

Kanerluktaq   bay

Kanertluk   fjord

Kayak (kiak)   single-person skin boat

Kongma (Kung-moo)   dwelling with snow walls and canvas or skin top

Kommotik   sledge

Kumik (kamik, kumming)   boots

Keeweewook   sink (verb)

Kobluna (kabloona, qavdluna)   white man

Nanook   white bear

Peelow (pilaut, panatoq)   large knife

Polnya   open water lead in the ice

Netchuk (nacheq)   seal
Nowyer (nauja)   white gull
Ooloo (ulo)   woman's knife
Seko (siko)   winter ice
Tupik (tupeq)   tent
Tooktoo (tukto)   caribou (reindeer)
Toolooa (Tulugaq, Toolooark)   raven
Umiak (Oomeak)   multi-person skin boat ("woman's boat"); also a
   white man's ship or boat.

Notes

CHAPTER ONE: FIRST CONTACT

1 For recollections of this meeting by the white men, see Sir John Ross, *Narrative of a Second Voyage in Search of a North-West Passage etc.*, 342–8, 309, and R. Huish, *The Last Voyage of Captain Sir John Ross*, 185–7: Inuit memories are preserved in L.A. Learmonth, "Ross Meets the Netchiliks," 10–13, and Knud Rasmussen, *The Netsilik Eskimos*, 27–8.

2 Rasmussen, *The Netsilik Eskimos*, 28.

3 Sir John Ross, *Narrative of a Second Voyage in Search of a North-West Passage etc.*, 316.

4 Ibid., 427.

5 Ibid., 415.

6 Ibid., 418.

7 Ibid.

8 Ibid., 720.

9 Back, *Narrative of the Arctic Land Expedition to the Mouth of the Great Fish River*, 390.

10 King, *Narrative of a Journey to the Shores of the Arctic Sea*, 68–9.

11 Back, *Narrative of the Arctic Land Expedition to the Mouth of the Great Fish River*, 438.

12 Rasmussen, *The Netsilik Eskimos*, 467.

13 Thomas Simpson, *Narrative of Discoveries on the North Coast of North America*, 365.

14 Ibid., 373–4.
15 Ibid., 375–7.
16 Ibid., 378–9.

CHAPTER TWO: THE INVESTIGATION

1 Rae, *Doctor John Rae's Correspondence with the Hudson's Bay Company on Arctic Exploration 1844–55*, lxxviii; in addition to this excellent edition by E.E. Rich, the primary source for Rae's expedition is the Rae correspondence held in the Hudson's Bay Company Archives, as E 15/9. His reports were published in Great Britain, Parliamentary Papers, Accounts and Papers (1856) vol. 41, no. 2124, and in Rae, "Sir John Franklin and his Crews," contemporary issues of *Household Words*, and the *Illustrated London News*.
2 Rae, "Sir John Franklin and his Crews," 16.
3 Hall Collection, book "B," 128–30.
4 Ibid., 130–1.
5 Ibid., 131–2.
6 Rae, "Sir John Franklin and his Crews," 19.
7 Great Britain, Parliamentary Papers, Accounts and Papers (1856) vol. 41, no. 2124, pp. 832–3; Rae, *Doctor John Rae's Correspondence*, 286–7; *Illustrated London News*, 4 November 1854.
8 Rae, "Sir John Franklin and his Crews," 16–17.
9 Primary source for Anderson's expedition is his Journal, held in the Hudson's Bay Company Archives as B/200/a/31 and published in *Canadian Field Naturalist* 54 and 55 and elsewhere; see also ADM/200; Great Britain, Parliamentary Papers, Accounts and Papers (1856) vol. 41, no. 2124.
10 McClintock, *The Voyage of the "Fox" in the Arctic Seas* (1859), 320–2.
11 Ibid., 210–11.
12 Ibid., 211–12.
13 Ibid., 227.
14 Ibid.
15 Ibid., 230.
16 Hall Collection, booklet marked "May 3 to 7 1866," box 8, 16–17.
17 Ibid., booklet marked "Jottings Apr 30 to May 5th 1866," box 8, 19.
18 The primary source for Hall's first expedition is C.F. Hall, *Life with the Esquimaux: A Narrative of Arctic Experience in Search of Survivors of Sir John Franklin's Expedition*; see also the biography of Hall by C. Loomis, *Weird and Tragic Shores*.

19 The primary source for Hall's second expedition is the Hall Collection held by the Smithsonian Institution. This collection has been edited by J.E. Nourse as *Narrative of the Second Arctic Expedition Commanded by Charles Francis Hall*. It was also utilized by Cooper for his *Island of the Lost* and by Loomis (see above).

20 Gilder published his accounts in a series for this employer, the New York *Herald*. These were subsequently edited and published as *Schwatka's Search*; Schwatka's journal was not discovered until 1965 and was edited and published by E.A. Stackpole as *The Long Arctic Search*; Klutschak's book was translated from German by William Barr as *Overland to Starvation Cove*.

CHAPTER THREE: THE WITNESSES

1 Fluhmann, *Second in Command*, 131.

2 Stefansson, *My Life with the Eskimos*, 252.

3 Ibid., 252–4.

4 Hall, *Life with the Esquimaux*, 220–1.

5 Ibid., 220.

6 Ibid., 244.

7 Ibid., 389.

8 Ibid., 398.

9 Ibid., 247.

10 Loomis, *Weird and Tragic Shores*, 113–14.

11 McClintock, *The Voyage of the "Fox"* (1859), 148.

12 Bird and Bird, "John Rae's Stone House," 35.

13 Stefansson, *My Life with the Eskimos*, 356.

14 Rae, *Narrative of an Expedition to the Shores of the Arctic Sea in 1846 and 1847*, 68.

15 Rae, "Rae on the Eskimos," 39.

16 Rasmussen, *The Netsilik Eskimos*, 29.

17 Ibid.

18 Rae, *Narrative of an Expedition to the Shores of the Arctic Sea in 1846 and 1847*, 122.

19 Nourse, *Narrative of the Second Arctic Expedition etc.*, 107.

20 Ibid., 590.

21 Ibid., 66.

22 Rae, *Narrative of an Expedition to the Shores of the Arctic Sea in 1846 and 1847*, 85, 95.

23 Nourse, *Narrative of the Second Arctic Expedition etc.*, 601.

24 Lyon, *Lyon's Private Journal*, 349.

25 McClintock, *The Voyage of the "Fox"* (1859), 227.

26 Nourse, *Narrative of the Second Arctic Expedition etc.*, 112–13.

27 W.E. Parry, *Journal of a Second Voyage for the Discovery of a North-west Passage*, 410–12.

28 Loomis, *Weird and Tragic Shores*, 189.

29 Hall Collection, Fieldnotes, book no. 31.

30 Ibid., book "B," 138.

31 Ibid., 138–9.

32 Rasmussen, *The Netsilik Eskimos*, 130.

33 Gibson, "Amundsen in King William Island," 36.

34 Rasmussen, *The Netsilik Eskimos*, 128.

35 Stefansson, *My Life with the Eskimos*, 354–7.

36 Ibid., 358–9.

37 Nourse, *Narrative of the Second Arctic Expedition etc.*, 588.

38 Hall Collection, book "B," 100.

39 Stefansson, *My Life with the Eskimos*, 250–1.

40 Gilder, *Schwatka's Search*, 302.

41 Stefansson, *My Life with the Eskimos*, 252.

42 Rae, "The lost Arctic Voyagers," 248.

43 Rae, *Doctor John Rae's Correspondence*, 239.

44 Rae, "The lost Arctic Voyagers," 248.

45 Gilder, *Schwatka's Search*, 303.

46 McClintock, *The Voyage of the "Fox"* (1859), 237.

47 Loomis, *Weird and Tragic Shores*, 75.

48 Hall, *Life with the Esquimaux*, 52.

49 Hall Collection, book "B," 100.

50 Nourse, *Narrative of the Second Arctic Expedition etc.*, 137.

51 Ibid., 64.

52 Hall Collection, Fieldnotes, book no. 24.

53 Gilder, *Schwatka's Search*, 302–3.

54 Barr, *Overland to Starvation Cove*, 201–2, 236–7.

CHAPTER FOUR: OMANEK AND ADAM BECK

1 Great Britain, Parliamentary Papers, Accounts and Papers (1851) vol. 33, no. 97, 80–3. A good deal was written in official circles about Adam Beck; see also Great Britain, Parliamentary Papers, Accounts and Papers (1852) vol. 50, nos. 390, 1435, 1436, and 1449. Beck's stories have been more accessibly published in

Wright, *Quest for Franklin*, 152–5, and Cyriax, "Adam Beck and the Franklin Search," 35–50.

2 Wright, *Quest for Franklin*, 155; Cyriax, "Adam Beck and the Franklin Search," 39.

3 Cyriax, "Adam Beck and the Franklin Search," 38–9.

4 Ibid., 46–7.

5 Ibid., 47 and footnote.

6 Ibid., 50.

7 Hall, *Life with the Esquimaux*, 52.

8 Dudley, "The Eskimo Place Names of Northern Cumberland Peninsula etc.," 347.

9 Lubbock, *The Arctic Whalers*, 303.

10 Ibid., 327.

11 Cyriax, "The Voyage of HMS *North Star*," 313.

12 Cyriax, "Adam Beck and the Franklin Search," 40.

13 Ibid., 45.

14 Binney, "In Search of Franklin," 21.

15 Rasmussen, *The Netsilik Eskimos*, 202.

16 Ibid., 50, 481.

17 Stefansson, *My Life with the Eskimos*, 288.

18 Rasmussen, *The Netsilik Eskimos*, 101, 106, 110.

19 Cyriax, "Captain Hall and the So-Called Survivors of the Franklin Expedition," 181.

20 King, *Narrative of a Journey to the Shores of the Arctic Sea etc.*, 68–9.

CHAPTER FIVE: POCTES BAY

1 Osborn, *Stray Leaves from an Arctic Journal*, 81–4.

2 Wright, *New Light on Franklin*, 77–82; Cyriax, "A Note on the Absence of Records," 30–40; Wilkinson, *Arctic Fever*, 102.

3 Anonymous, *Historic Tinned Foods*, 26–7; A.H. Markham, *Life of Sir John Franklin*, 245–6; Cyriax, *Sir John Franklin's Last Arctic Expedition*, 108–18.

4 Owen, *Fate of Franklin*, 271.

5 Kennedy, "Report on the Return of Lady Franklin's vessel etc.," 127.

6 A.H. Markham, *Life of Sir John Franklin*, 248; Cyriax, "A Note on the Absence of Records," 36–7.

7 Sir John Ross, *Narrative of a Second Voyage in Search of a Northwest Passage*, 416.

8 Ibid., 406, 410.

9 Ibid., 316.

10 Canada, *Arctic Pilot*, 162.

11 Cyriax, *Sir John Franklin's Last Arctic Expedition*, 124.

12 Sir John Ross, *Narrative of a Second Voyage in Search of a Northwest Passage*, cxxviii.

13 Barrow, *Voyages of Discovery and Research in the Arctic Regions*, 530.

14 Ibid.

15 Dunbar and Greenaway, *Arctic Canada from the Air*, 173.

16 Larsen, *Northwest Passage: The Voyage of the St. Roch*, 23.

17 De Roos, *North-West Passage*, 151.

18 Amundsen, *The Northwest Passage*, 68.

19 Ibid., 74.

20 Burwash, *Canada's Western Arctic*, 72.

21 Ibid.

22 McClintock, *The Voyage of the "Fox"* (1859), 232.

23 Ibid., 233.

CHAPTER SIX: A SEASON OF SEARCH

1 Great Britain, Parliamentary Papers, Accounts and Papers (1847–8) vol. 41, no. 264.

2 Owen, *Fate of Franklin*, 264.

3 Nourse, *Narrative of the Second Arctic Expedition etc.*, 610.

4 Wright, *Quest for Franklin*, 137; Sir John Ross, *Narrative of a Second Voyage in Search of a Northwest Passage* (map endpapers); McClintock, *The Voyage of the "Fox"* (1859), 236.

5 Hall Collection, book "B," 144.

6 McClintock, *The Voyage of the "Fox"* (1859), 228–9.

7 Hall Collection, book "B," 145.

8 Ibid., booklet marked "May 8–11th 1866" (box 8); book "B," 146.

9 O'Brien, *Alone across the Top of the World*, 49.

10 Cyriax, *Sir John Franklin's Last Arctic Expedition*, 132.

11 Stackpole, *The Long Arctic Search*, 75.

12 Gilder, *Schwatka's Search*, 133.

13 Stackpole, *The Long Arctic Search*, 76.

14 Gilder, *Schwatka's Search*, 147.

15 C.R. Markham, *Life of Sir Leopold McClintock*, 222; Cyriax, *Sir John Franklin's Last Arctic Expedition*, 133.

16 Nourse, *Narrative of the Second Arctic Expedition etc.*, 259.

17 Ibid., 276.

18 Hall Collection, book "B," 144.

19 Stackpole, *The Long Arctic Search*, 77; Royal Geographical Society, Cyriax Papers 2(a), 27–8.

20 Wonders, "Project Franklin," 64.

21 Royal Geographical Society, Cyriax Papers 2(a), 28.

22 Cyriax, "Recently Discovered Traces of Sir John Franklin's Expedition," 212.

23 Cyriax, *Sir John Franklin's Last Arctic Expedition*, 130; Cyriax, "The Two Franklin Expedition Records Found on King William Island," 183–5.

24 Richardson, *The Polar Regions*, 164 footnote.

25 Cyriax, *Sir John Franklin's Last Arctic Expedition*, 31.

26 Stackpole, *The Long Arctic Search*, 82.

27 Ibid.

CHAPTER SEVEN: CROZIER'S CHOICE

1 Wright, *New Light on Franklin*, 49–50.

2 A.H. Markham, *Life of Sir John Franklin*, 224; Wallace, *The Navy, The Company, and Richard King*, 118.

3 Cyriax, *Sir John Franklin's Last Arctic Expedition*, 153.

4 National Maritime Museum, Peglar Papers, AGC 36/4 to 36/18.

5 Wright, *Quest for Franklin*, 152.

6 A.H. Markham, *Life of Sir John Franklin*, 225.

7 Nourse, *Narrative of the Second Arctic Expedition etc.*, 589.

8 Stackpole, *The Long Arctic Search*, 69–71, 76–7; Gilder, *Schwatka's Search*, 96, 155; Barr, *Overland to Starvation Cove*, 81, 94.

9 McClintock, *The Voyage of the "Fox"* (1859), 242, 282.

10 O'Brien, *Alone across the Top of the World*, 222.

11 Based on data in Cyriax, "Arctic Sledge Travelling by Officers of the Royal Navy," 127–42; other data from Sir John Ross, *Narrative of a Second Voyage in Search of a Northwest Passage*, 644, 706.

12 Osborn, *Stray Leaves from an Arctic Journal*, 298.

13 Great Britain, Parliamentary Papers, Accounts and Papers (1847–8) vol. 41 no. 264.

14 Great Britain, Parliamentary Papers, Accounts and Papers (1850) vol. 50 no. 107.

15 Nourse, *Narrative of the Second Arctic Expedition etc.*, 334.

16 Sir John Ross, *Narrative of a Second Voyage in Search of a Northwest Passage*, 109.

17 Ibid., 706.

18 Huish, *The last Voyage of Captain Sir John Ross*, 672.

19 Cyriax, "Captain Hall and the So-Called Survivors of the Franklin Expedition," 172.

20 Great Britain, Parliamentary Papers, Accounts and Papers (1849) vol. 32 no. 188 and (1850) vol. 35 no. 107.

21 Bellot, *Memoirs and Journal of Lieut. Joseph Réné Bellot*, 146.

22 A.H. Markham, *Life of Sir John Franklin*, 238.

23 Cooper, *Island of the Lost*, 121.

24 Richardson, *The Polar Regions*, 169.

25 Gibson, "Sir John Franklin's Last Voyage," 27.

26 Back, *Narrative of the Arctic Land Expedition to the Mouth of the Great Fish River*, 325, 336, 341, 371.

27 Ibid., 438.

28 T. Simpson, *Narrative of Discoveries on the North Coast of North America etc.*, 380.

29 McClintock, *The Voyage of the "Fox"* (1859), 244–5.

30 Stackpole, *The Long Arctic Search*, 86.

31 McClintock, *The Voyage of the "Fox"* (1859), 261.

32 Ibid., 279.

33 Stackpole, *The Long Arctic Search*, 71, 79.

34 Ibid., 83, 87.

CHAPTER EIGHT: VICTORY POINT

1 Cyriax, "The Position of Victory Point," 496–507.

2 McClintock, *The Voyage of the "Fox"* (1859), 274.

3 Savours and Deacon, *Starving Sailors*, 106.

4 Beattie, "Elevated Bone Lead Levels in a Franklin Expedition Crewman," 144.

5 Cyriax, "A Historic Medicine Chest," 295–300.

6 McClintock, *The Voyage of the "Fox"* (1859), 275–6.

7 Lamb, *Franklin, Happy Voyager*, 276.

8 Royal Geographical Society, Cyriax Papers 1(a), 59.

9 McClintock, *The Voyage of the "Fox"* (1859), 336.

10 Stackpole, *The Long Arctic Search*, 74.

11 Burwash, *Canada's Western Arctic*, 92.

12 McClintock, *The Voyage of the "Fox"* (1859), 269.

13 Stackpole, *The Long Arctic Search*, 74.

14 Gilder, *Schwatka's Search*, 124–5.

15 Barr, *Overland to Starvation Cove*, 84.

16 Nourse, *Narrative of the Second Arctic Expedition etc.*, 276.

17 Fluhmann, *Second in Command*, 53.

18 Bell, *Lieut. John Irving, R.N. of H.M.S. "Terror"*, 73, 75, 112.

19 Ibid., 150.

20 Cyriax, "The Two Franklin Expedition Records Found on King William Island," 185.

21 Stackpole, *The Long Arctic Search*, 74.

CHAPTER NINE: INCIDENT AT TEEKEENU

1 O'Brien, *Alone across the Top of the World*, 49.

2 Burwash, *Canada's Western Arctic*, 70.

3 Hall Collection, book "A," 47.

4 Hall Collection, Fieldnotes, book no. 38.

5 Ibid.

6 Nourse, *Narrative of the Second Arctic Expedition etc.*, 606.

7 Hall Collection, Fieldnotes, book no. 38.

8 Nourse, *Narrative of the Second Arctic Expedition etc.*, 606.

9 Ibid.

10 Hall Collection, Fieldnotes, book no. 38.

11 Ibid., book no. 37.

12 Ibid., book no. 24.

13 Ibid., book no. 38.

14 Ibid., book no. 24.

15 Ibid., book no. 38.

16 Nourse, *Narrative of the Second Arctic Expedition etc.*, 64.

17 Ibid., 108.

18 Ibid., 591–2.

19 Gilder, *Schwatka's Search*, 89.

20 Ibid., 90–1.

21 Ibid., 91–2.

22 Hall Collection, Fieldnotes, book no. 38.

23 Barr, *Overland to Starvation Cove*, 74.

24 Fluhmann, *Second in Command*, 137.

25 Rasmussen, *The Netsilik Eskimos*, 129.

26 Ibid.

27 Nourse, *Narrative of the Second Arctic Expedition etc.*, 108.

28 Hall Collection, journal marked "No. 6, From Dec 6th to May 12 1865 Inclusive," 207 note 1.

29 Hall Collection, Fieldnotes, book no. 39.

30 McClintock, *The Voyage of the "Fox"* (1859), 249.

CHAPTER TEN: NUVERTARO

1 Gilder, *Schwatka's Search*, 316.
2 Hall Collection, Fieldnotes, book no. 38.
3 Ibid.
4 National Maritime Museum, box 62, plan 6132A (*Terror*).
5 Hall Collection, Fieldnotes, book no. 38.
6 Rae, "Sir John Franklin and his Crews," 16.
7 Hall Collection, Fieldnotes, book no. 25.
8 Gilder, *Schwatka's Search*, 93–4.
9 Stackpole, *The Long Arctic Search*, 63; Barr, *Overland to Starvation Cove*, 73–4.
10 Hall Collection, Fieldnotes, book no. 25.
11 Ibid., book no. 34.
12 Nourse, *Narrative of the Second Arctic Expedition etc.*, 398.
13 Hall Collection, Fieldnotes, book no. 40.
14 Gilder, *Schwatka's Search*, 84.
15 Ibid., 84–5.
16 Stackpole, *The Long Arctic Search*, 62.
17 Gilder, *Schwatka's Search*, 164.
18 Stackpole, *The Long Arctic Search*, 68.
19 McClintock, *The Voyage of the "Fox"* (1859), 236.
20 Hall Collection, book "B," 133.
21 Ibid., 129.
22 Gilder, *Schwatka's Search*, 106–8.
23 Stackpole, *The Long Arctic Search*, 67.
24 Barr, *Overland to Starvation Cove*, 73.
25 Gilder, *Schwatka's Search*, 107.
26 Barr, *Overland to Starvation Cove*, 73.
27 Schwatka to New York *Herald*, 29 October 1880.
28 Gilder, *Schwatka's Search*, 89.
29 Learmonth, "Notes on Franklin Relics," 122.
30 Barr, *Overland to Starvation Cove*, 73; Gilder, *Schwatka's Search*, 84.
31 Rae, "Sir John Franklin and his Crews," 16.
32 Rasmussen, *The Netsilik Eskimos*, 131.
33 Ibid., 101.
34 Ibid., 441 (photo facing).
35 Learmonth, "Notes on Franklin Relics," 123.

36 Gilder, *Schwatka's Search*, 210.

37 Barr, *Overland to Starvation Cove*, 134.

38 Ami, "Notes on the Adelaide Peninsula Skull," 319.

39 Gibson, "Sir John Franklin's Last Voyage," 25.

CHAPTER ELEVEN: TOONOONEE

1 Hall Collection, Fieldnotes, book no. 38.

2 Stackpole, *The Long Arctic Search*, 69.

3 Gilder, *Schwatka's Search*, 89.

4 McClintock, *The Voyage of the "Fox"* (1859), 233.

5 Ibid., 248–9.

6 Cyriax, "The Papers in the Possession of Harry Peglar etc.," 194.

7 Gilder, *Schwatka's Search*, 92.

8 Hall Collection, Fieldnotes, book no. 24.

9 Ibid.

10 Hall Collection, Fieldnotes, book no. 37.

11 Ibid., book "B," 142.

12 Ibid., 143.

13 Nourse, *Narrative of the Second Arctic Expedition etc.*, 595–6.

14 Hall Collection, Fieldnotes, book no. 37.

15 Ibid.

16 Ibid.

17 Ibid., book no. 25.

18 Ibid., book no. 29.

19 Stackpole, *The Long Arctic Search*, 84.

20 Gibson, "Sir John Franklin's Last Voyage," 28 (photo).

21 Hall Collection, Fieldnotes, book no. 31.

22 Fairholme Papers, S. Cracroft to Elizabeth Murray, 21 February 1873.

23 Hall Collection, Fieldnotes, book no. 31.

24 Beattie, "Elevated Bone Lead Levels in a Franklin Expedition Crewman," 142.

25 Beattie, "A Report on Newly Discovered Human Skeletal Remains etc.," 76.

26 Gilder, *Schwatka's Search*, 286.

27 Fluhmann, *Second in Command*, 140–1.

28 Hall Collection, Fieldnotes, 12 July 1866, 23.

29 Hall Collection, Fieldnotes, book no. 38.

30 Ibid.

CHAPTER TWELVE: KEEUNA

1 Hall Collection, Fieldnotes, book no. 39.
2 Gilder, *Schwatka's Search*, 106.
3 Hall Collection, Fieldnotes, book no. 29.
4 Ibid., book no. 34.
5 Ibid., book no. 31.
6 Ibid.
7 Ibid., book no. 34.
8 Ibid.
9 Ibid., book no. 38.
10 Gibson, "Sir John Franklin's Last Voyage," 24.
11 Hall Collection, Fieldnotes, book no. 30, book no. 34; Gibson, "Some Further Traces of the Franklin Retreat," 405; Stefansson, *Unsolved Mysteries of the Arctic*, 292.
12 Gibson, "Some Further Traces of the Franklin Retreat," 404.
13 Hall Collection, Fieldnotes, book no. 30.
14 Ibid., book no. 31.
15 Ibid.
16 Ibid., book no. 34.
17 Gibson, "Some Further Traces of the Franklin Retreat," 404–5.
18 Ibid., 405.
19 Hall Collection, Fieldnotes, book no. 30.
20 Ibid.
21 Stackpole, *The Long Arctic Search*, 71.
22 Amundsen, *The Northwest Passage*, vol. 2, 297, 310.
23 Hall Collection, book "B," 121–2.
24 Gibson, "Some Further Traces of the Franklin Retreat," 403.
25 Rasmussen, *The Netsilik Eskimos*, 73, 100.
26 Gibson, "Some Further Traces of the Franklin Retreat," 403.
27 Ibid., 405.
28 Ibid.
29 Ibid., 406.
30 Ibid.
31 Gilder, *Schwatka's Search*, 286.
32 Beattie, "Elevated Bone Lead Levels in a Franklin Expedition Crewman," 142.
33 Fluhmann, *Second in Command*, 141.
34 Gibson, "Some Further Traces of the Franklin Retreat," 406.
35 Ibid.

CHAPTER THIRTEEN: POOYETTA'S SEARCH

1 Hall Collection, book "B," 122.
2 T. Simpson, *Narrative of Discoveries on the North Coast of North America etc.*, 374.
3 Nourse, *Narrative of the Second Arctic Expedition etc.*, 401.
4 Rae, "Letter of Dr. John Rae to the British Admiralty," 285.
5 Rae, "Sir John Franklin and his Crews," 16.
6 Hall Collection, Fieldnotes, book no. 31.
7 Ibid., book no. 38.
8 Rasmussen, *The Netsilik Eskimos*, 104.
9 Hall Collection, Fieldnotes, book no. 38.
10 Gibson, "Sir John Franklin's Last Voyage," 24.
11 Stackpole, *The Long Arctic Search*, 74.
12 Gilder, *Schwatka's Search*, 106.
13 Ibid.
14 Hall Collection, Fieldnotes, book no. 40.
15 Stackpole, *The Long Arctic Search*, 74.
16 Hall Collection, Fieldnotes, book no. 31.
17 Ibid.
18 Hall Collection, book "B," 142.
19 Ibid., 135.
20 Ibid., 123.
21 Ibid., 136.
22 Ibid., 137.
23 Ibid.
24 Ibid., book no. 26.
25 Ibid., book no. 22.
26 Rasmussen, *The Netsilik Eskimos*, 99.
27 Hall Collection, Fieldnotes, book no. 24.
28 Gilder, *Schwatka's Search*, 108.
29 Stackpole, *The Long Arctic Search*, 63.
30 Gilder, *Schwatka's Search*, 107.
31 Rae, *Doctor John Rae's Correspondence*, 276.
32 Gilder, *Schwatka's Search*, 156; Barr, *Overland to Starvation Cove*, 94.
33 Stackpole, *The Long Arctic Search*, 80; Gilder, *Schwatka's Search*, 156.
34 Hall Collection, Fieldnotes, book no. 21.
35 Rasmussen, *The Netsilik Eskimos*, 479.
36 Stackpole, *The Long Arctic Search*, 74.
37 Gilder, *Schwatka's Search*, 106.

38 Hall Collection, book "B," 137–8.
39 Hall Collection, Fieldnotes, 12 July 1866, 22.

CHAPTER FOURTEEN: TOOLOOA AND AGLOOKA

1 Hall Collection, book "B," 5; Fieldnotes, book no. 37.
2 Gilder, *Schwatka's Search*, 301.
3 Ibid.
4 Huish, *The last Voyage of Captain Sir John Ross*, 220.
5 W.E. Parry, *Journal of a Second Voyage for the Discovery of a North-west Passage*, 430.
6 Sir John Ross, *Narrative of a Second Voyage in Search of a Northwest Passage*, 513; McClintock, *The Voyage of the "Fox"* (1859), 211.
7 Nourse, *Narrative of the Second Arctic Expedition etc.*, 590.
8 Hall Collection, Fieldnotes, 12 July 1866, 25.
9 Cyriax, "Captain Hall and the So-Called Survivors of the Franklin Expedition," 178.
10 Hall Collection, Fieldnotes, 12 July 1866, 23.
11 Ibid.
12 Nourse, *Narrative of the Second Arctic Expedition etc.*, 590.
13 ADM 37/6628, Muster Sheets of HMS *Fury*; W.E. Parry, *Journal of a Second Voyage for the Discovery of a Northwest Passage*, ii.
14 Gilder, *Schwatka's Search*, 90.
15 Stefansson, *The Friendly Arctic*, 442.
16 Nourse, *Narrative of the Second Arctic Expedition etc.*, 606.
17 Ibid., 255–6.
18 Ibid., 257.
19 Hall Collection, Fieldnotes, 12 July 1866, 24.
20 Royal Geographical Society, Cyriax Papers 2(c), 7.
21 Ibid., 1.
22 Hall Collection, Fieldnotes, book no. 26.
23 Sir John Ross, *Narrative of a Second Voyage in Search of a Northwest Passage*, 3.
24 Cyriax, "Captain Hall and the So-Called Survivors of the Franklin Expedition," 181.
25 Huish, *The last Voyage of Captain Sir John Ross*, 207, 239, 389.
26 Ibid., 243.
27 Ibid., 238–9.
28 Ibid., 237.
29 Ibid., 341–7.

30 Ibid., 414–15.

31 Ibid., 366–9.

32 Ibid., 255.

33 Ibid., 335.

34 Sir John Ross, *Narrative of a Second Voyage in Search of a Northwest Passage*, 645.

35 Huish, *The last Voyage of Captain Sir John Ross*, 222–32.

36 Rowley, "Rear-Admiral Sir John Ross etc.," 61.

37 Cyriax, "Captain Hall and the So-Called Survivors of the Franklin Expedition," 182.

38 Hall Collection, booklet marked "1866/April 29 May 1st" (box 8), 36.

39 Rae, "The lost Arctic Voyagers," 435.

40 Cyriax, "Captain Hall and the So-Called Survivors of the Franklin Expedition," 180.

41 Hall Collection, Fieldnotes, 12 July 1866, 20.

42 Hall Collection, booklet marked "1866/April 29 May 1st" (box 8), 36.

43 Ibid., 48.

44 Hall Collection, journal dated "Dec 6 1864–May 12 1865," book 6, 281–2.

45 Ibid., 282–3.

46 Sir John Ross, *Narrative of a Second Voyage in Search of a Northwest Passage*, 269.

47 Ibid., vol. 2, 60.

48 Rasmussen, *The Netsilik Eskimos*, 200, 191–2.

49 Hall Collection, Fieldnotes, book no. 37.

CHAPTER FIFTEEN: TOOLOOARK'S SHIPS

1 Nourse, *Narrative of the Second Arctic Expedition etc.*, 256–7.

2 Great Britain, Parliamentary Papers, Accounts and Papers (1851) vol. 33, no. 97.

3 McClintock, *The Voyage of the "Fox"* (1859), 227.

4 Ibid., 211.

5 Wright, *Quest for Franklin*, 231–2; Great Britain, Parliamentary Papers, Accounts and Papers (1850) vol. 35, no. 107.

6 Wright, *Quest for Franklin*, 232.

7 Cyriax, "Captain Hall and the So-Called Survivors of the Franklin Expedition," 181–2.

8 Huish, *The last Voyage of Captain Sir John Ross*, 191.

9 Ibid., 193.

10 Ibid., 415.

11 Sir John Ross, *Narrative of a Second Voyage in Search of a Northwest Passage*, 455.

12 Ibid., 456.

13 Ibid., 458–9.

14 Rasmussen, *The Netsilik Eskimos*, 28.

15 Rae, "The lost Arctic Voyagers," 435.

16 Parry, *Journal of a Second Voyage for the Discovery of a Northwest Passage*, 436–7; Murdock, "The Old Shipwreck," 42–3.

17 McClintock, *The Voyage of the "Fox"* (1859), 138.

18 Ibid., 146–7.

19 Cyriax, "Captain Hall and the So-Called Survivors of the Franklin Expedition," 181.

20 Hall Collection, Fieldnotes, book no. 28.

21 Ibid., book no. 26.

22 Ibid., book no. 28.

23 Gilder, *Schwatka's Search*, 90.

24 Cyriax, "Captain Hall and the So-Called Survivors of the Franklin Expedition," 181.

25 Nourse, *Narrative of the Second Arctic Expedition etc.*, 606.

26 Royal Geographical Society, Cyriax Papers 1(a), 13–14.

27 Hall Collection, Fieldnotes, book no. 38.

28 McClintock, *The Voyage of the "Fox"* (1859), 211.

29 Amundsen, *The Northwest Passage* vol. 2, 61.

30 Ibid.

31 Rasmussen, *The Netsilik Eskimos*, 130.

32 Rasmussen, "The Fifth Thule Expedition," 138.

33 Nourse, *Narrative of the Second Arctic Expedition etc.*, 592–3.

34 Hall Collection, Fieldnotes, book no. 38.

35 McClintock, *The Voyage of the "Fox"* (1859), 276–7.

36 Cyriax, "Captain Hall and the So-Called Survivors of the Franklin Expedition," 180.

37 McClintock, *The Voyage of the "Fox"* (1859), 277.

38 Rasmussen, *The Neitsilik Eskimos*, 221.

39 Hall Collection, booklet marked " 1866/April 29th May 1st," box 8, 48.

CHAPTER SIXTEEN: "THEN AGLOOKA WAS THE ESHEMUTA"

1 Barr, *Overland to Starvation Cove*, 100, 102.

2 Burwash, *Canada's Western Arctic*, 83, 112; *The Times* (London), 30 September 1930; Stefansson, *Unsolved Mysteries of the Arctic*, 150–2.

3 Burwash, *Canada's Western Arctic*, 112.

4 Ibid., 115.

5 Nourse, *Narrative of the Second Arctic Expedition etc.*, 277; Loomis, *Weird and Tragic Shores*, 206.

6 Burwash, *Canada's Western Arctic*, 115.

7 Ibid., 115.

8 Ibid.

9 Ibid., 115–16.

10 Ibid., 116.

11 Stefansson, *Unsolved Mysteries of the Arctic*, 152.

12 Wright, *Quest for Franklin*, 147.

13 Nourse, *Narrative of the Second Arctic Expedition etc.*, 417.

14 Wright, *Quest for Franklin*, 147.

15 Ibid., 146.

16 Stackpole, *The Long Arctic Search*, 75.

17 Ibid., 76.

18 Wright, *Quest for Franklin*, 149.

19 Sir John Ross, *Narrative of a Second Voyage in Search of a Northwest Passage*, 274.

20 Huish, *The last Voyage of Captain Sir John Ross*, 203.

21 Sir John Ross, *Narrative of a Second Voyage in Search of a Northwest Passage*, 625.

22 Ibid., 691.

23 Lyon, *Lyon's Private Journal*, 200.

24 Parry, *Journal of a Second Voyage for the Discovery of a Northwest Passage*, 244.

25 Ibid., 237.

26 McClintock, *The Voyage of the "Fox"* (1859), 139.

27 Lyon, *Lyon's Private Journal*, 399.

28 Parry, *Journal of a Second Voyage for the Discovery of a Northwest Passage*, 425.

29 Cyriax, "The Unsolved Problem of the Franklin Expedition Records Supposedly Buried on King William Island," 32.

30 Hall Collection, Hall to Jane Franklin, dated 9 January 1871.

31 Fluhmann, *Second in Command*, 137–8.

32 Nourse, *Narrative of a Second Arctic Expedition etc.*, 588.

33 Ibid., 590.

34 Ibid., 589.

35 Ibid., 109.

36 Hall Collection, book "A," 46.

37 Admiralty Muster Books – ADM 37/6669 (*Fury* – 1821 to 1823), ADM 37/6689 (*Hecla* – 1821 to 1823), ADM 38/1962 (*Terror* – 3 March to 20 June 1845), ADM 38/672 (*Erebus* – 4 March to 19 May 1845), ADM 38/9162 (Description Book *Terror* – 1843), Sir John Ross, *Narrative of a Second Voyage in Search of a Northwest Passage*, 5.

38 Stackpole, *The Long Arctic Search*, 77–9.

39 Barr, *Overland to Starvation Cove*, 93.

40 Gilder, *Schwatka's Search*, 289.

41 Sir John Ross, *Narrative of a Second Voyage in Search of a Northwest Passage*, 111, 194.

42 McClintock, *The Voyage of the "Fox"* (1859), 269.

43 Ibid.

CHAPTER SEVENTEEN: AGLOOKA'S SHIP

1 McClintock, *The Voyage of the "Fox"* (1859), 227.

2 Hall Collection, Fieldnotes, book no. 22.

3 Ibid., book no. 24.

4 Ibid., book no. 28.

5 Ibid.

6 McClintock, *The Voyage of the "Fox"* (1859), 227.

7 Hall Collection, Fieldnotes, book no. 22.

8 Nourse, *Narrative of the Second Arctic Expedition etc.*, 404.

9 Barr, *Overland to Starvation Cove*, 65, 230.

10 Stackpole, *The Long Arctic Search*, 55.

11 Gilder, *Schwatka's Search*, 79.

12 Great Britain, Parliamentary Papers, Accounts and Papers (1852) vol. 50 no. 501; Gould, *Oddities*, 103–6.

13 Wright, *New Light on Franklin*, 40.

14 Gilpin, "Outline of the Voyage of HMS *Enterprise* etc.," 8.

15 Royal Geographical Society, Cyriax Papers.

16 Miertsching, *Frozen Ships*, 152, 200.

17 Gilder, *Schwatka's Search*, 200.

18 Stackpole, *The Long Arctic Search*, 63; Gilder, *Schwatka's Search*, 104.

19 Cyriax, *Sir John Franklin's Last Arctic Expedition*, 193 and footnote.

20 Wright, *New Light on Franklin*, 38.

21 Barr, *Overland to Starvation Cove*, 230.

22 Stackpole, *The Long Arctic Search*, 63.

23 Barr, *Overland to Starvation Cove*, 65.

24 Stackpole, *The Long Arctic Search*, 55.

25 McClintock, *The Voyage of the "Fox"* (1859), 237.

26 Wright, *New Light on Franklin*, 52.

27 Sir John Ross, *Narrative of a Second Voyage in Search of a Northwest Passage*, 3.

28 Bell, *Lieut. John Irving, R.N. of H.M.S. "Terror,"* 117.

29 Stackpole, *The Long Arctic Search*, 56.

30 Barr, *Overland to Starvation Cove*, 131.

31 Stackpole, *The Long Arctic Search*, 55.

32 Hall Collection, Fieldnotes, book no. 28.

33 Nourse, *Narrative of the Second Arctic Expedition etc.*, 405.

34 Ibid.

35 Hall Collection, book "B," 95.

36 Cyriax, *Sir John Franklin's Last Arctic Expedition*, 184 (footnote).

37 Fluhmann, *Second in Command*, 101.

38 Stackpole, *The Long Arctic Search*, 55.

39 Barr, *Overland to Starvation Cove*, 65.

40 Rasmussen, *The Netsilik Eskimos*, 130.

41 Barr, *Overland to Starvation Cove*, 65.

42 McClintock, *The Voyage of the "Fox"* (1859), 227.

43 Ibid., 236–7.

44 Nourse, *Narrative of the Second Arctic Expedition etc.*, 592.

45 Gilder, *Schwatka's Search*, 85.

CHAPTER EIGHTEEN: KEEWEEWOO

1 Nourse, *Narrative of the Second Arctic Expedition etc.*, 398; Gilder, *Schwatka's Search*, 313.

2 Wright, *Quest for Franklin*, 222.

3 McClintock, *The Voyage of the "Fox"* (1859), 277.

4 Burwash, *Canada's Western Arctic*, 22.

5 Canada, *Arctic Pilot*, 175.

6 Nourse, *Narrative of the Second Arctic Expedition etc.*, 418.

7 Ibid., 404.

8 Ibid., 549.

9 Stackpole, *The Long Arctic Search*, 55.

10 Gilder, *Schwatka's Search*, 78.

11 Canadian chart no. 7731; US Hydrographic Service chart no. 6856.

12 Burwash, *Canada's Western Arctic*, 22.

13 Canada, *Arctic Pilot*, 183.

14 Canada, Department of National Defence, document s 3150–1 TD 5133 (DC Plans) dated 13 May 1965.

15 Personal communication with Dr E.F. Roots, 17 October 1985.

16 Wonders, "Project Franklin," 335.

17 Canada, *Arctic Pilot*, 183.

18 Rasmussen, *The Netsilik Eskimos*, 102–3.

CHAPTER NINETEEN: THE TRAIL TO SHARTOO

1 McClintock, *The Voyage of the "Fox"* (1859), 228.

2 Barr, *Overland to Starvation Cove*, 131.

3 Hall Collection, Fieldnotes, book no. 38.

4 Learmonth, "Notes on Franklin Relics," 123.

5 Gibson, "Sir John Franklin's Last Voyage," 25.

6 Ibid.

7 Hall Collection, Fieldnotes, book no. 34.

8 Ibid.

9 Rasmussen, *The Netsilik Eskimos*, 131.

10 Cyriax, "Recently Discovered Traces of Sir John Franklin's Expedition," 214.

11 Rasmussen, *The Netsilik Eskimos*, 130–1.

12 Anderson, "Chief Factor James Anderson's Back River Journal of 1855," 10.

13 Ibid., 22.

14 J.B. Tyrrell, "Story of a Franklin Search," 399; see also Cyriax, *Sir John Franklin's Last Arctic Expedition*, 185–6, and Anderson, "Chief Factor James Anderson's Back River Journal of 1855," 22 (footnote 174).

15 J.B. Tyrrell, "Story of a Franklin Search," 400.

16 Ibid., 400–1.

17 Ibid., 399.

18 Anderson, "Chief Factor James Anderson's Back River Journal of 1855," 11, 23.

19 Ibid., 23.

20 Ibid.

21 Gibson, "The Dease and Simpson Cairn," 44 (photo).

22 A. Simpson, *Life and Travels of Thomas Simpson*, 374.

23 Hall Collection, book "B," 146.

24 Hall Collection, Fieldnotes, book no. 35.

25 Rasmussen, *The Netsilik Eskimos*, 101.

26 Wright, *Quest for Franklin*, 174.

27 Cundy, *Beacon Six*, 237–9.

28 Hall Collection, Fieldnotes, book no. 35.

29 Ibid., book "B," 146.

30 A. Simpson, *Life and Travels of Thomas Simpson*, 376.

31 Hall Collection, book "B," 148–9.

32 Ibid., Fieldnotes, book no. 35.

33 Ibid., book "B," 154.

34 Rae, *Narrative of an Expedition to the Shores of the Arctic Sea in 1846 and 1847*, 106.

35 Ibid., 131.

36 Rae to New York *Herald*, dated 23 May and published 4 July 1880.

37 Rae, *Narrative of an Expedition to the Shores of the Arctic Sea in 1846 and 1847*, 75.

38 Rasmussen, *The Netsilik Eskimos*, 18, 22, 100, 104, 112.

39 Nourse, *Narrative of the Second Arctic Expedition etc.*, 114.

40 Rae to New York *Herald*, dated 23 May and published 4 July 1880.

41 Hall Collection, book "B," 131–2.

42 Rae, *Narrative of an Expedition to the Shores of the Arctic Sea in 1846 and 1847*, 51.

43 Ibid., 76.

44 Ibid., 89.

45 Nourse, *Narrative of the Second Arctic Expedition etc.*, 333.

46 Hall Collection, Fieldnotes, book no. 26.

47 Ibid., book no. 29.

48 Ibid., book no. 36.

49 Ibid., book "B," 144.

50 Nourse, *Narrative of the Second Arctic Expedition etc.*, 276.

51 Rasmussen, *The Netsilik Eskimos*, 96.

CHAPTER TWENTY: IN-NOOK-POO-ZHE-JOOK'S BOATS

1 Hall Collection, book "B," 140.

2 Nourse, *Narrative of the Second Arctic Expedition etc.*, 589.

3 Ibid., 590–1.

4 McClintock, *The Voyage of the "Fox"* (1859), 227.

5 Rasmussen, *The Netsilik Eskimos*, 120–1, 473.

6 Ibid., 121.

7 Barr, *Overland to Starvation Cove*, 72.

8 Ibid., 64.

9 Ibid., 64–5.

10 Rasmussen, *The Netsilik Eskimos*, 481.

11 Hall Collection, Fieldnotes, book no. 24.

12 Rasmussen, *The Netsilik Eskimos*, 26.

13 Ibid., 22.

14 Rae, *Narrative of an Expedition to the Shores of the Arctic Sea in 1846 and 1847*, 121–3.

15 Hall Collection, book "B," 131; Nourse, *Narrative of the Second Arctic Expedition etc.*, 259.

16 Nourse, *Narrative of the Second Arctic Expedition etc.*, 259–60, 276.

17 Ibid., 592.

18 Gilder, *Schwatka's Search*, 105–6; Barr, *Overland to Starvation Cove*, 73.

19 Nourse, *Narrative of the Second Arctic Expedition etc.*, 257.

20 Hall Collection, Fieldnotes, book no. 39.

21 Ibid., book "B," 139.

22 Nourse, *Narrative of the Second Arctic Expedition etc.*, 595.

23 Hall Collection, book "B," 132.

24 Ibid., 128.

25 Nourse, *Narrative of the Second Arctic Expedition etc.*, 109.

26 Ibid., 594–5.

27 Ibid., 588; Hall Collection, Fieldnotes, book no. 38.

28 Hall Collection, Fieldnotes, book no. 28.

29 Nourse, *Narrative of the Second Arctic Expedition etc.*, 33.

30 Hall Collection, Fieldnotes, book no. 28.

31 Nourse, *Narrative of the Second Arctic Expedition etc.*, 333.

32 Hall Collection, Fieldnotes, book no. 35; book "B," 133.

33 Ibid., book "B," 132–3.

34 Rae, "The lost Arctic Voyagers," 433–4.

35 Hall Collection, book "B," 134.

36 Ibid., 126.

37 McClintock, *The Voyage of the "Fox"* (1859), 262.

38 Ibid., 269.

39 Ibid., 264.

40 Gilder, *Schwatka's Search*, 155.

41 Ibid., 157.

42 Stackpole, *The Long Arctic Search*, 80.

43 Ibid.

44 Gilder, *Schwatka's Search*, xii.

45 McClintock, *The Voyage of the "Fox"* (1859), 264.

46 Gilder, *Schwatka's Search*, 285.

47 McClintock, *The Voyage of the "Fox,"* 5th edition (1881), 67.

48 C.R. Markham, *Life of Sir Leopold McClintock*, 281, 283.

49 Gilder, *Schwatka's Search*, 50.

50 National Maritime Museum to Woodman, 11 July 1990
   (ref H90/3474).

51 Nourse, *Narrative of the Second Arctic Expedition etc.*, 405.

52 Stackpole, *The Long Arctic Search*, 80.

53 Ibid., 69.

54 Beattie, "A Report on Newly Discovered Human Skeletal Remains
   etc.," 75–6.

55 Gilder, *Schwatka's Search*, 151, 157.

56 Hall Collection, book "B," 144.

57 Stackpole, *The Long Arctic Search*, 63.

58 Gilder, *Schwatka's Search*, 148.

CHAPTER TWENTY-ONE: TOO-SHOO-ART-THARIU

1 Hall Collection, Fieldnotes, book no. 38.

2 Ibid., book no. 22.

3 Nourse, *Narrative of the Second Arctic Expedition etc.*, 393.

4 Ibid., 109.

5 Ibid., 593–4.

6 Ibid., 108.

7 Loomis, *Weird and Tragic Shores*, 190.

8 Nourse, *Narrative of the Second Arctic Expedition etc.*, 591.

9 Fairholme Papers; *The Times* (London), Monday 17 October 1881.

10 Ibid.

11 Nourse, *Narrative of the Second Arctic Expedition etc.*, 592.

12 Ibid.

13 Mangles, *Papers and Despatches relating to the Arctic Searching Expeditions of 1850–51–52*, 81.

14 Rae, *Narrative of an Expedition to the Shores of the Arctic Sea in 1846 and 1847*, 5, 176.

15 Rae to New York *Herald*, dated 23 May and published 4 July 1880.

16 Rae, "Sir John Franklin and his Crews," 15.

17 Anderson, "Chief Factor James Anderson's Back River Journal of 1855," 22 footnote 173.

18 Loomis, *Weird and Tragic Shores*, 191.
19 King, *Narrative of a Journey to the Shores of the Arctic Sea etc.*, 68–9.
20 Anderson, "Chief Factor James Anderson's Back River Journal of 1855," 135.
21 Ibid., footnote 144.
22 Ibid., 135.
23 Ibid., 21–3.
24 Cyriax, "Captain Hall and the So-Called Survivors of the Franklin Expedition," 182–3.
25 Rae to New York *Herald*, dated 23 May and published 4 July 1880.
26 Rae, *Narrative of an Expedition to the Shores of the Arctic Sea in 1846 and 1847*, 133–4.
27 Ibid., 158–9.
28 Rae, *Doctor John Rae's Correspondence*, 41.
29 Rae, *Narrative of an Expedition to the Shores of the Arctic Sea in 1846 and 1847*, 120–3.
30 Ibid., 73.
31 Ibid., 136.
32 Ibid., 27, 181.
33 Nourse, *Narrative of the Second Arctic Expedition etc.*, 66, 180.
34 Ibid., 591–2.
35 Gibson, "Sir John Franklin's Last Voyage," 51 (photo and caption).
36 Nourse, *Narrative of the Second Arctic Expedition etc.*, 109.
37 Cyriax, "Captain Hall and the So-Called Survivors of the Franklin Expedition," 183.
38 Ibid.
39 Hall Collection, Fieldnotes, book no. 26.
40 Rae, "Sir John Franklin and his Crews," 16.
41 Hall Collection, Fieldnotes, book no. 28.
42 Anderson, "Chief Factor James Anderson's Back River Journal of 1855," 134–5.
43 Mowat, *Ordeal by Ice*, 323.
44 J.W. Tyrrell, *Across the Sub-Arctics of Canada*, 90, 95.
45 Ibid., 74–5.

CHAPTER TWENTY-TWO: THE VERDICT

1 Crouse, *Search for the Northwest Passage*, 462–3.
2 Carroll, *Through the Looking Glass*, 135.
3 Rasmussen, *The Netsilik Eskimos*, 84.

APPENDIX FOUR: LEAD POISONING

1 Beattie, *Frozen in Time*, 122.
2 Ibid., 123.
3 Kowal et al., "Did Solder Kill Franklin's Men?" 319–20.
4 Amy et al., "The Last Franklin Expedition: Report of a Postmortem Examination of a Crew Member," 117.
5 Trafton, "Did Lead Poisoning Contribute to the Deaths of Franklin Expedition Members?" 3.
6 Amy et al., "The Last Franklin Expedition: Report of a Postmortem Examination of a Crew Member," 117.

Bibliography

UNPUBLISHED SOURCES

MUSEUM OF ARMED FORCES HISTORY, NAVAL HISTORY SECTION
SMITHSONIAN INSTITUTION (WASHINGTON)
HALL COLLECTION (CAT # 58909–44–N)
This consists of relics, artifacts, notebooks, and miscellanea. This somewhat haphazard collection has been only imperfectly indexed, with
many loose or misplaced pages, numbering schemes, and unexplained
gaps which are very frustrating to the holders and those wishing to
make use of the material. Details given in the notes section should allow
the original items to be found without undue difficulty.

Of primary interest are Hall's original notebooks. The most significant
of these, and those most used in this book, cover his trip to King William
Island in May-June 1869. These have been numbered, perhaps by Hall,
from 21 (1 May 1869) through 39 (18 May 1869). Other notebooks are
unnumbered but have been roughly chronologically arranged. Hall's
"book A" and "book B" were prepared for Lady Franklin's use in January
1871 and are digests of the main information obtained. Copies of some
of this material are also available at the Royal Geographical Society.

ROYAL GEOGRAPHICAL SOCIETY ARCHIVES (LONDON): Cyriax Papers
  1(a) "Comment on *New Light on Franklin*" (17 July 1954) 179 pp.
  1(b) "Notes on *Quest for Franklin*" (n.d.) 61 pp.

2(a) Untitled; commenting on Wright's book *Quest for Franklin* (n.d.) 103 pp.

2(b) "Notes on *Quest for Franklin* by Noel Wright" (n.d.)

2(c) "Notes on *Quest for Franklin* by Adm. Noel Wright" (15 Dec. 1966)

4 Copies of Hall books "A" and "B" made for Jane Franklin dated 10 January 1871. Book "A" consists of pp 1–90, book "B" of pp 91–155.

5 Assorted pages from Hall's notebooks (photocopies), 1869.

6 Hall's notes for Thursday, 12 July 1866.

HUDSON'S BAY COMPANY ARCHIVES (WINNIPEG): Documents

B 200/9/31 (Anderson Journal)

B 239/K (Anderson expedition)

E 15/3, 15/8, 15/9 (Rae expeditions)

E 15/4 (Franklin expedition)

PUBLIC ARCHIVES (OTTAWA)

Fairholme Papers 1834–45 (notebook labelled "Letters and Journals W.F., G.F., J.F.")

PUBLIC RECORD OFFICE (LONDON): Documents

ADM 1 series:

1/1582 (George Back expedition)

1/2433, 2435 (John Ross 1829–33)

1/2436 (John Ross 1829–33)

1/5684, 5696 (McClintock 1857–60)

1/5714, 5718 (McClintock 1857–60)

1/5726, 5738 (McClintock 1857–60)

1/5743, 5754 (McClintock 1857–60)

ADM 7 series:

7/187 (Franklin expedition)

7/188 (J.C. Ross 1848–9)

7/200 (Anderson 1855)

ADM 37 series:

37/6669, 6689 (Muster Books *Fury* and *Hecla*)

ADM 38 series:

38/9162, 1962 (Muster Books *Terror*)

38/8045, 672 (Muster Books *Erebus*)

NATIONAL MARITIME MUSEUM (GREENWICH)

Documents

FRN/1 (Franklin Papers)

JOD/102 (Henry Piers Journal 14 Dec 1851–31 March 1852)

AGC 36/4 to 36/18 (Peglar Papers)

Ships' Plans (Press Box 62):

nos. 4434, 4436, 4437, 4438, 6137 (HMS *Erebus*)

nos. 4366, 6132, 6133A, 6136 (HMS *Terror*)

SCOTT POLAR RESEARCH INSTITUTE (CAMBRIDGE): Documents

MS 486 (John Ross Papers)

MS 655 (John Ross Memoirs)

MS 655/3 (John Ross Journal)

MS 1059 (John Ross Journal)

MS 248/303 (John Franklin Letters)

MS 248/363 (Couch Letter)

MS 248/449 (Osmer Letter)

MS 248/476 (Stanley Letter)

MS 312/3 (MacDonald Letter)

MS 1372 (Crozier Letter)

MS 787/1 (Rae Autobiography)

PUBLISHED SOURCES

Ami, H.M. "Notes on the Adelaide Peninsula Skull." *Proceedings and Transactions of the Royal Society of Canada* 22 (1928): 319–22.

Amy, R., R. Bahatnagar, E. Damkjar, and O. Beattie. "The Last Franklin Expedition: Report of a Postmortem Examination of a Crew Member." *Canadian Medical Association Journal* 135 (July 1986): 115–17.

Amundsen, Roald. *The Northwest Passage*. 2 volumes. London: Archibald Constable and Co. 1908.

– *To the North Magnetic Pole and through the Northwest Passage*. Seattle: Shorey Book Store 1967.

Anderson, James. *The Hudson Bay Expedition in Search of Sir John Franklin*. Introduction by S. Mickle. Reprinted from Canadian Women's Historical Society (Transaction 20). Toronto: Canadiana House 1969.

– "Chief Factor James Anderson's Back River Journal of 1855." *Canadian Field Naturalist* 54 (May–Dec. 1940): 63–7, 84–9, 107–9, 125–6, 134–6; and 55 (Jan.–March 1941): 9–11, 21–6, 38–44.

Anonymous. *Historic Tinned Foods*. Pamphlet no. 85. Greenford, Middlesex: International Tin Research and Development Corporation 1939.

– "Footnotes to the Franklin Search." *Beaver* 285 (Spring 1955): 46–51.

Bibliography

– *Narrative of a Voyage by Captain Ross in the years 1829, 30, 31, 32 and 33*. Clerkenwell Green: William Mason 1835.

Armstrong, Alexander. *A Personal Narrative of the Discovery of the North-West Passage*. London: Hurst and Blackett 1857.

Back, George. *Narrative of the Arctic Land Expedition to the Mouth of the Great Fish River*. London: John Murray 1836. Reprint Edmonton: Hurtig 1970.

– *Narrative of an Expedition in H.M.S. "Terror"*. London: John Murray 1838.

Ballantyne, R.M. *Hudson's Bay, or Everyday Life in the Wilds of North America*. 2nd edition. Edinburgh: Blackwood 1848.

Barr, William. *Overland to Starvation Cove: With the Inuit in Search of Franklin, 1878–1880*. Toronto: University of Toronto Press 1987.

Barrow, Sir John. *Voyages of Discovery and Research in the Arctic Regions From the Year 1818 to the Present Time*. London: John Murray 1846.

Beattie, Owen. "A Report on Newly Discovered Human Skeletal Remains from the Last Sir John Franklin Expedition." *Muskox* 33 (1983): 68–77.

– "Elevated Bone Lead Levels in a Franklin Expedition Crewman." In Sutherland, P.D., ed., *The Franklin Era in Canadian History, 1845–1859*. Ottawa: National Museum of Man 1985: 141–8.

Beattie, Owen, E. Damkjar, W. Kowal, and R. Amy. "Anatomy of an Autopsy." *Medical Post* 20 (1985): 1–2.

Beattie, Owen, and John Geiger. *Frozen in Time: Unlocking the Secrets of the Franklin Expedition*. Saskatoon, Saskatchewan: Western Producer Prairie Books 1987.

Beattie, Owen, W. Kowal, and H. Baadsgard. "Did Solder Kill Franklin's Men?" *Nature* 343 (January 1990): 319–20.

Beattie, Owen, and J.M. Savelle. "Discovery of Human Remains from Sir John Franklin's Last Expedition." *Historical Archeology* 17 (1983): 100–5.

Belcher, Sir Edward. *The Last of the Arctic Voyages*. London: L. Reeve 1855.

Bell, Benjamin, ed. *Lieut. John Irving, R.N. of H.M.S. "Terror": A memorial Sketch with Letters*. Edinburgh: David Douglas 1881.

Bellot, Joseph Réné. *Memoirs and Journal of Lieut. Joseph Rene Bellot*. London: Hurst and Blackett 1855.

Binney, I.W. "In Search of Franklin." *Sentinel* (January 1968): 20–3.

Bird, J.B. and M.M. "John Rae's Stone House." *Beaver* 284 (March 1954): 34–5.

Birket-Smith, Kaj. *Five Hundred Eskimo Words*. Copenhagen: Glydens-dalke Boghandel, Nordisk Forlag 1928. Reprint New York: AMS Press 1976.

Brown, John. *The North-West Passage and the Plans for the Search for Sir John Franklin, with sequel*. London: E. Stanford 1860.

Burns, Flora Hamilton. "H.M.S. *Herald* in Search of Franklin." *Beaver* 294 (Autumn 1963): 3–13.

Burwash, L.T. *Canada's Western Arctic*. Ottawa: King's Printer 1931.

– "The Franklin Search." *Canadian Geographical Journal* 1 (November 1930): 587–603.

– "Across Arctic Canada." *Geographical Journal* 74 (1929): 553–68.

– "The *Victory* Relics." *Beaver* 260 (December 1929): 311–12.

Canada, Government of. *Arctic Pilot* 3. 2nd edition. Ottawa: Queen's Printer 1968.

Carroll, Lewis. *Through the Looking Glass, and What Alice Found There*. London: Macmillan and Co. 1889.

Collinson, Sir Richard. *Journal of H.M.S. "Enterprise."* Edited by T.B. Collinson. London: Samson, Low, Maiston, Searle and Rivington 1889. Reprint New York: AMS Press 1976.

Cooke, Alan, and Clive Holland. *The Exploration of Northern Canada, 500 to 1920*. Toronto: McClelland and Stewart 1978.

Cooper, P.F. *Island of the Lost*. New York: G.P. Putnam's 1961.

– "A Trip to King William Island in 1954." *Arctic Circular* 8, no. 1 (1955): 8–11.

– "A Second Trip to King William Island." *Arctic Circular* 8, no. 4 (1955): 78–9.

Crouse, Nellis Maynard. *Search for the Northwest Passage*. New York: Columbia University Press 1934.

– *In Quest of the Western Ocean*. London: I.M. Dent and Sons 1928.

Cundy, Robert. *Beacon Six*. London: Eyre and Spottiswoode 1970.

Cyriax, R.J. *Sir John Franklin's Last Arctic Expedition*. London: Methuen and Co. 1939.

– "Sir J. Clark Ross and the Franklin Expedition." *Polar Record* 3 (1942): 528–40.

– "Captain Hall and the So-Called Survivors of the Franklin Expedition." *Polar Record* 4 (1944): 170–85.

– "A Historic Medicine Chest." *Canadian Medical Association Journal* 57 (1947): 295–300.

– "Recently Discovered Traces of Sir John Franklin's Expedition." *Geographical Journal* 117 (June 1951): 211–14.

– "The Position of Victory Point." *Polar Record* 6 (1952): 496–507.
– "The Two Franklin Expedition Records Found on King William Island." *Mariner's Mirror* 44 (1958): 179–89.
– "A Note on the Absence of Records." *Scottish Geographical Magazine* 75, no. 1 (1959): 30–40.
– "Adam Beck and the Franklin Search." *Mariner's Mirror* 48 (1962): 35–51.
– "Arctic Sledge Travelling by Officers of the Royal Navy." *Mariner's Mirror* 49 (1963): 127–42.
– "The Voyage of HMS *North Star*, 1849–50." *Mariner's Mirror* 50 (1964): 307–18.
– "Two Notebooks of C.F. Hall." *Geographical Journal* 131 (1965): 90–2.
– "The Unsolved Problem of the Franklin Expedition Records Supposedly Buried on King William Island." *Mariner's Mirror* 55 (1969): 23–32.
Cyriax, R.J., and A.G.E. Jones. "The Papers in the Possession of Harry Peglar, Captain of the Foretop, HMS *Terror* 1845." *Mariner's Mirror* 40 (1954): 186–95.
Cyriax, R.J., and J.M. Wordie. "Centenary of the Sailing of Sir John Franklin with the *Erebus* and *Terror*." *Geographical Journal* 106 (1945): 169–97.
Dease, Peter Warren, and Thomas Simpson. "Narrative of the Progress of Arctic Discoveries on the Northern Shore of America, in the summer of 1839." *Royal Geographical Society Journal* 10 (1841): 268–74.
De Roos, W. *North-West Passage*. London: Hollis and Carter 1980.
Dennett, J.F. *Voyages of Captains Parry, Ross, Franklin and G. Belzonio.* London: William Wright 1839.
Dickens, Charles. "The Lost Arctic Voyagers." *Household Words* 32 (Nov. 1854).
Dodge, E.S. *Northwest by Sea*. New York: Oxford University Press 1961.
– *The Polar Rosses*. New York: Faber and Faber 1973.
Dudley, K.F. "The Eskimo Place Names of Northern Cumberland Peninsula from Home Bay to Cape Dyer, Baffin Island NWT., Canada, with English Translations." *Arctic and Alpine Research* 4 (1972): 343–7.
Dunbar, Moira, and Keith R. Greenaway. *Arctic Canada from the Air*. Ottawa: Defence Research Board 1956.
Edwards, Deltus. *The Toll of the Arctic Seas*. London: Chapman and Hall 1910.
Fitzjames, James. "Journal of James Fitzjames Aboard *Erebus*, 1845." *Nautical Magazine and Naval Chronicle* 21 (1852): 158–65, 195–201.

Fluhmann, May. *Second in Command – Life of F.R.M. Crozier*. Yellowknife: Department of Information (North-West Territories) 1976.

Francis, Daniel. *Arctic Chase*. St John's, Newfoundland: Breakwater Books 1984.

– *Discovery of the North*. Edmonton: Hurtig 1986.

Franklin, John. *Narrative of a Journey to the Shores of the Polar Sea in the Years 1818–20–21–22*. London: John Murray, 1823. Reprint Edmonton: Hurtig 1969.

– *Narrative of a Second Expedition to the Shores of the Polar Sea in the Years 1825–1826–1827 … including an Account of the Progress of a Detachment to the Eastward by John Richardson*. London: John Murray 1828. Reprint Edmonton: Hurtig 1971.

Fraser, J.K. "Tracing Ross across Boothia." *Canadian Geographer* 2, no. 10 (1957): 40–60.

Galaburri, Richard. "The Franklin Records: A Problem for Further Investigation." *Musk-Ox* 32 (1983): 62–5.

Garn, Stanley. "Was the Ill-Fated Franklin Expedition a Victim of Lead Poisoning?" *Nutrition Reviews* 47 (October 1989): 322–3.

Gibson, William. "Some Further Traces of the Franklin Retreat." *Geographical Journal* 79 (May 1932): 402–8.

– "The Dease and Simpson Cairn." *Beaver* 264 (September 1933): 44–5.

– "Sir John Franklin's Last Voyage." *Beaver* 268 (June 1937): 44–75.

– "Amundsen in King William Island." *Beaver* 271 (June 1940): 32–8.

Gilder, William H. *Schwatka's Search: Sledging in the Arctic in Quest of Franklin Records*. New York: Charles Scribner's Sons 1881.

Gilpin, J.D. "Outline of the Voyage of HMS *Enterprise* and *Investigator* to Barrow Strait." *Nautical Magazine* 19 (1850): 8–9, 89–90, 160–70, 230.

Goodsir, Robert Anstruther. *An Arctic Voyage to Baffin's Bay and Lancaster Sound*. London: J. Van Voorst 1850.

Gould, Rupert T. *Oddities: A Book of Unexplained Facts*. London: G. Bles 1944.

Great Britain. Parliamentary Papers, Arctic Exploration (commonly known as the "Blue Books," 1848–1858).

– "Copies of Instructions to Sir John Franklin in reference to the arctic expedition of 1845." House of Commons Sessional Papers, Accounts and Papers 41, no. 264 (1847–8).

– "Extracts of any proceedings or correspondence of the Admiralty in reference to the Arctic expedition etc." House of Commons Sessional Papers, Accounts and Papers 32, no. 188 (1849).

– "Copies of any reports or statements from the officers employed in the arctic expedition ... in respect to the resumption of the search for Sir John Franklin's expedition etc." House of Commons Sessional Papers, Accounts and Papers 35, no. 107 (1850).

– "Copy or extracts from any correspondence or proceedings of the Board of Admiralty in relation to the arctic expedition etc." House of Commons Sessional Papers, Accounts and Papers 33, no. 97 (1851).

– "Return to and papers in connection with the later arctic expedition." House of Commons Sessional Papers, Accounts and Papers 50, no. 115 (1852).

– "Further correspondence which has been transmitted to the Admiralty, between Admiral Sir John Ross and the Danish Inspector-General, touching on the fate of the expedition under Sir John Franklin." House of Commons Sessional Papers, Accounts and Papers 50, no. 390 (1852).

– "Communications between the Admiralty and any Public Authorities at Home or Abroad, in reference to certain Vessels observed on an Iceberg in the North Atlantic in 1851, and supposed to have been abandoned." House of Commons Sessional Papers, Accounts and Papers 50, no. 501 (1852).

– "Report of the Committee appointed by the Lords Commissioners of the Admiralty to inquire into and report on the recent arctic expedition in search of Sir John Franklin etc." House of Commons Sessional Papers, Accounts and Papers 50, no. 1435 (1852).

– "Additional papers relative to the arctic expedition under the orders of Captain Austin and Mr. William Penny." House of Commons Sessional Papers, Accounts and Papers 50, no. 1436 (1852).

– "Further correspondence and proceedings connected with the arctic expeditions." House of Commons Sessional Papers, Accounts and Papers 50, no. 1449 (1852).

– "Further Papers Relative to the Recent Arctic Expeditions in Search of Sir John Franklin and the Crews of the *Erebus* and *Terror.*" House of Commons Sessional Papers, Accounts and Papers 35, no. 1898 (1854–5).

– "Further Papers Relative to the Recent Arctic Expeditions in Search of Sir John Franklin and the Crews of the *Erebus* and *Terror.*" House of Commons Sessional Papers, Accounts and Papers 41, no. 2124 (1856).

Hall, Charles Francis. *Life with the Esquimaux: A Narrative of Arctic Experience in Search of Survivors of Sir John Franklin's Expedition.* London: Sampson, Low, Sons and Marston 1862. Reprint Edmonton: Hurtig 1970.

Bibliography

Hearne, Samuel. *A Journey from Prince of Wales's Fort in Hudson's Bay to the Northern Ocean*. Reprint Toronto: Macmillan 1958.

Houston, C.S. *To the Arctic by Canoe*. Montreal: McGill University Press 1974.

– *Arctic Ordeal: The Journal of John Richardson, Surgeon-Naturalist with Franklin 1820–1822*. Kingston and Montreal: McGill-Queen's University Press 1984.

Huish, R. *The last Voyage of Captain Sir John Ross ... compiled from authentic informations and original documents transmitted by William Light, Purser's Steward through the Expedition*. London: Saunders 1836.

Huxley, Leonard. *Life and Letters of Sir Joseph Dalton Hooker*. London: John Murray 1918.

Inglefield, E.A. *A Summer Search for Sir John Franklin*. London: Thomas Harrison 1853.

Johnson, R.E. *Sir John Richardson*. London: Taylor and Francis 1976.

Jones, A.G.E. "Rear Admiral Sir William Edward Parry: A Different View." *Musk-Ox* 21 (1978): 3–10.

– "F.J. Hornby." *Mariner's Mirror* 41 (1955): 303–7.

– "Robert Martin: A Greenland Whaler." *Scottish Geographical Magazine* (Dec. 1969): 196–202.

– "The Voyage of HMS *Cove*." *Polar Record* 5 (1950): 543–56.

– "The Voyage of the *Enterprise* and *Investigator*, 1848–49." *Geographical Journal* 137 (June 1971): 165–79.

Jones, A.G.E., and R.J. Cyriax. "Lt. Edward Griffiths and the Franklin Expedition." *Mariner's Mirror* 39 (1953): 178–86.

Kennedy, William. *A Short Narrative of the Second Voyage of the "Prince Albert" in Search of Sir John Franklin*. London: W.H. Dalton 1853.

– "Report on the Return of Lady Franklin's vessel the *Prince Albert*, under the Command of Mr. Wm Kennedy, from the Arctic Regions." *Journal of the Royal Geographical Society* 23 (1853): 122–9.

Kerr, R. "Rae's Franklin Relics." *Beaver* 284 (March 1954): 25–7.

Ketchum, W.Q. "The Fate of Sir John Franklin." *Canadian Geographical Journal* 31 (December 1945): 300–3.

King, Richard. *Narrative of a Journey to the Shores of the Arctic Sea under the Command of Captain Back, RN*. London: Richard Bentley 1836.

– *The Franklin Search from First to Last*. London: John Churchill 1855.

Lamb, G.F. *Franklin, Happy Voyager*. London: Ernest Benn 1956.

Lambert, Richard S. *Franklin of the Arctic*. Toronto: McClelland and Stewart 1949.

Larsen, H. *Northwest Passage: The Voyage of the St. Roch*. Vancouver: Queen's Printer 1954.

Learmonth, L.A. "Notes on Franklin Relics." *Arctic* 1 (1948): 122–3.

– "Ross Meets the Netchiliks." *Beaver* 279 (September 1948): 10–13.

– "Recent Finds from Sir John Ross' Expedition 1829–1833." *Arctic* 3 (1950): 126–8.

– "A Divergent Opinion." *Beaver* 299 (Spring 1969): 32–3.

Loomis, Chauncey C. *Weird and Tragic Shores*. New York: A.A. Knopf 1971.

Lubbock, A. Basil. *The Arctic Whalers*. Glasgow: Brown, Son and Ferguson 1937.

Lyon, G. *Lyon's Private Journal*. London: John Murray 1824.

– *Brief Narrative of an Unsuccessful Attempt to reach Repulse Bay*. London: John Murray, 1825. Reprint Toronto: Coles Publishing 1971.

MacKay, Douglas. *The Honourable Company*. London: Cassell 1937.

MacKay, Douglas, and W.K. Lamb. "More Light on Thomas Simpson." *Beaver* 269 (September 1938): 26–31.

Mangles, James, ed. *Papers and Despatches relating to the Arctic Searching Expeditions of 1850–51–52*. 2nd edition. London: Francis and John Rivington 1852.

Manning, T.H. "Wreckage on Banks Island." *Beaver* 300 (Autumn 1969): 21.

Markham, Albert H. *A Whaling Cruise to Baffin's Bay*. 2nd edition. London: Samson, Lowe, and Marston 1875.

– "On Sledge Travelling." *Royal Geographical Society Proceedings* (December 1876): 110–20.

– *Life of Sir John Franklin*. London: George Philip and Son 1891.

Markham, Clements R. *Franklin's Footsteps*. London: Chapman and Hall 1853.

– "The Expedition of Lieutenant Schwatka to King William's Land." *Royal Geographical Society Proceedings* (November 1880): 657–62.

– *Life of Sir Leopold McClintock*. London: John Murray 1909.

– *The Lands of Silence*. Cambridge: Cambridge University Press 1921.

McClintock, Francis Leopold. *The Voyage of the "Fox" in the Arctic Seas: A Narrative of the Discovery of the Fate of Sir John Franklin and His Companions*. Philadelphia: Porter and Coates 1859. Reprint Edmonton: Hurtig Publishers 1972.

– *The Voyage of the "Fox" in the Arctic Seas: A Narrative of the Discovery of the Fate of Sir John Franklin and His Companions*. 5th edition. London: John Murray 1881.

– "Discoveries by the late Expedition in Search of Sir John Franklin and his Party." *Royal Geographical Society Proceedings* 4 (1859): 2–13.

– "Narrative of the Expedition in Search of Sir John Franklin and his Party." *Royal Geographical Society Journal* 31 (1861): 1–13.

– "On Arctic Sledge Travelling." *Royal Geographical Society Proceedings* (June 1875): 464–79.

M'Clure, Robert. *The Discovery of the North-West Passage.* Edited by S. Osborn. London: Longman, Brown, Green and Longmans 1856. Reprint Edmonton: Hurtig 1969.

McCormick, R. *Narrative of a Boat Expedition up Wellington Channel.* London: Eyre and Spottiswoode 1854.

– *Voyages of Discovery in Arctic and Antarctic Seas.* 2 volumes. London: Sampson, Low, Marston, Searle and Rivington 1884.

McDougall, George F. *The Eventful Voyage of HM Discovery Ship Resolute, 1852–53–54.* London: Longmans, Brown, Green, Longmans and Roberts 1857.

McIlraith, John. *Life of Sir John Richardson.* London: Longman, Green and Co. 1868.

McKenzie, W.G. "A Further Clue in the Franklin Mystery." *Beaver* 299 (Spring 1969): 28–32.

Miertsching, Johann. *Frozen Ships: The Arctic Diary of Johann Miertsching, 1850–1854.* Translated and edited by L.H. Neatby. Toronto: Macmillan 1967.

Mogg, W. "HMS Hecla and Fury in Prince Regent Inlet." *Polar Record* 12 (1964): 11–28.

Mowat, Farley. *Ordeal by Ice.* Boston: Atlantic Little Brown 1960.

Murdock, P.E. "The Old Shipwreck." *Beaver* 284 (March 1954): 42–3.

Nanton, Paul. *Arctic Breakthrough.* Toronto: Clarke Irwin 1970.

Neatby, L.H. *Conquest of the Last Frontier.* Athens, Ohio: Ohio University Press 1966.

– *In Quest of the Northwest Passage.* Toronto: Longmans, Green and Co. 1958.

– *Search for Franklin.* New York: Walker 1970.

– "Joe and Hannah." *Beaver* 290 (Autumn 1969): 16–21.

Nelson, J.H. "The last Voyage of HMS *Investigator.*" *Polar Record* 13 (1967): 763–8.

Nourse, J.E., ed. *Narrative of the Second Arctic Expedition Commanded by Charles Francis Hall.* Washington: Government Printing Office 1879.

O'Brien, Jack. *Alone across the Top of the World.* Chicago: John C. Winston Co. 1935.

Osborn, Sherard. *Stray Leaves from an Arctic Journal.* London: Longman, Brown, Green and Longmans 1852.

– *Captain Sir John Franklin.* London: Bradbury and Evans 1860.

– *The Career, Last Voyage and Fate of Sir John Franklin.* Edinburgh: William Blackwood and Sons 1865.

Oswalt, Wendell H. *Eskimos and Explorers.* Novato, California: Chandler and Sharp 1979.

Owen, Roderick. *Fate of Franklin.* London: Hutchinson 1978.

Parry, Ann. *Parry of the Arctic.* London: Chatto and Windus 1963.

Parry, Edward. *Memoirs of Rear Admiral Sir W. Edward Parry, Kt.* London: Longman, Brown, Green, Longmans and Roberts 1857.

Parry, William Edward. *Journal of a Voyage for the Discovery of a Northwest Passage ... performed in the Years 1819–20 in H.M.S. "Hecla" and "Griper."* London: John Murray 1821. Reprint New York: Greenwood Press 1968.

– *Journal of a Second Voyage for the Discovery of a Northwest Passage ... performed in the Years 1821–22–23 in H.M.S. "Fury" and "Hecla."* London: John Murray 1824. Reprint New York: Greenwood Press 1969.

– *Journals of the 1st, 2nd, & 3rd Voyages for the Discovery of a Northwest Passage from Atlantic to Pacific in 1819–20–21–22–23–24–25 under orders of Capt. W.E. Parry.* London: John Murray 1828.

Passwater, Richard A., and Elmer M. Cranton. *Trace Elements, Hair Analysis and Nutrition.* New Canaan, Connecticut: Keats Publishing 1983.

Rae, John. *Narrative of an Expedition to the Shores of the Arctic Sea in 1846 and 1847.* London: John Murray 1850. Reprint Toronto: Canadiana House 1970.

– *Doctor John Rae's Correspondence with the Hudson's Bay Company on Arctic Exploration 1844–55.* Edited by E.E. Rich and A.M. Johnson, with introduction by J.M. Wordie and R.J. Cyriax. London: Hudson's Bay Record Society 1953.

– "The lost Arctic Voyagers." *Household Words* (23 Dec. 1854): 433–7.

– "Sir John Franklin and his Crews." *Household Words* (3 Feb. 1855): 12–20.

– "Letter of Dr. John Rae to the British Admiralty." *American Geographical Society of New York Journal* 12 (1880): 284–8.

– "Arctic Exploration." Rae to New York *Herald* dated 23 May 1880, published 4 July 1880.

– "Rae on the Eskimos." *Beaver* 284 (March 1954): 38–41.

Rasmussen, Knud J. *The Netsilik Eskimos: Report of the 5th Thule Expedition.* 8, no. 1–2. Copenhagen: Glydensdalke Boghandel, Nordisk Forlag 1931. Reprint New York: AMS Press 1976.

– "The Fifth Thule Expedition." *Geographical Journal* 67 (1926): 123–38.

Bibliography

Richardson, John. *Arctic Searching Expeditions.* 2 volumes. London: Longman, Brown, Green and Longmans 1851.

– *The Polar Regions.* Edinburgh: Adam and Charles Black 1861.

Ross, James Clark. *Voyages of Discovery and Research in the Southern and Antarctic Seas.* Reprint London: David and Charles Reprints 1969.

Ross, Sir John. *A Voyage of Discovery Made for the Purpose of Exploring Baffin Bay.* London: Longman, Hurst, Rees, Arme and Brown 1819.

– *Narrative of a Second Voyage in Search of a North West Passage, and of a residence in the Arctic Regions during the years 1829–30–31–32–33; with Appendix.* 2 volumes. London: A.W. Webster 1835.

Ross, M.J. *Ross in the Antarctic.* Whitby: Caedmon Press 1982.

Ross, W. Gillies. *Whaling and Eskimos: Hudson Bay 1860–1915.* Ottawa: National Museum of Man 1975.

Rowley, Graham. "Rear-Admiral Sir John Ross, RN, 1777–1856: Archival Material in the Scott Polar Research Institute." *Polar Record* 15 (1970): 61–2.

Savours, A., and M. Deacon. *Starving Sailors: The Influence of Nutrition upon Naval and Maritime History.* London: National Maritime Museum 1981.

Scoresby, William. *An Account of the Arctic Regions with a History and Description of the Northern Whale Fishery.* Reprint Newton Abbot, Devon: David and Charles Reprints 1969.

– *The Franklin Expedition.* London: Longman, Brown, Green and Longmans 1850.

Scoresby, Rev. William. *Memorials of the Sea.* London: Longman, Brown, Green and Longmans 1851.

Seemann, B. *Narrative of the Voyage of HMS "Herald" during the years 1845–51, under the command of Captain Henry Kellett, R.N.* London: Reeve and Co. 1853.

Simmonds, P.L. *Sir John Franklin and the Arctic Regions.* Buffalo: George H. Derby and Co. 1852.

Simpson, Alexander. *Life and Travels of Thomas Simpson.* London: Richard Bentley 1845.

Simpson, George. *Journal of Occurrences in the Athabasca Department.* Reprint. Edited by E.E. Rich. Toronto: Champlain Society 1938.

Simpson, Thomas. *Narrative of Discoveries on the North Coast of North America During the Years 1836–39.* London: Richard Bentley 1843.

Skewes, J. Henry. *Sir John Franklin: The True Secret of His Fate.* London: Bemrose and Sons 1889.

Snow, W.P. *Voyage of the "Prince Albert" in search of Sir John Franklin.* London: Longman, Brown, Green, and Longmans 1851.

Stackpole, E.A., ed. *The Long Arctic Search*. Chester, Connecticut: Pequot Press 1977.

Stamp, Tom and Cordelia. *William Scoresby*. Whitby: Caedmon of Whitby Press 1976.

Starbuck, Alexander. *A History of American Whale Fishery*. New York: Argosy Antiquarian 1964.

Stefansson, Vilhjalmur. *My Life with the Eskimos*. New York: Macmillan 1927.

– *The Friendly Arctic*. New York: Macmillan 1944.

– *Unsolved Mysteries of the Arctic*. New York: Collier Books 1962.

– "Rae's Arctic Correspondence." *Beaver* 284 (March 1954): 36–7.

Stevenson, John. "The Unsolved Death of Thomas Simpson, Explorer." *Beaver* 266 (June 1935): 17–20, 64–6.

Sutherland, P.C. *Journal of a Voyage in Baffin's Bay and Barrow Straits in the years 1850–51, performed by HM Ships "Lady Franklin" and "Sophia" under the command of Mr. William Penny, in search of the missing crews of HM Ships "Erebus" and "Terror."* London: Longman, Brown, Green, and Longmans 1852.

Thomson, G.M. *The Search for the Northwest Passage*. New York: Macmillan 1975.

Trafton, Stephen J. "Did Lead Poisoning Contribute to the Deaths of Franklin Expedition Members?" *Information North* 15 (November 1989): 1–4.

Traill, H.D. *Life of Sir John Franklin, R.N.* London: John Murray 1896.

Tyrrell, J.B. "A Story of a Franklin Search Expedition." *Transactions of the Royal Canadian Institute* 8 (1910): 393–402.

Tyrrell, J.W. *Across the Sub-Arctics of Canada*. London: T. Fisher Unwin 1898. Reprint Toronto: Coles Publishing Co. 1973.

Wallace, Hugh N. *The Navy, The Company, and Richard King*. Montreal and London: McGill-Queen's University Press 1980.

Wallace, R.C. "Rae of the Arctic." *Beaver* 284 (March 1954): 28–33.

Walsh, R.T. "Quest in the North." *Sentinel* 10 (May 1974): 23–4.

Wilkinson, Douglas. *Arctic Fever*. Toronto: Clarke Irwin and Co. 1971.

Wilson, M. "Sir John Ross' Last Expedition in Search of Sir John Franklin." *Musk-Ox* 13 (1973): 3–11.

Wonders, W.G. "Search for Franklin." *Canadian Geographical Journal* 76 (1968): 116–27.

– "Project Franklin." *Polar Record* 14 (1968): 63–5.

Woodward, Frances J. *Portrait of Jane – A Life of Lady Franklin*. London: Hodder and Stoughton 1951.

Bibliography

– "The Franklin Search in 1850." *Polar Record* 5 (1950): 532–42.

Wright, Noel. *Quest for Franklin*. London: Heinemann 1959.

– *New Light on Franklin*. Ipswich: W.J. Cowell 1949.

Young, A.W. *The Search for Sir John Franklin*. London: J. Griffin and Co. 1875.

– *The Cruise of the "Pandora."* London: William Clowes and Sons 1876.

Index

Index